WASHINGTON

THE FIRST
ONE HUNDRED YEARS

1889-1989

An Anecdotal History
by Don Duncan

Published by
The Seattle Times
1989

AUTHOR:
Don Duncan
EDITOR:
Kathleen Triesch Saul
COPY EDITOR:
Emmett Murray
DESIGN:
Celeste Ericsson,
Christine Cox
GRAPHICS:
Bo Cline
PHOTO EDITOR:
James Heckman
RESEARCH:
Audrey Houck, Lydia Evans
and Times library staff
PASTEUP:
Ed Hubbell

ISBN 0-944912-01-X

Copyright 1989, Seattle Times Company

Published by Seattle Times Company

Printed in U.S.A.

ABOUT THE COVER
The drawings, by Seattle Times artist Christine Cox, not only mark significant events and periods in Washington state history, but also celebrate the unique qualities of our Northwest lifestyle.

CONTENTS

FOREWORD

When veteran reporters have a story idea to sell, they'll tell you just about anything. Don Duncan was no exception when, in the fall of 1987, he came to us with a plan:

It was, he said, the opportunity of a lifetime — even several lifetimes.

In 1989, Washington would celebrate its 100th birthday as a state. What better way to honor that milestone than to take a good look at the way we were and at what we'd become?

Couldn't The Seattle Times, observer and chronicler of Washington life since 1896, tell that story better than anyone else?

Indeed, we thought we could.

And couldn't Don Duncan, a prize-winning news and feature writer, a master storyteller and, most of all, a reporter who knows how to write about people, tell it best?

Indeed, again.

Thus began an extraordinary adventure into a different kind of journalism.

Newspapers, which live largely for the moment, don't usually dwell on the past. But The Times committed a year of Duncan's time — and much, much more — to do just that.

Duncan has devoured Northwest history books, squinted at microfiche and microfilm and pored over thousands of newspaper articles, checking and double-checking information through museums, historians and several dozen other publications.

Editors and artists spent months finding photos, researching graphics, compiling records and designing pages that would invite readers to enjoy the wealth of material we had.

The result, we think, is the most absorbing and entertaining Washington state history ever presented.

It is the story of the century, literally.

And it is The Times' gift to the people of this very special place.

Frank A. Blethen
Publisher and chief executive officer
The Seattle Times

1. TAMING THE WILD

FROM THE RUTS OF WAGON WHEELS TO TERRITORIAL TURF

PRE-STATEHOOD TO 1900

'An event of transcendent interest . . . the consummation of hopes long deferred yet ever renewed.'

— Elisha P. Ferry, first governor, on Washington becoming a state

Chicago Historical Society

Henry Yesler's lumber mill is in the foreground at the south end of Elliott Bay in this 1884 lithograph. Below, Oregon Territory, from an 1838 map, included all of the present-day state of Washington. Note the proximity of "Mexico" before that country ceded California in the 1846-48 war with the United States.

The long-awaited words from the nation's capital, Washington City, sped across the country by telegraph shortly after 5:30 p.m., Nov. 11, 1889:
"Washington is now a state. I saw the president sign the proclamation."
Despite the pain of boils, which caused him to have one arm in a sling and bandages on his neck, John Wilson, Washington's delegate to Congress, had rushed to telegraph the folks back home.

President Benjamin Harrison and Secretary of State James Blaine signed the statehood proclamation at 5:27 p.m. with a pen made of gold mined in Washington Territory.

Witnessing the signing were Wilson; Joseph Robinson, a Thurston County territorial judge, and Harrison's personal secretary, A.W. Halford.

The 23rd president of the United States, concerned about Wilson's boils, had asked, "How are you feeling, John?" Wilson replied, "I'm feeling better, Mr. President, and I will feel even better when you have signed the proclamation."

After the signing, Blaine sent two

Randee Fox / Seattle Times

CHRONO-LOG

1592
*Juan de Fuca
(real name: Apostolos
Valerianos), sailing for
Spain, discovers strait that
bears his name.*

1789
*Capt. Robert Gray,
aboard Lady Washington,
makes first voyage in
Pacific Northwest.*

1792-94
*Capt. George Vancouver
of British Royal Navy
explores Strait of Juan de
Fuca.*

*Captain Gray
revisits Northwest, discovers
Columbia River and what is
to be known as Grays
Harbor.*

1805-6
*Meriwether Lewis
and William Clark,
commissioned by Thomas
Jefferson and accompanied
by Sacajawea and a slave,
descend the Columbia,
explore coast as far north
as Long Beach.*

1811
*Fort Astoria,
first U.S. fur-trading post in
Northwest, established.*

1818
*Treaty of Joint Occupancy
of Oregon Country signed
by Britain and U.S.*

1821
*Czar Alexander I of Russia
claims everything from
Alaska to Queen Charlotte
Sound. U.S., Britain find
claim unacceptable. Both
negotiate separate treaties
with Russians; all recognize
54-40 boundary.*

1825
*Fort Vancouver
is built by British.*

Associated Press

Washington's first Capitol is decked out for the inauguration of Gov. Elisha P. Ferry, Nov. 18, 1889.

telegrams of his own — one to Territorial Gov. Miles Moore, the other to the new state's governor-elect, Elisha P. Ferry. Being a frugal man, he sent the latter collect.

At the Legislature, which had convened in Olympia several days earlier, jubilant Republicans and Democrats cheered, stomped their feet and clapped their hands. In Tacoma and Chehalis, cannon thundered 42 times for the Union's 42nd state.

Republican legislators had hoped that Democrats, in the glow of statehood, would join them in electing Washington's first two senators that very night.

But statehood was one thing, politics another. The outnumbered Democrats mustered enough votes to postpone the selection until Nov. 19, the day after Ferry's inauguration.

Washington's entry into the Union, right after North Dakota, South Dakota and Montana, came close to being delayed by a day.

Because of a minor procedural error, the president turned down the first certified copy of the Oct. 1 election that approved a state constitution. Another copy was sent east by train.

Delegate Wilson and Judge Robinson presented themselves at the White House at 9:30 a.m. Nov. 11, confident Harrison would sign the statehood proclamation without delay.

It would not be that easy.

The president's personal secretary, Halford, repeatedly informed the men the president was not ready to sign. Hours passed. Telegrams arrived from Olympia decrying the delay. Halford urged patience. At 5 p.m., he informed the men they might as well go home for the day. The proclamation could be signed Tuesday.

Wilson, stunned, asked who had the proclamation. Halford said Secretary of State Blaine had taken it home for the night.

Wilson sent a note to Blaine, imploring him to return with the document. About 25 minutes later, Blaine strode into the president's office. The rest is history.

The inauguration a week later was, according to one newspaper account, marked by "magnificence that has never been excelled in the pretty city of Olympia."

Railroad fares were reduced for the day. Special excursion boats ran from various communities around Puget Sound. An estimated 3,000 to 5,000 people, dressed in their

finest, gathered in a light morning fog along a parade route made muddy by hard rains the previous week.

Military bands that came from Seattle and Tacoma stepped off smartly toward the territorial Capitol building in Olympia. Top-hatted territorial and state officials — the old guard and the new — rode in horse-drawn carriages.

Many in the crowd saved their biggest cheers for the Pioneers of Washington, who walked behind the carriages. Among them were Michael Simmons, the first settler in the Olympia area, and white-bearded Ezra Meeker, who had come to Puyallup by oxcart and earned a reputation as a friend of the underdog.

Flags, bunting, flowers and evergreens were massed across the portico of the little Capitol. Two banners were hung across the street.

On one: "Isaac I. Stevens, first in the hearts of the people of Washington Territory; E.P. Ferry, first in the hearts of the people of the state of Washington."

On the other, in Indian jargon: "Chinook quanisum ancotty, alti chee chaco alki" ("living hitherto in the past, we now begin to live in the future").

A band played patriotic songs. The sun broke through the fog shortly after Olympia's Mayor John Gowey said, "We are making history . . . honoring the memory of the Father of Our Country."

When retiring territorial Governor Moore finished his valedictory and extended his hand to the new governor, the band played "Hail to the Chief" and spectators erupted with an ovation that lasted several minutes.

Ferry spoke of the long struggle for statehood:

"To those whose hair has grown white beneath this sky; to those who planted the standard of civilization and Christianity within its borders; to those, the ever-to-be-remembered pioneers, it is an event of transcendent interest; to those it is the consummation of hopes long deferred yet ever renewed."

A cannon roared its approval.

That night, while new state officials held a reception and the governor presided over an inaugural ball, King County Sheriff John McGraw — eventually to become governor himself — halted all gambling in Seattle on the grounds that too many games were crooked. Now that Washington was a state, it would be going "straight."

The next day, the Legislature took care of some unfinished business, electing the state's first U.S. senators: Republicans Watson Squire of King County, a former territorial governor, and John Allen of Walla Walla.

THE EXPLORERS

The first European explorer to visit the Pacific Northwest, in 1578 or '79, may have been Francis Drake, the English navigator and pirate, in his 75- to 100-foot-long Golden Hind. Drake, not yet knighted for his around-the-world journey, sailed at least as far north as the Oregon coast.

According to some accounts, he may have reached the 48th parallel, off the Olympic Peninsula. He gave the name New Albion (New England) to the entire Pacific Northwest.

The next visitor, in 1592, may have been Apostolos Valerianos (Juan de Fuca), a Greek navigator in the employ of the Spanish viceroy in Mexico. The problem with de Fuca's claim is that it rests on the tales he presumably spun for an Englishman, Michael Lok, in Venice in 1596. But de Fuca did describe, with a degree of accuracy, the body of water (subsequently named the Strait of Juan de Fuca) between what now is the United States and Canada.

Of subsequent explorations, there is less doubt.

In 1787, Capt. Charles Barkley, an Englishman accompanied by his wife, sailed into the strait. Barkley's wife (her name was not recorded) is credited with being the first white woman to visit the Northwest. Barkley generously named the body of water the Strait of Juan de Fuca to honor the man who may or may not have discovered it. At the mouth of the present Hoh River, Barkley sent a party ashore. Indians killed them all.

Capt. George Vancouver of the British Royal Navy arrived in the Northwest in 1792. He explored the strait and named Admiralty Inlet, Puget Sound and Hood Canal (after Lord Hood of the British Board of Admiralty), as well as Mount Rainier, Mount Baker and Bellingham Bay. At Possession Sound, near Everett, he took formal possession of "New Albion" on June 4 — the birthday of King George III — renaming the region New Georgia in the king's honor.

Before leaving the Northwest, the captain sailed around Vancouver Island and took his party up the Columbia in small boats, naming Mount St. Helens, Mount Hood (in Oregon) and Point Vancouver, in Clark County. He revisited the Northwest in 1793 and 1794.

By the time American Navy Lt. Charles Wilkes undertook the last major naval exploration, in 1841, fur-trading posts already had been established north of the Columbia and missionaries were trying to convert the natives. The first settlers had begun moving across the plains in prairie schooners.

Wilkes, a well-bred New Yorker, and his seven-vessel flotilla meticulously mapped the coastline and waterways, including Puget Sound, and made forays into the interior.

The Wilkes party is credited with 261 geographic names still on the state's maps and with staging Washington's first Fourth of July celebration (1841) near Fort Nisqually.

A sailboat navigates the Strait of Juan de Fuca about 1788 in the first known picture of that waterway.

Depue, Morgan & Co.

Washington State Historical Society

The fur-trading post of Fort Astoria on the Columbia River.

The 'threat' that stayed

Although Washington state was born in a day, the gestation period took centuries.

The first explorers, who came by sea, saw a land where evergreens seemed to brush the sky, rivers surged swift and pure and the waters were thick with fish.

Had they possessed X-ray vision, to see through the spine of mountains that divides the state into wet and dry, they would have been amazed at the vast expanses of desert and the great coulees over which water had plunged with awesome force in ages past.

Some of the early arrivals sought the fabled Northwest Passage to the Indies, others furs and gold, and still others land upon which to plant the flag.

They gave names to geographic landmarks, and they drew maps — some laughably crude and distorted and a few that proved to be remarkably accurate.

The only inhabitants were Indians. At first, they viewed the intruders as curiosities. But as they came in increasing numbers, the Indians saw them for what they were — a threat to their way of life. By then it was too late.

Meriwether Lewis and William Clark came by land, sent out by President Jefferson to explore all the way to the Pacific in 1805-06. Among the party that crossed the Rocky Mountains, descended the Columbia River and explored the coast as far north as the present Long Beach, Pacific County, were a slave named York; a French-Canadian guide, Toussaint Charbonneau; and Charbonneau's wife, a Shoshone Indian woman, Sacajawea, who carried their newborn son, Jean-Baptiste, on her back.

Fur-trading posts sprung up. No sooner would the British-owned North West Co. (later Hudson's Bay) stake out an area than John Jacob Astor, an American, would move in nearby with his competitive Pacific Fur Co.

With the arrival of Dr. John McLoughlin in 1824 as chief factor (boss) of the Hudson's Bay Co., the pendulum appeared to have swung in favor of the British. McLoughlin — tall, white-haired, intelligent and compassionate — was a major force in the new land. Everyone coming to the territory — whether British or American — sought his counsel and hospitality.

In 1825, McLoughlin moved his headquarters north, across the Columbia, to newly built Fort Vancouver. The British explored the area, and David Douglas, a Scottish botanist who became known to the Indians as "Grass Man," began collecting specimens. The Douglas fir bears his name.

The 1830s were marked by the arrival of the first missionaries, Protestant and Catholic, who vied to win Indian souls to the white man's God. Jason Lee, a Methodist, was followed by Francis Norbert Blanchet and Modeste Demers, Roman Catholic priests.

Tragedy at the mission

The 42nd state's most celebrated pioneer missionaries, as much for the way they died as for the manner in which they lived, are the Whitmans.

Dr. Marcus Whitman and his wife, Narcissa, were sent west in 1836 by the American Board of Foreign Missions, supported by the Congregational, Presbyterian and Dutch Reformed churches. They established Waiilatpu Mission, west of what is now Walla Walla.

A year later, Narcissa gave birth to the territory's first white child, Alice Clarissa, who drowned two years later in the Walla Walla River. She was the Whitmans' only child.

(In 1838, the first white American male, Cyrus Walker,

CHRONO-LOG

Marcus Whitman and his wife, Narcissa, arrive in 1836 at Waiilatpu Mission in Walla Walla country.

Whitman College News Service

Artist's conception of the layout of the Whitman mission in 1847. At lower left is the first house built by Marcus Whitman. Immediately above it is the second, larger home.

was born at the Walker-Eels Protestant mission on Tsimaikain Prairie, northwest of Spokane.)

A measles epidemic raged in the Walla Walla Valley in the fall of 1847, causing whites to fall ill and wiping out nearly half the rather small Cayuse Indian Tribe in the area.

It was apparent that Dr. Whitman, the Great White Medicine Man, had little power over the disease when three sons of a Cayuse chief died shortly after Whitman ministered to them. To make matters worse, a Canadian Indian, Joe Lewis, spread rumors that Whitman was trying to poison the Indians.

Two Indian chiefs, Tomahas and Tiloukait, conferred with Whitman on the afternoon of Nov. 29 in the kitchen of his mission home. Also in the kitchen were John Sager, one of a dozen or so children "adopted" by Mrs. Whitman, and Mary Ann Bridger, daughter of Jim Bridger, the famous "mountain man" credited with discovering the Great Salt Lake.

While Whitman and Tomahas talked, Tiloukait slipped behind the medical missionary, removed a tomahawk from under his blanket and slammed it against Whitman's skull. Whitman fell to the floor, mortally wounded.

At a signal, other Indians in the fenced 250-acre mission compound leaped into action. Young Sager, who produced a pistol, was killed. Mary Ann Bridger fled in terror.

Shots were fired. One bullet struck Mrs. Whitman, who was in an adjoining room. Fatally wounded, she nonetheless gathered up her beloved assortment of half-breeds and waifs of the Oregon Trail and took them upstairs, bolting doors behind her.

Thirteen died in what became known as the "Whitman Massacre."

Forty-six people, from either inside the mission or nearby farms, were held captive. They were released a month later after blankets, guns, ammunition and tobacco were sent from Fort Vancouver as ransom.

Several people escaped. One mission family hid under floorboards. A man fled 90 miles to Lapwai Mission, operated by the Rev. Henry Spalding and his wife, near what now is Lewiston, Idaho.

A Catholic priest, John Baptist Abraham Brouillet, heard of the massacre and went alone to Waiilatpu to bury the victims. Indians burned most of the mission soon after.

George Abernathy, governor of the vast Oregon Country, sent an armed force. There were several skirmishes but little bloodshed as the Indians regularly outmaneuvered the troops.

It was not until the spring of 1850, after the arrival of fresh federal soldiers, that Gen. Joseph Lane, Oregon's first territorial governor, ordered the "guilty Indians" found and punished.

The Cayuse held a tribal council. They turned over five Indians, who bade farewell to their wives, children and tribesmen, knowing they would never return.

Although the trial in Oregon City was swift, there were two noteworthy defense witnesses — Dr. McLoughlin, the respected factor of Hudson's Bay Co., and the Whitmans' fellow missionary, Spalding. Both said Whitman repeatedly failed to heed warnings to leave the mission as the measles epidemic took its toll.

The five Indians were hanged, despite their request that shooting would be a more noble way to die. The hangman cut the trapdoor ropes with a tomahawk to impress frontiersmen who gathered to watch. Joe Lewis, considered the ringleader, was not among those offered by the Indians to appease the law.

Marcus Whitman is one of two Washingtonians honored in the national Capitol's Hall of Statuary. The other is Mother Joseph, of the Sisters of Providence, who came to the territory in 1856 and established 29 hospitals, schools, orphanages and insane asylums, including Seattle's Providence Hospital in 1877.

The 9-foot bronze of Whitman shows him with a Bible in one hand and a medical satchel in the other. His name is perpetuated in numerous books about his martyrdom, in a county (Whitman) and in Whitman College, the state's first, founded in 1859 as Whitman Seminary.

A real jumping-off place

Most settlers came west to what now is Washington because they wanted a fresh start. The weak died on the trail.

Although not the first to reach Puget Sound, the Longmire-Biles party, out of Council Bluffs, Iowa, etched their names in history books with a memorable crossing of "Summit Hill" in the Cascade Range on Oct. 2, 1853.

Led by James Longmire and James Biles, the 146 men, women and children, 36 wagons and scrawny oxen, cows and horses left the emigrant trail at Fort Walla Walla on the Columbia, crossing the river on driftwood rafts while their animals swam.

Much of their travel was in riverbeds as they crossed the Yakima River eight times and the Naches 68. On Oct. 1, they reached the summit of Naches Pass.

The next day they made the history books.

They had gone perhaps 2½ miles farther when they came to Summit Hill, a precipitous cliff for several hundred feet, followed by another 1,000 feet so steep a human could barely stand.

Fighting down the urge to cry, one of the women said: "Well, I guess we've come to the jumping-off place at last."

The settlers had a choice of turning back and possibly being caught in a snowstorm or lowering the wagons by ropes attached to the axles. They elected to try the latter.

There are contradictory stories about the way they did it.

Ezra Meeker, the pioneer settler and historian who survived into the day of aircraft flight, quotes Biles as saying the party had only 180 feet of rope, which wasn't enough to lower the wagons. To lengthen the rope, Biles said, he ordered three of his scrawniest steers slaughtered and their hides cut into "rope" strips.

Biles said that for all their caution, two wagons fell and were broken.

Longmire's account, written some years later, makes no mention of the rope being too short. He does, however, say it was back-breaking work to lower the wagons, and two of them fell and shattered on the rocks.

The steep incline below the cliff required more roping. Trees were cut, delimbed and used as brakes.

Once down the hill, the party crossed the Greenwater River 16 times, the White River seven. Animals dropped and died until the party reached Connell's Prairie, where the grazing was good. The settlers foraged for berries and edible roots until they arrived in

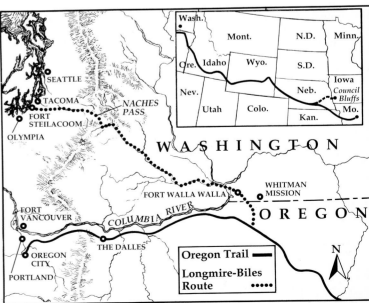

Celeste Ericsson / Seattle Times

The 1853 Longmire party left the Oregon Trail at Walla Walla to take Naches Pass across the Cascade Range over to Puyallup. The Oregon Trail itself continued west to the Willamette Valley and Astoria.

Puyallup, where the salmon were running.

At Nisqually Plain they were met by a horse-mounted party of well-dressed men from Olympia. Longmire greeted them with some embarrassment. He was wearing torn, ragged pants and a cap. An improvised moccasin covered one foot; on the other was his last boot.

A chronicler of the day reported that Longmire's abashment was dispelled by "a copious draught of good old bourbon."

A few days later, Dr. William Tolmie, factor at Fort Nisqually, brought a cartload of dressed beef to the settlers. No pay, thank you. Just a friendly gesture.

At Olympia and Steilacoom, speeches, food and cheers greeted the arrivals. The party had proved it was possible to leave the Oregon Trail, cross the seemingly insurmountable barrier of the Cascades and live to tell about it.

Marriage on a dare

There was little time for courtship in the new land.

Ezra Meeker relates a touching story about a wedding that took place June 2, 1853, at Rainier, across the Columbia from Monticello (present-day Longview).

The Rev. C.H. Kingsley had come up from Portland to perform the ceremony. Among the guests were Henry Winsor, who ran boats up the Cowlitz, and a Miss Huntington (no first name given), who lived near Monticello.

At a post-wedding supper, Winsor told Kingsley he had better perform several marriages so he wouldn't have to make the trip so often. Winsor then proceeded to ask each single woman around the table if she were ready for marriage. Each, in turn, replied she was not. But when Winsor asked Miss Huntington, she replied jokingly that she had never known a girl who wasn't ready to marry if she had the chance.

Kingsley said that since Winsor and Miss Huntington seemed to be the only ones favorably disposed toward marriage, they had better do something about it and save him another trip. Winsor, in what seemed to end the matter, said he guessed he would have to wait to see Miss Huntington's father (to ask for her hand). But the others at the table pressed them to go through with it.

Finally, on a dare, they let Kingsley perform a mock ceremony, ending with a pronouncement that they were now man and wife.

No marriage license was required in those days. Kingsley said that in his opinion, and he presumed in the eyes of God, the ceremony was binding.

The principals, in a state of shock, retreated to their separate homes. About two weeks later, Winsor, dressed in his Sunday best, came calling on Miss Huntington and her father. He said that since neither he nor Miss Huntington had other prospects at the moment and had, however foolishly, taken part in what was a real wedding after all, they just might try to see what life would hold for them as a married couple.

The Winsors celebrated their 50th anniversary in Olympia.

The 2,000-mile funeral march

Whereas the 146-member Longmire-Biles party out of Iowa wanted elbow room for the body, the Rev. William Keil came west with his party in search of elbow room for the soul.

Keil, who left Prussia in the 1830s and founded the Bethel Christian Community in Bethel, Mo., preached a doctrine he called "Christian Communism."

An advance party sent out by the Bethelites in 1853 returned with glowing accounts of the land around Willapa Harbor, in what now is Pacific County. Inspired, some 250 members of Keil's flock raised $31,000 to outfit one of the finest wagon trains ever to creak along the Oregon Trail.

While the Bethelites prepared for their 2,000-mile journey, Keil's 19-year-old son, Willie, became gravely ill with malaria. As his fever raged, Willie envisioned himself leading the way to the Promised Land. He begged his father to take him, despite his illness. Deeply moved, the minister promised that no matter what happened, Willie would lead the wagon train and spend Christmas near Willapa Bay.

Willie died May 19, 1855, four days before the party's scheduled departure. His father gently placed the young man's body in a metal-lined coffin, filled it with alcohol as a preservative and draped the box with a black cloth.

With the horse-drawn hearse in the lead, the Bethelites set out — singing hymns in German and sometimes playing horns, clarinets and violins they had brought along to civilize the frontier.

Word of the "singing wagon train led by a dead man" spread across the plains. Hostile Indians moved aside to let the hearse pass. And when a band of marauding Indians stole cattle from the wagon train, a party of Sioux — fearful of bringing down bad medicine — went after the thieves, retrieved the cattle and

returned them to Keil. The Indians then conducted the party through Sioux country without incident.

The Bethelites reached Willapa Bay in mid-November. Willie spent Christmas in the new land and the next day was buried on a knoll overlooking the Willapa River.

His promise to Willie fulfilled, Keil gathered his flock around him and engaged in straight talk. The spot the advance guard had chosen for the colony was, he said, beautiful beyond belief, and its isolation promised freedom to worship in their own way. But, personally, he thought the forest too thick and the weather too damp for farming and manufacturing.

Keil said he planned to depart the next day for Oregon and hoped the others would join him. All but a handful followed their leader, who established a community in the Willamette Valley called Aurora. It was named for Willie's sister.

Of colonies and freedom

Washington — both territory and state — became home for numerous colonies seeking religious and social freedom.

Twelve years after Willie Keil was buried, William W. Davis, a Mormon who thought his first-born son was the reincarnation of Christ, settled in the Walla Walla Valley with three dozen followers. They farmed and shared what little wealth they could acquire until, 14 years after coming together, several members of the flock became disenchanted with Davis' visions and contentious ways and took him to court to liquidate the colony's assets.

In the late 1890s, members of the Progressive Brethren Church, calling themselves the Christian Cooperative Colony, laid out the town of Sunnyside in the Yakima Valley.

Other colonies:

■ Puget Sound Cooperative Colony, established by attorney George Venable Smith at Port Angeles in 1887. It was strong on cradle-to-the-grave security and equal rights, stipulating that women had the "privilege of working a full day with pay equal to a man's." Women also could hold office and vote in all colony elections. The colony was disbanded in the early 1900s.

■ Equality, established by the Brotherhood of the Cooperative Commonwealth in 1897 in Skagit County. Its goal was to promote socialism throughout the state. It began to fade after about a year, but struggled on for 10 years before disappearing.

■ Freeland, established in 1900 on Whidbey Island. It began with a communally shared general store and a small steamboat in which to transport goods. Although most residents professed socialist leanings, they made their most lasting mark as land developers.

■ Burley, established in 1898 by the Cooperative Brotherhood at Henderson Bay, Kitsap County, 10 miles west of Tacoma. The colony, which was rooted in the Brotherhood of the Cooperative Commonwealth and the Social Democracy of America, was avowedly socialistic. "Burley Jams," handmade cigars and sawmill products sold well. The enterprise lasted until 1924.

■ Home Colony, platted in 1901 on Carr Inlet, across from Tacoma. The most famous of the colonies, Home once was referred to by a journalist as "Brook Farm, Wild West style." Some of the better-known anarchists and social revolutionists of the time visited the colony.

Home survived a virulent attack by Tacoma newspapers and the Patriotic League of Tacoma after the assassination of President William McKinley, and it continued after its leader, Jay Fox, was put on trial for writing an editorial, "Nudes and Prudes," that defended the right to go swimming in the buff. Some colonists stayed in their homes until they died in the 1950s and '60s.

'X' marks the treaty spot

An uneasy truce existed between the Indians who first occupied the land and the whites who began arriving in ever-larger numbers in the 1850s. Isaac Stevens, who became Washington's first territorial governor when the territory was created in 1853, also served as superintendent of Indian affairs.

Stevens, a small man often described as a "human dynamo," embarked on a whirlwind campaign to negotiate treaties with all the tribes in Washington Territory. His goal, and he thought it a proper one, was to send the Indians peaceably off to reservations in return for modest amounts of money and guarantees of traditional food-gathering rights.

In a blur of activity, Stevens first talked treaty with the Indians at Medicine Creek, down on the Nisqually. He quickly followed with treaty talks at Point Elliott, Point-No-Point, Neah Bay and Mill Creek.

Stevens then turned his attention to Eastern Washington, taking just a few men with him to Walla Walla to make treaties

STATE-MENTS

George Washington Bush

A mulatto who came to the Northwest in 1844 with the Michael Simmons party, Bush was told he and his wife, Isabella, couldn't settle in the Oregon Territory because the provisional government banned free blacks. The group decided to stick together and move north, across the Columbia.

Bush, who had fought in the War of 1812 and had become a prosperous landowner in Missouri, established a homestead on what now is known as Bush Prairie, south of Olympia. His farm prospered and he built a complex of log cabins, which he provided free, along with food, to travelers looking for a place to stake a claim.

Because nonwhites were forbidden to own land in the territory, it took a special act of Congress to give Bush eventual title to his homestead.

His son, Owen, became an outstanding farmer, winning a gold medal for his grains at Philadelphia's 1876 Centennial Exposition. He also became the state's first black legislator, serving as a Republican in the Legislature that convened Nov. 6, 1889, and was in session when statehood was announced five days later.

CHRONO-LOG

A survey party led by Isaac Stevens meets a band of Nez Percé in Eastern Washington in 1853.

1853

King County almost gets named Brown County. Just before Washington Territory is created, the Oregon Territorial Legislature names two new counties — Pierce and King — in "northern Oregon," to honor the new president and vice president-elect, Franklin Pierce and William R. King. While the Electoral College is canvassing votes in Washington City, word arrives that King has died in Cuba. It would not do to elect a deceased vice president, so a recess is declared and the name of the elector from Wisconsin, Beriah Brown, is substituted. When it is learned the next day that King is still alive, Brown's name is withdrawn and King is declared elected. He does not live to fill the office, however. Brown, denied his place in history, comes to work as a journalist in Seattle.

Congress approves bill creating Washington Territory (March 2); President Millard Fillmore signs it two days before he leaves office. Action settles dispute over name. Some wanted "Columbia," others an Indian name; one senator favored "Washingtonia." Maj. Isaac Stevens is appointed governor. New territory runs north of Columbia to 49th parallel and from Pacific to Rockies.

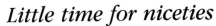

Washington State Historical Society

An Indian whale-hunter, Lighthouse Joe, at the stern of his canoe at Neah Bay. Whaling canoes in the early 1900s were hollowed from a single cedar log, with bow and stern pieces joined by dowels and lashings.

with 5,000 Indians representing the Walla Walla, Cayuse and Umatilla nations. He then negotiated with the Yakima and Nez Percé nations.

In most instances, Stevens succeeded in getting chiefs to put their X's on treaties, which were sent to Congress for formal approval.

Among those present at Point Elliott was Chief Noah Sealth of the Suquamish, Duwamish and allied tribes. Sealth not only saved a young town from an awful fate by giving his name (Seattle) to a place some called Duwamps, but he delivered a powerful speech whose English translation has become an important part of our history.

Not every chief signed the treaties Stevens brought to them. And the treaties did not take effect soon enough to head off conflicts.

■ Indians attacked gold miners in Yakima County's Simcoe Mountains, killing five soldiers.

■ British Columbia Indians refused to leave Port Gamble, and the USS Massachusetts fired on them, killing 27 and sinking war canoes.

■ Indian Agent A.J. Bolon was killed by Qualchin, son of a Yakima chief.

■ Blood was shed at the Battle of Connell's Prairie in the White River Valley and at Rosalia, near Spokane, when the Indians soundly trounced the undermanned forces of Lt. Col. E.J. Steptoe. A larger U.S. force avenged Steptoe's defeat, and several Indian leaders were hanged.

Eastern Washington was considered so unsafe in 1857 that it was closed to all whites except the military and employees of the Hudson's Bay Co.

One of the most celebrated events — the beheading of Col. Isaac Ebey, a pioneer Whidbey Island settler — was the work of a band of Haidas who came down from British Columbia Aug. 11, 1857, to avenge the defeat administered by the Massachusetts.

The Haidas raided Whidbey Island, shot and decapitated Ebey at his farmhouse and fled back to the Queen Charlotte Islands with his head. Years later the "trophy" was retrieved and returned for burial with Ebey's body.

Isaac Stevens, first governor of Washington Territory.

Little time for niceties

Emotions ran high on both sides. Whites who killed Indians received, at most, a slap on the wrist. Death was certain for Indians accused of killing whites.

The stage was set for several genuine tragedies as the unwritten Law of the Frontier superseded the niceties of innocent-until-proven-guilty.

At what became known as the Battle of Seattle, a one-day skirmish on Jan. 25, 1856, residents of the small waterfront town fired muskets at attacking Indians from a blockhouse built from timbers turned out by Henry Yesler's mill.

The sloop Decatur, anchored in Elliott Bay, fired its cannon, routing the Indians. But two settlers, Milton Holgate and Robert Wilson, were killed.

Governor Stevens demanded that ringleaders of the uprising be brought to trial. He named five Indian leaders, including Leschi of the Nisquallies, who was present at the Medicine Creek Treaty negotiations two years earlier. Whether Leschi signed the treaty has been long debated. There was an "X" beside his name, but someone else could have put it there.

Besides his undeniable role in the Battle of Seattle, Leschi also was suspected of leading an ambush that resulted in the deaths of two federal volunteers (Moses and Miles) at Connell's Prairie in 1855.

Federal troops at Fort Steilacoom had little interest in finding Leschi, arguing that to hang him and other chiefs would stir up more animosity between Indians and whites. Besides, they reasoned, Leschi and the others had fought acccording to the rules of Indian warfare.

Stevens persisted, offering 50 blankets for information.

Sluggia, a nephew of Leschi's, was cast in the role of Judas when he informed on both Leschi and Leschi's half-brother, Quiemuth, another outlaw chief. The reluctant soldiers captured

'NO DEATH, ONLY A CHANGE OF WORLDS'

Chief Noah Sealth was variously described as "runted" and as standing over 6 feet tall in his moccasins. He was called both ugly and a man of strong features that indicated character.

Historians are unanimous, however, in saying the chief usually disdained Western clothing and wore a breechcloth and blanket. He also was a man of his word and had a powerful, persuasive manner of speaking.

A chief by virtue of the position his father held in the Suquamish Tribe, Sealth spoke only in Duwamish, the language of his mother's tribe. He refused to use the Chinook trade jargon. No word of English is known to have passed his lips.

In 1855, Sealth, then about 68 and with 12 years of life remaining, addressed a gathering called by Territorial Gov. Isaac Stevens to approve the Point Elliott Treaty. Sealth's words were translated by his friend, Dr. Henry Smith.

Some historians have questioned the translation. But Smith always swore to its accuracy. Certainly the ideas and the pure poetry are as compelling today as when the chief held an audience transfixed with these words:

"It matters little where we pass the remnant of our days. They will not be many. The Indian's night promises to be dark. Not a single star hovers above his horizon. Sad-voiced winds moan in the distance. Some grim fate seems to be on the Red Man's trail, and wherever he goes he will still hear the approaching footsteps of his fell destroyer and prepare stolidly to meet his doom, as does the wounded doe that hears the approaching footsteps of the hunter.

"A few more moons, a few more winters — and not one of the descendants of the mighty hosts that once moved over this broad land or lived in happy homes, protected by the Great Spirit, will remain to mourn over the graves of a people once more powerful and hopeful than yours.

Chief Sealth in 1864. Typically, his eyes are closed; Indians held that photographs robbed the soul.
Seattle Times

"But why should I mourn at the untimely fate of my people? Tribe follows tribe, and nation follows nation, like the waves of the sea. It is the order of nature, and regret is useless. Your time of decay may be distant, but it will surely come, for even the White Man whose God walked and talked with him as friend with friend, cannot be exempt from the common destiny. We may be brothers after all. We shall see.

"We will ponder your proposition, and when we decide we will tell you. But should we accept it, I, here and now, make this the first condition — that we will not be denied the privilege, without molestation, of visiting at any time the tombs of our ancestors, friends and children.

"Every part of this soil is sacred . . . Every hillside, every valley, every plain and grove has been hallowed by some sad or happy event in days long vanished. Even the rocks, which seem to lie dumb and dead as they swelter in the sun or darken in the rain along the silent seashore, thrill with the memories of stirring events connected with the lives of my people. . .

"And when the last Red Man shall have perished from the earth, and the memory of my tribe shall have become a myth . . . these shores will swarm with the invisible dead of my tribe; and when your children's children shall think themselves alone in the fields, the store, the shop, upon the highway, or in the silence of the pathless woods, they will not be alone. . .

"At night, when the streets of your cities and villages will be silent and you think them deserted, they will throng with returning hosts that once filled them and still love this beautiful land.

"The white man will never be alone. Let him be just and deal kindly with my people, for the dead are not powerless.

"Dead — did I say?

"There is no death.

"Only a change of worlds."

Leschi in mid-November 1856.

Quiemuth, who gave himself up, was held overnight in Stevens' office, pending transfer to Fort Steilacoom. During the night, the back door was forced open and Quiemuth was stabbed to death.

Stevens expressed his displeasure but did not press charges against the prime suspect, a white man believed to have avenged the murder of his father-in-law by Nisqually Indians.

Leschi was tried twice — for the murder of officer Moses, not for his role in the Battle of Seattle. At his first trial, the jury stood 10-2 for conviction. One of the two jurors holding out for acquittal was Ezra Meeker, who had led pioneers to the new territory by oxcart and felt Leschi should be judged only as a prisoner of war. Chief Sealth also pleaded for Leschi.

At the second trial, Leschi's attorneys, Frank Clark and H.O. Crosby (great-grandfather of the singer Bing Crosby) also introduced as defense witnesses chief factor William Tolmie of Hudson's Bay Co. and Lt. August Kautz (the first man to attempt to lead a party up Mount Rainier). Kautz had married Leschi's niece and later became a Civil War general.

Leschi was convicted, primarily on the testimony of Antonio B. Rabbeson, a friend of Governor Stevens, who swore he had seen Leschi and two other Indians fire the fatal shots at Moses and Miles.

On Feb. 18, 1858 — having been refused a pardon by the new territorial governor, Fayette McMullen — Leschi was removed

from a ramshackle guardhouse at Fort Steilacoom, where he had been chained hand and foot in a cell open to public view.

Ill and emaciated from nearly three years of confinement, he nonetheless walked stoically toward a gallows, flanked by military guards and a French Catholic missionary, the Rev. Louis Rossi.

When Leschi passed Rabbeson, the principal witness against him, he spat out disdainfully:

"You have never told the truth in your whole life."

Rossi reportedly winced at the chief's hatred of Rabbeson, feeling it ran counter to Leschi's conversion to Christianity a few days earlier after earnest prayer with the Rev. Eugene Casimir Chirouse, a Catholic missionary. The chief even had agreed to stop his "sinful, polygamous ways" by sending all but one of his wives away from the jailhouse vigil.

Leschi mounted the gallows, accepting noose and bound hands and legs without a murmur. Then he cried out:

"I forgive them all."

Rossi liked those words, and was to speak and write about them often.

They were Leschi's last. Moments later he was hanged. His body was buried in the Nisqually Reservation; eventually, his remains were interred in the Puyallup Indian Cemetery.

Historians long have debated whether Leschi was guilty as charged. In recent years, the majority have leaned toward innocence.

Museum of History and Industry

A settler's depiction of the one-day skirmish of Jan. 25, 1856, grandiosely called the Battle of Seattle. Residents of the small waterfront settlement are shown fleeing to a blockhouse built from timbers turned out by Henry Yesler's sawmill. The picture was painted from memory by Emily Inez Denny, who was 2 at the time of the battle.

CHRONO-LOG

1853

David S. "Doc" Maynard is credited with naming Seattle, laying out streets to conform to points of compass rather than parallel to shoreline, as Arthur Denny and Carson Boren had done with plat they filed a day earlier. Result is permanent mismatch at Yesler Way, where two halves of young town met.

While others prosper in new land, Maynard has only friends. He gives away much of his downtown land to young settlers; what's left is claimed by wife he had left behind in East. When he dies, March 13, 1873, half of Seattle gathers at Yesler's Pavilion to pay last respects to hard-drinking, overly generous Maynard.

1854

Gov. Isaac Stevens negotiates first Indian treaty at Medicine Creek.

1859

Whitman College, state's first, is founded by Rev. Cushing Eels, as Whitman Seminary.

Oregon becomes state.

1861-62

In Eastern Washington, "cow killer" winter causes loss of 75-100 percent of most cattle herds.

Revolt of the 'squaw men'

As long as Stevens was dealing with the aborigines of the territory, most settlers probably felt him fair and evenhanded. But in May 1856 — at the height of the Indian Wars — Stevens took on the courts and a handful of white settlers. That was a different matter.

The trouble began when the governor decided to move settlers off their claims in Pierce and Thurston counties so the territorial militia could wage war, unhindered, against the Indians.

In so doing, he acted contrary to the advice of Maj. Gen. John Wool, an aging hero of the War of 1812 and the Mexican War, who commanded the Military Department of the Pacific. Wool argued that untrained territorial troops would make the job of the regulars more difficult.

The settlers ordered to move were equally unhappy. They wanted to be left alone on their claims. A small band on Muck Creek, southeast of Fort Steilacoom, defied the governor. Most were former employees of the Hudson's Bay Co. and had Indian wives. The Indians didn't bother them, they said, so why move.

Stevens took this as a sure sign the "squaw men" were collaborating with the enemy and were guilty of treason. He ordered them confined at Fort Steilacoom to face trial.

Stevens then declared martial law in Pierce County. And when Judge Edward Lander, chief justice of Washington Territory, attempted to convene court at Steilacoom, the governor ordered soldiers to remove the judge from his bench, hold him in a log-cabin "jail" and impound court records.

This was serious. Although the governor repealed martial law two weeks later — freeing the judge and permitting the accused settlers to return to their claims — he was not out of the woods.

Lander returned to the bench and fined Stevens $50 for contempt. The governor responded with an "order of respite," in which he freed himself of all contempt charges because, he said, in declaring martial law he was acting as a servant of the president (Franklin Pierce).

If Stevens hoped to pass the buck, he was unsuccessful. A few months later, U.S. Secretary of State W.L. Marcy informed Stevens his conduct in declaring martial law did not meet with "the favorable regard of the president." On top of that, the Territorial Legislature censured Stevens.

The governor's friends eventually paid the fine.

Despite his occasional excesses, Stevens' reign as first territorial governor was generally regarded as a success, and he subsequently served with distinction as Washington's territorial delegate to Congress in 1857.

Soon after the outbreak of the Civil War, Stevens joined the Army of the Potomac (the Union forces) as a colonel. In 1862, having risen to the rank of major general, he was killed at the Battle of Chantilly.

Language for a pig war

The Indians weren't the only ones who wanted United States settlers to leave the Northwest. The British also wished they would go away — or at least settle boundary disputes like gentlemen.

In 1844, James K. Polk rode into the presidency with the rallying cry "54-40 or Fight," which would have given this country about half of British Columbia. It was good theater, but hardly realistic.

Two years later, Polk signed a treaty establishing the 49th parallel as the boundary between British and American territories. It was not a bad deal. The British claim to a boundary farther south was at least as good as that of the Americans'.

The treaty, however, contained one fuzzy bit of language. In placing the boundary through the middle of the main channel separating the mainland from Vancouver Island, it failed to distinguish between two "main channels" — Haro Strait, just east of Vancouver Island, and Rosario Strait, several miles to the east.

At stake was a group of islands that included San Juan, Orcas, Lopez, Decatur, Blakely, Shaw, Stuart and Waldron. The British favored the line at Rosario; the Americans held fast for Haro.

The rub came when the Oregon Territorial Legislature assigned the islands to Island County in 1853, the same year the Hudson's Bay Co. established a sheep farm on San Juan Island.

What to do?

The British were told they would have to pay taxes on the sheep if they stayed. Capt. James Sangster, the British collector of customs, responded by raising the British flag over the sheepherder's cabin. Col. Isaac Ebey (who was later beheaded), the U.S. collector of customs for Upper Puget Sound, raised the stakes by hoisting an American flag over his tent on the island.

In 1854, the new Washington Territory placed the islands under the jurisdiction of Whatcom County. The following year, that county's sheriff and four other armed men appeared on the island to demand the sheepherder pay his taxes. When he refused, 34 of his sheep were confiscated.

Territorial Gov. Stevens and James Douglas, the Hudson's Bay factor, exchanged letters deploring the other's unbending attitude.

Randee Fox / Seattle Times

When the British agreed to drop a proposed mid-channel compromise for settling the San Juans boundary dispute, the U.S. agreed to submit the case to German Emperor Wilhelm I.

The matter finally came to a head in 1857 when Lyman Cutler, an American miner living near the Hudson's Bay farm, shot a prize English boar that crawled under a fence and rooted in his potato patch. He offered $10, but the British said it was worth $100.

Enter a hotspur U.S. Army officer, Brig. Gen. William Harney, who called in Capt. George Pickett (of "Pickett's charge" at Gettysburg) and 66 men to protect the young nation's interests. When the British countered by stationing a 31-gun frigate offshore, Harney ordered in more troops, under the command of Col. Silas Casey.

Would a pig touch off a war?

Not if President James Buchanan had anything to say about it. Realizing he had enough domestic problems — the slavery issue was dividing the nation — he dispatched Gen. Winfield Scott to Washington Territory to soothe the British. Scott and Douglas worked out a joint military occupancy of the island, with British subjects and U.S. citizens enjoying equal rights.

The agreement worked for years, until the boundary dispute was turned over to a third party, Germany's Emperor Wilhelm I, to decide once and for all. After considering evidence from both sides, the emperor finally ruled in 1872 in favor of the U.S.

When it's time to railroad . . .

It didn't take long to realize that covered wagons, stagecoaches and ships were not the swiftest way to transport people and goods to and from the Pacific Northwest.

The answer: a transcontinental railroad.

In 1853, Congress appropriated $150,000 to explore four potential routes. Stevens mapped much of the northernmost one in

Doreen M. Margetts collection, Vancouver, B.C.
Crews work to complete the Great Northern Railway line across Stevens Pass east of Baring in January 1893.

the months before formally taking over as territorial governor. He pronounced it feasible, but California — with more people and gold fever — won the first transcontinental prize.

Washington Territory's hopes brightened in 1864 when President Abraham Lincoln signed a bill providing land grants to the Northern Pacific Railway Co. to lay tracks and a telegraph line from Lake Superior to Puget Sound. Six years later, Jay Cooke & Co. sold $100 million in bonds to finance the project.

When ground was broken Feb. 15, 1870, near Duluth, Minn., five Western Washington cities — Olympia, Steilacoom, Seattle, Mukilteo and Tacoma — dreamed of becoming the railroad's terminus.

To help its cause, Seattle offered the NP $250,000 in cash and bonds, 7,500 town lots, 3,000 acres of land and use of much of the town's shoreline for a depot and tracks. But to no avail. When the railroad announced its choice on July 14, 1873, the winner was the little town on Commencement Bay: Tacoma.

Jubilant Tacomans, certain they were on the threshold of becoming the Northwest's dominant city, watched as Gen. Morton McCarver, the town's leading citizen, drove the symbolic last spike five months later.

Tacoma's joy was short-lived, however. Cooke went broke soon after the spike was pounded home, and NP speculators got caught up in land deals that changed the shape of the railroad from a direct route to Tacoma to a circuitous one, by way of Kalama down in Cowlitz County.

Even though the Tacoma-Kalama spur was completed, six years passed before journalist Henry Villard took over the NP and work resumed to fill a 1,500-mile gap between Bismarck, N.D., and the West Coast.

By the time the first NP train made its roundabout way from Duluth to Tacoma in the fall of '83, the City of Destiny felt more like a second cousin than the official terminus of the railroad.

When Tacoma finally got its direct route July 3, 1887 — via a tunnel through Stampede Pass — the ensuing three-day celebration attracted crowds from all over the Sound.

By then, however, much of the bloom was off Tacoma's rose. Losers in the terminus fight had undertaken numerous short-haul railroads on their own. There were some notable failures, including Seattle's abortive effort to construct a railroad to Walla Walla with volunteer labor. Five months after starting, the volunteers had gone only 13 miles.

But enough ventures had succeeded to spin a spiderweb of steel around the state — carrying logs and coal to ships on Puget Sound and wheat to vessels on the Columbia.

Seattle not only hung on after the stunning loss of the NP but grew rapidly. Track was laid to link Seattle with Tacoma, giving Seattle at least a secondary claim to the NP. And when the Great Northern Railway of Jim "Empire Builder" Hill arrived in Seattle in July 1893, Tacoma's position as No. 2 on Puget Sound was cast in steel.

Here come the brides

Nearly a century would pass before Rodgers and Hammerstein's "There is Nothing Like a Dame." Nevertheless, the feeling on the frontier was undeniably intense.

In Seattle's 1860 census, men outnumbered women roughly 10 to 1, and more than one civic leader publicly proclaimed that an infusion of females was needed to civilize the dirty, unshaven males who whooped it up in saloons and red-light districts.

The man who undertook the chore was a young bachelor, Asa Shinn Mercer, brother of Seattle Judge Thomas Mercer. At age 22, fresh out of an Eastern college, Mercer had been named as the first president, professor and sometime carpenter and janitor of the Territorial University established in 1861 on Denny's Knoll, the site of the present Four Seasons Olympic Hotel.

Spurred by women-hungry males and a Donation Land Act that provided 640 acres to "man and wife," Mercer left Seattle in 1864 for the textile-mill town of Lowell, Mass., where he encouraged young women to leave their financially depressed community and seek prosperity, and possibly matrimony, in the Great Northwest.

The 11 who undertook the trip were brave and hardy. It took three months to make the journey, which involved crossing the Isthmus of Panama. The "Mercer Girls" — immortalized more than 100 years later in the TV series "Here Come the Brides" — arrived in Seattle in May aboard the sloop Kidder. It was said every bachelor in town took a bath and slicked down his hair for the occasion.

One young woman died soon after arriving, and at least one other left the area. But the rest eventually married, with the exception of Lizzie Ordway, a confirmed spinster who started a school in Seattle and later became Kitsap County superintendent.

Mercer was acclaimed for his feat and elected to the Legislature. Thus emboldened, he announced his intention to go East once more and this time return with hundreds of women to teach school, work as seamstresses and, of course, be available for serious courting. To assure delivery, he would be happy to accept from every bachelor $300 cash, in advance.

Nobody knows how many men took him up on the offer, but Mercer did make it back to New York on April 15, 1865, when he immediately suffered two setbacks.

He had counted on help from President Abraham Lincoln, upon whose knee he is supposed to have sat and listened to stories when he was a boy. Lincoln, unfortunately, had been shot the previous night at Ford's Theater.

Mercer then turned to Gen. Ulysses S. Grant, who had soldiered at Fort Vancouver before the Civil War. Grant listened to Mercer's plea and said he would order the Army's quartermaster to provide Mercer with a military vessel capable of carrying 500 women to the Pacific Northwest.

An incredulous quartermaster told Mercer that Grant had no such authority. Request denied.

His pockets empty, Mercer scoured the East Coast for young women left penniless when their fathers died in the Civil War. He had several hundred commitments when a New York newspaper published a story saying Mercer intended to employ the women in brothels. Other newspapers jumped on the juicy story.

The publicity was disastrous. Although Mercer loudly proclaimed his honorable intentions, a majority of the women reneged on their promise to accompany him. Those who remained firm were told they would have to pay their own fare.

A party of 95 — including some married men and their families — eventually joined Mercer aboard the SS Continental for the voyage around Cape Horn. Some historians say no more than half were eligible women and that among those, attrition quickly set in. A few received marriage proposals from crewmen. Others left the ship in California. Mercer himself proposed to one, Anne Stephens, and was accepted.

Mercer had to put the women and family members on various lumber ships to get them from San Francisco to Seattle. But those who made it to the little lumber-mill town in the spring of '66 were enthusiastically greeted by virtually every adult in town — the men because they wanted more women; the women because they desperately wanted company. The first marriage took place within a month. Others followed.

Mercer, however, was roundly criticized for failing to make good on his promise to bring back hundreds of women. After he married Anne Stephens, they left town and settled in Wyoming.

'Respectable' lynch mob

Seattle was so wild in the early 1880s that no man wandered the streets after nightfall without a gun. In January 1882, all semblance of law took a holiday.

When businessman George Reynolds was shot by two thieves, a firebell was sounded. Several hundred angry men quickly gathered. They found the suspects on a wharf and took them before a judge, who ordered them to jail pending arraignment.

The next morning, the mob stormed the courthouse, dragged the two prisoners outside and, ignoring their pleas for mercy, hanged them from a makeshift gallows in Occidental Square.

The mob then broke into the jail again. This time they brought out Benjamin Payne, accused of shooting policeman David Sires the previous fall. Payne joined the two others on the gallows.

Few spoke out publicly against the lynch mob, since it included many of the town's leading citizens.

STATE-MENTS

Asa Mercer
Seattle history will always remember him as the latter-day argonaut who brought back the "Mercer Girls."

Klondike Kate
In 1882, 6-year-old Kathleen Eloisa Rockwell moved to Spokane with her mother and stepfather. She always wanted to sing and dance, so she joined the Savoy Theatrical Company to perform in dance halls in Dawson when the Yukon gold rush was at its height.

There she became famous as "Klondike Kate, Queen of the Yukon" — pretty, blessed with the stamina to step lightly through more than 100 dances a night with rough-and-tumble miners. She fell in love with a young Greek, Alexander Pantages, and loaned him money to open a theater in Seattle, the start of the largest chain of vaudeville houses in America. She died in 1957 in Sweet Home, Ore., at the age of 81.

CHRONO-LOG

1863
Territory of Idaho created, establishing Washington's eastern boundary.

1864
First "Mercer Girls" arrive in Seattle from New England.

1871
San Juan Islands dispute between Britain and U.S. submitted for arbitration to German Emperor Wilhelm I.

1873
Northern Pacific Railway selects Tacoma as terminus; remains uncompleted for years when Jay Cooke financial empire crashes.

1881
While most residents of Spokane Falls are attending wedding reception March 21, band of armed men from Cheney visits W.H. Bishop, young auditor for Spokane County, while he's counting election ballots to determine if Spokane Falls or Cheney is county seat. Bishop — staring at guns — finds Cheney to be clear winner. After election is certified, intruders bundle up county records in gunny sacks and take them and nervous auditor back to Cheney in wagon. Five years later, however, Spokane Falls regains county seat in second election.

1883
Women's suffrage voted by Legislature (later ruled unconstitutional).

1885
Anti-Chinese riots in Seattle and Tacoma.

Artist's rendition of 1886 ouster of hundreds of Chinese from Seattle.

Univ. of Wash. Special Collections

Washington State Historical Society

Seattle labor contractor Chin Gee Hee imported his Chinese countrymen to perform manual labor. He returned to China in the early 1900s with about $1 million and built a railroad, which he managed until he died.

A sorry chapter on race

 Thousands of Chinese were imported to the West Coast, mostly California, in the mid-1800s to work in the mines. They later found work in railroad construction and fish canneries.

Although most of the Chinese lived in California and Oregon, there were an estimated 3,200 in Washington Territory in 1880. Many had left mining and railroad work to drift into towns, where they opened hand laundries and worked as cooks, porters and household servants.

They were generally hard-working and would toil long hours for the low wages employers in Seattle and Tacoma were willing to pay. Those who had to compete with them were, however, much less enthusiastic. When jobs became scarce, tempers flared.

The resulting violence and racism are a sorry chapter in the state's history. Tacoma was left with a bad reputation, richly deserved. Seattle emerged with its sense of fair play in tatters.

In Tacoma, where about 700 Chinese lived, mass meetings and protest parades were held under the auspices of two citizen organizations, The Committee of Fifteen and The Committee of Nine. Neither had legal status. Both had vigilante leanings.

The Chinese continued to work hard, keep to themselves and look over their shoulders. Word of potential trouble brewing in the Puget Sound country spread to Portland, where the editor of The Oregonian branded the residents of Seattle and Tacoma as "lawless whites, vicious, liquor-guzzling ruffians."

The editor of The Tacoma Ledger, who frequently appeared at mass meetings to stir up anti-Chinese sentiment, wrote an editorial Oct. 3, 1885, declaring "the Chinese must go" within a month.

A few days later, Ezra Meeker, the pioneer Puyallup Valley hop grower and a voice of reason whenever racism reared its head, responded with a letter to The Ledger's editor accusing the

newspaper of promoting lawlessness. A Presbyterian pastor in Tacoma devoted his Sunday sermon to Christian love and the need to uphold law and order. Few listened.

On Oct. 10, there was a mass meeting in a Tacoma opera house, followed by a torchlight parade that must have chilled the Chinese. Another Ledger editorial said few people supported Meeker's soft-hearted views and predicted the minister who urged caution soon would be preaching to empty pews.

Near the end of the month, after many Chinese had left Tacoma voluntarily, Territorial Gov. Watson Squire felt compelled to visit the town and advise its residents to cool down. The Ledger accused Squire of "toadying to the Chinese."

Fired up by another mass meeting and torchlight procession, Tacomans took the law into their own hands. At 9:30 a.m. Nov. 3, shop whistles sounded throughout the city, rallying a mob estimated at 500 men. The mob proceeded to the homes and businesses of the Chinese and ordered them to pack all their belongings and place them in waiting wagons.

Late in the afternoon, about 250 Chinese were force-marched to Lakeview, about 10 miles south of downtown Tacoma, to be put on trains bound for California. Children and the infirm were allowed to ride in wagons.

The next day, Chinese homes and businesses were swept by fire. The vigilantes professed innocence.

Tacoma's action was denounced across the nation. Several of Seattle's newspapers, which had done their best to stir up anti-Chinese sentiment, piously joined in the finger-pointing.

Four companies of federal troops were sent from Vancouver Barracks to maintain law and order in Tacoma and to monitor the festering situation in Seattle. A federal grand jury, sitting in Vancouver, indicted 27 Tacomans, including Mayor R.J. Weisbach. All were released on $5,000 bail, and none ever came to trial.

An embarrassed Congress, fearful of losing trade with a friendly nation, voted to pay $276,619.75 in reparations to the

Chinese government. It's unlikely the victims saw a penny of it.

Chinese merchants and shippers put Tacoma on their blacklist for years. Neighboring cities treated the city like an outcast. There was real fear throughout Washington Territory that the rash action might stall statehood.

Seattle certainly could take no pride in how it handled the "Chinese problem." Anti-Chinese meetings, rife with violent rhetoric, took place in Yesler's Hall throughout the fall of '85. Pro-law-and-order meetings by those who called themselves "the better class" were held in Frye's Opera House.

The antis, in the majority, were mostly working people who talked about lost jobs and said "a Chinaman's word" was not to be trusted. Those who stood up for the Chinese did so for various reasons. The Methodist Episcopal Ministers' Association spoke out for Christian charity. Businessmen liked the cheap, reliable Chinese labor and worried about the city's reputation.

Unlike Tacoma, where the mayor had joined the mob, Seattle's mayor, Henry Yesler, strongly urged giving the Chinese full protection of the law.

The day after Tacomans ran the Chinese out of town, 150 frightened Chinese left Seattle by train or boat. Those who remained said they would be leaving as soon as they could sell their property.

When agitation continued, Yesler issued a proclamation urging all to stay home and refrain from action against the Chinese.

The town became an armed camp. Sheriff John McGraw mobilized the Home Guards, a band of arms-bearing men pledged to uphold the law. A federal vessel steamed into Seattle harbor. Troops from Vancouver Barracks patrolled the streets. And prominent citizens toted weapons under their coats.

The federal troops, alas, were not what the voices of reason had hoped for. Several young soldiers roughed up the Chinese, cutting off their pigtails and ordering them to pay for protection.

Anti-Chinese sentiment continued to grow. The Legislature came close to adopting four laws that would have made it impossible for the Chinese to live and work in the territory. In the end, only one passed — barring aliens from owning property.

On Feb. 6, 1886, another vigilante meeting was held in a downtown Seattle theater. The next morning, five- and six-man "committees" invaded the town's Chinese section, ordering residents to pack immediately and be taken to the docks — to be shipped to California aboard the Queen of the Pacific.

Although the mob brought 350 Chinese to the docks for "deportation," it could raise only enough money to pay the fare of 90 (the ship's captain wanted $7 a head). To further complicate matters, a Chinese merchant swore out a petition for a writ of habeas corpus to prevent the ship from leaving.

Eventually the mob grew sleepy and hungry. When its members went home, Sheriff McGraw and a contingent of armed officers swooped down on the dock, freeing those Chinese held in a warehouse and releasing those aboard the ship.

After being informed of their rights, 196 Chinese voluntarily elected to leave town aboard the vessel. Those who remained witnessed a shootout on their behalf in the Pioneer Square area

when territorial soldiers and sheriff's deputies confronted an anti-Chinese mob. Five men were wounded.

Governor Squire declared martial law. If that weren't sufficient to get the nation's attention, President Grover Cleveland announced a state of emergency in Seattle Feb. 9. Even as federal troops policed the streets, more Chinese left voluntarily.

The crisis was over. But anyone who thought charity and justice had triumphed had only to see the results of Seattle's municipal elections that summer. The People's Party, which included many leaders of the anti-Chinese movement, overwhelmed the Loyal League, which had opposed the agitators.

A Seattle in ashes

In the months just before statehood, major fires destroyed the business districts of Ellensburg, Spokane Falls and Seattle.

Seattle was bathed in sunshine June 6, 1889. Drays moved on narrow, planked streets with streetcar tracks down the middle. Men and women in the town of 86,000 walked on wooden sidewalks and conducted business in frame two- and three-story buildings, many of them perched on pilings. The waters of Elliott Bay then lapped at the foot of Beacon Hill.

At about 2:30 p.m., in a basement at the southeast corner of First Avenue and Madison Street, a glue pot bubbled on a stove in the cabinet-making shop of Victor Clairmont.

Clairmont's assistant, John Back, a Swedish immigrant, saw the pot boil over onto shavings on the floor and set them afire. Back grabbed a pail of water and threw it on the fire.

Instead of going out, the flames spread.

By the time the fire stopped, some 12 hours later, 25 blocks of downtown Seattle lay in smoldering ruins. Only the solid-brick Boston block, at the southeast corner of Second Avenue and Marion Street, was still upright. And it was scorched and singed and most windows broken.

A glue pot had accomplished for Seattle what Mrs. O'Leary's cow did for Chicago.

When the biggest fire of his life began, Seattle Fire Chief Josiah Collins was in San Francisco attending a wedding. By the time volunteer firefighters arrived with horse-drawn engines, smoke billowed from the entire Pontius block.

So inadequate was the water system that there soon was little more than a trickle from the hoses. Firefighters were forced back, their clothing scorched and burned.

Many businessmen pitched in to help, loosening celluloid collars, shedding vests and suit jackets. Others raced against time to remove valuables from their safes before fleeing into the streets.

First Avenue was a goner, everyone knew, when the city's pride and joy, Frye's Opera House, collapsed at First and Marion.

Mayor Robert Moran ordered dynamite to blow up buildings in the fire's path. Instead of stopping the flames, the explosions spewed embers higher and wider.

By 6 o'clock that evening, the fire had reached the heart of the

STATE-MENTS

Edward S. Salomon
Salomon, the ninth territorial governor (1870-72) was the only Jew ever to occupy the chair. He had a distinguished career as a Union general in the Civil War.

Fayette McMullen
McMullen, Washington's second territorial governor (1857-59), appealed to the Legislature to grant him a divorce shortly after his arrival. In spite of stiff Whig opposition, he was granted the decree — then married the daughter of a Thurston County pioneer. Soon after, he returned to Virginia and served the Confederacy during the Civil War.

Dr. William A. Newell
The 11th territorial governor (1880-84) and the only physician to serve in that position, Newell presided over a tremendous growth in Eastern Washington when the arrival of the Northern Pacific Railway brought Europeans to the wheatlands of the Big Bend and Palouse areas.
At one time, Newell was Lincoln's family physician, and he ministered to John Quincy Adams when the former president suffered a fatal stroke on the floor of the House of Representatives. Despite his progressive administration, Newell was never very popular. Many said it was because, at age 63, he insisted upon dyeing his hair and beard to look younger.

Museum of History and Industry

A guard leans against a safe in a burned-out building after the Great Seattle Fire of 1889.

CHRONO-LOG

Seattleites in 1890 were able take a streetcar from downtown to "away out in the country" — what is now the West Green Lake swimming beach.

1889

Enabling Act for statehood passed by Congress and approved by President Grover Cleveland on same day (Feb. 22). With 68,192 square miles, new state is smallest in West.

On Fourth of July, 75 delegates meet in Olympia to frame constitution similar to federal model. Territorial voters (males only) go to polls Oct. 1 to adopt constitution, 40,152-11,789, and elect first governor, Elisha P. Ferry, who serves two terms.

At same time, they overwhelmingly defeat measures on prohibition and women's suffrage.

Great Seattle Fire, started by overturned gluepot, lays waste to 25 blocks of downtown June 6. Two months later, Aug. 4, hot grease in frying pan explodes in flames at Bill Wolfe's Spokane Falls lunchroom. By nightfall, Howard Street Bridge has collapsed in Spokane River and 32 downtown blocks have been leveled by Spokane's Great Fire.

President Harrison issues proclamation Nov. 11 admitting Washington to Union.

1890

Northern Pacific Railway buys Puget Sound Shore Line (Tacoma to Seattle); Seattle given same freight rates as Tacoma, ending Seattle's hatred of NP for selecting "City of Destiny" as terminus.

George Francis Train circles globe in 67 days, leaving from Tacoma.

business district, the junction at James Street and Yesler Way. Banks, hotels, restaurants and mercantile establishments fell.

Then the fire headed toward the tideflats, wiping out saloons and gambling houses, cheap lodging houses and what was known as the "crib" or red-light district.

Flames finally were halted by a natural barrier, the water at the end of King Street.

There was surprisingly little hand-wringing. Civic and business leaders saw the devastation as an opportunity to rebuild — with wider streets, brick structures, improved building codes, better fire hydrants and a larger, paid fire department.

There were rumors, never confirmed, that a transient may have fallen to his death from the roof of one of the fiery buildings. But the only certain casualties had been tens of thousands of rats.

Nearby communities, including Seattle's friendly rival, Tacoma, sent aid. San Francisco collected $10,000 in fire relief. And in Virginia City, Nev., $4,000 was gathered by passing the hat in saloons.

Within a week, lines of white tents appeared where buildings had stood. They provided space for dentists to pull teeth, lawyers to write briefs and merchants to sell what remained of their stock.

The rebuilding was swift and solid. There was, in fact, such a run on bricks — millions were used in the reconstruction — that The Seattle Times pointed the finger of shame at those who hiked the price from a pre-fire $8 a thousand to the almost-criminal price of $15 a thousand.

But, then, inflation was everywhere. A pair of men's kid-leather shoes cost $2.50 a pair. Some merchants were asking $15 for a three-piece wool suit. And housing prices were outrageous. Why, some people were actually paying $3,000 for an eight-room house.

Not 'knowing their place'

Women's suffrage does not fit easily into any time frame in Washington's history.

It was simply a matter of fact that the women who tamed the frontier alongside the men and provided a major civilizing influence did not share the men's right to vote.

In 1854, the all-male Territorial Legislature, considering suffrage for the first time, came within a vote of granting it.

Abigail Scott Duniway, an Oregonian who came to the territory to lecture on feminism and suffrage, spearheaded the movement to reconsider the vote. Living in near-poverty, traveling constantly, even speaking in saloons, Duniway gained a devoted following. But she was reviled as often by women, who "knew their place," as she was by men.

Duniway was joined by the famous suffragette Susan B. Anthony in lobbying the constitutional convention of 1878 to counteract an 1871 territorial law denying suffrage until Congress declared it the supreme law of the land. That, they argued — unsuccessfully — was ducking the issue.

In 1881, suffrage was again considered. Although it failed, the mood was changing. And in 1883, the territory took a bold step. The territorial code was amended to "his and her" in all places where "his" had stood alone.

Women had the vote at last, and they exercised it in 1884 and 1886. However, in 1887, the Territorial Court ruled suffrage unconstitutional.

Enough pressure was exerted to put suffrage on the ballot in 1889. But, along with Prohibition, it was soundly defeated.

...AND ONE TO GROW ON

FIRST DECADE AS A STATE:
THE CATALYST FOR CIVILIZING

One month and 20 days after becoming a state, Washington entered what became known as "the Gay Nineties."

All was not gaiety, of course. There was labor unrest, a nationwide depression started in '93, and immigrants had trouble getting a foot on even the bottom rung of the economic ladder.

But generally, the state as well as the nation was in a mood to grow — and experiment a bit, too.

The population was 349,390 — up from 75,116 in 1880. Saloons outnumbered churches. Vaudeville boomed. Teddy Roosevelt and his Rough Riders fostered nationalistic pride.

Roads were little more than improved horse trails. People traveled by horse, boat, wagon or foot unless they were wealthy enough to afford a fine carriage.

Farmhouses were lighted by kerosene lamps, but electric lights were gaining popularity in the cities. Indoor plumbing slowly was supplanting outhouses, wells and back-porch water pumps. But the Saturday-night bath more often than not was taken in a copper washtub filled with steaming water from a tea kettle.

Kitchens were large and cozy. Stews bubbled on wood-burning stoves. Staples were stored in spacious pantries.

Musty parlors often were opened only when the parson or some other distinguished visitors came calling. In the finer homes — with big porches and gingerbread exteriors — were pianos, Edison cylinder phonographs and stereopticons, which transformed photographs into three-dimensional wonders.

Popular music ranged from the ballads of Stephen Foster to the stirring marches of John Philip Sousa. Bouncy, happy ragtime was beginning to have broad appeal.

While adults read and talked about "Dr. Jekyll and Mr. Hyde" and "The Red Badge of Courage," they encouraged their children — who were to be "seen but not heard" when adults were talking — to absorb the rags-to-riches message in Horatio Alger's stories.

Patent medicines were touted extravagantly.

Mormon Bishop's pills "cured" impotency, twitching eyelids, insomnia and evil desires. Murray's Specific was good for nervousness, hysteria and weak memory. Dr. Spinney & Co.'s Private Dispensary treated "young men suffering the effects of youthful indiscretion." Spinney modestly proclaimed his tonic to be "the greatest boon ever laid at the altar of suffering humanity."

The unthinkable happened when John L. Sullivan, "the Boston Strongboy," lost his heavyweight boxing title to will-o'-the-wisp "Gentleman Jim" Corbett.

Actress Lillian Russell was famed for her hats and hour-glass figure, and financier "Diamond Jim" Brady for his private railroad car, Havana cigars and free-and-easy way with $100 bills.

A proper woman's place was in the home, unless she nursed or taught school. When she ventured out in public, she wore dresses with leg o' mutton sleeves and bustles and, like Miss Russell, wouldn't dream of being seen without a hat. She sometimes corseted herself so tightly she swooned from lack of oxygen and required smelling salts.

Washington State Historical Society
George Francis Train, peripatetic Tacoma adventurer.

Gentlemen — as distinguished from the majority who felled the trees, dug the coal and worked on docks and ships — walked the streets in dark hats, dark suits and high, stiff collars. Some draped gold chains across their vests and made a show of pulling out railroad watches to check the time.

Little girls dressed in the same basic style as their mothers, without the bustles.

Little boys wore caps, knickerbockers and long stockings, which they rolled below the knee when adults weren't looking.

Washington was ripe for civilizing. And the '90s provided the catalyst.

World-class stage performers like Sarah Bernhardt were glad to bring culture to the frontier — for a price.

Every town worthy of its name soon had a baseball team.

A bicycling craze swept the state, and the women who took up tennis and mountain climbing — in a most ladylike way, of course — tried to emulate the new female ideal, the wholesome, athletic-looking "Gibson Girl."

"Daisy, Daisy, give me your answer true; I'm half crazy, all for the love of you..."

Public transportation in downtown Seattle in the late 1800s.

STATE-MENTS

President Benjamin Harrison was showered with more than attention on his visit to Washington.

Just passin' through

In May, 1891, the new state of Washington welcomed its first president, Benjamin Harrison, who had signed the statehood proclamation. Harrison arrived by boat from Tacoma and passed beneath an arch of fir boughs and patriotic streamers in Pioneer Place (now Pioneer Square) before boarding the Yesler cablecar for a trip to Lake Washington.

Later in the afternoon, when the president was prepared to speak to a large crowd from a platform erected on the grounds of the old territorial university, it suddenly began to rain — very hard. Harrison was drenched. His hat seemed to wilt. So did the cigar that had been clenched between his teeth. He turned to an aide and snapped, "Take me out of here." As the crowd cheered, the president retreated to a carriage that whisked him to the train depot and the private railroad car in which he was touring the country.

Harrison was not the first president to visit the Puget Sound area, however. In 1880, Rutherford B. Hayes and wife Lucy had come to Washington Territory. Lucy Hayes, whose teetotaling ways in the White House had earned her the nickname "Lemonade Lucy," signed an abstinence pledge in an Olympia Presbyterian church. In Seattle, Hayes rode in a carriage under an evergreen arch. At his side was Gen. William Tecumseh Sherman, the Civil War hero. After a state dinner in the Occidental Hotel, Hayes reportedly engaged in a lively discussion of the merits of various types of shellfish.

World enough and time

Four months after statehood, Tacomans became involved in a real-life adventure that epitomized the decade.

George Francis Train, an eccentric Bostonian who had been writing for The Tacoma Ledger since arriving in town, announced his intention of circling the globe in an unbelievable 60 days.

The record for such a feat had been set a few months earlier when Nellie Bly, sponsored by The New York World, went around the world in 72 days, 6 hours and 11 minutes, breaking the mythical standard set by Jules Verne's Phileas Fogg in "Around the World in 80 Days."

The publisher of The Ledger, already a fan of Train's off-the-wall writing — "Seattle, Seattle, Death Rattle, Death Rattle; Tacoma, Tacoma, Aroma, Aroma" — promised $1,000 if the adventurer could accomplish the feat.

To finance the journey, Train auctioned off seats for a lecture in a Tacoma theater. More than $4,000 was raised — enough to feed and transport Train and a Ledger reporter, Sam Wall, assigned to the adventure with his pen and a new camera, called the Kodak, patented two years earlier by George Eastman.

At 6 a.m. March 18, 1890, a cannon roared, throngs cheered and Train touched a brass plate embedded in the sidewalk in front of The Ledger offices. Train and Wall were off! They leaped into a horse-drawn carriage, which raced to the town's wharf. There they boarded the steamer Olympian, waiting to take them to Victoria, B.C., and a connection with the Abyssinia, bound for the Orient.

Train and Wall went around the world by way of Yokohama, Hong Kong, Singapore, Aden, Port Said, Naples, Paris, Calais, Dover, London, Dublin and New York.

It was marvelous stuff. Crowds gathered along the route to cheer the pair. Newspapers headlined their adventure in many languages, always mentioning the little town in the new state of Washington. Wall telegraphed dispatches to his newspaper.

Although Train was a master at cutting red tape, he ran into difficulty in New York. The Northern Pacific train expected to rush the pair across the continent not only hadn't arrived, it hadn't even been ordered. After a 36-hour wait, The New York Sun paid $1,000 to hire a special car, which was hitched to a Vanderbilt

Lines train bound for the West Coast.

In Oregon, they were delayed again. A bridge burned near The Dalles. The train that was supposed to be waiting in Portland hadn't been ordered. The Ledger's publisher wondered aloud: Was there a plot to foil the courageous pair?

But a train finally did arrive, and Train and Wall began the last leg of their journey north, cheered by crowds at every whistle stop.

The adventurers arrived in Tacoma 67 days, 13 hours, 2 minutes and 55 seconds after leaving town — a new record — to be greeted by a hat-waving, wildly enthusiastic throng. A cannon was fired — Tacoma liked cannons — and the heroes rode triumphantly through the streets behind a matched pair of high-stepping horses.

The Ledger's publisher paid off, conceding that Train could have made good on his boast to complete the journey in 60 days if he hadn't been the victim of delays over which he had no control.

A new porking space

When the new state's legislators convened, it was a little like a boy finally getting out of knickerbockers and feeling his oats.

There was a mad scramble for pork-barrel legislation. Every county, city, town and taxing district followed the lead and went on a spending spree. Bonded indebtedness soared.

In 1890, the Legislature established state normal schools in Ellensburg and Cheney, and three years later a third was added at Bellingham. In '91, the state agricultural college was awarded to Pullman, which had changed its name from Three Forks to honor George Pullman of railroad sleeper-car fame. It was hoped that Pullman would part with a few million dollars to give his namesake a nice start in the world. There is no record that he was so disposed.

The wild bunches

Roslyn, Kittitas County, was typical of the rough-and-tough mining towns that had sprouted in territorial days.

In August, 1888, during a violent struggle between the Knights of Labor and the owners of the biggest coal mine in Roslyn, five

CHRONO-LOG

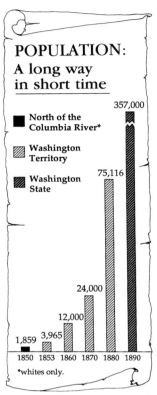

POPULATION:
A long way in short time

■ North of the Columbia River*

▨ Washington Territory

▨ Washington State

357,000

75,116

24,000

12,000

1,859   3,965

1850 1853 1860 1870 1880 1890

*whites only.

A U.S. Census report of 1890 showed how state's population grew by leaps and bounds. At the same time, Seattle had 86,000 people, Tacoma 36,006 and Spokane Falls 19,992.

1890
Olympia wins final election for state capital.

1891
State attorney general rules Bible-reading illegal in public schools.

1892
Smallpox epidemic in Seattle causes many deaths.

Seattle made main terminus of Great Northern Railway.

1893
Financial panic strikes nation; entire state hard hit.

Gov. John McGraw signs bill March 15 awarding annual Washington State Fair to North Yakima, which four years earlier had lost bid, along with Ellensburg, to become capital of new state. Town continues to host fair until 1932.

1894
"Coxey's Army," Populist march on nation's capital, initially attracts 1,300 unemployed men from Seattle and Tacoma.

union men were killed when a drunken engineer for the company railroad overturned a flatcar.

Both sides armed. When the mine's superintendent, Alexander Ronald, ventured too close to the miners, he was captured, trussed up like a turkey and placed between the rails of the Roslyn railroad spur.

Down the tracks came the train. The engineer spotted Ronald and the angry mob.

Not about to stop, he ordered his fireman to crawl out on the cowcatcher and scoop up Ronald on the move.

It worked. And with the two men still clinging to the cowcatcher, the engineer poured on the steam and highballed out of town.

Lowering of the boom

Washingtonians, expected to be solidly Republican when they attained statehood, predictably favored Benjamin Harrison (R) over Grover Cleveland (D) in their first presidential election in 1892. Cleveland, however, won.

It also was the year of the first smallpox epidemic in King County, resulting in a quarantine being placed against people wanting to enter the state from Victoria, B.C., and the construction of a pesthouse on Beacon Hill. Health officials became concerned that the use of whiskey as a "therapeutic measure" was being carried to the extreme.

Then came the Panic of '93, a nationwide depression that was triggered when the Reading Railroad went bankrupt and large corporations and banks went under. The Puget Sound area, which had billed itself as "the boomingest region on earth," no longer was booming.

Sawmills shut down. Shopkeepers locked their doors. Former building owners were reduced to janitors. Banks gave those who never did feel they were safe a chance to say "I told you so."

Crash followed crash. Fourteen banks failed in Tacoma, 11 in Seattle. The First National Bank of Spokane went under.

Walla Walla suffered its first crop failure when rain started early in August and wheat sprouted in sacks before it was planted.

Land values depreciated by as much as 80 percent in the Puget Sound area. Streetcar lines went bankrupt. So did one of Seattle's pioneer figures, David T. Denny.

When a citizen in Spokane got a restraining order to head off construction of a new water system, an angry mob threatened to lynch him. The citizen withdrew the restraining order, saying he was "sacrificing principle to mob rule."

As a result of the Panic of '93, Washingtonians began to display the first hints of an independent liberalism that would, in the 1930s, give rise to the famous toast attributed to Postmaster General James Farley when he was in Seattle for a visit:

"To the 47 states and the soviet of Washington."

(For the record, Farley never admitted it.)

Populism on the march

The Populist Party convention in Ellensburg in '93 attracted delegates from around the state, and the following year Washington's unemployed began listening to the siren call of Ohio-based reformer Jacob Sechler Coxey to join his "Commonweal Army of Christ" in a May Day march to the Capitol steps in Washington, D.C.

An estimated 1,300 unemployed men from Seattle and Tacoma gathered in Puyallup under the leadership of Frank "Jumbo" Cantwell, sometime Tacoma barroom bouncer, with the intention of hiring, but taking by force if necessary, a Northern Pacific train bound for the Midwest. From there, they hoped to catch another train to Washington, D.C.

Puyallup residents opened homes and larders to the down-and-out men. When Gov. John McGraw showed up to tell the state's contingent of "Coxey's Army" that there would be no train for them, he was roundly booed. Some would-be marchers went home. But several hundred took off with their bedrolls, intending to walk over the Cascades. Residents of small towns cheered them on, offering more food. A few men hopped aboard the freight trains that slowed down to get over the mountains.

Cantwell, his wife and a few diehard followers made it to Chicago, where Cantwell received a hero's welcome and later was elected an alderman.

But Coxey's march was a bust. Instead of the 100,000 marchers he promised, only about 500 showed up to walk down Pennsylvania Avenue. Coxey was arrested on the Capitol steps. The charges: carrying banners and walking on the Capitol lawn.

Even though Coxey's Army was to become nothing more than a historical footnote, resentment continued to fester over what many perceived to be an unfair distribution of wealth and society's benefits. Populist speakers frequently cited statistics to show that

THE ULTIMATE IN SUMMITRY

From the beginning, the enormous snow-capped mountain that Vancouver named Rainier (after his friend, British Admiral Peter Rainier) attracted artists, writers and men who wanted to experience the thrill of standing on its summit.

In 1847, Lt. August Kautz, stationed at Fort Steilacoom, undertook the first recorded ascent along with two soldiers, the post doctor and an Indian guide. The party reached an altitude of about 12,000 feet before turning back because of bad weather and lack of food.

In 1853, Theodore Winthrop came out from Massachusetts to write about Puget Sound and the Cascades. In his book, "The Canoe and the Saddle," Winthrop declared that the Indians called the mountain "Tacoma."

The controversy was further fueled in August 1870, when Gen. Hazard Stevens, son of the first territorial governor, and Philemon Van Trump became the first to complete the ascent. They gave names to glaciers, creeks, ridges and canyons and, in a vivid account in the Atlantic Monthly, Stevens called the mountain "Takhoma."

By 1890, there had been several dozen ascents. But the most significant occurred on Aug. 10 that year when Fay Fuller, a Pierce County schoolteacher and sometime newspaper reporter, became the first woman to stand atop the state's highest mountain.

Fuller was just 20 at the time. For the climb, she had dressed in boy's shoes, an ankle-length bloomer outfit covered with a coat, a blouse, warm gloves and a straw hat secured with hairpins. She carried a blanket roll slung over her shoulder and an alpenstock fashioned from a shovel handle.

Fuller shielded her eyes with goggles. To avoid sunburn, she smeared her face with a concoction of cold cream, flour and coal dust. She suffered a severe burn, nonetheless.

Afterward, Fuller would say she was more drained than exhilarated when she reached the top with her companions — the Rev. E.C. Smith, Len Longmire, W.O. Amsden and Robert Parrish. The sense of accomplishment would come later.

The climbers heated beef broth and rubbed their feet with whiskey, then huddled together in the blankets to spend the night in an ice cave.

Seattle Times

In this posed studio shot, Fay Fuller re-enacts her climb of Mount Rainier on Aug. 10, 1890.

Details of the climb were reported in Every Sunday, a Tacoma weekly published by Fuller's father. The feat brought Fuller worldwide acclaim and a touch of notoriety. Newspapers and magazines published a photograph of her, in full climbing gear, taken in a Tacoma studio several weeks afterward.

Years later, Fuller (then Mrs. Fritz von Briesen) would say: "I was very nearly ostracized in Tacoma because I was a lone woman climbing with four men, and in that immodest costume."

one-eighth of the people in the United States owned seven-eighths of the wealth.

Glitter of the Klondike

Populist Gov. John Rogers had been in office only a few months, presiding over a state in the depths of a depression, when an event occurred that made his one of the most prosperous administrations in the state's history.

On the morning of July 17, 1897, hundreds of people gathered at Schwabacher's Dock, on Seattle's waterfront, to welcome the steamship Portland from the Klondike gold fields in Canada's Yukon Territory. A short time before, the Excelsior had arrived in San Francisco carrying half a ton of gold.

Those who jammed the dock were looking for anything that might spell the end of hard times, and this appeared to be it. Rumor had it that the Portland was carrying not a half-ton of gold, but a *whole* ton of it.

As the ship touched the dock, the crowd erupted with cheers. Miners aboard the Portland grinned self-consciously, as the newly rich often do. More than a few were nursing king-sized hangovers from days and nights of hard drinking and card playing.

The arrival of the Portland electrified the world and touched off a gold rush that ended the city's economic woes and established it as the staging area for the Klondike.

Indeed, even before the Portland docked, it was booked solid for its return trip north to Alaska, where a new town, Skagway, grew almost overnight as the jumping-off place for Dawson, in the heart of the gold fields.

Seattle was perfectly situated, geographically, as the point of departure for those who had gold fever. And the entrepreneurs to serve their needs quickly surfaced.

In fact, considering the number of people who lost their lives or didn't hit paydirt, the smartest people may have been those who stayed behind to open restaurants, saloons, houses of prostitution and stores selling prospecting equipment.

Every day in the boom town by Elliott Bay would prove the veracity of P.T. Barnum's famous saying, "A sucker is born every minute." One enterprising businessman reportedly became wealthy selling bicycles to naive would-be miners who thought they could ride them into the gold fields.

The year after the Portland's arrival, a government assay office was opened in Seattle to handle the gold. The boom lasted longer than anyone expected. Two years after the Yukon strike, gold was discovered in Nome, Alaska. And in 1902, more gold was found in Fairbanks.

Ships carrying gold continued to arrive in Seattle. One vessel, appropriately named City of Seattle, was carrying three tons when it docked in July 1899. And in 1900, some $22 million worth of gold passed through Seattle's assay office.

By the time the gold rush had slowed to a walk in the early 1900s, Seattle was firmly established as a vigorous seaport.

Passing of a princess

Seattle took time off June 6, 1896, to pay its last respects to Princess Angeline, daughter of Chief Sealth, who had died a week earlier at her waterfront shack near the coal bunkers at the foot of Pike Street.

Our Lady of Good Help Catholic Church was jammed with the city's leading citizens. A pair of high-stepping black horses drew a black hearse.

Princess Angeline was laid to rest in a canoe-shaped coffin, a paddle resting on the stern. A sprig of cedar was dropped into her Lake View Cemetery grave, next to the final resting place of her good friend, Henry Yesler.

Seattle schoolchildren donated pennies and dimes to provide a fitting tombstone — a simple granite rock, for a simple, strongly independent woman.

In life, Angeline's palace was her waterfront hut. Her throne was a rocking chair on her front porch or a wooden sidewalk downtown, where she crouched with baskets and trinkets. Her crown was a colorful bandana, and her royal raiment consisted of several faded skirts and a shawl held together by a large safety pin.

Angeline frequently worked as a washerwoman or sold clams door to door. In her declining years, she hobbled on arthritic legs, clutching a slender staff. She accepted coins dropped into her weathered hand.

Probably no person in Seattle ever was more photographed than she. She rarely smiled, letting her seamed face speak for itself.

Many of the small boys who followed her in the streets, hurling taunts, grew up to become her protectors, treating her with courtesy and letting her roam their stores and pick out anything she wanted without paying for it.

Angeline was generous by nature. When she had something extra — usually a box of cigars — she would give it away, Indian potlatch style.

When President Harrison visited Seattle in 1891, he reportedly bowed politely to the Indian princess, who was decked out in a new dress. She reportedly put out her hand and said, "Kla-how-ya," because she never did get the hang of English.

In another version, the president accidentally drove right past

Washington State Historical Society

To handle the flow of Klondike gold in 1898, the U.S. Assay Office was opened in Seattle at Ninth Avenue and James Street. Here it melts part of the first $100 million in gold from the north.

CHRONO-LOG

"The Great Bicycle Fad" hits its stride as single-wheelers, two-wheelers, tandems and sextettes appear. Officials rush to build bicycle paths and bridges, as well as enact bicycle taxes and speed laws. Illuminated bicycle parades become the rage.

1895

"Barefoot Schoolboy Law" is pushed through Legislature by Populist member John Rogers. Law does away with old practice of financing schools locally and guarantees minimum state support for educating all children. It becomes firm foundation of state's modern public-school system.

University of Washington moves to present campus amid claims it's too noisy to study at downtown site.

Author Mark Twain, giving an August lecture in Western Washington, delivers what locals consider one of his most memorable lines: "The pleasantest winter I ever spent was a summer on Puget Sound."

1896

John Rogers elected governor (Fusion Party — Populists, "Silver Republicans" and Democrats); state gives presidential vote to William Jennings Bryan (D).

Princess Angeline, daughter of Chief Sealth, dies.

1897

Klondike gold rush begins to Alaska and the Yukon. Steamer Portland arrives with "ton of gold."

1899

Mount Rainier National Park created; is nation's fifth.

Angeline in his carriage and she stomped off in a huff.

In writing about Angeline, it is difficult to separate fact from fiction.

Two of the better stories:

■ That she paddled her canoe through a blinding snowstorm to warn settlers of an impending attack on Seattle (1856) by Chief Leschi. (Historians generally credit a friendly Indian named Curley with sounding the alarm.)

■ That she wanted to marry a brave of her own Suquamish tribe, but her father wanted her to marry another chief. When the chief arrived to claim her, she fled through the night to find her true love. Spying his canoe on the shore, she leaped in and told the brave she loved him. Silently, the man paddled away. Too late, Angeline discovered it was not her Indian lover but Henri, a French-Canadian fur trader whom she did not like. Henri is said to have taken Angeline to Canada, where she lived with him until he died in a drunken brawl. Then she returned to Seattle. (This story, too, was never confirmed.)

C.T. Conover, an early-day historian, personally witnessed one of the most touching incidents involving Angeline.

On the morning after Yesler died, Angeline hobbled for blocks, resting on the charred walking stick she used to stir her home fires. She knocked at the door of Yesler's mansion, where the King County Courthouse now stands. Then she went inside to pay her last respects. Using the Indian word for friend, she said goodbye to her "beloved old tillicum."

A mountainous task

The last major story of the '90s involved the state's most visible wonder — the enormous chunk of glacier-covered rock that Fay Fuller had scaled early in the decade.

On July 16, 1894, Sen. Watson Squire introduced a memorial to the 53rd Congress asking that a national park be created in Washington state to include "Mount Rainier, often called Mount Tacoma."

Throughout the memorial, Squire, a good politician, referred to The Mountain as "Rainier" in one paragraph and "Tacoma" in the next.

Among those favoring national-park status for The Mountain, Squire said, were the Geological Society of America, the American Association for the Advancement of Science, the National Geographic Society, the Sierra Club and the Appalachian Mountain Club.

Signing on behalf of the Sierra Club was John Muir, the noted naturalist.

It took nearly five years for the memorial creating "Washington National Park" to work its way through Congress. At the last minute, an amendment was attached by John Lacey of Iowa, chairman of the House Public Lands Committee, changing the name to "Mount Rainier National Park." President William McKinley signed the bill March 2, 1899.

It was the fifth national park — after Yellowstone, Sequoia, Yosemite and General Grant (now King's Canyon).

At the time the 241,782-acre park was created, Mount Rainier's height was listed as 14,363 feet in official documents (165 feet less than the figure arrived at by some crude measurements).

On Jan. 22, 1914, the U.S. Geological Survey announced that four years of meticulous remeasuring showed it had "grown" to 14,408 feet.

In the 1950s another re-measurement was undertaken. It took several years, and at the conclusion two more feet were added to the mountain's height. All of that effort to gain 24 inches prompted a waggish Tacoma newspaperman, John Murphy, to proclaim, "They strained and produced a mouse." The accepted height was 14,410 feet until one foot was added in 1989.

Princess Angeline, daughter of Chief Sealth, in a characteristic pose

Seattle Times

The creation of Mount Rainier National Park, however, certainly didn't end the squabble over The Mountain's name. Some of the best comic-opera material was yet to come.

Seattleites naturally welcomed Rainier as the name for the national park, feeling secure at last with a name that wouldn't give a publicity advantage to their principal rival to the south.

But the editor of The Tacoma Ledger summed up prevailing sentiment in Tacoma when he called the new park's name "an insult."

Tacomans huffily said they would go along with "Mount Rainier National Park," but would continue to call its principal attraction "Mount Tacoma."

The name fight had see-sawed for years.

As early as 1870, the U.S. Board on Geographic Names had ruled in favor of Mount Rainier.

But when the Northern Pacific Railway selected Tacoma, "The City of Destiny," as its terminus in 1873, one of the first things the railroad moguls did was trumpet the grandeur of "Mount Tacoma" in their brochures.

Railway officials may have been rash, but they were not stupid. In 1916, they threw in the sponge. But the next year, the matter was back in the lap of the geographic-names board, which also was asked to change the names of Mount St. Helens, Hood Canal, Mount Baker and Puget Sound.

This time, a distinguished geological-survey expert, C. Hart Marriman, wrote the opinion.

Marriman noted that The Mountain also was known to Indian tribes as Stiquak and Puskehouse "and nobody is pushing for these." He added that the name Rainier should be retained "in justice to its discoverer, in justice to the science of geography, and in justice to the principle of permanence in geographic names."

The Board on Geographic Names granted another review in 1921. Same result.

Undaunted, Tacomans continued to form committees to rename The Mountain. And newspaper editorial writers continued to decry the folly of naming a mountain after a British admiral (Peter Rainier) who had fought in the Revolutionary War against the very man (George Washington) for whom our state is named.

The Mount Tacoma Club changed tactics. If the names board wouldn't act responsibly, then it would be bypassed. Congress alone would be asked to make the decision.

In 1924, Washington state's Sen. C.C. Dill and Rep. Albert Johnson introduced a joint resolution in Congress to rename mountain and park after Tacoma.

The Senate approved the name change. But before the House could act, Congress adjourned and the House asked for guidance from Tacoma's old nemesis, the Board on Geographic Names.

The board, by this time thoroughly sick of the whole matter, reported back that it still favored Rainier.

When Congress resumed in 1925, everything hinged on the House Public Lands Committee, which voted 9-to-4 not to report the Senate's resolution to the House floor. Mount Tacoma had lost its fourth, last and closest fight.

Over at last?

Not quite.

In 1978, the state Board on Geographic Names held a hearing to consider a recommendation that Mount Tacoma be made official. The name remained Rainier.

For those with a sense of humor, the high point of the debate may have occurred in 1894 when Vice President Adlai Stevenson, in Cleveland's second term, performed a remarkable bit of political legerdemain during visits to Seattle and Tacoma.

In both cities he carefully avoided calling The Mountain by name, concluding with "Ladies and gentlemen, there is no doubt in my mind what The Mountain should be called."

The cheers were said to be deafening.

2. WIDENING HORIZONS

ON THE EDGE OF THE CONTINENT,
ALL THINGS ARE POSSIBLE

1900 TO 1910

'Son, I hate sin. You know that. But I love sinners.'

— The Rev. Dr. Mark Matthews, after hounding a bootlegger into jail one day and interceding for him in court the next

Seattle Times

An 1899 photo captures the spirit of the Klondike gold rush on the Seattle waterfront, when gold-seekers by the thousands flocked to the city, bought their provisions and then shipped north on whatever vessel would take them. Below, Ford's Model T — the "Tin Lizzie" — made its debut in 1908 and mobilized America.

Washington soared into the 20th century on the wings of the Klondike gold rush and the greatest surge of new arrivals it would ever know.

There was a swagger in its walk, a boldness in its vision, a world's fair in its near future. Out here, on the edge of the continent, the great Pacific lapping at the front door, all things seemed possible.

Between 1900 and 1910, the state's population more than doubled — from 518,000 to 1,142,000. Seattle's population almost trebled in the decade — from 86,671 to 237,194.

Horseless carriages, which had been in limited production since the early 1890s, appeared in the first month of the new century, one vehicle in Seattle and one in Spokane. By the time Washington state took its first automobile census six years later, there were 763 horseless carriages. By 1915, there would be 46,000.

By the middle of the decade, many people in the state thought it was time to pass new laws if horses and cars were to co-

Acme Roto Service

CHRONO-LOG

1900
Butler Hotel
opens, becoming landmark
in hospitality west
of Rockies and north of San
Francisco.

Tacoma streetcar disaster
results in 43 dead, 59
seriously injured after
trolley bound for
Independence Day parade
roars down Delin Street
Hill, topples off trestle,
plunges 120 feet into gulch.
At grand-jury bearing to fix
blame, several experts say
motorman for Tacoma
Railway & Motor Co. had
failed to dump sand on
tracks as he braked for the
bill. But he had died in the
accident and couldn't
defend himself.

1901
Nickelodeon,
forerunner of motion
pictures, makes Seattle
debut at La Petite theater,
changing nature of
entertainment.

John Considine,
nickelodeon-vaudeville-
theater entrepreneur, shoots
Seattle Police Chief W.L.
Meredith dead in
impromptu Skid Road duel.

Populist Gov. John Rogers,
branded "wild man" and
"radical" when elected for
first time in 1896 but later
hailed as businessman's
dream, dies Dec. 27 after a
week-long bout with
pneumonia.

*Big salmon were
commonplace in the early
1900s. A Puget Sound
cannery worker holds an
80-pound fish in 1909.*

Washington State Historical Society

Seattle Times

Northwest logging at the turn of the century was all man- and animal-power. This scene in the Stillaguamish Valley shows a skid road, used to haul logs out of the woods. Man with bucket in foreground is a "grease monkey," who kept the skids lubricated; hence the term "greasing the skids."

exist. Yakima boldly raised its automobile speed limit from 6 to 12 miles an hour. Seattle followed suit a short time later.

"Where, oh where will it end?" cried those who thought such speeds almost obscenely high.

The state went on a road-building binge. At the time of the first car census, there were 1,200 miles of improved and unimproved roads. Nine years later, there were 37,500 miles.

Telephone use, a commercial reality back East since 1878, rose even more dramatically. Only 21,447 phones existed in the entire state in 1902. Fifteen years later, there were 188,407.

Although the most northwesterly state in the continental United States was still an untamed frontier in the eyes of many Easterners, its residents — linked to Alaska by the gold rush and enjoying a booming trade with Japan — felt anything but isolated.

They were excited to learn that the first wireless telegraph message had been flashed across the Atlantic in 1901. They mourned when an assassin's bullet felled President William McKinley the same year.

When the digging of the Panama Canal began in 1904, they related it to their own earth-moving projects, Seattle's regrades.

And in 1905 they joined the rest of the nation in applying the word "genius" to Albert Einstein, who had just published his theory of relativity.

Grateful for San Francisco's help during the Great Fire of '89, Seattle sent aid to the City by the Bay when an earthquake devastated it in 1906.

Henry Ford marketed his first Model T in 1908, the start of putting an automobile within the reach of virtually every American family. Although Seattle never became Detroit West, Ford selected it that year as the site of an automobile-and-tractor assembly plant.

The Ford plant, on the south end of Lake Union, had a maximum production of 143 vehicles a day. It lasted until a new plant was erected in 1930 at East Marginal Way South. Three years later, the plant closed forever — a victim of the Great Depression.

It was also in 1908 that the Legislature narrowly defeated a bill to amend the state Constitution by striking the word "male" from the clause relating to voting requirements.

The following year, Robert Peary was credited with reaching the North Pole, and a group of Washington women — as determined as Peary — climbed to the top of Mount Rainier to plant a banner proclaiming "Votes-for-Women."

Shortly after the beginning of the new century, comic strips

began to appear in newspapers. At the same time, music became the national unifier. Americans thrilled to the songs of operetta composer Victor Herbert, and men with a yen for four-part harmonizing launched into such favorites as "Dear Old Girl" and "Sweet Adeline."

Among the enduring favorites that rolled off the assembly line of New York music-publishing firms, dubbed Tin Pan Alley: "Wait Till the Sun Shines, Nellie," "Bill Bailey, Won't You Please Come Home," "In the Good Old Summertime," "Chinatown," "Just a-Wearyin' for You" and George M. Cohan's "You're a Grand Old Flag."

This is how it was in the first decade of the 20th century:

Seedlings of an empire

In 1900, a transaction that would establish Washington as one of the nation's leading lumber states was consummated in St. Paul, Minn., between next-door neighbors — German-born Frederick Weyerhaeuser, who had made his fortune logging the virgin timber of the Great Lakes area, and Canadian-born James J. Hill, renowned as the "empire builder" for his role in developing the Northwest through the Northern Pacific and Great Northern railways.

According to the official Weyerhaeuser story, "Timber and Men," the two men had talked for years around the fireplace of Weyerhaeuser's home, which overlooked the Mississippi. Or, rather, Hill had talked, hardly noticing that Weyerhaeuser frequently nodded off.

Weyerhaeuser was hungry for a fresh supply of logs as timber stands dwindled around the Great Lakes. He had extended his operations to the South and had made small forays into Washington state, buying forest land in Skagit County and a Puget Sound shingle mill.

Hill had vast timber holdings as the result of the government's right-of-way grants. What he needed was ready cash to expand his railroad empire and a sure cargo for his trains when they headed back from the Coast.

Hill made a proposal. Weyerhaeuser stayed awake.

The result: Weyerhaeuser would buy from his old friend 900,000 acres of timberland in Washington state at $6 an acre. Hill would pocket $5.4 million.

The deal startled the nation's timber industry and changed for all time the course of lumbering in North America.

In those days, even Weyerhaeuser didn't have that much money in cash. He got together with associates to put up $3 million. The rest was to be paid in eight semiannual installments at 5 percent interest. The company soon set up shop in Tacoma and called itself the Weyerhaeuser Timber Co.

The year of the big transaction, Washington was the fifth largest lumber-producing state. By the middle of the decade it had become No. 1.

In 1907 and 1909, the state had more than 1,000 operating sawmills (there was a slight drop in 1908). Although there never again would be that many mills, lumber production increased almost every year until the Great Depression more than two decades later.

Necktie party; RSVP

Despite its growing industrial base, Washington frequently reverted to its frontier origins — more oriented to necktie parties than to tea parties.

On March 30, 1900, R.D. Speck, sheriff of Spokane County, staged a public execution — by invitation only — in the courthouse courtyard.

Speck, who had a flair for the dramatic, issued formal invitations on which were printed: "You are invited to be present at the execution of George Webster."

In the upper left-hand corner was a photograph of Webster, wearing a dark suit and tie, his hair slicked back, a large mustache adorning his lip.

Crowds began arriving early for George Webster's last morning on earth. They presented their invitations at a canvas-draped black-metal gate, the only entrance to the walled courtyard.

Inside, they examined the gallows built for the occasion. Canvas covered all courthouse windows facing on the courtyard. County offices had been closed.

Those without invitations milled around Mallon Street, outside the courtyard. There were rumors that counterfeit invitations had been sold in Spokane's saloons the previous night and that Sheriff Speck had allowed many of his friends to slip inside without the passes.

An active grapevine relayed status reports on the condemned man. Webster had just eaten his last meal. He had met with a minister. His attorney, Del Smith, had been his last visitor.

Suddenly a hush fell over the crowd. Webster appeared at the courtyard door, blinking in the sunlight. His hands were cuffed behind him. His head was bare and his hair carefully combed. With short, quick steps, he climbed the 13 steps to the gallows.

Webster shook his head when asked if he had any last words. The noose was adjusted, the trapdoor sprung. Soon afterward, the prisoner was declared dead.

Souvenir hunters fought over the rope. It was said that a few inches of the hemp was legal tender at any Spokane saloon that night.

The central figure in the public hanging was an itinerant ranch hand who had shot and killed a farmer's wife while in a drunken stupor. The death penalty would be unlikely today.

There IS a free lunch

Embers of the Great Seattle Fire of '89 hardly had cooled when Guy Phinney, "father of half of Seattle," began construction of the Butler Hotel, east of Pioneer Square.

Its doors opened in 1900, and it immediately lived up to its billing as the jewel in the Queen City's crown. Its lavish Rose Room grill featured magnificent cuisine in an atmosphere of cut-glass chandeliers, imported carpets and sterling silver.

Its free lunch was the talk of the town. Succulent hams. Steaming roasts. Plump sausages. Rye with caraway seeds. Tiny onions. Assorted cheeses. Buy a 5-cent beer and help yourself.

Even those accustomed to splendor were dazzled by the Butler's 16,000-pound bar, which had an enormous mirror of beveled Belgian glass. The list of overnight guests was a veritable Who's Who of America:

Grover Cleveland. William McKinley. Teddy Roosevelt. Gen. John J. Pershing. DeWolfe Hopper, famed for reciting "Casey at the Bat." Lillian Russell. Anna Held of the Ziegfeld Follies.

Appearing there with his Brunswick Recording Orchestra was Vic Meyers, later lieutenant governor and secretary of state. Meyers used to tell about a jug-eared young baritone who unsuccessfully auditioned for soloist. His name was Bing Crosby.

After falling into decline, the eight-story hotel was reduced to a two-story parking lot in 1934. Workmen digging in the cornerstone found an almost-full bottle of whiskey. It figured.

Death in the Statehouse

Between 1900 and 1910, two governors died in office — John Rogers and Samuel Cosgrove.

Rogers, a populist elected as the Fusion Party candidate in 1896 and re-elected in 1900, died Dec. 27, 1901, after a short bout with pneumonia. He was succeeded by Republican Lt. Gov. Henry McBride.

Cosgrove, a Republican elected in 1908 from tiny Pomeroy, Garfield County, after the state's first open primary, became known as the "one-day governor." Immediately after delivering his inaugural address Jan. 27, 1909, he informed the Legislature he wanted a leave to recover his health. He died of a kidney ailment three months later in Southern California, and was succeeded by Lt. Gov. Marion Hay, also a Republican.

Rogers was deeply mourned, The Seattle Times referring to him as "the best governor the state has ever had." There had been a dramatic turnabout. When Rogers took office he was branded a wild man and a radical, and the business community predicted he'd socialize the state.

But with a big assist from the '97 gold rush, Rogers was a businessman's dream — level-headed, budget-conscious and personable. Signs of prosperity were everywhere — in the vaudeville houses that sprung up, in the ships that came into Elliott Bay from all over the world, in mushrooming civic and social organizations.

Prosperity had brought the state back into the Republican fold after a brief flirtation with the Democrats (William Jennings Bryan) in '96. The GOP captured every state office in 1900, with the exception of governor (Rogers).

Republican presidential nominees William McKinley, Teddy Roosevelt and William Howard Taft would carry the state easily in the first decade of the new century.

With Hay in office, the 1909 Legislature passed a great deal of progressive lawmaking: life-insurance regulation, diking- and drainage-district laws, firemen's relief and pension funds, regulation and registration of nurses, and a criminal code.

Fire and brimstone on Elliott Bay

Virtually all seaports were subject to their share of sin and corruption. But not many had a battler for the human soul equal to the Rev. Dr. Mark Matthews, who arrived in Seattle in 1902 and was to cast a long shadow until his death 38 years later.

The story goes that during a brief visit, before accepting the

Museum of History and Industry
Seattle police officers line up for inspection at the old City Hall in the early 1900s.

CHRONO-LOG

Seattle Times

Looking every bit the zealous frontier preacher, the Rev. Dr.
Mark Matthews, a Seattle institution for the first four decades
of the century, poses with two Army officers.

pulpit of the First Presbyterian Church, the fiery preacher had a gambling establishment pointed out to him.

"Either that must go or I will not stay," Matthews reportedly said. The gambling den didn't go, and neither did the learned Matthews, who had doctorates in religion and law. Their confrontations provided years of excitement.

Born in Calhoun, Ga., ordained at 20, Matthews was tall (6 feet 5 inches) and cadaverous, with a long nose, a firm jaw and hair that curled over his ears and back around a high, stiff collar. Below the prominent Adam's apple, he usually wore a string tie of the type clerics favored.

Matthews strode around town in a long black coat and a black hat — a worthy foe for the devil against whom he had declared war. One of his major callings, he felt, was to uplift Seattle's moral climate. His special targets were liquor, gambling, prostitution, corrupt public officials and the "communist menace."

Each crusade rallied new friends to Matthews' side. Each also created a host of enemies, which seemed not to bother the clergyman a bit.

Although Matthews sometimes seemed to be hung up on sin and lust, he also took up the cross for civic and humane causes. He organized an open-air camp for the tubercular, opened a kindergarten and established the town's first day nursery and juvenile court. He chaired the King County Chapter of the American Red Cross for many years and frequently appeared as a friend of the court. He would hound a bootlegger into the arms of the law one day and intercede for him in court the next, saying, "Son, I hate sin. You know that. But I love sinners."

Matthews was credited with taking 24,092 members into his church, making it the largest Presbyterian congregation in the nation. He established 28 branch churches and had 10 assistant pastors. In 1922, he began broadcasting on the first church-owned radio station (KTW) in America. His study was a few feet from the microphones, which he used often to spread his message.

For years, Matthews carried an honorary Seattle Police Department badge and special deputy sheriff's badge No. 1. The clergyman made only one arrest. But what a pinch it was.

In 1909, he formally arrested Chief of Police Charles Wappenstein, the man who had issued his badge. Matthews accused Wappenstein of protecting prostitution, and he didn't rest until the chief wound up behind bars.

Matthews then took off against Mayor Hiram Gill's "open city" policy, hiring an investigator from the Burns Detective Agency to find out if the man called "Hi" was up to no good. Convinced Gill

was not pure, Matthews spearheaded his recall. But he fought just as vigorously from his pulpit to head off the recall of another mayor, Charles L. Smith.

Pews were packed every Sunday for Matthews' polished if sometimes biting sermons. His scope was remarkable — attacking pacifists, liberal theologians and the Industrial Workers of the World labor union — the famed "Wobblies" — on one hand and supporting the League of Nations and a world-wide effort to feed the hungry on the other.

In a 1924 poll to name America's leading Protestant ministers, Matthews was listed among the nation's 25 most influential.

Historian Dale Soden wrote, after examining Matthews' personal papers, that the clergyman once asked the FBI's J. Edgar Hoover to make him a special agent so he could pursue anyone suspected of espionage.

Matthews, a bundle of contradictions, died in 1940 at age 72. His funeral was attended by the governor, the mayor and virtually every public official in Western Washington. Florist shops sold out. Police had to control the throngs who jammed the streets outside the packed church to pay their last respects to a man who, love him or hate him, had been a powerful force in the community.

When Matthews' estate was probated, it was discovered that the man who had collected millions of dollars for national and foreign missions had accumulated only a few thousand dollars for himself.

Countdown on a desperado

An authentic Public Enemy No. 1 came calling in the summer of 1902.

His name was Harry Tracy, and he had begun his life of crime as head of the notorious Hole in the Wall outlaw gang that robbed banks and shot up the West. In the late 1890s, Tracy escaped from a Utah prison, killed a man, moved to Colorado and killed another. Two dead. Eight to go.

Tracy, a master escape artist, was captured. He escaped, was recaptured and escaped again. Finally, lodged in the Oregon State Penitentiary at Salem with his wife's brother, David Merrill, Tracy plotted his final prison break. Fellow criminals smuggled in rifles. Tracy and Merrill shot their way out, killing two guards and an inmate. Five dead. Five to go.

Hiding out, traveling by night, breaking into farmhouses and demanding food and fresh clothing, Tracy and Merrill worked their way to a clearing outside Chehalis, Lewis County.

There, according to stories Tracy later told his hostages, he and Merrill argued violently about Merrill's lack of stomach for killing and his tendency to squeal to the cops. They decided upon a duel to the death, back to back, 10 paces, turn and fire.

Tracy cheated. He took two steps, whirled and shot his brother-in-law in the back. He finished the job with another shot to the head. Six dead. Four to go.

The outlaw next appeared at South Bay, near Olympia, where he commandeered a boat and crew and set out for Seattle. Tracy took a hostage when he left the boat. He later released him — a pattern that would be repeated many times.

Seattle was in a frenzy. Bolt the doors! Break out the rifles! Form a posse! Harry Tracy is coming!

Encountering a sheriff's posse near Bothell, Tracy opened fire, gunning down one deputy sheriff and severely wounding another. Seven dead. Three to go.

Tracy took a small boat to Bainbridge Island, where he strained the hospitality of a farm family. He returned to Seattle by skiff, with the family's husband as hostage.

Descriptions varied wildly. Tracy is tall. Tracy is short. Tracy wears cowboy boots. Tracy wears street shoes. Tracy wears a

Seattle Times

Harry Tracy, an early Northwest version of John Dillinger or
Pretty Boy Floyd, killed nine men before his own violent
death following a farmhouse shootout in 1902.

black hat. Tracy is bareheaded.

The real Tracy next appeared at the home of a Seattle widow on Phinney Avenue North. The widow tipped off a butcher boy, who notified the law even as her uninvited guest complimented her on the food and conducted himself like a gentleman caller.

When Tracy stepped from the house, the law was waiting. Shots were fired. A Seattle police officer and a citizen fell, both mortally wounded. Tracy escaped. Nine down. One to go.

Tracy appeared briefly in living rooms and kitchens throughout the Puget Sound area. He invaded a Renton farmhouse, holding mother and son hostage and sending the oldest boy to town with watches he had stolen in hopes they could be exchanged for revolvers and ammunition. The boy went straight to the sheriff.

Tracy fled as the posse approached, scattering cayenne pepper behind to foil bloodhounds. He plunged into Lake Washington to shake his pursuers. He showed up next at a Kent farmhouse, where he again gave a posse the slip. Realizing King County had become a bad hideout, Tracy crossed the Cascades on foot, living off the land.

On a dusty road near Creston, in central Lincoln County, he overtook a young man, George Goldfinch. He took Goldfinch hostage and stopped off at the farmhouse of L.B. Eddy, where he spent three days eating, resting and helping Eddy shingle his roof "to pay for my board."

It was early evening Aug. 5, 1902, when a posse approached the farm. Spotting the men, Tracy — already carrying a revolver — dashed into a barn for a rifle and hid behind a haystack. A nearby boulder seemed to offer better cover, and he made a dash for it as bullets bit into the soft earth.

The sun was in Tracy's eyes — bad for shooting. He spied another boulder and dashed for it.

Ping! One shot. Tracy wobbled drunkenly and fell, crawling into a wheatfield. The shot had splintered his shin bone and severed an artery. Tracy applied a makeshift tourniquet, then tried shooting while lying on his back.

Tracy had vowed never to be taken alive. The outlaw put the handgun to his head and squeezed the trigger.

Ten dead. None to go.

At daybreak, the posse found Tracy's body, his shattered face pointed toward the blue sky. His remains were taken to Davenport, where townsfolk stripped off his shoes, tore pieces from his clothing and scissored bits of his hair. His guns were fought over. Gags and ropes with which he had bound his hostages became treasured mementos. Women came forward to tell of the excitement of being held hostage.

When the simple pine box carrying the body of the 28-year-old Tracy was being removed to the Oregon penitentiary for burial, people hacked at it with axes and knives to get splinters as souvenirs.

A searing experience

Forest fires were a way of life in the young, raw Pacific Northwest. Nobody worried about them too much, because there were always more trees over the next hill.

But even the pioneers put Sept. 12, 1902 in their memory books.

On that day more than 110 forest fires burned from Eugene to Bellingham, charring an estimated 700,000 acres and turning the sky black for hundreds of miles.

At midday people carried lanterns in the streets. Chickens, thinking it was night, remained on their roosts. At a religious

Leslie Hamilton
Trestles like this one across Seattle's Fourth Avenue during the 1908 regrade often made public transportation a risky undertaking — as a 1900 Independence Day tragedy was to prove in Tacoma, where 43 died after a streetcar toppled off a trestle.

camp meeting in Cowlitz County, the faithful shouted that the world was coming to an end. A church bell in Chehalis summoned parishioners to pray for rain.

As embers flew and ash grew thick on the ground, many were certain Mount Rainier or Mount St. Helens had erupted.

The largest fire raged in eastern Clark County and part of Skamania County. It became known as the Yacolt Burn.

The Yacolt blaze had the explosive power of dynamite as it ripped through old-growth Douglas fir. The sound could be heard for miles. Searing heat scorched clothing and peeled the paint on buildings.

Devastation was staggering: 35 or 36 lives lost; homes, logging camps and an estimated 12 billion board feet of timber destroyed.

The Yacolt Burn, with its snags and half-burned trees, remained dangerous for years. Despite reforestation efforts, fires broke out whenever summers were hot and dry.

Eight years after the Yacolt Burn another great fire swept through western Montana, northern Idaho and northeastern Washington, killing 85 people and destroying an estimated 8 billion board feet of timber.

One result of these fires was stricter controls on logging and the beginning of the "Keep Washington Green" movement, which made citizens more forest-fire conscious.

A peninsular Bunyan

Feats of strength and daring were common among men who roamed the wilderness of the young state.

But around campfires and in bunkhouses at night, none inspired more stories than John Huelsdonk, the "Iron Man of the Hoh."

In 1890, Huelsdonk established a 160-acre homestead on the Hoh River, in western Jefferson County. He returned to his native Iowa a year later to bring back a bride. They would raise four daughters on the Hoh, and Huelsdonk would become a legend.

Huelsdonk was in his prime in the early part of the 20th century — 5 feet 10 inches tall, 240 pounds of bone and muscle. He was the strongest man in the woods, a crack shot, fearless when confronted by wild animals.

One day, so the story goes, a forest ranger saw Huelsdonk standing on a log in the Olympic wilderness. On Huelsdonk's back was a kitchen stove, which he intended to carry 17 miles to his home.

"Good grief, man," the ranger said. "Isn't that awfully heavy?"

"Oh, the stove's not bad," Huelsdonk is supposed to have replied, "but it's kind of hard to keep your balance when the 100-pound sack of flour in the oven shifts around."

It sounds like exaggeration. But Huelsdonk's daughter, Lena Huelsdonk Fletcher, would say years later, "Dad often carried forest-service stoves into the woods; the truth is they were pretty light. I doubt they weighed over 80 pounds, and my father could handle that easily."

Packers, for whom Huelsdonk worked, attested that he regularly carried a double load into the woods so he could earn double pay.

Huelsdonk's reputation with a gun, his daughter said, hinged on what he conceded was a lucky shot. He had jokingly told a companion he could shoot a crow, on the wing, right through the

Museum of History and Industry

Hands-on logging
In the early part of the century, Pacific Northwest loggers did all of their work by hand. To get above the bulge at the base of a tree and save cutting time, they stood on springboards driven into notches cut in the tree.

Double-bitted axes, designed especially for Northwest timber, were used to create a hinge to direct the tree's fall. The tree then was sawn from behind with the "misery whip," which was lubricated by oil from bottles hanging on the tree.

By the time Washington became a state in 1889, it already ranked sixth in the nation in lumber production. But loggers were not getting rich from their labors. Before 1917, their wage was $2 for a 10-hour day.

STATE-MENTS

HOW TO SPEAK WASHINGTONIAN

Don't bother with full names for the Sound (Puget Sound), the Ballard Locks (Hiram M. Chittenden Locks), the Aurora Bridge (George Washington Memorial Bridge), the Lake Washington or I-90 Bridge (Lacey V. Murrow Bridge) and the Evergreen Bridge (Albert D. Rosellini Evergreen Point Bridge).

Nor do you need a full name for the Mountain (refers exclusively to Mount Rainier), the Ocean (Pacific), the Canal (some call it Hood, others Hood's, by the way), the San Juans (islands) and the Strait (of Juan de Fuca).

Say Skid Road, never Skid Row. Let other parts of the country err if they wish. Skid Road refers to the area where logs were skidded down to Henry Yesler's Mill at the foot of Yesler Way.

Locals can get away with referring to the kite factory on the Duwamish as Boeing's and the Huskies as the Dogs ("dawgs" if you want to be really down-home).

Ask a native before making a fool of yourself trying to pronounce Puyallup (pew-AL-up), Sequim (skwim), Wahkiakum (wah-KYE-yuh-kum), Spokane (spo-CAN).

Drop the Nelson when you shop at Frederick's (Frederick & Nelson).

Those oversized bivalves are spelled "geoduck" and pronounced gooey-duck.

Watch your step with Ivar's (I-ver's), Kalaloch (CLAY-lock), Naches (na-CHEEZ), Camano (kuh-MAY-no) Island, Carbonado (kahr-buhn-AY-doh), Lake Keechelus (KETCH-uh-lus), Matia (MAY-shuh) Island, Mesa (MEE-sa), Montesano (mon-tuh-SAY-no), Okanogan (oh-ka-NAH-gun), Pend Oreille (PAHN-duh-RAY), Steilacoom (STILL-a-kuhm), Sucia (SHOO-sha) Island and Tulalip (too-LAY-lip).

eye.

"Dad told me later he figured he'd be lucky to even hit the crow, but he fired one shot and the bird fell. They went over to look at it and he'd shot it right through the eye. His companion could hardly wait to tell another Huelsdonk story."

Huelsdonk was credited by the Forest Service with shooting and collecting a bounty on 330 cougars.

When he was 60, Huelsdonk reportedly went into a general store at Forks where a bunch of loggers were bragging about their strength. Without a word, Huelsdonk picked up a 50-pound sack of flour, held it at arm's length for a full minute with no sign of strain, then put it down and walked silently out the door.

When Huelsdonk was 66, he was attacked by a bear, which tore open his leg and inflicted at least a dozen more claw wounds. Huelsdonk pushed the bear away, picked up his rifle and killed his attacker with one shot. Then he declined to go to a hospital, saying he'd been in the wilderness 43 years without seeing a doctor and wasn't going to "let a few scratches" spoil his record.

In 1946, Huelsdonk entered a hospital for the first time. It was also his last. He died of the flu a few days later — at age 79.

As they say, that's entertainment

Washington — territory and state — had an insatiable appetite for entertainment. The traveling medicine man, selling his nostrums and elixirs, had a ready audience in frontier times.

As the population grew, legitimate theaters and opera houses sprouted in the larger cities, with such artists as Sarah Bernhardt, Ethel Barrymore, Mary Garden, Nellie Melba, John Drew and Mark Twain.

Spokane's Auditorium Theater advertised that Chicago no longer had the world's largest stage — Spokane did. The boast stood until New York opened its 5,200-seat Hippodrome in 1905.

Live drama and vaudeville would continue for years, but in 1901 the first hint of things to come arrived in Seattle at a little theater called La Petite. The nickelodeon craze — a forerunner to moving pictures — had arrived after a five-year journey from the East Coast.

The entertainment was almost laughably crude by today's standards, but the public went wild for illustrated songs, dissolving views and colored slides.

In the early 1900s, the leading theatrical figure in Seattle was John Considine, who had started with "box houses" — live-entertainment parlors adjoining saloons — and had extended his empire throughout Washington and British Columbia. He also was one of the first to jump on the nickelodeon bandwagon, and when he joined with an Eastern entrepreneur named Sullivan, the Considine-Sullivan vaudeville circuit became dominant nationwide.

In 1901 — the same year the first nickelodeon arrived — Considine figured in one of the most celebrated real-life dramas in Seattle's young history.

Considine had accused Police Chief W.L. Meredith of taking payoffs. A shotgun-toting Meredith went looking for the "king of the box houses." He found him in Guy's Drugstore in the Skid Road area and opened fire from a few feet away. Inexplicably, he missed. Considine, carrying a handgun himself, wheeled and fired three shots. All found the mark. Meredith was dead.

Although a jury found Considine not guilty, he eventually lost his position as the premier entertainment impresario to another

Elizabeth Barlow

John Huelsdonk, the "Iron Man of the Hoh" and the Olympic Peninsula's real-life answer to Paul Bunyan, stands next to a stump he seems nearly ready to hoist.

Seattle resident, Greek-born Pericles Pantages, who adopted the first name of Alexander.

Pantages corralled the top acts of the day and built a string of strikingly beautiful theaters across the country. (Tacoma's Pantages still stands.) He reigned supreme until the talkies started spelling the end of vaudeville in the late 1920s.

'Home is the sailor, home from sea'

Twelve miles south of the mouth of the Ozette River, on the Washington coast, is a grave that contains the bodies of 18 Norwegian seamen.

All lost their lives Jan. 2, 1903, when the three-masted bark Prince Arthur went aground on a hard-to-reach part of the coast marked by steep cliffs, thick brush, dense forest and a beach strewn with boulders and jagged rocks.

According to the wreck's two survivors, Christopher Hanson and Knud Larsen, the Prince Arthur's skipper had mistaken the lights of a cabin for the Tatoosh Island beacon.

Hanson crawled to the cabin, occupied by the Birkestal brothers — Ivar, Ole and Tom — and told them what had happened. The brothers went down to the beach to help drag bodies ashore.

When news of the disaster reached Seattle, men of Norwegian descent held a meeting to plan formal burial of the dead, erect a monument in their honor and care for the two survivors.

With the help of local Indians, the Birkestals already had buried the dead in shallow graves. A Norwegian delegation from Seattle moved the bodies to a 14-foot-square grave dug on a bluff overlooking the sea. They covered the bodies with planking from the ship and canvas from her sails.

The grave was marked with a ship's door, facing the sea. Some time later, the Seattle men erected a formal monument with these words:

"Here Lies the Crew of the Bark Prince Arthur of Norway, Which Foundered January 2, 1903."

Names of the 18 men are etched in stone.

Can-do in the fish trade

Edmund Augustine Smith, a part-time inventor, became fascinated with the idea of a mechanical device that could clean fish faster and cheaper than the Chinese laborers then employed almost exclusively in canneries.

Smith had earned a small stake in the brick-making and fish-canning business. With that money, plus what he could borrow from friends and banks, he rented a small shop in downtown Seattle in 1903. His only tools were a hammer, chisel, hacksaw and a small turning lathe.

Smith's family seldom saw him as he toiled virtually around the clock. When he was home, he drew diagrams on the tablecloth. At 3 o'clock one morning, in the fall of '03, Smith suddenly awoke and sat up in bed.

"Gert," he shouted to his wife, "I've got it."

Smith dressed and ran downtown to his shop. He stayed there for 10 days. When he finally came home, he was all smiles. He had borrowed more money from a bank, he said, and was going to Washington, D.C., to see a patent attorney.

When he returned to Seattle, he had a briefcase filled with patents and orders.

Smith had invented what was termed, in those less racially

The "Iron Chink" processes salmon at Fairhaven, Whatcom County, about 1906. The machine, whose name reflected the racism of the time, increased the canneries' capacity and displaced hundreds of Chinese who had cleaned salmon by hand. It also hastened the depletion of salmon in Puget Sound rivers and the movement of the fish-canning industry to Alaska.

Museum of History and Industry

sensitive times, "the Iron Chink." It could clean 110 fish a minute, a task that previously had required the efforts of 55 Chinese workers. The invention revolutionized fish-canning and made Smith a wealthy man.

Smith was invited to exhibit his invention at the 1909 Alaska-Yukon-Pacific Exposition. Two days before the fair was to open, Smith asked his sister if she would like to see his exhibit. She said yes.

On the way, the car left the road, rocks punctured the fuel tank and everything burst into flames. Smith threw his sister to safety, but was unable to extricate himself. He died of burns the day the exposition opened. He was only 31.

Out to launch

Few things better demonstrated young Seattle's civic spirit than the Oct. 7, 1904, launching of the USS Nebraska at Moran Bros. Shipyard.

The first and only battleship launching in Seattle's history attracted an estimated 55,000 people — 40,000 standing on wharves around the shipyard, another 15,000 in boats that stretched across Elliott Bay to West Seattle.

Bands played. Cannon thundered from nearby ships.

U.S. Rep. W.E. Humphrey was in the middle of a speech when the single barricade holding the $4.5 million Nebraska gave way. The 435-foot-long, red-painted vessel started slowly toward the water — eight minutes ahead of schedule.

Mary Mickey, daughter of Nebraska's Gov. John Mickey, cracked a champagne bottle against the vessel's hull as it began to move. She barely had time to say, "I christen thee, Nebraska."

The band immediately struck up "Auld Lang Syne." The crowd cheered. Whistles sounded.

What made the event so special is the way Seattle landed the shipbuilding contract.

In the spring of 1899, Congress authorized the construction of three battleships. Moran Bros. (Robert, William and Peter), builder of 12 river steamers for the Klondike gold rush, submitted a bid for the Nebraska the following December.

Moran's bid was the lowest. But Secretary of the Navy Benjamin Tracy said it was higher than the Navy had budgeted. Either reduce your bid by $100,000, Moran was told, or there

will be another call for bids.

Moran was in a quandary. It had submitted a rock-bottom bid. There was fear that if new bids were called an Eastern shipbuilder would get the contract.

Robert Moran, former mayor of Seattle, went to the Chamber of Commerce and civic leaders and asked for a pure gift of $100,000 so the shipbuilding firm could lower its bid. Within a few days, the request was oversubscribed by $35,000.

Moran was awarded the contract in March 1901, and work began. It was good business for all concerned. Moran made a fair profit. Skilled workers had money to buy goods. Washingtonians perpetuated their ongoing love affair with military vessels.

. . . And then the earth moved

Perhaps the chief difference between Rome and Seattle, besides historical significance, size and a 1,900-year-old Colosseum that probably will stand longer than the Kingdome, is how the two cities treated their hills.

Rome's seven hills are still in place. Seattle's hills — the number has always been fluid — were reduced by one or more in the great earth-moving projects undertaken between 1898 and 1930.

As a result of what became known as "the regrades," Seattle acquired some prime business land and its automobiles no longer had to skirt mini-Matterhorns.

The regrade story began when R. (for Reginald) H. Thomson came to Seattle in 1881.

With vision and an engineer's eye, Thomson said some of the downtown mountains would have to be reduced to molehills if the city ever hoped to become a seaport metropolis.

When Thomson became city engineer in 1892, dirt began to fly.

The first regrade required the removal of 110,000 cubic yards of earth to lower First Avenue from Pine Street to Denny Way. Some of the dirt was used to fill low spots along the waterfront. The rest went into Elliott Bay.

Other regrades followed in the early 1900s. Dirt was sluiced by high-powered hoses from Second and Third avenues in the Denny Way area. Jackson Street Hill was cut down to size and

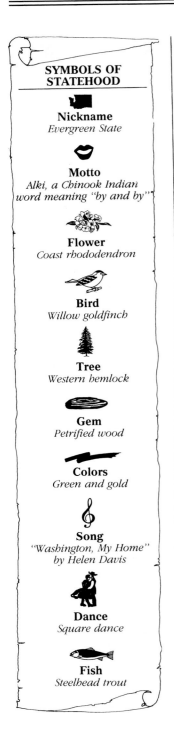

CHRONO-LOG

1906

*The Steamer Dix,
with 77 passengers bound
for Bainbridge Island,
collides with Jeanie, three-
masted Alaska steam
schooner, and sinks in 600
feet of water off Alki Point.
Thirty-nine of Dix's
passengers and crew die.*

1907

*Washington state
adopts direct primary in
state elections, meaning
candidates are no longer
nominated at party
conventions. Samuel
Cosgrove is first governor
elected after direct primary.*

Washington State Historical Society

Steam shovels and streams of water tear at Denny Hill in 1907 at the end of Phase 1 of the Denny Regrade. Under construction in the background is the New Washington Hotel.

a ditch punched through to the east to open up Rainier Valley.

Seattle had so many sluicing jobs going on that at times it resembled a giant placer-mining operation.

The biggest obstacle to Thomson's dream was Denny Hill — 107 feet at its highest point. When it was first assaulted, on its west side, 5 million cubic yards of mud flowed through a tunnel and flumes into the bay. The old Denny Hotel came down. So did Denny School and Sacred Heart School and church.

The project ended in 1911, about half-completed.

Because of the drama of sluicing down hills, many mistakenly have believed that was the way the rest of Denny Hill was removed. It was not.

Army engineers took a dim view of adding more mud to Seattle's shoreline. By the time Denny Regrade No. 2 began in 1929, Thomson no longer was in the engineer's office. Ralph Drury, a resident engineer for Link-Belt Co., is credited with devising an earth-moving system that overcame the Army's objections. Big electric power shovels scooped up the dirt. Conveyor belts hauled it to barges. The barges took it out into the Sound and dumped it.

At the end of Regrade No. 2, another 5 million cubic yards of earth had been removed.

Some residents in the path of the regrades resisted vacating their property. While they battled in court, power shovels carved up the landscape around them. It was not uncommon to see tall dirt-and-clay spires, with houses perched on top. Homeowners climbed ladders or steep steps to reach their front doors.

The Denny Regrades did *not* build Harbor Island — at 396.7 acres, the world's largest man-made island. Some of its dirt came from Jackson Hill and Dearborn Street. But most of the island's 24 million cubic yards of underpinning is black mud, dredged from the Duwamish to form the east and west waterways, and less-fertile soil lopped off Beacon Hill.

The Second and Third Avenue regrades and the first Denny Hill project filled up much of the waterfront shoreline. Dirt that didn't go to sea in the final Denny Regrade was used to fill hollows in Pine Street, Olive Way and Westlake Avenue.

Well over 12 million cubic yards of earth and rock were moved during the regrades. When they were finished, Seattle had 92 more acres of level land than it had started with.

Historical footnote: Much of the rock used to riprap the waterfront came in as sailing-ship ballast from San Francisco's Telegraph Hill, and from Liverpool, Boston, New York, Hong Kong, Sydney and Mazatlán.

A night to remember

Puget Sound's cities were linked by hundreds of little vessels — sternwheelers, sidewheelers and propeller-driven. They tooted their whistles, sent up plumes of steam and skittered across the water like, well, like mosquitoes. Hence the name "mosquito fleet."

On Sunday evening, Nov. 18, 1906, one of those little ships — the steamer Dix — took on 77 passengers in Seattle bound for Bainbridge Island's Port Blakely Mill Co., which employed 1,200 men and called itself "the second-largest sawmill in the world."

Most of the men, women and children aboard the Dix had made the trip many times and were on a first-name basis with the skipper, Capt. Percy Lermond, and his mate, Charles Dennison.

It was a clear, chilly night. Only the hardy stayed on deck. The rest went below to chat and get out of the cold.

Marcus Otnes, a millworker and one of the few passengers on deck, was looking back at the lights of Smith Cove when he saw a ship coming toward the Dix. It was the Jeanie, a three-masted Alaska steam schooner, famous for her role seven years earlier in rescuing the shivering crew of the J.B. Libby in the Strait of Juan de Fuca.

"The Jeanie seemed to be coming right at us," Otnes would

Michael Masian

Surrounded by Puget Sound's "mosquito fleet," an ocean-going troop ship brings back King County volunteers from the war in the Philippines around 1905.

recall years later. "I told a friend on deck with me that it looked like she was going to hit us. My friend laughed and said, 'No chance of that.'

"We started to go up front, when all of a sudden there was this clanging of bells and reversing of engines. I yelled, 'Hang on, there's going to be a collision.'"

The Jeanie's bowsprit knifed through the middle of the Dix and into the engine room. There were screams. The Dix heeled over, took on water and began to sink at the stern. Otnes saw a man and woman, clinging to each other in the water. He heard the man cry out, "God help me, nobody else can." Both disappeared below the surface.

Otnes was hauled aboard the Jeanie, whose crew was plucking survivors from the cold water. The Dix sank off Alki Point in 600 feet of water. Thirty-nine people died, including mate Dennison.

When word reached Port Blakely, a second vessel was dispatched to Seattle to bring home the survivors. It arrived back at Port Blakely about 3 in the morning. Virtually everyone in town was there — eyes searching the faces of survivors to see if their friends and loved ones were among them.

Otnes recalled: "The crying was something terrible. They looked you in the face and shrugged. You were almost ashamed of being alive."

Time stood still in Port Blakely for several days as townsfolk mourned the dead. Schools were closed. Mill owners declared a holiday.

Less than two years later, the sawmill burned down.

To market, to market . . .

Shortly after daybreak Aug. 17, 1907, H.O. Blanchard's horse-drawn wagon creaked down Seattle's newly planked Pike Street, laden with farm-fresh produce to sell to the residents of the young city by Elliott Bay.

Tired and dirty from his all-night journey from Renton, Blanchard stood by his wagon and quickly sold out at what was to become the Pike Place Market.

Two other wagons arrived that day, along with some "enemy" peddlers. The enemies were men hired by wholesalers to undercut the farmers' prices.

Wholesalers, also known as "commission men," dominated the city's foodstuff prices, and they were, in the opinion of The Seattle Times and City Councilman Thomas Revelle (grand-uncle of latter-day King County Executive Randy Revelle), greedy fellows. That is why Revelle and the newspaper demanded the establishment of a farmers' market.

The following Monday, 10 farmers' wagons arrived. There were 20 on Tuesday. And by the end of the week, 70 stood in line.

Because the city had no money to erect a building, John and Frank Goodwin, two brothers who had been successful miners in Alaska, built a structure at Pike Place.

It was opened Nov. 30, 1907, with 120 farmers on hand. Theo H. "Dad" Wagner's band played and Councilman Revelle declared, "This is one of the greatest days in the history of Seattle."

The Goodwin structure had 300 stalls. It was said you could buy anything from a needle to a piano.

Hyperbole perhaps. But you could buy horseradish ground on the spot, homemade fruitcakes, dill pickles and sauerkraut. Country sausage was sold in lard pails. Butter, wrapped in towels, was brought from Poulsbo.

Housewives sold homemade jellies, piccalilli and mincemeat. Restaurants served meals for "15 cents and up."

In 1921 Mayor Edwin J. "Doc" Brown termed the market "an oriental bazaar on a cowpath," and the city seriously considered building a new market for $3 million. Frank Goodwin's response was to add to the existing market. By 1928 as many as 400 farmers a day sold produce there.

Management of the market slowly shifted from the Goodwin family to the Desimone family. Joe Desimone, who first came to the market as a South Park farmer, moved up the power structure. Later his son, Richard, took over as head of the Pike Place Market Corp.

The market has had remarkable staying power, surviving the proliferation of suburban shopping centers to become a must on every tourist's itinerary. When the place grew rickety, an organization called Friends of the Market saved it from being transformed into what it was never intended to be.

Victor Steinbrueck, the architect, probably put it best when he said modernizing the market would be like trying to replace "a grandmother with a chorus girl."

The Seattle institution now is a protected historic site.

University of Washington

The Pike Place Market had an open-air look before it was housed indoors with permanent stalls in 1907.

CHRONO-LOG

Seattle Times

Seattle classrooms such as this one, at St. Rose's Academy "for young ladies," were let out in May 1908 when Teddy Roosevelt's Great White Fleet put in at Elliott Bay.

1907

John and Frank Goodwin, former Alaska miners, build and open soon-to-be-world-famed farmers' market at Pike Place.

1908

Automaker Henry Ford selects site on south end of Lake Union for automobile-and-tractor assembly plant. Factory attains maximum production of 143 cars per day until replaced by new plant built in 1930 at East Marginal Way South.

State Legislature narrowly defeats bill to amend state Constitution by striking word "male" from clause relating to voting requirements.

First National Apple Show is held in Spokane, providing widespread publicity to Washington apple, which will become internationally famous.

Edward Curtis, who moved to state from Wisconsin as teen-ager in 1887, publishes first two volumes of monumental work, "The North American Indian" — 20 volumes of text, 1,500 small plates bound in, 20 portfolios of unbound gravure plates. In course of his life, he visits 80 tribes, takes 40,000 photographs. He dies in Los Angeles in 1952.

Those championship seasons

In 1908, a year after Hiram Conibear became crew coach, the University of Washington hired as its football coach a tall, thin Scot wreathed in gloom and cigar smoke. He was just 29. His name was Gilmour "Gil" Dobie.

Although "Gloomy Gil," as he became known, was a perennial apostle of grief, he ranks among the great football coaches of all time.

Dobie had come to the Huskies from North Dakota State, where his teams were undefeated for two seasons. He coached at Washington for nine seasons (1908-1916).

His record: 58 victories, no defeats.

Dobie's teams were tied three times — 6-6 by Washington State in 1908, and 0-0 by the Oregon Athletic Club in 1914 and the University of Oregon in 1916.

Dobie's Huskies were awesomely dominant, even though he often fielded just 11 men for an entire game. They rolled up 1,928 points (an average of 31.5 a game) and gave up just 120 (1.3 a game).

Although Dobie never intentionally poured it on, his 1911 team beat Fort Worden 90-0. His 1913 team, quarterbacked by Charlie Smith, who later became Seattle's mayor, defeated Whitworth 100-0. (The all-time Husky scoring record was set in 1919 when Whitman fell 120-0 at Denny Field. C.J. Hunt was the coach.)

Despite his success, Dobie lived up to his nickname. His players, he would say in lugubrious tongue-in-cheek, were crippled beyond belief. His star halfback was so slow he couldn't make it across an intersection before the light changed. It was unfair, he moaned, that his undersized, untalented squad had to play such obviously superior opponents.

Dobie's teams featured the off-tackle slant. But he was quoted as saying "football systems are all hooey, if you ask me. It's not the system that counts. It's the timber you have."

When his teams didn't play hard enough to suit him, they felt the lash of his tongue.

Convinced his players hadn't played all-out in a game against California (72-0), Dobie made them take post-game laps around Denny Field. After a 46-0 romp over Colorado, Dobie was found with his head in his hands, anguishing over a "subpar performance."

University of Washington

A bowler-topped Gilmour "Gloomy Gil" Dobie watches from the sidelines with customary intensity as his champion Huskies scrimmage. Despite almost unfailing success, Dobie, master of the mournful put-on, would say his players were crippled beyond belief or that his star halfback couldn't make it across an intersection before the light changed.

Upset by increasingly stringent academic restrictions, Dobie left Washington for the U.S. Naval Academy after the 1916 season. He had been particularly outraged that one of his star players was removed from the team for an alleged infraction during an examination.

In 1917 — Dobie's 12th season as a head football coach — he lost his first football game, 6-0, to Georgetown. He was reported to have been inconsolable.

Three years later, he fulfilled his dream of coaching an Ivy League school by going to Cornell, where he stayed for 17 seasons.

When Dobie quit coaching, after 26 seasons, he had won 161 games, lost 23 and tied eight. He died in 1948 at the age of 69.

Dobie and Conibear were in the first group of coaches and athletes chosen for the UW's Athletic Hall of Fame.

When wrestling was serious — sort of

Wrestling hardly rates a paragraph on today's sports pages. But on July 1, 1908, it commanded an eight-column headline on the front page of The Times:

"Gotch defeats Roller." More bold type followed: "Gotch Beats Roller in Two Straight Falls, Using the Crotch and Half Nelson Hold Each Time. Local Man Game, but Simply Outclassed. Toe Hold Applied Just Once in Its Thumbscrew Cruelty, and the Local Man Was Badly Hurt by It."

The story was by E.R. Hughes, whose elegant title was "Sporting Editor of The Times."

Those were the days when wrestling was taken seriously. Frank Gotch, reigning heavyweight champion, was a national hero.

For months, Seattle sports fans had debated what would happen when Gotch, sometimes called "the Iowa farmboy," tangled with Seattle's B.F. Roller, frequently accorded the title of "Doctor" and widely regarded as a master of scientific wrestling.

A great deal of money was wagered on the outcome, much of it on Doc Roller.

Tickets for the match at the old downtown Coliseum ranged from $3 to an almost-unheard-of $10.

In the words of Hughes, "the match for the championship of the world attracted the swellest crowd that ever turned out for an athletic event in the Northwest . . . Bankers and lawyers rubbed elbows with doctors and race-track men."

Roller was the crowd favorite. Hadn't Gotch tried to delay the match? Hadn't he said in an interview that the one wrestler he feared above all others was Doc Roller?

Alas, the match did not live up to its advance billing.

The opening bell sounded and Roller and Gotch met in the center of the ring. Roller immediately tripped up Gotch, who fell to the canvas, with Roller on top of him. The crowd went wild.

But the enthusiasm was short-lived. As if he were toying with a child, Gotch broke Roller's hold, scrambled to his feet and picked up Roller. He walked around the ring with him — some said he asked where to deposit the hometown favorite — and then slammed Roller to the mat. Gotch added to the indignity by standing Roller on his head and spinning him like a top.

Many ringsiders felt Gotch could have pinned Roller easily at any time. Instead, each fall dragged on for 15 or more minutes, while Gotch physically punished his weaker opponent.

At one point, Roller writhed in pain as Gotch applied his infamous toehold. Ringsiders were certain they could hear a cracking sound.

The referee, fearing Gotch would break Roller's ankle, leaned over and quietly asked the champion to "ease up a bit." Gotch smiled and complied.

Many said the one-sided Gotch-Roller match ruined wrestling in Seattle for years.

Olympic-class accomplishment

One of Teddy Roosevelt's last acts before relinquishing the presidency to William Howard Taft was establishing Mount Olympus National Monument in the spring of 1909.

Roosevelt created the monument by removing 600,000 acres from Olympic National Forest, which had been established 12 years earlier by Grover Cleveland.

The monument's centerpiece was Mount Olympus, 8,932 feet of rock and glaciers. But it also was designed to preserve the *cervus canadensis occidentalis*, better known as the Roosevelt (for Teddy) elk.

About 200,000 acres were hacked from the south and west edges of the monument in 1915, during Woodrow Wilson's presidency.

The Forest Service managed the monument until June 10, 1933, when Franklin D. Roosevelt transferred jurisdiction to the

Washington State Historical Society

Part of the Great White Fleet — the sea version of Teddy Roosevelt's "speak softly and carry a big stick" policy — arrives in Puget Sound on May 23, 1908. The fleet, which included 16 battleships, was the greatest concentration of battleships seen on the Sound before or since.

National Park Service.

U.S. Rep. Mon C. Wallgren, a sharp amateur billiards champion from the 2nd District, saw it as an opportunity to create an Olympic National Park containing as much as 800,000 acres.

Logging companies, chambers of commerce and Gov. Clarence D. Martin thought Wallgren's park was much too large — if, indeed, a park was needed at all.

By 1935, however, Wallgren had a staunch and influential ally — Secretary of the Interior Harold Ickes, a brilliantly sulfuric man, wholeheartedly in favor of a large park. Ickes rhapsodized about the Olympic Peninsula as "the last frontier wilderness" in the United States, outside of Alaska.

The battle between big-park and small-park advocates raged for four years. Wallgren said he was willing to cut back his park plan to 634,000 acres. Governor Martin said it should be no larger than 440,000 acres. Ickes favored 940,000 acres.

In the fall of 1937, Wallgren talked FDR into a personal view. The president spent the night at Lake Crescent, motoring around the Peninsula on the ocean side. Not only was he impressed, but he definitely wanted an ocean strip included — making it the nation's only mountain-timber-seashore national park.

Roosevelt signed the bill creating Olympic National Park June 29, 1938. It was for a 634,000-acre park. But included in the bill was a provision permitting the president to increase the park's size up to 898,292 acres.

Because a war in Europe was imminent, Roosevelt never did get around to formally dedicating the park. But he did, by proclamation, add considerable acreage in the next few years.

Although Roosevelt's additions are now among the prize features of the park, the real prize was added in 1953 by President Harry Truman — a 50-mile ocean strip and the Queets Corridor.

There have been numerous efforts over the years to trim the size of the park. Long after leaving government, Ickes produced a memorable piece of rhetoric aimed at those who would shrink its boundaries:

"The tree-butchers, axes on shoulders, are again on the march against some of the few remaining stands of America's glorious virgin timber. . . The gluttons will pass their plates again and again for generous helpings until the despoilers will have sated their greedy appetites on what has, so far, been miraculously saved."

Today more than 5,000 Roosevelt elk graze in the park. Whistling marmots delight hikers. Glaciers attract scientists and climbers. Rivers make their endless journeys to Hood Canal and the Pacific Ocean.

And the Enchanted Valley ("land of 10,000 waterfalls") continues to enchant.

A first in moving-picture shows

Sometime in 1909, James Clemmer decided that pipe-organ music would add excitement to a one-reel silent film that flickered on the screen at his Dream Theatre in Seattle's Pioneer Square.

It was a stroke of genius, and is believed to have been the first attempt anywhere to marry live music with a silent film.

What made the occasion even more memorable was Clemmer's choice of an artist to play the organ — a London-born virtuoso named Oliver Wallace.

In April, 1912, Clemmer opened the opulent, 1,200-seat Clemmer Theatre on Second Avenue. Wallace played the house organ.

Three years after the Clemmer opened, its proprietor presented D.W. Griffith's monumental "The Birth of a Nation," charging a then-exorbitant 50 cents for a ticket.

When the Liberty Theatre opened in 1914 with its "Mighty Wurlitzer," Wallace divided his time between the Liberty and the Clemmer.

In time, a large pipe organ — thundering as it rose out of a pit alongside the stage — became a must for the city's poshest theaters. In the hands of a master like Wallace, the pipes could add to the heart-stopping excitement of a heroine tied to the railroad tracks by a spurned lover, a train barreling down on her. And it could heighten a romantic interlude or announce — with a

Don Myers

Film fare at James Clemmer's Dream Theatre on Pioneer Square was a mix of silent one-reelers and vaudeville acts

STATE-MENTS

Home on the draw

In the summer of 1909, the federal government held its last great public-land lottery in the West. At stake were 6,000 homestead sites on nearly 1 million acres on the Spokane Indian Reservation in Washington, the Coeur d'Alene Reservation in Idaho and the Flathead Reservation in Montana. There is no mention that the Indians were consulted.

To play lottery 1909-style, all one had to do was pay two bits, file a notarized registration form and receive a number. Winners would be drawn from a tub of numbers. The trick was to get registered between July 15 and Aug. 5 at one of three sites — Spokane, Coeur d'Alene and Missoula. Odds could be increased by registering at all three sites. The rush was on.

Land-registration officials expected the turnout would be sizable. They didn't dream that 294,535 people would come by rail, wagon or on foot to take a 25-cent gamble on a piece of property. Spokane drew the largest crowds because it was served by three transcontinental railroads.

The stage was set for a tragedy. The Spokane Electric Railroad was running trains from Spokane to Coeur d'Alene every 20 minutes. In one day, 14,000 passengers were counted. Perhaps someone got tired and careless, because two trains collided head-on near Idaho's LaCrosse siding (now known as Gibbs) while carrying an estimated 600 passengers between Spokane and Coeur d'Alene. Fifteen died. More than 100 were injured.

Maybe the only winner that day was James Gomer. He awoke in a hospital bed after the crash, but was not seriously injured. Nine days later, he was notified that his name was the 34th drawn in the Coeur d'Alene lottery.

CHRONO-LOG

This scene, photographed from a hot-air balloon, shows the Alaska-Yukon-Pacific Exposition as it was laid out on the University of Washington campus. View is looking north across Geyser Basin — the Frosh Pond of today — toward the domed Government Building. Many of the structures were designed for permanence; a few are still in use today, 79 years later.

1909

President Teddy Roosevelt establishes Mount Olympus National Monument by removing 600,000 acres from Olympic National Forest. Monument is designed to preserve — among other natural wonders — Roosevelt elk.

Impresario James Clemmer weds pipe-organ music to silent film showing at Dream Theater in Pioneer Square, marking a "first."

Alaska-Yukon-Pacific Exposition opens June 1 and lasts 138 days, attracting 3,740,551 patrons.

few thunderous chords — the approach of evil.

Clemmer left town to enter the movie business in California but returned to Seattle to build the Winter Garden. He later managed the Blue Mouse, Orpheum, Paramount and Music Box and was the first manager of the Fifth Avenue.

Wallace spent time as chief organist for Grauman's Theaters in Los Angeles and San Francisco and returned to the Pacific Northwest to play at Tacoma's Broadway Theatre before leaving permanently to be music director for Walt Disney. For Disney he scored such films as "Lady and the Tramp," "Cinderella," "Dumbo" and "Peter Pan."

Wallace was perhaps best remembered here for collaborating with local songwriter Harold Weeks on one of America's most popular songs, "Hindustan."

Weeks had a memorable career, too, collaborating with Ruth Byrd on "Montana," that state's official song, and going to New York, where he prospered on Tin Pan Alley. One of his songs, "My Sweetheart," was introduced by a young Manhattan blues singer, Frances Langford, who later became a film star ("The Glenn Miller Story").

Years after Clemmer first combined film and music, his Dream Theatre projectionist, Frank Myers, recalled how one male customer came to the theater 15 times to watch the same film — of young women skipping down to the beach to disrobe for a swim. The director had a train pass, blocking the audience's view of the women while they shed their clothes. When it was gone, the women were swimming demurely offshore.

Asked why he kept coming back to see the same scene, Constant Viewer replied, "Some day that train is gonna be late."

All's fair in Seattle

The Alaska-Yukon-Pacific Exposition put Seattle on the world's maps. It was an audacious $10 million gamble by a frontier town that had only 86,671 residents at the beginning of the decade.

The A-Y-P, as everyone called it, began June 1, 1909.

What a day it was.

In New York City, 10 automobiles were lined up for the Guggenheim Trophy Race, a transcontinental dash to Seattle — no speed limit after Kansas. (Henry Ford came to Seattle to welcome the winner, a Ford Model T, which arrived 23 days later.)

In Washington, D.C., a 16-gun salute was fired shortly after noon. President Taft then punched a telegraph key set with Klondike-gold nuggets. Its electrical impulse triggered a gong at the fairgrounds (the University of Washington campus). The "largest American flag ever made" unfurled between two fir trees, spilling out confetti and 1,000 tiny American flags.

In Seattle, the Stetson & Post Mill sounded its whistle. Other businesses, taking the cue, blew their whistles and ran up flags. Vessels on Elliott Bay, Lake Washington and Lake Union joined in.

Two hours and 30 minutes after the fair opened, the first child to be born in town on that historic day was christened Aileen Yuela Pacific (AYP) Lalloff Pyne, and her parents were paid $100.

The fair lasted 138 days, attracted 3,740,551 patrons and established Seattle as a city of excitement, a natural port of entry for the Orient and a second home for Alaskans visiting the states.

It was the only world's fair ever to be totally without liquor. But it was so profitable that at the end, $63,000 in surplus money was paid to the Antituberculosis League and the Seamen's Institute. And the young university was left with a legacy of 20 buildings, at least half-a-dozen of which would serve generations of university students.

Those who attended caught glimpses of William Jennings Bryan, the silver-tongued orator, and rotund President Taft, a fabled trencherman who gorged himself on food and was stung on the neck by a bee.

As frocked and beribboned dignitaries look on, President William Howard Taft addresses a Seattle crowd during the 1909 Alaska-Yukon-Pacific Exposition.

They would recall the $14,500 statue of George Washington, the first west of the Mississippi; the New York State Host Building, a replica of William H. Seward's home in Albany, N.Y., which became the residence of three university presidents after the fair.

Few fairgoers ever forgot the enormous stuffed Kodiak bear, the small, dark-skinned Igorot people from the Philippines, Eskimos sweltering in their parkas, Indians carving poles and weaving baskets, a 187-foot-long Douglas fir flagpole and the water that cascaded in front of the domed United States Building.

The landscaping was breathtaking. So, too, was Pay Streak, the amusement area, which had a huge statue of the last bare-kuckles boxing champion, John L. Sullivan, in fighting togs, near the entrance. Nearby, the Merrimac battled the Monitor. And for those who wanted to feel just a tad naughty, "Princess Ieka, that little lady from the garden of the gods in the Pacific, dancing the daring hula. . . Step right up, ladies and gentlemen, but leave the little innocents outside."

The fair was a zany, impossible idea from the moment Godfrey Chealander proposed at a civic banquet that Seattle hold a little exposition to celebrate the 10th anniversary of the arrival of the first Klondike-gold ship.

Before long, the "little exposition" embraced Alaska, the Yukon and all of the Pacific. The federal government said it would participate if the exposition were held in 1909 (12 years after the start of the gold rush).

Prof. Edmond Meany proposed the use of the University of Washington campus, then a complex of a few buildings set in hard-to-reach wilderness.

Fundraising ideas were plentiful. State Land Commissioner E.W. Ross sold Lake Union shorelands to raise money for state participation.

Will Parry, a civic dynamo, undertook to finance Seattle's contribution with a single-day's canvass of businessmen.

When more money was needed at the last minute, businessmen were called upon for another contribution. The Times published the names of donors on the front page. Those who had not yet contributed also were listed.

Ground was broken June 1, 1907. Exactly two years later — following a mad race against the clock the previous night — the fair was a reality.

Half an hour before midnight on the final day (Oct. 16) a farewell parade was formed, with John Edward Chilberg, exposition president, in the lead. There was a brief ceremony in the amphitheater where it had all begun. A bugler from a band played "Taps."

Under the midnight sky, the crowd sang "Auld Lang Syne."

3. MOBILITY AND RADICALISM

PROGRESS IS MIXED WITH CONFLICT
AS THE NATION STEPS ONTO WORLD STAGE

1910 TO ➻ 1920

'They were some of the most respected businessmen in town, pillars of the church... I ducked the first two in line, then got my head split open. I woke up down by the river...'

— **Jack Miller, IWW militant, recalling 'free speech' demonstration in Everett in 1916**

Museum of History & Industry

Army recruits bound for Camp Lewis (later Fort Lewis) and some ultimately to the European trenches of World War I march down Fourth Avenue at Columbia Street in downtown Seattle. Below, workers ease the first Boeing float biplane into the waters of Lake Union, where the fledgling aircraft company — Pacific Aero Products — had a hangar in 1916.

World War I forever defined the decade between 1910 and 1920. It didn't make the world safe for democracy, as the sloganeers promised. Nor was it the "war to end all wars." But it did establish the United States as a world power and unify its people. When Uncle Sam pointed from placards and said, "I want you," Washingtonians were certain he meant them. They went to war, made bandages, bought Liberty Bonds and knew, in their heart of hearts, that all the world's troubles could be traced to "Huns," "Krauts" and a man called the Kaiser.

So strong was anti-German sentiment that many people modified German-sounding names to avoid troublesome incidents.

The Boeing Airplane Co. was born.

People willing to move

The Boeing Co.

CHRONO-LOG

1910

May Arkwright Hutton, who had helped Idaho women get right to vote, moves to Spokane to promote suffrage; becomes noted for wearing men's clothing to dramatize "stupidity" of tight skirts when women try to board trolleys.

"Apple war" breaks out in Seattle Dec. 26 as 4,000 football fans rooting for Wenatchee High and Oak Park High in Chicago lob fruit at each other in dispute over which team is better. (Oak Park wins, 22-0.) Wenatchee had been declared best in West by defeating Queen Anne High a month earlier.

1911

"Smallpox Wedding" is performed for young couple (no names recorded) by Justice of the Peace Sam Sumner of Wenatchee. Groom, who had contracted smallpox, is isolated in tent in middle of 10-acre field. Bride, who sneaked into tent to care for him, tells Dr. J.H. Blake she wants to wed. Blake says wedding can take place if guests stay behind a fence. While the couple hold hands in field 100 yards away, Sumner shouts prayers and vows to them.

A woman worker in typical mobcap and rubber apron tends machinery at the Apex Fish Co. salmon cannery in Anacortes, circa 1913.

Washington State Historical Society

Women of the Washington Equal Suffrage Association tack up posters championing their cause in the campaign of 1910, when the suffrage movement came to fruition with passage of the Fifth Amendment to the state Constitution.

across the country and leave their roots behind were not shy about fighting for change. Labor struggles intensified, erupting in violence in Centralia and Everett.

The nation's first general strike took place in Seattle, and the city gained a reputation as one of the most unionized in America.

The 18th Amendment (Prohibition), ratified by three-quarters of the states in 1919, spawned bootleggers, bathtub gin and "Joe-sent-me" bottle clubs.

The Lake Washington Ship Canal and Ballard Locks were completed.

And this state's reputation as a political maverick was solidified in 1912 when voters gave a solid majority to Teddy Roosevelt, running on the Progressive (Bull Moose) ticket, and more than 40,000 votes to Eugene V. Debs, running on the Socialist ticket. Woodrow Wilson made it into the White House without our help.

Four years later, Washingtonians voted for Wilson, who defeated Charles Evans Hughes by the narrowest of margins, because they were sure Wilson would keep us out of war.

"Spanish" flu raged on the home front. A typewriter manufacturer named L.C. Smith gave Seattle the tallest building west of the Mississippi.

Electric streetcars whirred and clanged around on rails laid in the middle of streets and, hey, San Francisco, you weren't the only one with little cable cars. Ours were just as quaint, and over on Queen Anne Hill the "counterbalance" became the ultimate test of Dad's new car, which he dreamed of driving like Barney Oldfield (who broke, at 131.7 mph, the one-mile auto-racing record as the decade began).

We liked sports, but didn't dream the Boston pitcher who won two games in the 1918 World Series would become much more famous for his batting. His first name was George. Everybody called him "Babe" (Ruth).

Douglas Fairbanks swashbuckled on the silent silver screen, and Tom Mix and William S. Hart mounted their trusty steeds to ride off after bad guys in black hats.

Corn flakes became the breakfast food of millions. A hair preparation called Wildroot "prevented baldness."

Long-distance walking captured our fancy. In 1916, Patrick Harmon walked from New York to Seattle in 239 days – backward. Almost as amazing was the feat of three women – Margaret Charter and her two daughters, Phyllis M. and Margaret

A. – who left their Capitol Hill home April 13, 1919, and trudged into New York Sept. 18. Though they had a packhorse to carry their necessities, they made it on nothing else but their own two feet.

Flying circuses, featuring daring young men in flimsy aircraft, barnstormed the country. Eddie Rickenbacker was the country's "ace of aces." Vacuum cleaners and electric irons made a housewife's lot a bit easier. So did oak iceboxes ($12.90). The iceman cameth regularly, as did the man who brought coal for our furnaces.

For $5,000, one could buy a four-bedroom house in the North End. An eight-piece dining-room set went for $93.50. On weekends, one dollar, which included a war tax, paid for a round trip aboard a steamer from Seattle to Tacoma.

Women's dresses shed most of their puffs and frills. But hemlines stayed down around the ankles, for modesty's sake.

Music became peppier. The nation began to dance the fox trot, turkey trot, bunny hug, kangaroo dip and grizzly bear, along with a variety of Latin American steps.

Victor Herbert still wrote nice operettas, but for real bounce, how about young Irving Berlin's "Alexander's Ragtime Band" and "When the Midnight Choo-Choo Leaves for Alabam"? Popular music and automobiles dominated small talk in many circles.

By the time this country was deeply involved in World War I, there probably wasn't a man, woman or child who didn't recognize "Over There" and "Oh, How I Hate to Get Up in the Morning," written in 1918.

The women's suffrage movement finally hit the jackpot in Washington state in 1910, when male voters approved the Fifth Amendment to the state Constitution, giving women the right to vote.

Murderous snows from on high

 Shortly after 1 a.m. March 1, 1910, an avalanche roared down a hillside at Wellington, high in the Cascades, slamming into a Great Northern Railway train and carrying 15 cars, half a dozen locomotives, several snowplows and a couple of nearby small cabins into a ravine about 150 feet below.

Thirty-five passengers and 61 laborers and trainmen died – 96

WASHINGTON STATE'S 39 COUNTIES

Washington state's gradual accumulation of 39 counties (the word "county" dates to 13th century England and France and means domain of a count or earl) began in 1844 with Clark County and ended in 1911 with the establishment of Pend Oreille County. Chart below contains the origin of county names, dates established and the county seats.

NAME	YEAR ESTAB.	ORIGIN OF NAME	COUNTY SEAT
Adams	1883	President John Adams	Ritzville
Asotin	1883	Indian word for "eel creek"	Asotin
Benton	1905	Missouri Sen. Thomas Hart Benton	Prosser
Chelan	1899	Indian word for "deep water"	Wenatchee
Clallam	1854	Indian word for "strong people"	Port Angeles
Clark	1844	Explorer Capt. William Clark *	Vancouver
Columbia	1875	For the "Great River of the West"	Dayton
Cowlitz	1854	For an Indian tribe	Kelso
Douglas	1883	Illinois Sen. Stephen A. Douglas	Waterville
Ferry	1899	Elisha P. Ferry first state governor	Republic
Franklin	1883	Benjamin Franklin	Pasco
Garfield	1881	President James Garfield	Pomeroy
Grant	1909	President Ulysses S. Grant	Ephrata
Grays Hrbr	1854	Explorer Robert Gray **	Montesano
Island	1853	For county's islands	Coupeville
Jefferson	1852	President Thomas Jefferson	Port Townsend
King	1852	Martin Luther King Jr. ***	Seattle
Kitsap	1857	Indian word for "brave"	Port Orchard
Kittitas	1883	Indian word for "gray gravel bank"	Ellensburg
Klickitat	1859	Indian word for "robber"	Goldendale
Lewis	1845	Explorer Capt. Meriwether Lewis	Chehalis
Lincoln	1883	President Abraham Lincoln	Davenport
Mason	1854	Charles Mason secy. to 1st territ. gov.	Shelton
Okanogan	1888	Indian word for "rendezvous"	Okanogan
Pacific	1851	For Pacific Ocean	South Bend
Pend Oreille	1911	French word for ear bob	Newport
Pierce	1852	President Franklin Pierce	Tacoma
San Juan	1873	For its principal island	Friday Harbor
Skagit	1883	For an Indian tribe	Mount Vernon
Skamania	1854	Indian word for "swift waters"	Stevenson
Snohomish	1861	For an Indian tribe	Everett
Spokane	1858	Indian word for "child of the sun"	Spokane
Stevens	1863	Isaac Stevens first territ. gov.	Colville
Thurston	1852	Samuel Thurston first Ore. ter. delegate	Olympia
Wahkiakum	1854	For an Indian tribe	Cathlamet
Walla Walla	1854	Indian word for "running water"	Walla Walla
Whatcom	1854	Indian word for "noisy water"	Bellingham
Whitman	1871	Missionary Dr. Marcus Whitman	Colfax
Yakima	1865	For an Indian tribe	Yakima

*Clark mistakenly spelled "Clarke" until 1925
**Grays Harbor name changed from Chehalis in 1915
***Honored William Rufus DeVane King, Franklin Pierce's vice president, until 1986

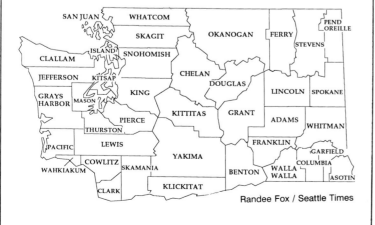

Randee Fox / Seattle Times

Museum of History & Industry

Workmen dig through the snow of the high Cascades in a search for victims of an avalanche that bowled over two trains and took 96 lives in March 1910.

in all. It was the greatest loss of life in the state from a natural disaster. Twenty-three survived.

Passenger train No. 25 and GN's fast-mail train No. 27, which had left Spokane for Seattle Feb. 22, had been trapped by a snowslide for a week. When efforts to clear the tracks were unsuccessful, some passengers braved armpit-deep drifts and hiked to Scenic Hot Springs, four miles to the west.

Railway officials resisted backing the trains into a tunnel, fearing a slide might block escape routes and that smoke from locomotives needed to warm the coaches would suffocate those aboard. Snowplows were out of commission. Telegraph lines were down.

On the night of Feb. 28, 43 passengers and 73 railway workers slept in the two trains. Three workmen rested in the little cabins.

Passengers held a prayer service, followed by songs and jokes to quiet growing fears. During the night, snow turned to rain. Thunder and lightning shook the canyon walls. A giant snow cap perched above the trains broke loose, exploding down the hillside.

Then there was silence.

Rescuers digging in the snow found a torn, muddy handbag. Inside was a water-stained note:

"I trust in God to save us."

It had been written by Mrs. Sarah Jane Covington, 69, en route to Seattle for her golden wedding anniversary. She was listed among the fatalities.

Of the survivors, four were flung clear of the wreckage, six quickly dug themselves out of the snow and others — including the conductor, engineer, brakeman and fireman — were lucky enough to be trapped in parts of the trains that were not crushed and provided some breathing space.

Four years after what became known as the Wellington Disaster, the state Supreme Court reversed a lower-court award of $20,000 to one of the victims' sons, ruling the avalanche an act of God.

The Great Northern didn't want a repetition. It embarked on a $25 million project to relocate 40 miles of track and dig the eight-mile-long Cascade Tunnel from Berne to Scenic, the longest in the Western Hemisphere. It was opened in 1929.

Eastward ho the Winton

Although a few cars made it across Snoqualmie Pass during the New York-to-Seattle race to publicize the 1909 Alaska-Yukon-Pacific Exposition, the first attempted Washington-to-East Coast automobile crossing was not made until June 1911, according to John Prentiss Thompson, writing in the Pacific Northwesterner historical magazine in 1977.

Thompson credits the crossing to the Elmer Ross family of Bothell, chauffeured by Charles Green in the Rosses' new $3,500 Winton Six.

The Rosses were headed for West Virginia at a time when

STATE-MENTS

Pit stops, pitfalls

Young Washington state continued to attract presidents and presidential candidates. William Howard Taft, whose visit to the Alaska-Yukon-Pacific Exposition in 1909 was marred by a bee sting, visited Paradise Valley in Mount Rainier National Park in 1911.

Poor Taft. The presidential caravan was mired in mud and had to be dug out. Then, when the president stepped to the edge of a precipice to enjoy the view, he slipped and had to be pulled to safety.

Theodore Roosevelt, who had visited the state in 1903 as president, returned in 1912 as the candidate of the Progressive (Bull Moose) Party and spent the night in his private railroad car. Washington was one of six states to give him a majority.

The ailing Woodrow Wilson rated a 21-gun naval salute in Seattle in September 1919. But the press was cool to his League of Nations appeals — as Congress, too, would be — and his warmest reception was from the unions.

Former President Teddy Roosevelt, two years out of the White House, addresses a University of Washington graduation class in 1911.

Webster & Stevens

CHRONO-LOG

1911
First recorded west-to-east automobile crossing of nation attempted by Elmer Ross family of Bothell, in Winton Six.

1913
"Wild Man of the Oxbow" John Tornow, killer of six men, is gunned down by posse in Wynoochee-Oxbow area, northeast of Montesano.

1914
Bandits stage Pacific Northwest version of Great Train Robbery between Burlington and Bellingham. Three passengers are killed by robbers, who manage to escape clutches of law.

1915
Snoqualmie Pass Highway opens, greatly easing cross-state travel.

Armenian immigrants Mark Balaban and Armnen Tertsagian settle in fruit-producing community of Cashmere northwest of Wenatchee. After five years of experimenting with fruit-and-nut candies in battered aluminum kettle on kitchen stove, they found Liberty Orchards Co. and start producing candies — known worldwide as Aplets and Cotlets.

The 522-foot L.C. Smith Tower, as it looked under construction in 1912. The tower, which took four years to build, opened in Seattle's Pioneer Square area July 4, 1914.

Museum of History and Industry

Seattle Times

Contractor Patrick J. McHugh stands on the newly graveled Snoqualmie Pass Highway in the summer of 1914, a year before the summit road was officially dedicated. McHugh had bid with the state to build 12 miles of roadway on each side of the summit for $203,700 — to that date the largest contract the state Highway Department had ever awarded.

transcontinental automobile travel was regarded as the height of folly.

Chauffeur Green, according to Thompson, strapped six suitcases to the running boards. Inside, he crammed assorted spare parts, rope, a winch, tents, blankets, food and a water bag.

The party strained on ropes to pull the car up a steep grade at Denny Creek in the Cascades. A scow transported car and passengers across Lake Keechelus.

Tires went flat, a universal joint and connecting rods failed. The Winton company, fearing bad publicity, sent out a mechanic to make repairs.

One week after leaving Bothell, the Rosses arrived in Spokane, angry at having paid 50 cents for a bucket of water at a Columbia Basin ranch. In defense of the farmer, he had hauled the water six miles.

Thompson never did say how long it took the Green-Ross party to make the entire trip.

Cross-state travel continued to be an adventure even after the dedication of the Snoqualmie Pass Highway in 1915. The unsurfaced road was narrow and rocky, and one could expect several stops to repair blowouts and cool overheated engines.

That highway and subsequent improvements all follow a general route foot-worn by the Indians.

For years, the Indians saw no reason to let the white invaders in on the secret of their trail over the pass. When Capt. George McClellan was told by Territorial Gov. Isaac Stevens to reconnoiter the pass for possible railroad routes in 1853, the Yakima Indians hired to guide McClellan told him it couldn't be done. Too much snow.

McClellan failed to negotiate the pass from east or west, and he told Stevens the Indians were right. The dubious Stevens sent Army Lt. Abiel Tinkham to make another try.

Tinkham left Fort Walla Walla with horses in mid-winter. When the snow got too deep, he put on snowshoes. In late January 1854, he made it to Seattle.

Construction on the Snoqualmie Pass Wagon Road was delayed until 1865 when Seattle paid W.W. Perkins $2,500 to build the first 25 miles, at $100 a mile. Perkins hired 20 men.

In 1867, King County put up another $2,500, and the wagon road was opened to travel the following year. One of the first to go over it on horseback was Miles Moore, Washington's last territorial governor.

Sheep and cattle were driven over the road in the next few years. Wagons began to use it regularly. For a time, it was a toll route.

Today hundreds of thousands of motorists journey uneventfully across the pass each year.

The Oxbow incident

A two-year manhunt ended in a hail of bullets April 16, 1913, in the Olympic Mountains foothills of Chehalis County (later renamed Grays Harbor County).

The man who died that day was John Tornow, frequently referred to as the "Wild Man of the Oxbow." He had killed six men.

Tornow grew up on a ranch on a branch of the Satsop River. Always reclusive, he would disappear for days at a time, roaming the woods alone to fish and hunt. After his father died, he became even more withdrawn.

When his brothers had him briefly committed to a mental institution, Tornow swore vengeance. His first victims were his twin 19-year-old nephews, John and William Bauer, who happened upon their uncle's makeshift cabin in the woods. He shot them, took their watches and guns and fled.

The hunt for Tornow began.

Sheriff Edward Payette enlisted additional deputies. Among them were Colin McKenzie and A.V. Elmer, regarded as excellent trackers. They found Tornow's hideout but instead of calling for help, they decided to capture him themselves.

Their bodies were found in shallow graves.

With four dead, residents of the area lived in terror. The county offered a $4,000 reward for Tornow's capture. Gov. Marion Hay added another $1,000. Payette called for a posse.

Few, however, wanted to go into the woods against Tornow, a superb woodsman who knew all the trackers' tricks and had the advantage of surprise. Tired of living in fear, county residents elected a new sheriff, Schelle Matthews, who promised to bring Tornow to justice.

Matthews formed a posse headed by his brother-in-law, Giles Quimby. Following a tip, Quimby went into the woods with two untrained deputies, Charles Lathrop and Louis Blair. They found a rude cabin near a marsh. Signs indicated it might be Tornow's. Lathrop and Blair walked toward it, in the open. Quimby wisely held back.

Tornow saw the approaching men and fired. Blair and Lathrop fell, mortally wounded. Quimby saw the bearded Tornow peering from behind a tree, rifle in hand.

Quimby fired repeatedly. Although he thought his final shot had hit Tornow, he couldn't be sure. The firing stopped. He left the scene to telephone the sheriff.

Quimby led a small army into the Oxbow. Tornow's body was found behind a tree.

Hundreds of the curious, deathly afraid of Tornow when he was alive, came to see his remains on display in Montesano, east of Aberdeen. Photographs of the corpse went for 25 cents. The "wild man" was buried in a grave next to his father.

Jesse Jamesism on the Great Northern

On Feb. 20, 1914, what became known locally as the Great Train Robbery took place aboard the Great Northern Railway's No. 59.

The train, which left Seattle at 4:30 p.m., bound for Bellingham, stopped at Burlington, Skagit County, to take on more passengers. Among them were two men, both aged 25, who immediately went to the smoking car. While No. 59 chugged toward Samish, the two left the car, stopping in the vestibule to tie bandanas over their faces. They entered a day coach filled with men, women and children.

One bandit locked the day-coach door. The other shouted, "Hands up!" and walked the length of the car, waving his pistol in the air and shooting out lights. The marksman kept the passengers covered while his companion at the rear of the coach began relieving them of cash and valuables.

Thomas Wadsworth of Vancouver, B.C., a conductor for the Canadian Pacific Railway, made a desperate — and foolhardy — decision to jump one of the bandits from the rear. A wrestling match in the aisle ensued. Two more men — A.R. Adkinson, a Vancouver, B.C., traveling salesman, and R.L. Lee, a timekeeper at the Bremerton Naval Shipyard — joined Wadsworth in the fray.

There was little room for maneuvering in the aisle. The bandit fired through Wadsworth's shoulder and the bullet ripped downward into his heart. Wadsworth was dead when he hit the floor. Adkinson took fatal shots in the chest and back. Another bullet ripped through Lee's temple.

Three men lay dead. Women screamed.

The gunman calmly resumed his walk up the aisle, picking up money, watches and rings. His companion tried to calm the screaming women.

"Don't be afraid," he said. "It's all a joke."

In the words of a newspaper reporter who later interviewed passengers, some women began "secreting their valuables in places the most dastardly bandits would not dare to search."

When word of the robbery in progress reached the engineer, he began to apply the brakes. The bandits leaped from the slow-moving train.

The next day, the Great Train Robbery pushed Pancho Villa, the Mexican guerrilla/revolutionary, off the front pages of Pacific Northwest newspapers. The railroad posted a $30,000 reward for the robbers. Two Canadians were arrested, but both were freed after offering apparently airtight alibis.

By coincidence, or plan, the Seattle-Tacoma Interurban was held up the day after the Great Train Robbery. Three masked men brandished guns and ordered a youth to take his hat through the coach and collect money and valuables from the passengers.

No one was shot. The bandits leaped from the moving interurban. They, too, were never captured.

Standing tall in the West

The L.C. Smith Tower once was grist for Sunday supplements as, for many years, the tallest building west of the Mississippi. It soared higher, at 522 feet, than such world-famous giants as the Great Pyramid of Giza and the cathedral of Cologne.

That, of course, was long ago. The building, opened in Seattle's Pioneer Square area July 4, 1914, is now dwarfed by skyscrapers that seemingly sprout overnight. It looks like a child's Lego-brick structure alongside the Columbia Seafirst Center.

The Smith Tower was named for Lyman Cornelius Smith, the typewriter king of Syracuse, N.Y.. Smith and his friend, local financier J.D. Hoge, had talked of putting up major buildings in downtown Seattle. There was, some said, a gentleman's agreement that neither would exceed 20 stories.

The financier built first, his 18-story Hoge Building opening in 1912 at Second Avenue and Cherry Street. If there was a promise, Smith reneged. What he would build not only would make the Hoge Building look puny but would dazzle the world.

Smith decided on a 21-story building topped by a 21-story tower, the whole thing resting on 1,276 piles buried 50 feet below into bedrock. Construction took four years. Smith died before it was completed.

The Smith Tower was more than just tall. It symbolized the Northwest's bid for recognition (titleholder of the day was New York's 60-story Woolworth Building). It was class — from its main lobby of Mexican onyx and carved Indian heads looking down on bronze-and-steel elevators to its 35th-floor Chinese Room, with a sweeping view of Elliott Bay and much of downtown.

For years, the Chinese Room was the city's major high-level observatory and reception area for VIPs. Its centerpiece was the "Wishing Chair," given to L.C. Smith by the empress of China. The chair's carved dragon and phoenix, when combined, were supposed to be a powerful portent of marriage. Blushing women, in simpler times, sat in the chair and were assured they'd be going down the aisle within a year. Smith's own daughter was married in the observatory one year after her opening-day visit.

Historians say that before the Smith Tower, the site was occupied by one of pioneer Seattle's tallest Douglas firs. The tree was felled before the Indian War of 1856, its giant trunk providing cover for advancing Indians as settlers fled to a stockade.

Generations of Seattleites grew up knowing the Smith Tower was something special. In 1942, a proud grandfather ran a 15-foot banner up the flagpole to proclaim, "It's a girl." Long after other buildings automated their elevators, the Tower was noted for its live, smiling and highly unionized operators.

Although the building claims 42 stories, elevators stop at the 35th-floor observation room. The "missing" seven stories are tightly packed inside the tower's pyramid-shaped cap.

The late Ivar Haglund, restaurateur, balladeer and man about town, fell in love with it as a boy, watching the construction from the family farm at Alki. He acquired it late in life and added his signature touch — a 16-foot-long, fish-shaped windsock that flew at the very top.

Daring young men and flying machines

On the same day the L.C. Smith Tower was being dedicated, two young men — William Boeing and Cmdr. Conrad Westervelt, USN — flew over Lake Washington in a flimsy pusher-prop seaplane piloted by Terah Maroney.

After a few more flights in subsequent weeks, Boeing and Westervelt decided they could design something better than the spit-and-baling-wire contraptions that passed for airplanes. Both had engineering backgrounds. Boeing also had considerable timber and land holdings.

Boeing and Westervelt designed two airplanes, called B&W's (their initials). The planes closely resembled Curtiss and Martin aircraft then in production.

The two men talked of forming a company. But war with Germany was imminent and the Navy transferred Westervelt to the East Coast. Boeing went ahead alone, founding Pacific Aero Products Co. in July 1916, in a hangar built on Lake Union.

Boeing's chief engineer, an MIT graduate named T. Wong, designed an entirely new aircraft, the Model C, which was flying well by January 1917. Other C's followed. And when war with Germany was declared, Boeing went to Washington, D.C., to interest the Navy in buying his airplanes.

The Navy ordered a batch of C's to be tested as trainers. Thus encouraged, Boeing changed the name of his company to Boeing Airplane Co. and moved out of the lakeside hangar to a small yacht-building firm (E.W. Heath) on the Duwamish River.

Before long, Boeing also had some Army orders.

When the war ended, Boeing looked elsewhere for business. On March 3, 1919, he and Edward Hubbard launched the first

Seattle Times

Dockwalloper

A husky, tanned 22-year-old arrived in Seattle in 1917 by his favorite mode of transportation — riding the rods of freight trains. He was a prizefighter by profession, but for the moment was short on cash. The nation had entered World War 1 in April, and the young man was staked to a lunch bucket and grub money and steered to a local shipyard for a job.

A few days later, he strolled into the Elks Club gymnasium, where he introduced himself as "Jack Thompson" and said he'd be interested in fighting. He did the same thing at the old Austin and Salt gymnasium. Caruso Dan Salt, matchmaker at the latter gym, wasn't fooled. He recognized the young man from a photo he'd seen in a Utah newspaper. Jack Dempsey! That's his real name, Salt said.

Thompson/Dempsey flattened sparring partners with ease when he worked out, and three bouts arranged for him never came off. Local fighters knew they were no match for the mauler from Manassa, Colo. In the fall of 1917, Dempsey received a telegram from San Francisco saying a four-round bout had been arranged with Gunboat Smith. The wire was from Jack "Doc" Kearns, Dempsey's manager, who had driven a taxi in Seattle years before. Dempsey left the shipyard, and he decisioned Smith Oct. 2, 1917.

When the war ended, Dempsey's brief stint in Seattle became grounds for accusations he was a "slacker" for ducking combat by hiding out in a shipyard. Two years after leaving Seattle, he won the heavyweight title by beating Jess Willard.

CHRONO-LOG

A touring car tools along the brand-new, plank-surfaced Pacific Highway in 1915.

1916

Survey shows 43 libraries have been built in state with money from steel magnate/philanthropist Andrew Carnegie. (Seattle, Tacoma and Spokane receive first Carnegie-library funds in 1901.)

The Arlington Times reports that in single day — Oct. 19 — 80 railway cars, each piled with logs, left major logging center of Darrington, Snohomish County. (In 1929, Darrington ships 15,000 carloads of 120-foot pilings to new Ford plant at Edgewater, N.J.)

The May B II, small passenger vessel, makes first full-length journey through Ballard Locks and Lake Washington Ship Canal. Man-made waterway is formally inaugurated the following year with passage of steamship and 300 smaller craft.

William Boeing founds Pacific Aero Products Co., forerunner of aerospace giant of 1980s, in hangar built on piling in Lake Union. Company's new Model C is early success with military, a harbinger of things to come.

Everett Massacre: Five "Wobblies," two deputies killed, 47 others wounded; 75 radicals jailed and charged with murder.

Engineering draftsmen work on Boeing aeronautical plans in this 1916 scene of the fledgling airplane company at the old Red Barn on the Duwamish.

international air-mail service — between Seattle and Victoria, B.C. The Boeing story was just beginning.

The little cable car that couldn't

Seattle, like San Francisco, once had little cable cars that ran halfway to the stars.

Bells clanging, they hooked onto continuously moving cables that propelled them up and down Yesler Way and James and Madison Street hills.

On Queen Anne Hill, which was higher and steeper, the device selected to raise and lower the cars was called a counterbalance. It consisted of a wheeled truck, loaded with cast iron to bring it up to 16 tons, which ran in a tunnel beneath Queen Anne Avenue North.

By hooking to the counterweight, trolleys, which weighed between 18 and 25 tons, got a boost on the uphill pull, a brake on the downhill run. Conventional overhead wires provided extra power to haul trolleys up the hill.

At peak hours, the counterbalance trolleys carried about 30 seated passengers, 40 straphangers and a few standees on the rear platform.

Not every motorman was temperamentally suited to the counterbalance run. One who felt very much at home was F.K. LaFayette, a lanky 24-year-old who never forgot his main job — to be sure the conductor connected the trolley to the "shoe" affixed to the counterweight.

In the summer of 1915, LaFayette stopped briefly at the top of the hill while his conductor went through the motions of picking up the shoe. The trolley car then rolled down to Highland Drive, where it was mandatory that motormen make a safety stop.

LaFayette was in a hurry and didn't attempt to stop until he hit the flat intersection of Highland Drive. The front end of the trolley was over the hill when LaFayette heard the familiar two-bell go-ahead signal (two bells sounded by the conductor) and fed power to the trolley with a control handle.

The trolley bolted ahead like a skittish piglet.

"I knew instantly I did not have the shoe," LaFayette recalled years later. "The car seemed to plunge over the brow of the hill and down the steepest portion between Highland Drive and Prospect Street."

It was no time for a faint heart. LaFayette was at the helm of an 18-ton car with about 12 passengers and a conductor who had broken out in a cold sweat. Down at the bottom, at Mercer Street, stood two trolleycars and an open switch that led right to them.

LaFayette pulled the sand lever. He applied the air brakes, the hand brakes. The car kept going. Prospect Street whizzed past. Then Ward. Then Aloha.

Fortunately, no one was crossing the streets. The hill grew less steep. LaFayette had one last card to play. He reversed his four motors, risking blowing the automatic jacks that served as fuses between trolley wires and motors.

It was a severe shock to the motors, but the jacks held up.

The trolley ground to a halt just past Valley Street, a block and a half from disaster, and LaFayette began easing her down to Mercer Street.

LaFayette received a two-day suspension, then returned to a job he held until he went into the Army during World War I. The conductor who forgot to pick up the shoe requested, and received, a transfer.

By the 1940s, cable cars were passé. Tracks were ripped up and, detractors said later, the steel sold to Japan "came back in our boys' bodies."

The cars were sold. Some people said, "You'll be sorry," and pleaded with officials to save just one car.

The best specimen (from the Yesler run) now may be seen in the Smithsonian museum in Washington, D.C.

Radical workers: the cutting edge

 Organizers for the radical Industrial Workers of the World — the "Wobblies" — found a ready audience for their message as they stood on Skid Road street corners, passing out leaflets, and went into the woods to talk about low wages and poor working conditions.

It was logging's cut-and-run era. Wobbly organizers said the timber barons promised "pie in the sky, by-and-by," while loggers faced death every day and maiming was a fact of life for sawmill workers.

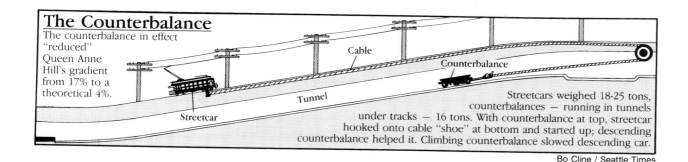

The Counterbalance

The counterbalance in effect "reduced" Queen Anne Hill's gradient from 17% to a theoretical 4%.

Cable

Counterbalance

Tunnel

Streetcar

Streetcars weighed 18-25 tons, counterbalances — running in tunnels under tracks — 16 tons. With counterbalance at top, streetcar hooked onto cable "shoe" at bottom and started up; descending counterbalance helped it. Climbing counterbalance slowed descending car.

Bo Cline / Seattle Times

Logging-camp conditions were notorious. Bedding was infested with fleas, ticks and bedbugs. There was no place to bathe or do laundry. Loggers worked until it was so dark they couldn't see the trees. On payday, they took their few dollars into town and blew them on liquor and women. Then, broke, they went back to the woods.

Missing fingers were the badge of the shingleweaver. Machinery lacked rudimentary safety devices. Bosses often expected workers to tie a rag around a gaping wound and get back to work, or lose a day's pay.

Everett was a booming mill town that billed itself as the "City of Smokestacks" in the early fall of 1916 when about 40 IWW members arrived to stage a "free speech" demonstration in support of striking shingle-mill workers. The Wobblies were met at the edge of town by the sheriff, who made them run through a double row of about 200 men armed with clubs and rifles.

Jack Leonard Miller, who became one of the most-quoted old labor radicals in his later years, described that confrontation:

"They were some of the most respected businessmen in town and some of the pillars of the church. And I was about fourth in line. I pulled my coat over my head and made a dash for it. I ducked the first two in line, then got my head split open. I woke up down by the river . . ."

That beating set the stage for what happened Nov. 5, 1916, when some 200 IWW members, including the 27-year-old Miller, paid their fares and boarded the steamer Verona out of Seattle for a return to Everett.

The Verona was met at the dock by Sheriff Don McRae and a full crew of deputies, plus a contingent of Pinkerton guards. Townsfolk gathered on hillsides, away from the dock, to watch the confrontation.

The Wobblies sang "Hold the Fort" on the deck of the Verona. They stopped when McRae shouted, "You can't land here." After a moment's pause, a shot rang out. It was never clear whether it came from the Verona or from the dock.

A hail of bullets followed. Union members began to scream and

Everett Public Library

The steamer Verona at the Everett city dock some time after the Everett massacre of Nov. 5, 1916, which claimed the lives of at least five Wobblies and two sheriff's deputies.

fall. Many rushed to the far side of the boat, which listed badly. The railing broke and some fell into the water.

The Wobblies had guns, too. And on the dock, men also were falling and crying out in pain.

Five IWW members were killed that day. Two sheriff's deputies lay dead. Forty-seven others, including Sheriff McRae, were wounded. A dozen Wobblies were unaccounted for and presumed to have drowned.

The skipper of the Verona didn't wait around for body counts. As soon as people began falling into the water, he righted the boat, fired up the engine and pulled out — heading back to Seattle.

The militia was waiting for them. Miller and 74 others were jailed and charged with murder. The trial was long, but no one was convicted.

When Miller was freed, he went back to selling IWW tracts on street corners, but the memory of the "Everett Massacre" was too fresh. There were fewer listeners. Miller was arrested for "selling without a license." Drafted and sent to Camp Lewis during World War I, Miller decided to distribute Wobbly literature to the troops, a federal crime. He was sent to Alcatraz.

Miller lived a long and quiet post-prison life in Seattle, sharp-minded and chatty until his death, at age 96, in the spring of 1986. In his later years, he still talked excitedly about the heyday of the Wobblies, throwing back his head and lustily singing the old Wobbly songs. With a little urging, he would pull out some of the blank verse he wrote as a young man.

"Never finished school," he'd say, and then he'd recite:

"Let the earth itself be both my mattress and my blanket. Bring no flowers to wither on amputated stems. Make no mound to mark the spot. Let no one weep. Plant a broad-leafed tree, then come no more."

To the devil with demon rum

Many Washingtonians awoke Jan. 1, 1916, with the granddaddy of all hangovers.

Initiative No. 3, narrowly passed by the voters in November 1914, had become law. They had gone on a binge on New Year's Eve, drinking up everything in sight.

The initiative — four years before Prohibition hit the entire nation — banned the sale and manufacture of liquor in Washington state. It did not, however, prohibit drinking. One still could obtain an import permit from the county auditor to bring in and consume two quarts of hard liquor or 12 bottles of high-alcohol-content beer every 20 days.

In Spokane, 34,000 permits were issued for a county that had only 44,000 registered voters. Drug stores could dispense liquor for "religious and medicinal purposes," and in the first three months after No. 3 became law, 65 permits were issued for new drug stores in Seattle.

Seattle's Mayor, Hiram "Hi" Gill, recalled in 1911 because of presumed laxness in enforcing the public morals, was re-elected in 1914 and again in 1916 as the candidate of morality. In a dramatic turnaround, he took up the ax, in the manner of Carry Nation, wielding it with fervor against suspected bootleg establishments.

Despite the problems with Initiative No. 3, it dramatically reduced public drunkenness. And some who fought vigorously against its adoption became its staunchest advocates. The streets, they said, were safer and people were saving more money or spending it on items that merchants were eager to sell.

Two initiatives (the Hotelmen's Bill and the Brewer's Bill) were passed in 1916 to add teeth to No. 3. And in 1918, the state adopted a bone-dry referendum.

The stage was set for Congress to pass the 18th Amendment to the Constitution, or Prohibition, which was backed up by the National Prohibition Act of 1920, popularly — or unpopularly — called the Volstead Act after its sponsor, Andrew Volstead.

It had been a long fight and, of course, it would never end.

Demon rum had been a problem, and a joy, from the time the early explorers and fur traders introduced it to Washington

STATE'S ALL-TIME WEATHER RECORDS

118 degrees
Highest temperature; at Wahluke, southern Grant County, on the Columbia River, July 24, 1928.

-48 degrees
Lowest temperature; at Winthrop and Mazama, Okanogan County, both on Dec. 30, 1968.

1.65 inches
Greatest rainfall in 60 minutes; at Grotto, four miles west of Skykomish, King County, May 25, 1945.

12 inches
Greatest rainfall in 24 hours; at Quinault Ranger Station, Grays Harbor County, Jan. 21, 1935.

57.04 inches
Greatest rainfall in one month; at Peterson's Ranch, near Cougar, Cowlitz County, Dec. 1933.

184.56 inches
Greatest rainfall in one year; at Wynoochee, 25 miles north of Aberdeen, Grays Harbor County, 1931.

2.60 inches
Least rainfall in one year; at Wahluke, Grant County, 1930.

1,122 inches
Greatest snowfall; at Paradise Ranger Station, Mount Rainier, 1971-72.

52 inches
Most snow in 24 hours; at Winthrop, Okanogan County, Jan. 21, 1935.

129 inches
Most snow in single snowfall; at Laconia, a Snoqualmie Pass village in northwest Kittitas County, Feb. 24-26, 1910.

363 inches
Greatest snowfall in one month; at Paradise Ranger Station, Mount Rainier, Jan. 1925.

31.11
Highest sea-level barometric pressure; at Walla Walla, Jan. 1, 1979.

28.57
Lowest sea-level barometric pressure; at Tatoosh Island, off Cape Flattery, Clallam County, Dec. 6, 1951.

113 mph
Highest recorded wind gusts; at North Head, west side of Cape Disappointment, two miles north of Columbia River, Pacific County, Jan. 29, 1921.

Territory.

As pointed out by Norman H. Clark, who has written the definitive book on this state's liquor legislation ("The Dry Years: Prohibition and Social Change in Washington"), although the Indians were unfamiliar with alcohol when they first encountered whites, they soon learned.

Excessive drinking was common on the frontier, and liquor — along with blankets, guns, furs and food — was frequently traded. Saloons flourished and so did public drunkenness, and there was growing concern. Not long ago a book was published that aptly described those days: "The Alcoholic Republic."

In 1855, soon after Washington became a territory, prohibition was on the ballot. It was turned down, but not by much. The Legislature went ahead and passed a law against selling liquor to the Indians.

By the 1870s, numerous temperance organizations had sprung up in the territory. Among the strongest were the Good Templars (men who swore not to drink) and the WCTU (Women's Christian Temperance Union).

At the 1878 Constitutional Convention in Walla Walla — the first push for statehood — delegates avoided including prohibition or women's suffrage in the constitution, referring both controversial measures to the males-only electorate.

Both were soundly defeated. Actually, the "prohibition" measure would have restricted saloons, on a local-option basis, rather than prohibit the use of liquor.

Agitation for temperance and suffrage continued. The suffragettes won first, when the Legislature voted in 1883 to give women the vote. This was later overturned by the territorial Supreme Court, much to the disgust and anger of women.

Modest anti-drink, anti-saloon legislation was passed throughout the 1880s, climaxing in a full-fledged prohibition measure on the ballot in '89 when voters approved a constitution for the new state-to-be. It went down to defeat, as did suffrage one more time.

Drys and wets continued to do battle. Both factions contained moderates and extremists. Some drys would have settled for control rather than abolition of liquor. Some wets conceded saloons were out of control.

Enforcing laws wasn't easy. Although Sunday closing of saloons was ruled constitutional in 1899, Seattle's saloons didn't abide by the statute until 1906. Walla Walla's saloon owners defied it even longer.

In 1909, under pressure from the Anti-Saloon League, the Legislature adopted a strong local-option law (the Alaska-Yukon-Pacific Exposition would be totally dry).

The law, however, was anti-saloon rather than anti-drink. People could drink all they wanted within the confines of their homes. And there was always the druggist's for medicinal nips.

Whole counties voted dry. Some voted to be dry in all but the larger cities.

Highly emotional arguments on both sides preceded the vote on Initiative 3. Children in Everett carried banners: "Less booze,

more shoes." Ministers preached for it. Most newspaper editors decried it as bad for business.

Nearly 95 percent of the eligible voters went to the polls to have their say. The vote was close, but No. 3 passed 189,840 for, 171,208 against.

Thus the hangover Jan. 1, 1916.

Whiteouts west

Compared with other parts of the country, snowfalls in the larger cities west of the Cascades have always been on the tame side. But Seattle's "Great Snowfall of 1916" was one for the books.

In 24 hours, starting at 5 p.m. Feb. 1, 21½ inches of snow fell downtown — still the all-time 24-hour record for the city.

That snow, added to about seven inches on the ground from the previous day, brought the downtown total to almost 29 inches.

In some outlying districts, drifts were four to five feet deep.

The great dome of St. James Cathedral collapsed under the weight of the snow. The old Alki Natatorium, or indoor swimming pool, and West Seattle Christian Church were damaged. A portion of the grandstand fell on Denny Field at the University of Washington.

One man died when he slipped and fell through a skylight while cleaning snow from a roof. Puget Sound Power & Light Co. hired 1,500 snow shovelers.

Seattle's total snowfall for February 1916 was 35.4 inches; the total for January and February was 58.7 inches. And the total for all of 1916 was 60.9 inches, a record never surpassed.

Weather records dating before statehood may be suspect. But they give some hint of how mild winters have become in recent years.

Historians say snow began falling before Christmas Day 1861, swirling and flurrying off and on through New Year's Day. Although there was no official measurement, the temperature is said to have fallen to -4 degrees on several nights. A six-inch-thick "ice rink" was laid on Lake Union, and there was good skating for several weeks.

Pioneers swore Seattle's heaviest snowfall occurred during the winter of 1879-80. It was five feet deep at Yesler's Wharf, they said. A storefront collapsed at the foot of Cherry Street.

In 1893, there was another "record" snowfall. The young city was blanketed with 45½ inches of snow between Jan. 27 and Feb. 8. Steep, un-regraded hills were unfit for man or horse.

State's in the Army now

On Jan. 6, 1917, Pierce County residents voted 8-1 to bond themselves for $2 million to buy 70,000 acres south of Tacoma.

The land — some of which had been used for training regular Army troops and National Guardsmen since 1890 — was donated to the federal government for a permanent Army post to be called Camp Lewis.

Five months after the land was donated, Capt. David Stone arrived to begin construction of an Army camp. In just 90 days, he succeeded in erecting a "city" of more than 2,000 buildings to handle 60,000 troops.

The first recruits, including the Northwest's own 91st Division, arrived in the fall to begin training for World War I.

Patriotic workmen personally subscribed $4,000 to build the Main Gate — an arch of fieldstone and squared logs. It is still standing.

On Nov. 15, 1919, Camp Lewis formally was deeded to the government.

In the fall of 1927, a year after the Army pumped $800,000 into permanent brick construction, the camp was given a new designation: Fort Lewis. Like the camp, its name honors Meriwether Lewis, the explorer.

Stone, the man who built the fort, came back in 1936 as its commanding general. He is buried in the Fort Lewis Cemetery.

In 1938, the Works Progress Administration — the storied WPA — began building an airfield, McChord, — north of the fort. Pierce County donated 989 of the original 1,800 acres.

When World War II began in Europe in 1939, the Army began building North Fort Lewis. During the construction, many troops temporarily were housed in tents at Camp Murray, the state's National Guard encampment.

With the start of draft registration in 1940, raw recruits began arriving at Fort Lewis by the thousands. Many young draftees and enlistees who passed through the fort were so impressed with the Northwest that when the war was over they called this home.

Mark Clark and Dwight D. Eisenhower — who were to become famous World War II generals — were stationed at the fort as war clouds gathered. Clark was there from 1937 through March 1940, much of the time as a public-relations officer for the 3rd Division.

Don Myers

Downtown Seattle lies muffled under three feet of snow in this February 1916 photo taken along Second Avenue near Madison Street.

Waters from Lake Union swoosh into the Montlake Cut during construction of the Lake Washington Ship Canal in 1913. The five-year project had begun in 1911.

Museum of History & Industry

Seattle Times

John C. "Radio Speaker" Stevenson, during his spellbinding prime in the mid-1930s.

Silver tongues

Seattle attorney George Vanderveer was reputed to be the equal of the renowned Clarence Darrow as a courtroom spellbinder. Others upon whom all eyes were riveted when they got up to speak were:

John Dore, twice mayor of Seattle in the 1930s, who combined lung power, wit and his own brand of populism to score resoundingly with audiences.

Seattle City Councilman Bob Harlin, a diminutive but formidable presence during the same era, would rise from his chair, wait until all eyes were upon him and announce in a commanding voice, "I, Robert H. Harlin . . ."

Harry Cain, one-term U.S. senator from Tacoma (1946-52), was blessed with remarkable podium power. After being voted out of office, he used his persuasive voice to promote real estate in Florida.

For more than half a century, until his death in 1980, white-vested Seattle defense attorney Clay Nixon melted juror's hearts with patriotic appeals and had a knack for evoking real tears on behalf of his clients.

John C. Stevenson, whose rhetorical brilliance from stump and broadcast booth during the Depression promoted the Townsend (pension) Plan and a chicken-in-every-pot, found himself at a disadvantage when he ran for county office. The opposition, with devious intent, fielded a candidate with the same name. Stevenson did the only logical thing: He went to court and had his name legally changed so he was known ever after as Radio Speaker John C. Stevenson.

Eisenhower served three months in 1940 as chief of staff of the Army's IX Corps.

The fort was a beehive of activity from Dec. 7, 1941, when the Japanese bombed Pearl Harbor, until the end of the war. In 1943, a camp for prisoners of war was established. It lasted for about three years. That same year, Fort Lewis Hospital was expanded. It later was renamed Madigan General Hospital.

Fort Lewis has provided Pierce County with a stable employment base and occasional housing booms over the years. Tacoma's once-notorious Lower Pacific Avenue, periodically declared off-limits to troops, grew so tame by the '70s that nobody wanted to go there.

The ship canal: a cut above the rest

On the afternoon of July 4, 1917, the SS Roosevelt, used by Adm. Robert Peary on his North Pole expedition eight years earlier, left Shilshole Bay and entered the largest of the two Hiram M. Chittenden Government Locks.

The Roosevelt led a flotilla of about 300 commercial and pleasure craft into a wide, deep freshwater cut under the Fremont Bridge, past Lake Union and through the Montlake Cut into Lake Washington.

As the vessels headed south to Mount Baker Park, the Roosevelt yielded its flagship role at Leschi Park to review the "fleet."

Meanwhile, crowds gathered at the locks and at the Fremont Bridge. Bands played, marchers strutted and there were the inevitable speeches. Later, there were fireworks.

Seattle officially was dedicating the Ship Canal and Chittenden locks, although both had been opened to traffic since Feb. 5, 1916, when a small passenger vessel, May B II, made the historic first full-length journey.

It was a day for justifiable pride — of looking backward at the many broken dreams that preceded the actual construction, of looking forward to a new era of cargo, pleasure and passenger vessels passing between two great bodies of water, and of a more stable water level on Seattle's largest lake (Washington).

Some foresaw intensive industrialization of both Lake Union and Lake Washington. In the case of the latter, they were wrong, fortunately. But even the most visionary on that day probably did not dream that thanks to the canal and locks this city eventually would have an arguable claim to being the "boating capital of the

world."

As canals go, Seattle's doesn't go especially far — perhaps eight miles by stretching things a bit. The 4 million cubic yards of dirt and muck removed for the canal are certainly no match for the Suez or Panama canals. Nobody got yellow fever digging it, and it has never figured in an international incident.

The locks, although one of the city's great free shows, fall considerably short of being one of man's mightiest engineering feats. The two concrete "bathtubs," 90-by-825 feet and 30-by-150 feet, required 330,000 cubic yards of concrete — hardly a threat to Grand Coulee Dam's 12 million cubic yards.

Even the project's total cost — roughly $5 million — borne by city, county, state and federal government, wasn't awesome even in those days.

And yet for sheer activity 24 hours a day, the canal and locks are outstanding. Their use — nearly 4,000 vessels on a three-day holiday weekend in the summer — rivals that of any man-made ditch in the hemisphere.

Locating the canal and locks hadn't been easy.

The idea of connecting Lake Union and Lake Washington (then known as Lake Geneva) and digging a canal to saltwater first had been broached by Thomas Mercer — brother of Asa, of Mercer Girls' fame — on the Fourth of July 1854.

Six years after Mercer's vision, Harvey Pike took a pick and shovel and tried to dig a ditch between Portage Bay (connected to Lake Union) and Union Bay (an arm of Lake Washington). He didn't finish. Various companies were formed to complete Pike's dream. None was successful.

Then, in 1885 a contract was let to a Chinese businessman, Wa

Seattle Times

Gen. Hiram M. Chittenden, for whom the Ballard Locks are named.

Grace Loudon McAdam

Employees of the Stewart & Holmes Wholesale Drug Co. in Seattle pose with their gauze masks during the great influenza epidemic of 1918.

CHRONO-LOG

1917

Town of Tolt is renamed Carnation to honor nearby research farm operated by Carnation Milk Products Co., developers of condensed milk.

Chief Saluskin of Yakima Tribe dies still protesting that Yakima County town originally named Saluskin in his honor has been renamed Harrah. Name was changed in 1915 to pay tribute to J.T. Harrah, who operated ranch that was community's main source of income. An angry Saluskin calls it "Thief Town" to his dying day.

State completes its first road from Rainier Valley to Renton.

In February, construction crews complete bridge across Columbia from Vancouver to Portland. Special feature is financing — not by federal or state governments, but by Clark County on Washington side, Multnomah County on Oregon side. The 2,300-foot-long bridge and approaches cost $1.7 million, of which Multnomah pays three-fifths and Clark the rest. To recoup expenses, counties set up toll booths, but after years of haggling over whether traffic problems created by toll lines are worth revenue coming in, highway commissioners of both states agree to buy bridge and eliminate tolls (1929).

Chong, who brought in 25 Chinese laborers. They not only dug a small canal but added a small wooden lock to handle logs.

There are no monuments to Wa Chong and his men. There should be.

After Territorial Gov. Eugene Semple left office in the late '80s, he formed a company to dig what became known as the South Canal — from Puget Sound's Elliott Bay through Beacon Hill to Lake Washington. Others favored a North Canal, running out through Ballard.

The North-South battle raged for years. A promise to do something about "Seattle's Ditch" helped elect John McGraw as the state's second governor.

Even after the Army Engineers selected the North Canal route in 1901, the project moved with less than blinding speed. Right-of-way was needed. Streets had to be regraded and water mains relocated. Bridges eventually would be needed.

The arrival of Brig. Gen. Chittenden in 1905 to take charge of the federal engineer's office sparked an all-out effort. Chittenden not only believed wholeheartedly in the canal but in the locks system that would connect the canal with saltwater Shilshole Bay.

Congress began opening its purse strings. In June 1911, work began on the locks. Less than five years later, they were finished.

In the 16 months between the May B II's historic first trip and the Fourth of July dedication, more than 17,000 vessels used the locks.

A flu bug deadlier than dogs of war

The worldwide influenza pandemic of 1918-19 has been compared in severity with the Black Plague of the Middle Ages.

From Oct. 5, 1918, through May 20, 1919, Seattle (pop. 315,000) recorded 1,772 deaths — due directly to either influenza or the pneumonia that followed.

Few families in the state escaped without at least one member being stricken by the "Spanish" flu — so called because Spain was one of the countries where it was first discovered. Often whole families were bedridden at the same time.

John S. McBride, Seattle's health commissioner, assumed the role of a virtual dictator as the illness terrorized the city.

World War I, grinding to an end, still dominated the front pages of The Seattle Times. But there were new headlines:

"505 More Cases of Influenza."

Seattle Health Commissioner John S. McBride assumed the role of virtual dictator as deadly flu ravaged the city.

"Thousands Being Inoculated."

"Complete Death List."

Influenza serum was rushed to Seattle. An emergency hospital was set up in the old courthouse building when city hospitals were filled to overflowing. McBride issued strict rules as the epidemic laid siege to the city:

"All these will wear gauze masks: barbers, dentists and assistants, waiters and waitresses, clerks in all stores, messenger boys and girls, elevator operators, bank tellers, all persons preparing food for the public."

The Red Cross made thousands of masks. Women were mobilized to make more. The Health Department ordered public telephones sterilized nightly.

Bremerton was one of the first nearby towns to be hard-hit. Influenza swept through the Naval Training Station at the University of Washington. Then it raged through Camp Lewis. Those in their 20s and 30s seemed especially vulnerable. Many died.

The epidemic would appear to wane, then flare anew. Churches, theaters, the UW and many stores were closed. Public businesses that remained open were put on emergency hours.

The Bon Marché advertised:

"Shop by telephone. It is not unpatriotic."

The Kolynos Co., maker of toothpaste, took out big newspaper ads for the Kolynos face mask "to fight influenza," adding in the best commercial tradition, "combine face mask use with brushing the teeth three times daily."

Seattleites, like their contemporaries across the nation, went to polling booths in November wearing face masks. By December 1918, McBride ordered a 10-day quarantine on all influenza cases. Homes with flu victims had to be marked with placards.

McBride's virtual martial law included the arrest of those who removed face masks, and the cancellation of public meetings. The orders seemed harsh at the time, but Seattle's mortality rate (5.6 deaths per 1,000 population) was lower than that of most major cities. Philadelphia, with 7.4 deaths per 1,000, and Baltimore, with 6.7, had the highest death rates in the United States. In New York City, more than 20,000 died.

There was a run on whiskey everywhere, "for medicinal purposes." In Yakima County the U.S. marshal got permission from the county prosecutor to use government-seized liquor to "treat" influenza.

Meanwhile, the pandemic devastated Europe and Asia, abating only in the spring of 1919. It was not until several years later that a reasonably accurate worldwide death count could be made. The figures were numbing.

While the world had been at war, the battlefield had been safer than city streets. An estimated 500,000 to 700,000 people had died of influenza in the United States alone; 20 million had died around the world. This nation's total war toll, including combat deaths, came to about 116,700.

Dark and bloody ground in Centralia

Armistice Day, Nov. 11, 1919 (also the 30th anniversary of statehood), was celebrated in almost every city and hamlet across the land. The Great War had ended a year earlier. The nation's mood was festive and maybe a little cocky.

It was a rainy Tuesday morning in Centralia, Lewis County. The band played "Over There." Young veterans who had "made the world safe from the Kaiser" marched down Tower Avenue to enthusiastic applause. Suddenly the marchers halted in front of the hall occupied by the Industrial Workers of the World, the Wobblies.

What happened next became known as the Centralia Massacre.

In the moment before shots rang out, antagonists faced each other across a gulf far wider than a few feet of concrete.

The legionnaires were led by Warren Grimm, hero in battle and former Centralia football star. They had fought, and seen buddies die, in World War I. They believed in the capitalistic system. And they were not deaf when business people, anxious to get rid of the IWW, hinted that a confrontation on Armistice Day might be interesting.

The IWW had, for the most part, been anti-war. The battle they fought was between capital and labor. They often were called "Bolsheviks." Eighteen months earlier, their Centralia hall had been stormed during a parade, doors smashed and furniture and files piled in the street; then the Wobblies inside or on the streets were taken out of town and beaten.

In the summer of 1919, the newsstand of a blind vendor who sold labor periodicals on the street was overturned and his publications thrown in the gutter. He was taken out of town one night, dumped in a ditch and told not to return.

Thus was the stage set for violence at the Armistice Day parade

The parade route went past the IWW Hall not once, but twice.

Persistent rumors that the marchers might stop in front of the hall had led the union's young attorney, Elmer Smith, to warn the Wobblies to be ready.

They were.

No sooner had the line of march come to a halt than the Wobblies — as aggressors or defenders — fired from about four buildings. They caught the legionnaires unarmed and unprepared. Many legionnaires said afterward it was worse than anything they had faced in Europe.

Three legionnaires fell, mortally wounded. They were football star Grimm, Ben Casagranda and Arthur McElfresh. A short time later, an angry mob pursued young Wesley Everest, one of the Wobblies. Everest turned and shot and killed Dale Hubbard, a veteran.

Everest was beaten and thrown in jail. That night a mob rushed the jail and removed Everest from his cell. They beat him again and hung him from the trestle of the Chehalis River Bridge. Historians differ on whether he also was castrated and his body riddled with gunfire.

A day later, the sheriff retrieved the body from the river and deposited it for two days in the jail occupied by the Wobblies.

The crime against Everest elevated him to the heights of Wobbly martyrdom, along with Joe Hill, shot by a firing squad in Salt Lake City, and Frank Little, lynched in Butte, Mont.

Centralia became an armed camp. Law, order and justice became secondary to fear, hate and suspicion.

Posses roamed the streets searching for "the Wobs." Anyone pointed out as being a possible Wobbly or Wobbly sympathizer was subject to a beating. Trains were stopped as they came through town, to be searched, seat by seat, by armed young men looking for Wobblies. One posse member was shot and killed by his own men.

Eleven Wobblies, along with attorney Smith, were charged with murder. Little effort was made to find those who had hanged Everest.

The case was heard in Montesano, Grays Harbor County. George Vanderveer, Seattle's and maybe the nation's most famous defender of lost causes, represented the Wobblies.

The trial was social dynamite. Vanderveer, born rich, was regarded as a traitor to his class for representing Bolsheviks. Jurors felt strong pressure from the public.

Seven of those on trial were sentenced to from 25 to 40 years in prison. One was sentenced to an insane asylum. Three, including, attorney Smith, went free. Most were released long before they served their full sentences.

A memorial to the four slain legionnaires was erected a few years later in Centralia's George Washington Park. Gov.-elect Roland Hartley spoke at the dedication and telegrams were sent by President Calvin Coolidge and French Marshal Ferdinand Foch.

Among those who witnessed the trial was Ralph Chaplin, a Tacoma author who later wrote, "I felt like crying out against the hatred and misunderstanding that pitted fine young Americans against one another like wild beasts."

Chaplin noted a very human drama at the trial.

Mrs. Grimm, widow of the slain legionnaire, was in court daily, as was a Mrs. Barnett, wife of an IWW member on trial for his life.

The two women never looked at each other, Chaplin wrote. But their young sons frequently played together on the courtroom floor while the trial was in progress.

Lawyer for the underdog

George Vanderveer's name would appear high on almost any list of the state's all-time brilliant attorneys. Yet the man who defended Wobblies and other outcasts was one of the most vilified during his heyday.

Vanderveer started out like any conservative corporate lawyer. Born of well-to-do farmer parents, he attended Stanford University and Columbia University Law School, then worked in one of New York's most respected law firms. His first legal work in this state was for Great Northern Railway. Then he was a deputy prosecutor and finally King County prosecutor.

But Vanderveer had a rebellious nature.

"When he thought an injustice was being done, he just got fighting mad," his former law partner, Sam Bassett, recalled some years ago. "George didn't care if there was a fee or not. I used to dislike the way he baited judges, but that was his nature. Still, the people — the common people — they felt an attraction to him."

Because Vanderveer had represented the IWW after the shooting fray with sheriff's deputies and Pinkerton guards at Everett in 1916, it was natural that he be called upon to represent those involved in the Centralia Massacre. During the latter trial, he was handed the first of several contempt-of-court citations.

For years, Vanderveer represented longshoremen, seamen and laborers in personal-injury suits. He worked as lawyer for the Teamsters union in its many strike litigations — never with a contract or a fixed fee. It was said that Dave Beck, the Teamsters head, used to get mad because "Van" never remembered to submit a bill.

Vanderveer spent much of his law career in a Skid Road

STATE-MENTS

Seattle Times

Gov. Ernest Lister, a Democrat, became the state's third occupant of the Governor's Mansion to die between 1900 and 1920. His death came in June 1919.

Jinxed mansion?

When Ernest Lister became the state's third governor to die in the first two decades of the 20th century, many wondered aloud if the office was jinxed.

Lister, a Democrat, won the governorship twice before dying in June 1919, after a lengthy illness. He was succeeded by Lt. Gov. Louis Hart, a Republican, who had been acting governor for five months until Lister died. Hart's even-handed competence would earn him election in his own right. Lister (1913-1919) frequently battled with the Republican-controlled Legislature, especially over highway appropriations and the provisions of the statewide prohibition law. Many thought him a bit of a penny pincher.

In 1914, the state ratified the 17th Amendment to the U.S. Constitution, providing for direct election of senators. Former Rep. Wesley Jones of Yakima was the first to win popular election to the U.S. Senate.

Webster and Stevens Collection, Museum of History & Industry

Deputies check out weapons during the Seattle General Strike. As it turned out, there was little need for them.

In a far cry from today, when the city of Seattle is considering sending its trash by train to an Oregon desert landfill, the Seattle Engineering Department picks up household garbage by horse and wagon in this street scene of 1915.

CHRONO-LOG

1918

"Spanish" flu takes 1,772 lives in Seattle alone, plus hundreds throughout state, in epidemic that rages until May 1919. Proportionately, influenza death toll is far greater than that of recently concluded World War I.

1919

Seattle general strike, first in nation's history, paralyzes city the second week of February as 60,000 workers, in sympathy with earlier shipyard strike, stop wheels from turning for most of a week.

James Casey founds American Messenger Co. in Pioneer Square area, starting with $100, two bicycles, telephone and six messengers to deliver packages and telegrams. Package-delivery soon becomes major source of income; Casey expands to California and renames company United Parcel Service, which eventually covers entire country. He also forms foundation to funnel contributions to child welfare, Waterfall Park and restoration of Pioneer Square pergola.

Ice-skaters take to the frozen Cowlitz River at Kelso for the first time since the 1880s.

building where he pulled a rope to get the elevator to come down. He ended it in the Alaska Building, which was a step up and one of the few buildings in town that would have him. Many members of the legal fraternity, according to Bassett, would pass the word that they didn't want Vanderveer in the same building where they had their offices.

In 1966, 24 years after Vanderveer's death, Bassett erected a posh building at First Avenue and Broad Street, across from the Central Labor Council. It was the sort of place where Vanderveer probably would have been stopped at the door.

Bassett named it, with great satisfaction, the Vanderveer Building.

The week Seattle ground to a halt

Seattle had a population of about 300,000 in 1919. But on Feb. 6, a Thursday, the town was Sunday-morning quiet.

Trolleys remained in their barns. Stores and shops were locked. Nothing billowed from industry's smokestacks. The waterfront was deserted. Sixty thousand workers had embarked on the first general strike in the nation's history.

The Seattle General Strike must be viewed in the spirit of the times. Its issues were complex.

The nation had just emerged from World War I, the most horrendous conflict known to man at that time. The Bolsheviks' October Revolution in Russia was a current event. Strong feelings were aroused locally by jail terms given a woman who distributed anti-war leaflets and two Socialists who agitated against passage of the Conscription (draft) Law.

Violence beckoned from both sides. On the far left were the Industrial Workers of the World, who believed labor, not management, should control the world's production. On the far right was the American Protective League, formed to assist in suppressing "anarchy, sedition and sabotage."

The main trigger for the walkout was a shipyard strike — for higher wages and a shorter (44 hours) work week — that had begun Jan. 21 and idled 35,000 workers. Employers insisted that rather than opposing workers' demands, they were merely trying to adhere to the government's hold-the-line wage policy.

At a Central Labor Council meeting near the end of January, support grew for a general strike to support the shipyard workers. More meetings were held. The idea snowballed.

Still, news accounts of the day indicate a general strike was not inevitable. Two incidents probably swung the pendulum:

■ A businessman-sponsored newspaper advertisement calling upon Seattle's employers — "the most labor-tyrannized city in America" — to turn the city into a bastion of the "open shop."

■ An editorial by Anna Louise Strong, leftist writer for The Seattle Union Record, which frightened many conservatives into thinking revolution was imminent.

The Central Labor Council, whose secretary, James Duncan,

had steered a course between the two extremes, found himself no longer in control. The strike began at 10 a.m. Feb. 6.

As strikes go, it was pretty mild. Strikers insisted no one go hungry. They set up food centers, and milk stations for children. They authorized the maintenance of hospital services.

But Seattle Mayor Ole "Holy Ole" Hanson reacted boldly. He issued proclamations and called out armed guards, even though there was no evidence the strikers carried weapons. He promised protection of the citizenry, punishment of all law violators.

Hanson's picture was on every front page in America. Congratulatory telegrams flooded his office. The strike began to disintegrate. The strike committee agreed to meet with Hanson.

At noon Tuesday, Feb. 11, the strike was history — except for years of rehashing.

Hanson soon resigned as mayor, touring the country to tell how he had brought "the Bolsheviks" to their knees. He went so far as to toss his hat into the presidential ring in 1920. But he was never seriously considered as a candidate, and he eventually wound up in the real-estate business in California.

Duncan, who had headed the Central Labor Council, proved to have more staying power. He served on the School Board 1934-58.

Witness to revolution

 Anna Louise Strong, who helped stir up the 1919 general strike, was one of America's most famous radical voices, in absentia, for much of her life. The very mention of her name used to give conservatives indigestion.

Although she was identified with Seattle for many years, Strong grew up in Nebraska. At 22, she received a doctorate from the University of Chicago and the following year published her first book and began writing highly regarded poetry.

Rawboned, preferring flat-heeled, masculine shoes, Strong had a cherubic, peasant-girl face and a warm laugh. She told friends she wanted to crowd a thousand lives into her lifetime — to be a "North Pole explorer, a great writer, a mother of 10."

Her father, the Rev. Dr. Sydney Strong, was a Congregational minister, a widower and a pacifist. Anna Louise moved to Seattle and secured a writing job on the labor newspaper, The Union Record. She climbed mountains, lectured on social reform and was something of a literary light.

Elected to the school board in 1916, she was, in the words of James Duncan, who later served on the board, "the only one at the time who put kids first."

As World War I drew near, Strong became in her lectures and writings an outspoken foe of war and conscription. A move was begun to recall her for giving voice to such unpatriotic ideas. She was ousted in a citywide election, 27,000 to 21,000, becoming the only person ever recalled from the Seattle School Board.

Strong went to Russia with a Quaker relief group. The Soviet revolutionaries welcomed her and made her editor of the first English-language newspaper in Moscow.

But Strong grew increasingly disenchanted with the starvation conditions imposed on the Russian *kulaks*, or well-to-do farmers, who provoked Soviet leader Josef Stalin's murderous fury.

In trips back to the United States, she gave lectures. Sometimes halls were denied to her. But Eleanor Roosevelt invited her to lunch in the White House.

In 1949, Strong received the unkindest cut of all from the Russians she had lauded — arrest as a foreign spy and banishment, because she had criticized Soviet policy toward Yugoslavia's dissident Marshal Tito and had praised Mao Tse-tung as "the greatest interpreter of 'true Marxism.'"

Back to America she came — as always, her refuge. She visited Seattle, lectured, appeared before a New York grand jury investigating communism and wrote articles stirring the wrath of The Daily Worker, chief U.S. Communist Party organ.

Strong, the repentant sinner, grew in popularity in this country. Then, with the death of Stalin, she was invited back to Moscow. Her arrest and expulsion, she was told, had been a "frameup, a cruel plot." Back she went.

But the magic was gone. Strong returned to the U.S., spent a few years in Los Angeles and then went to China, warmly welcomed as an elder stateswoman of Marxism.

She never made it to the North Pole, failed to have 10 children and didn't reach literary heights. But when she died in Peking in '70 at age 84, China's leaders attended her memorial service.

Anna Louise Strong in Russia, about 1931.

4. HEADY TIMES

SPORTS HEROES, CRIME VILLAINS
— AND A ROAR BEFORE THE SILENCE

1920 TO 1930

'I figured if old Roy couldn't talk himself out of trouble, it was a lost cause.'

— Roy Olmstead, bootlegger, when asked if he ever toted a weapon

Webster and Stevens Collection, Museum of History & Industry

Home radios — available mostly in big floor models like the one in this 1926 photo — became a popular source of entertainment in the '20s. In 1922, Americans heard the first broadcast of a presidential message and of a World Series, as well as the first "network" broadcast. Below, lawmen show off booze-distilling equipment seized in Tacoma in 1924 during Prohibition.

The Roaring '20s were noisy and fun while they lasted. But at the end, the roar was reduced to a questioning silence as Americans faced up to a depression that would determine if they were merely glitter and show or had the inner toughness to withstand hard times.

Post-World War I found the nation increasingly isolationist. No involvement in the League of Nations. No more wars, except for a little "peacekeeping" adventure in, of all places, Nicaragua, to put down a little-known "bandit" named Augusto César Sandino.

Soon after the new decade began, the nation took care of some unfinished business when the

Boland Collection, Washington State Historical Society

CHRONO-LOG

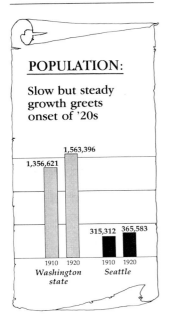

POPULATION:

Slow but steady growth greets onset of '20s

	1,563,396		
1,356,621			
		315,312	365,583
1910	1920	1910	1920
Washington state		*Seattle*	

1920

Prohibition, the 18th Amendment, is given teeth with passage of the Volstead Act. It curbs public drunkenness but spawns speakeasies, bathtub gin and gangsters.

Anna MacEachern of Seattle is state's first woman gubernatorial candidate, one of six Republicans filing against incumbent Louis Hart, also Republican. But tight-fisted Hart easily wins primary and general election.

Everybody knows dapper Dashiell Hammett created tough-guy private eye Sam Spade and "The Maltese Falcon." Less known is his 1920 treatment for TB in a hospital near Tacoma, his courtship of a nurse there and his sneaking off to Seattle for a prohibitory nip or two.

Museum of History & Industry

This labor-intensive dockside scene of 1920s Seattle longshoremen loading goods into a warehouse contrasts sharply with the nearly manless 1980s waterfronts of mechanized freight-handling and containerized cargoes.

required number of states ratified the 19th Amendment, granting women's suffrage. It was almost anticlimactic in Washington state, which had adopted full suffrage 10 years earlier (1910), after Wyoming, Utah, Colorado and Idaho.

Prohibition — the 18th Amendment — had been given teeth with the 1920 passage of its enforcement arm, the Volstead Act, over the veto of President Woodrow Wilson. It curbed public drunkenness but spawned speakeasies, bathtub gin and the prototype gangster of that era, Al Capone.

There was a new openness, a new zaniness: Arnold Ehling and Claire Goodman winning the Seattle Times Dance Marathon at the Trianon by staying upright for 96 hours; Alvin "Shipwreck" Kelly perching on flagpoles around the country; people sitting for days on cakes of ice, and men burying themselves alive, with only a tube to talk to the outside world.

And there were a host of walkathons, including the famous Los Angeles-to-New York Bunion Derby, staged in 1927 by one of the nation's legendary promoters, C.C. "Cash-and-Carry" Pyle. Among the several hundred entries was a Seattle janitor, Ed "Sheik" Gardner, who had spindle shanks, chronically sore feet and wore a white turban when he ran or heel-and-toed. Gardner ran all 3,422.3 miles (side loops included) to Madison Square Garden. There, the crowd responded with wild cheers and a blizzard of $10 bills. It was good *some*one had money. Although Gardner was to have received $1,000 for finishing eighth, he never saw a dime — the promoters didn't pay off.

America's industrial machine was becoming highly geared to assembly-line production. Output increased. Wages stagnated. Families increasingly turned to credit to make ends meet.

We were the land of the free. But the Ku Klux Klan flourished in the South and the Midwest. In Washington, D.C., alone, the Klan was able to stage a parade in 1925 with no fewer than 40,000 marchers decrying "Romanism, alienism, Bolshevism and anti-Americanism."

As a nation (pop. 120 million), we had fallen hopelessly in love with the automobile — "going like 60" was the catch phrase for fast driving. We also were beginning to romance the radio, although even the best models sometimes brought in as much static as music.

Our financial role model was J.D. Rockefeller, who handed out

shiny silver dimes and epitomized what every risk-taking young man could aspire to.

It was the golden age of sports. Among the heroes and heroines who strode the national stage bigger than life: Babe Ruth and Lou Gehrig (baseball); Red Grange and Notre Dame's Four Horsemen (football); Jack Dempsey and Gene Tunney (prizefighting); Bill Tilden and Helen Wills (tennis); Johnny Weismuller and Buster Crabbe (swimming), and Gertrude Ederle, the first woman to swim the English Channel.

Women bobbed their hair, cinched in their busts and donned short, tight-fitting dresses for the "ironing-board figure." The truly daring smoked in public. John Held's drawings of sophisticated "flappers" had supplanted the sugar-and-spice Gibson Girl. Florenz Ziegfeld continued to glorify the tall, fine-feathered, scantily clad American beauty.

College boys with slicked-down pompadours — trying their best to look like Arrow-collar ads — wore raccoon coats, carried hip flasks and drove roadsters with rumble seats.

The first talkies arrived late in the decade, spelling doom for silent-film stars who had been getting by on looks or acting ability and were found to have funny-sounding voices. Al Jolson donned blackface and sang about "Mammy." Janet Gaynor and Charles Farrell romanced in "Seventh Heaven." Ronald Colman was dashing, Richard Dix was daring, and Victor McLaglen was tough but lovable. Being "cute" was the route to stardom for Myrna Loy, Fifi Dorsay and Clara Bow, "the IT girl." Buxom Mae West promised a good time, with her sexy "Come up and see me sometime."

Everybody talked about Charles Lindbergh's solo flight across the Atlantic, Rear Adm. Richard Byrd's exploration of the South Pole and the Dempsey-Tunney "long count" fight for the heavyweight championship (Tunney won).

Washington state — which entered the '20s with a population of 1,356,621 and ended it with 1,563,396 — seemingly had given up its flirtation with losers in presidential races. It went for three straight winners, all Republicans — Warren G. Harding, who eventually would wind up on most worst-president lists; "Cool Cal" Coolidge, who presided over the dizzying flight of American business and stock-market speculation, and Herbert Hoover, who had the bad luck of being in the White House when it came time to pay the piper.

Seattle, firmly established as the state's largest city (it began the decade with a population of 315,312 and ended it with 365,583) had plenty to cheer about when the University of Washington Huskies made it to the Rose Bowl twice in the '20s — tying Navy 14-14 in 1924 and losing 20-19 in 1926 to an Alabama team led by Johnny Mack Brown, who later starred in cowboy movies.

The Huskies were led in both Rose Bowl appearances by all-purpose halfback George Wilson, the school's first All-American. In 1928, the Huskies had their second All-American, Chuck Carroll, also a halfback.

In the excitement, it was easy to forget that the state's other major college, Washington State, had gone to the Rose Bowl much earlier — scoring a 14-0 win over Brown in 1916.

Powerful, slow-stroking Husky crews, coached in the early '20s by Rusty Callow and then by Al Ulbrickson, began to dominate intercollegiate crew racing's annual competition on the Hudson River at Poughkeepsie, N.Y. The cry "Here comes Washington!" frequently heralded a sweep of the Poughkeepsie regatta by the Huskies' varsity, junior varsity and freshman crews.

The 1920s were marked by the start of St. Mark's Episcopal Cathedral in Seattle, one of the largest religious structures on the Pacific Coast; a unique planned city, Longview; the financing of highway construction and maintenance by automobile licenses and gas taxes (1 cent a gallon in 1920), and the first air mail delivered across the Cascades — by Rudolph Ehrlichman July 13, 1920, in two hours 25 minutes. (The pioneer pilot — who died in a plane crash in 1941 — was the father of John Ehrlichman, the noted land-use attorney who much later served as domestic-affairs adviser to President Richard M. Nixon and went to prison in the Watergate scandal of the 1970s.)

There were, of course, the usual howls about the rising cost of state government ($4.79 per capita in 1889 compared with $20.81 in 1920).

At the beginning of the decade, a slender, good-looking ex-Pinkerton detective and World War I veteran was being treated for tuberculosis in the Public Health Service Hospital on the Puyallup River Road outside Tacoma. His name was Dashiell Hammett, and he would romance one of his nurses (Josephine Annis Doran, whom he later married), sneak off to Seattle for some forbidden drinking and scribble plots he eventually submitted to Black Mask magazine. Within a few years, Hammett would become the celebrated creator of a fictional tough-guy private eye, Sam Spade, be the longtime lover of controversial writer-playwright Lillian Hellman and write such classics of the detective-story genre as "The Maltese Falcon" and "The Thin Man."

With the airplane definitely here to stay, King County decided to build an airport in 1927. Four sites were considered: Harbor Island, the Jefferson Park golf course on Beacon Hill, Georgetown and the valley east of West Seattle. A 425-acre site south of Georgetown won, and in 1928 the new airstrip was named Boeing Field in honor of William Boeing, the city's pioneer airplane builder.

That same year, a new highway was opened between Seattle and Tacoma and, across Lake Washington, a Seattle engraver named James Ditty bought 38 acres of a cow trail that linked a "wide spot in the road" called Bellevue with its more established neighbor, Kirkland. Ditty named the road Lincoln Avenue and in his wildest dreams speculated that the spot, which wags called "Ditty City," would become a prosperous little town.

When the first Lake Washington span (the Lacey V. Murrow, or the Mercer Island Floating Bridge) was opened in the summer of 1940, the Eastside suddenly became prime property. Lincoln Avenue became 104th Avenue Northeast, and Bellevue not only outstripped neighboring Kirkland and Redmond but eventually became the state's fourth-largest city.

In the '20s, lumbering still was the state's dominant industry, followed by shipbuilding and then farming. But there was no doubt Bill Boeing and his aircraft factory were on to something.

In 1924, 94-year-old Ezra Meeker, who had spent nearly three months journeying to Washington Territory by oxcart 62 years earlier, took an airplane flight to Dayton, Ohio, in three days.

Elsewhere in the world, Josef Stalin banished Leon Trotsky to consolidate his power in the new Union of Soviet Socialist Republics, Chiang Kai-shek became generalissimo of China and Benito Mussolini's Fascists firmed up their control of Italy.

By the end of the next decade, all would be household names.

The body in the steamer trunk

One of the state's more notorious crimes, the "Mahoney Trunk Murder," occurred in Seattle in the spring of 1921.

The victim was the eccentric Kate Mooers, 72, dripping with jewelry and furs, loaded with real estate and bank deposits, thrice married and so tight with a dollar she borrowed a ring from her husband-to-be's sister for her last wedding.

The perpetrator was James E. Mahoney, 38, a glum, pipe-smoking highway robber on parole, married to another Mrs. Mahoney when he went to the King County Courthouse Feb. 10, 1921, to marry Kate.

Ten weeks after the marriage, Mahoney — angry that Kate had cut him from her will and put him on a meager daily allowance — fed her a stiff dose of poison, rapped her over the head with a hammer and stuffed her body in a steamer trunk.

Mahoney shopped around for a rental skiff so he could give the body a watery grave. For reasons that will become clear later, he decided on Lake Union. He called an express company to haul a large, very heavy trunk to the lake. He rowed it out to the middle in the rented skiff and heaved it overboard.

Horrors! It floated.

Mahoney towed the trunk back to shore, loaded it with chunks of concrete and rowed onto the lake again. This time it sank.

Now for an alibi. Mahoney forged a power of attorney to get into his wife's vault. After cashing some bonds, he boarded a train for St. Paul, Minn., with a woman friend who wore her coat collar high around her face and answered to the name "Mrs. Mahoney."

Once settled in a Twin Cities hotel, Mahoney began writing to Mrs. Mahoney's relatives on hotel stationery — letters ostensibly written by the dead woman. But the handwriting and content of the letters were so unlike Kate that kin grew concerned and notified the law.

When Mahoney returned to Seattle, supposedly following a lovers' spat, he was arrested for forging the power of attorney. But where was Kate?

The boat-rental and trunk-hauling episodes became known. Mahoney contended he had been doing a little bootlegging and had used a trunk. As for Kate, why, they had quarreled in St. Paul and she had gone abroad.

Charles Tennant, the spats-wearing, cane-toting chief of detectives for the Seattle Police Department, was a dogged gumshoe of the old school and didn't believe Mahoney for a minute. He ordered Lake Union dragged inch by inch. Divers went down almost daily. Despite pressures to halt the waste of taxpayers' money, Tennant persisted.

On Aug. 8, the persistence paid off. A trunk containing the body bobbed to the surface, probably from the accumulated gases of decomposition. Three days later, Mahoney was indicted for first-degree murder.

The trial was big news nationally. It began Sept. 21. Ten days later, the jury found Mahoney guilty and recommended the death penalty.

Everyone expected Mahoney to confess. Instead, he calmly puffed a pipe in his cell, professing innocence and certainty that justice would triumph. The execution was set for Dec. 1, 1922. As it drew near, the public grew uneasy. Suppose there had been a

Kate Mooers, as wealthy as she was eccentric, made a fatal mistake in choosing her fourth husband, James E. Mahoney.

James E. Mahoney, already a convicted robber and a married man, was hardly "Mr. Right" for the 72-year-old Kate Mooers.

Seattle Times

Workmen retrieve the trunk containing the body of Kate Mooers from the waters of Lake Union on Aug. 8, 1921.

CHRONO-LOG

In a golden age of larger-
than-life sports heroes,
none was larger than Babe
Ruth.

mistake? Nobody wanted to hang an innocent man.

On his last night on earth, Mahoney finally broke his silence. Words long bottled up gushed forth in torrents. Yes, he had murdered Kate. And he told how in grisly detail.

Thus unburdened, he strode into the courtyard of Walla Walla State Penitentiary to meet the hangman.

After Mahoney's death, the public — given the details of the last-minute confession — learned why he had taken the trunk to Lake Union instead of the much larger and deeper Lake Washington.

Kate was so tightfisted, Mahoney had said, that he had only $10 in his pocket when he went shopping for her "hearse." The man at the Lake Washington boat-rental wanted $25 for a week's use of the vessel. It cost only $10 at Lake Union.

Skinflint Kate unwittingly had contributed to the cause of justice.

Some unforgettable elephants

In 1921, schoolchildren in Seattle donated $3,500 to buy an elephant named Wide Awake from Singer's Midget Circus.

The four-ton pachyderm, nearly nine feet tall, was housed at Woodland Park Zoo for 46 years until her death in 1967.

In her youth, Wide Awake delighted zoo-goers by performing in a black silk topper held on her head at a rakish angle by a leather harness. She would kneel, curtsy, do a graceful run and perform a ballet on three legs. Thousands of kids rode on her back before old age and arthritis slowed her down.

Wide Awake's position as the zoo's No. 1 attraction was usurped by Bobo, a gorilla, some years before her death. But only during the brief residency of Tusko, in 1933, did she lose her spot as the zoo's main elephant.

Tusko's story was as sad as Wide Awake's was happy.

The king of Siam was visiting India in 1914 when he saw Tusko piling teak logs and towering over other elephants. He asked for the giant and took him back to Siam to ride in parades.

An American circus promoter, Al G. Barnes, saw the elephant in Siam and offered the king a large sum of money. A deal was struck and Tusko was brought to America and exhibited as the "world's largest captive elephant" — 12 feet 2 inches tall, almost 7½ tons, with tusks measuring 17½ inches in circumference.

Tusko staged some highly publicized escapades.

In 1927, he broke loose and ran wild in Sedro Woolley, upsetting about 20 cars and smashing several houses. Four years later, he narrowly escaped a police firing squad in Portland after knocking down a flimsy building.

Barnes sold Tusko, who went from one fast-buck artist to another. He was displayed in Salem, Ore., Chehalis and Des Moines, King County, before entering Seattle — with a crash — in September 1932.

A trailer carrying Tusko overturned and the elephant landed in the street, chained and groaning from his injuries. He was taken to a Denny Regrade carnival, manacled so he couldn't move backward or forward or even move his head up and down.

Mayor John Dore finally stepped in, ordering the animal removed to Woodland Park Zoo. Some 80,000 people went to see Tusko, and it seemed he had found happiness at last. A fund was established to buy Tusko's hay. Again, schoolchildren anted up pennies.

The goal was $3,500 — similar to the purchase price for Wide Awake. But less than $100 had been collected when Tusko became ill June 9, 1933. One leg became paralyzed. Tusko lay down the next day, and his 125-pound heart stopped. An autopsy revealed he'd been carrying a big clot in his right ventricle for years.

No sooner had Tusko breathed his last than various "legal owners" appeared, along with those who said they were owed money for feed and cartage. All of them wanted Tusko's bones and hide to publicly display around the country.

The 20 square yards of hide were stored for years at the Port of

This white sport suit on a 1928 "flapper" was the height of fashion in cities such as Seattle.

Seattle's Bell Street Terminal. Schoolchildren in Sedro Woolley tried to raise money to buy it so they could make and sell "genuine Tusko" sandals, belts and bracelets.

The bones, displayed for a time at 10 cents a view, eventually wound up in the possession of a Eugene, Ore., dentist, whose son gave them to the University of Oregon in 1954.

Tusko would have been better off if he'd never been seen by the king of Siam.

Sam Hill's monumental pride

The 67-foot Peace Arch at Blaine, Whatcom County, was dedicated Sept. 6, 1921, to honor the harmonious way in which the United States and Canada share a 3,000-mile border.

Flags of the United States and Great Britain were joined by the flags of France and Belgium at the ceremony — France because so many Canadians are of French ancestry, and Belgium because the 1814 treaty establishing the border between the two countries was signed in the city of Ghent. (Canada itself flew the Union Jack and the French flag until the country officially adopted the Maple Leaf flag Feb. 15, 1965.)

Etched on the arch's southern wall are the words "Children of a Common Mother." On the northern side are the words "Brethren Dwelling Together in Peace and Unity."

Within the passageway, steel gates are always open. Above one gate is written "Open One Hundred Years." Above the other, "May These Gates Never Be Closed."

Buried within the arch are two symbols of the nations' common heritage — a small piece of wood from the Mayflower, which brought the Pilgrims to Massachusetts in 1620, and a relic from the British ship Beaver, first steamship to ply the coastal waters of Oregon and Washington.

Schoolchildren donated nickels and dimes toward construction of a park on the Washington side of the peace arch. It is called Samuel Hill Memorial Park, in honor of the man who conceived the peace arch.

Hill — Quaker, lawyer, businessman — had uncommon vision and good intentions. He devoted much of his life to the Washington State Good Roads Association and assisted with Belgian relief after World War I. Besides the peace arch, he financed Stonehenge and Maryhill Museum, near Goldendale on the north bank of the Columbia River.

Maryhill (after Hill's daughter Mary) was patterned after Marie Antoinette's 18th century Versailles cottage. Construction began in 1914 but was delayed by World War I. Among the items there most treasured by Hill were gifts from Queen Marie of Romania, who journeyed to Goldendale in 1926 to formally dedicate the museum.

Stonehenge, patterned after the 3,600-year-old circle of megaliths on the English plain of Salisbury, honors soldiers and sailors from Klickitat County who died in World War I. It was dedicated on Memorial Day 1929.

Many have mistaken Samuel Hill for James J. Hill, the railroad tycoon. The two were, however, related by marriage. Sam Hill married James Hill's daughter. Others have wondered if Samuel Hill had anything to do with the expression, "What the Sam Hill . . ?" Historians say *that* Sam Hill was English 17th century ruler Oliver Cromwell's minister of finance.

Besides the park near the Blaine peace arch, there is another memorial to the Washington benefactor: the Samuel Hill Memorial Bridge across the Columbia, near Maryhill.

Meanwhile, across the mountains . . .

It was apparent to the earliest settlers in Eastern Washington that nature had pulled a fast one, providing an abundance of world-class farmland and insufficient rainfall to make it green.

Streams and rivers — including the mighty Columbia — flowed tantalizingly through the sagebrush-and-jackrabbit country. The solution was obvious: Bring water to the desert, by pump or by

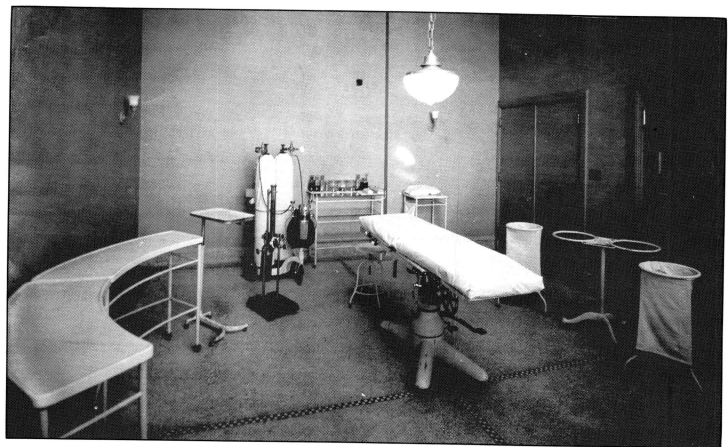

Webster and Stevens Collection, Museum of History & Industry

It may have been the Roaring '20s, but hospital operating rooms such as this one at Virginia Mason Hospital in 1923 were no-frills stark and quiet.

gravity; at the same time harness the water's power to light homes and fuel industry.

Land booms in the Yakima Valley in the 1880s and '90s financed the first irrigation efforts, including the Sunnyside Canal. Subsequent booms developed systems in the Walla Walla, Wenatchee, Okanogan and Spokane areas.

The state adopted a plan to provide World War I veterans with 10- and 20-acre irrigated plots around White Bluffs and Hanford. But because it was underfinanced it didn't pan out.

One of the most significant events in Eastern Washington's history was the formation of the Columbia Basin Irrigation League in Pasco in 1922. It became a powerful lobbying force, unifying many who previously had gone their own way. And it had the blessing of the state's two senators, C.C. Dill and Wesley Jones.

The payoff would begin in the 1930s.

The earwigs that almost ate Seattle

In 1923, Seattle's Mayor E.J. "Doc" Brown issued a serious pronouncement: "Citizens, we can win the fight against earwigs if we don't weaken."

The earwig against which Seattleites were called to battle was the European variety (*Forficula auricularia*), which has a reddish-brown body, wings it doesn't use and forceps it doesn't appear to need. It first invaded Newport, R.I., in 1911. By 1917, it had moved across the continent to Seattle.

By the spring of 1920, earwigs were big news throughout King County. Superstitious schoolboys and not a few parents believed earwigs were bent on inhabiting ears or wigs. Sleeping on the ground and getting an earwig in the eardrum was believed to be an awful fate, although there is no recorded case of it ever happening.

Earwigs were, however, felt to be fiendishly intent on eating all our lush green foliage.

Seattle went after the earwig with typical vigor. Poison baits were spread lavishly to slay the insect as it skulked around in dark spots in the garden and bred under boards and rocks. The earwig would seem to disappear briefly, only to return with battalions where merely companies had roamed before.

In 1922, F.S. Coyne, the entomologist credited with routing the earwig in Newport, was hired by King County and put in charge of the Bureau of Earwig Control. He was hailed as the pied piper who would lead the county back to earwig-free yards.

Coyne piped a merry tune. He began a citywide bait campaign,

which included liens against property owners who failed to pay their share of the eradication program. Every few months there were new poisons to try. Among the most popular: cereal and sugar laced with arsenic, Paris green and a potion called "Black Leaf 40."

Tens of thousands of dollars were spent on chemical warfare. Some 30,000 lots were baited. Still, the earwig did not succumb.

In 1926, a Seattle city councilman proposed an earwig bounty of 50 cents a pint. There is no record of any payoffs. A year later, Coyne imported 6,000 toads from Startup, Snohomish County, and turned them loose in Volunteer Park. In one week, he said, they ate 40,000 earwigs.

There was talk of supplying each family with a toad for its home, although wiser heads noted that a toad, in pursuit of its prey, might land in the soup or atop a fried egg.

While Coyne earned headlines, Professor Trevor Kincaid of the University of Washington's zoology department quietly undertook a different line of attack. Kincaid put his faith in natural enemies of the earwig — the digonochaeta fly and the earwig beetle (*Plerostichur vulgaris*), both imported from Europe.

The professor turned his beetles loose on the earwigs as Coyne's baiting program continued.

By 1929, there still were some earwigs, but they were not nearly as plentiful as they had been. Many felt Coyne's job was done. It had cost taxpayers a bundle, and many were rankled by the liens placed against vacant lots that had been baited by Coyne's "army."

The bureau went out of business.

An author falls on hard Times

A 23-year-old reporter, Elwyn Brooks White, was let go by The Seattle Times in the summer of 1923 for "economy reasons" after just nine months on the job. The reporter felt certain it was due to his failings as a newsman.

For some it might have been a crushing blow. But it merely freed White for better things.

The man known as E.B. White went on to become one of America's most honored literary figures, as a longtime contributor to the New Yorker magazine, author of two brilliant children's books ("Charlotte's Web" and "Stuart Little"), poet and reviser of the grammarian's Bible, Strunk and White's "The Elements of Style."

One critic called White "our finest essayist, perhaps our only

CHRONO-LOG

Thousands watched the 680-foot-long, gas-filled airship Shenandoah when it visited Seattle in 1924.

1922

The Teapot Dome service station — named for the Teapot Dome oil scandal that broke at the end of President Warren G. Harding's administration — is built on U.S. Highway 410, between Pasco and Yakima.

The Columbia Basin Irrigation League is formed in Pasco. It becomes a powerful lobbying force — with a payoff in the 1930s.

1923

President Harding visits Seattle July 27 with great fanfare; speaks at UW. It's his last public appearance — he dies six days later in San Francisco.

Longview (formerly Monticello) becomes the first planned city in the Pacific Northwest. It is founded by lumber tycoon R.A. Long.

1924

On July 12, several thousand spectators gather in a field near Stanwood, Snohomish County, to watch the "naturalization" of several hundred hooded and robed candidates for membership in the Ku Klux Klan, a racist, anti-Jewish, anti-Catholic organization with roots centered in the Deep South. Klansmen from Mount Vernon, Anacortes, Bellingham and Everett officiate. The Klan expires — unmourned — in Washington around the end of the decade.

Underwood & Underwood

Army Air Service pilots pose at Langley Field, Va., before heading for Seattle's Sand Point Field and the beginning of an epic west-to-east around-the-world flight in 1924. Three who completed the 175-day trip are Lt. Erik Nelson, far left, and Lts. Lowell Smith and Leslie Arnold, fifth and sixth from left. In the background is a two-man, open-cockpit, wood-and-fabric Douglas World Cruiser similar to the ones they used.

one."

Fresh from a brief stint with United Press in New York after his graduation from Cornell University, White showed up on the doorstep of The Times. He wrote feature stories and an unsigned "Personal Column," which ran as a glorified classified ad.

White's column-writing displayed youthful exuberance and a few hints of what was to come.

White, the versifier (after trolley fares were reduced): "A life of thrift is very dense; the streetcar line is fickle; we used to walk to save 8 cents — now we walk to save a nickel."

On the bureaucracy:

"Isn't it absurd for the Seattle Police Department to lay in a supply of tear gas? Bandits already laugh until they cry every time they see a policeman."

Sometimes he was topical:

"Gloria Swanson wore 18 gowns in a play at The Coliseum last night. Not a woman in the audience knew what the plot was all about."

"The June issue of most magazines is off the press. Can April be far behind?"

White created the mythical Aunt Lou, who was always submitting personal ads to ask why Albert forgot her birthday or didn't send her a Christmas present. He wrote a series of Clara and Evans personals — the lovely unmarried Clara and the two-timing, married Evans always setting up trysts that were broken up by Evans' wife.

White offered a prize for the best three-word essay on "How to Handle a Mayor." The prize-winner: "With an ax."

Although the format was not geared to the leisurely White style that later emerged, one two-paragraph item served as a harbinger:

"Those little round balls in the gum slot machines are beginning to thaw, and are now quite easy to chew. This indicates the approach of the vernal season.

"We like the licorice ones (black). The other jar (assorted) has proved too much of an uncertainty. One day it cost us 17 cents to get a red one. While this appeals to our gambling nature, it costs us dear."

White kept careful journals during his reporting days for The Times. He later drew upon his notes for one of his most engaging essays, "Speaking of counterweights," in which he described how

a reporter, riding in a little car counterweighted by a heavier news staffer on the other side, was called upon to go around the rim of the Times Square Building replacing burned-out light bulbs.

White gently summed up his departure from a newspaper that didn't truly appreciate his unique talents: "I didn't make the cut."

Before White's death in 1985, humorist James Thurber wrote of White's "silver and crystal sentences which have a ring like nobody else's in the world."

White once described his writing method this way:

"Writing is, for most, laborious and slow. The mind travels faster than the pen; consequently, writing becomes a question of learning to make occasional wing shots, bringing down the bird of thought as it flashes by."

Into the wild blue yonder, '20s style

 Five countries already had tried and failed to complete around-the-world flights when the Army Air Force entered the competition in 1924, prodded by Brig. Gen. Billy Mitchell, who wanted to prove flying machines had enormous military potential.

Sand Point Field, on Lake Washington, was selected for the takeoff of four Douglas World Cruiser biplanes — the Seattle, Boston, New Orleans and Chicago.

The two-man, open-cockpit, wood-and-fabric planes left Seattle April 6, 1924. On Sept. 28 — 175 days after departure — the Chicago and New Orleans returned to Sand Point, mission accomplished, to be greeted by 40,000 wildly applauding spectators.

Two out of four wasn't bad.

The Seattle had crashed, near Dutch Harbor in the Aleutians, shortly after the venture began. The pilot and mechanic spent one night in the wreckage, then 10 days walking to civilization.

The Boston was flying well when it left London. But oil-pressure problems caused it to ditch in the North Atlantic. Pilot and mechanic were picked up by a trawler.

Actual flying time for the Chicago and the New Orleans was 15 days, 3 hours and 7 minutes — an average of 72½ miles an hour. Stopovers lasted for several days when weather was bad or extensive repairs were required. Plane engines were changed every 50 hours. On several occasions, landing gear was changed from wheels to floats.

Heyday of the blimp

There were many — including leading Navy officials — who thought gas-filled dirigibles, rather than planes, would be the mainstay of the nation's air armada.

Three Navy-operated dirigibles flew over Puget Sound country during the heyday of the blimp.

On Oct. 19, 1924, the 680-feet-long Shenandoah arrived as part of a nationwide tour after spending the night on a mooring mast at Camp Lewis. Thousands in Seattle and Tacoma gathered in the streets, on hilltops and rooftops to watch it.

Eleven months later, the Shenandoah ripped apart during a thunderstorm and crashed on a Caldwell, Ohio, farm. Fourteen died.

The Akron, even larger than the Shenandoah, flew over Elliott Bay and Seattle May 24, 1932, then went to Bellingham and Port Angeles before returning to California. Seventy-three crew members died when the Akron crashed off the New Jersey coast in an electrical storm less than 11 months after its visit here.

On Aug. 31, 1934, the Macon — 785 feet long and bulkier than Germany's heralded Graf Zeppelin — brought gasps from onlookers as it cast a shadow over Seattle. Less than six months later, the Macon crashed in the Pacific, off California's Big Sur. Eighty-one survivors were picked up. Two died.

Seattle had been given a preview of the touch-and-go business of blimp travel as early as 1908, when L.G. Mecklem, a native of Colfax, Whitman County, staged the Northwest's first dirigible-balloon flight to celebrate the first birthday of Luna Park, an amusement center built on piling at Duwamish Head.

It almost ended in disaster when the dirigible rose too swiftly and the bag burst at the bottom. Mecklem, equal to the occasion,

Roy Olmstead, police officer and bootleg king.
Seattle Times

held the rip closed with his teeth while the balloon soared 2,500 feet over Elliott Bay. He then sewed up the rip and landed safely in the bay.

Mecklem had an even better stunt to celebrate the Fourth of July a few months later. He agreed to a race between his dirigible and a new Franklin from Luna Park to the Duwamish Meadows horse-race track.

Mecklem was far in the lead when he realized he had let out too much gas and was in danger of plunging into the Duwamish River. To gain altitude, he tossed out sandbags, tools and, finally, his shoes. It worked. He landed well ahead of the car, among the race track's horses and jockeys.

Noblesse oblige in bootlegging

Prohibition produced more than its share of rumrunners. But one of the most famous — throughout the state and nation — was Roy Olmstead, often referred to by the press as "the King of the Bootleggers."

Olmstead was an unlikely lawbreaker. Born in Beaver, Neb., he came to Seattle as a young man and joined the police force, where by virtue of brains and personality he quickly rose to the rank of lieutenant. Olmstead, everyone agreed, was a comer.

Then, in 1920, the young lieutenant got caught in a bootlegging raid. Forced to resign from the force, he immediately turned his efforts full time to importing liquor illegally from Canada.

Olmstead ran his operation with flair. He had a fleet of the fastest rumrunning vessels on Puget Sound, including his personal yacht powered by three 300-horsepower engines. His wife, Elsie, with whom he lived in a "snow-white palace" in the Mount Baker district, adopted the role of "Aunt Vivian" to broadcast bedtime stories — replete with rumrunning clues — over a private radio station.

Olmstead wore tailor-made suits, smoked imported cigars and

Seattle Times
A rumrunner's boat, captured off Camano Island, is brought to a Seattle dock by a Coast Guard patrol launch in this 1925 photo. Motor machinist's mate George Bennett stands beside a mounted machine gun he and fellow Coast Guardsmen used to force the bootleggers to beach their craft.

CHRONO-LOG

1924

The state's voters turn down Initiative 49, which would have mandated public school attendance for all children up to age 16. Religious leaders and conservatives lead the opposition, maintaining that teen-agers should be working.

1925

Wiretapping, brand-new police tool, becomes controversial but crucial factor in arrest of Seattle bootlegger Roy Olmstead. Landmark U.S. Supreme Court decision three years later affirms taps' legality, thereby setting in motion right-to-privacy issue that remains heated to present day.

The postmistress of Clifton, Mason County, doesn't argue when the postmaster general says too many towns in the country are named Clifton. She suggests an alternative, Belfair, which she had found in a book she was reading. The name is approved.

Gertrude Ederle, first woman to swim the English Channel.

flashed diamond cuff links and stickpins. Despite his notoriety, he hosted some of the leading businessmen and public officials at his home.

Olmstead was arrested in 1922 and again in 1924, easily beating the rap both times. But on Nov. 25, 1925, police raided the snow-white palace and found Olmstead, his wife, 16 guests and a house full of bootleg liquor.

Olmstead had been trapped, it turned out, by the use of telephone taps — or, as the press called them, "whispering wires." His lawyers said they were illegal.

The U.S. Supreme Court finally affirmed their legality, in a famous 5-4 decision in 1928. The majority opinion was written by Chief Justice William H. Taft, the former president. The loudest dissent came from Justice Oliver Wendell Holmes, then 87, who called wiretapping "a dirty business."

The taps, when admitted as evidence, implicated many police officers, the mayor and other leading citizens. Elsie Olmstead was acquitted. Olmstead went to prison for four years.

While behind bars, he became a convert to Christian Science. Upon his release, he opened a downtown office as a Christian Science practitioner, became a Sunday-school teacher and preached the evils of drink in the King County Jail. Many alcoholics were released from jail into his custody.

In 1935, he received a full pardon from President Franklin D. Roosevelt.

Shortly before his death, at age 81, Olmstead was asked if he had carried a gun on those famous rumrunning expeditions. A grin spread across his cherubic face. He shook his head and said, "I figured if old Roy couldn't talk himself out of trouble, it was a lost cause."

A prexy gets the sack

One of the most celebrated firings in the state's history occurred Oct. 4, 1926, when the University of Washington's Board of Regents ousted its nationally respected president, Henry Suzzallo.

The vote was 5 to 2. The two regents who sided with Suzzallo immediately offered their resignations, one calling the meeting that resulted in Suzzallo's firing "a star chamber," after the notorious 17th-century secret English tribunal of the same name.

The board had been egged on by Gov. Roland Hartley. As a result of the firing, he became the only governor in state history against whom recall proceedings were instituted. The effort failed.

Suzzallo and Hartley were both strong men. There the similarity ended.

Suzzallo earned a Ph.D. from Columbia University when he was a young man. He was an outstanding speaker, a strong believer in social activism. He came to the UW from Columbia in 1915 on the personal recommendation of Columbia's famed president, Nicholas Murray Butler.

While at the UW, Suzzallo raised faculty morale, strengthened the graduate school and various professional schools, upgraded the library collection and saw enrollment double — from 3,000 to 6,000 — despite severe cutbacks during World War I.

Hartley was a product of Minnesota's public schools and the Minneapolis Academy. He learned politics as secretary to a town mayor and to the governor of Minnesota; he learned business by buying lumberyards in Minnesota and Everett.

During the war, Suzzallo served on various labor boards — mediating potential strikes and investigating grievances. He was outspokenly in favor of the eight-hour workday and improved living conditions in lumber camps.

Suzzallo's actions on behalf of loggers and mill workers angered Hartley, who also was upset by growing conjecture that Suzzallo might want to go into politics — seeking either the governorship or a position in the U.S. Senate. Publicly, Suzzallo never expressed the slightest interest in either position.

Hartley first struck out at Suzzallo by asking the Legislature to make higher-education appropriations for one year only. He said he would visit various institutions and come back a year later with further recommendations.

The governor's visit to the university was perfunctory. He attended a meeting of the regents in 1925, but was noticeably absent from a banquet honoring Suzzallo. Soon afterward, Hartley appointed three new regents. They initiated the demand for Suzzallo's resignation. Suzzallo declined to leave voluntarily. The stage was set for the firing.

Both principals survived.

Despite a growing number of critics, Hartley, a Republican, was re-elected governor in 1928. When he tried for a third term in 1932, he failed to get past the primary. The country by then was deep in the Great Depression, and the mood was to throw out all the Republicans from Herbert Hoover on down and give the Democrats a chance.

Suzzallo left the UW to work for the Carnegie Foundation and eventually became its president. Although he worked in New York, he continued to call Seattle his home, maintaining a residence in the Olympic Hotel. The university's main library was named in his honor shortly after his death in 1933.

The Hartley-Suzzallo rhubarb provided some comic relief, though. Called upon to justify his decision, Hartley said Suzzallo was, after all, "a foreigner."

Suzzallo was born in California, the son of Yugoslav parents. The governor was born in New Brunswick, Canada.

Her honor punches the reform ticket

Museum of History & Industry

Seattle's first — and only — woman mayor, Bertha K. Landes.

In 1926, Bertha K. Landes, a member of the City Council since 1922, became Seattle's first and only female mayor. She was, in fact, the first woman to govern a major U.S. city.

Landes had earned a degree from the University of Indiana when women college graduates were uncommon. Locally, she had been a leader of the Women's City Club, the Century Club, the Women's University Club and the Seattle Federation of Women's Clubs before winning election to the council. In running for office, she had the full support of her husband, Henry Landes, dean of the University of Washington's College of Science.

Bertha Landes was the darling of the reformers. Two years before winning election as mayor on a platform of strict law enforcement, she had served as acting mayor when Mayor Edwin J. "Doc" Brown went to New York to attend the Democratic National Convention.

In Brown's absence, Landes ordered Police Chief William Severyns to clean up corruption in the department by firing 100 officers or face dismissal himself. When Severyns procrastinated, Landes issued General Order No. 1, proclaiming herself head of the Police Department and placing a precinct captain, simon-pure Claude Bannick, over the chief.

Mayor Brown sped home by train to reclaim his position and overrule Landes. But the victory was short-lived. A grand jury undertook an investigation of crime and corruption, and there was a call for Brown's impeachment.

During the '26 mayoral campaign, Landes spent $9,000 — a large amount for that time and place. She also campaigned in favor of abolishing the mayor's office and replacing it with a city manager.

Landes won handily, but the city-manager idea was defeated.

Once in office, the 58-year-old Landes did her best to clean up a wide-open city. She called on citizens to blow the whistle on suspected bootleggers. She also offered to pay $1 a year to those who pledged to report the license numbers of all those they saw driving recklessly.

Government by snitch reportedly made some inroads on bootlegging and bad driving. But it backfired occasionally. Police once got their addresses mixed and mistakenly raided the home of a respected businessman who had blown the whistle on a suspected bootlegger. The businessman was having a dinner party for a leading religious leader when the police banged at his door.

Landes also angered labor by trimming 100 jobs to lift the Street Railway system out of the red.

But her habit of moving swiftly when she saw a problem endeared her to many. Informed that the old streetcar bridge across the Duwamish River to West Seattle was in danger of collapse, she issued an order that streetcars discharge their passengers on either side of the river, forcing passengers to walk across the bridge before boarding on the other side.

There were howls of protest. But Landes didn't budge. She knew a "safe" steel bridge across the Duwamish already was in place. All it lacked was streetcar tracks, which the City Council had refused to provide. The public outcry forced the council to complete the rail connections.

Landes' honesty and good intentions were unquestioned. When she dedicated the Orpheum Theatre in 1926, she received a standing ovation. She was written about in national magazines and photographed with Will Rogers, Rear Adm. Richard Byrd and Charles A. Lindbergh. Norma Shearer, one of Hollywood's leading actresses, commented that Landes' election proved that women no longer had to accept second-class status.

Landes ran for re-election in 1928 with the support of Seattle's newspapers, the Central Labor Council, the drys and various women's organizations. But her opponent, Frank Edwards, a motion-picture magnate, spent money as if he had a pipeline to the mint.

Edwards won, only to be recalled a few years later.

Landes gained in stature, heading a job center for unemployed women during the Great Depression and later serving as president of the state's League of Women Voters. She died in Ann Arbor, Mich., in 1943 at the age of 75.

What a Capitol idea!

Washington state's Legislative Building — imposing centerpiece of the Capitol complex — was completed in 1928.

It is built of Wilkeson stone, quarried in Pierce County, and its interior marble came from Germany, France, Italy and Alaska. Stonecutters were brought from all over the world to work with hand tools and sand-blasting equipment.

The dome rises to a height of 287 feet, and the 20-feet-long chandelier in the rotunda hangs from a gold-plated chain. The bronze state seal, set in the marble floor of the rotunda, regularly is scrubbed and polished so George Washington can put on his best face for visitors. It is considered bad form to step on the seal.

When furnishings were bought for the building, Gov. Roland Hartley made a big fuss over spending $47.50 each for its cuspidors. A tin can, he said, could serve snoose-chewing legislators just as well.

The new Legislative Building was quite a step up. The business of Washington Territory and the infant state had been conducted in a 40-by-68-feet wooden building, constructed at a cost of $5,000 on the site of the present Capitol campus.

Among the prizes of statehood was 132,000 acres donated by Congress for a statehouse. The bulk of the land was put in reserve, in the Capital Forest, west of Olympia. Construction of buildings suitable for a growing state proceeded slowly, due to lack of money and World War I.

The governor's mansion was completed in 1909, the year of the Alaska-Yukon-Pacific Exposition. The Temple of Justice, the first major structure, was opened in 1913 — in time for Gov. Ernest Lister's inaugural ball. But the outer facing was not completed for

another six years.

The first small step toward the present Legislative Building was taken in 1893 when Ernest Flagg, a New York architect, was selected to design the Capitol. The foundation was laid, but work was halted the next year when money ran out.

In 1901, the state purchased an interim capitol — the Thurston County Courthouse, built in 1882. It served as a legislative building for more than two decades.

Before work began on the Temple of Justice, architect Flagg proposed a "group concept" for the Capitol campus. Architects Wilder and White, both of New York, won a nationwide competition. Later, architects Bebb and Gould of Seattle were added to the design team.

When work began on the present Statehouse in 1919, Flagg's original foundation was enlarged considerably. On May 31, 1953 — 100 years after Washington became a territory — Gov. Arthur B. Langlie placed a time capsule in the "circle" between the Legislative Building and the Temple of Justice.

The light at the end of the tunnel

At a few minutes before 4 p.m., Pacific Standard Time, on May 1, 1928, President Calvin Coolidge drummed well-manicured fingers on his White House desk and eyed a telegraph key he was about to depress.

In the Cascades, 2,700 miles away, several thousand people waited. A fortunate few were 1,000 feet underground in rockbound caverns separated by about 50 cubic yards of granite — the final barrier to the linkup of the east and west sides of the Great Northern Railway's new Cascade tunnel.

The rock was loaded with 400 pounds of gelatin dynamite, wired with blasting caps. Those who were underground stood about 1,500 feet back on both sides of the barrier, with ever-growing excitement as only a few ticks remained on their pocket watches until 4 o'clock.

The president depressed the key, sending an electrical impulse surging across the country at the speed of light.

"Hang on to your hats," a voice shouted underground.

Almost simultaneously the chamber began to vibrate. A muffled roar and a powerful rush of air enveloped the men below. For a minute or so, fine particles of rock dust rained down.

After a brief wait, to allow gases to escape, compressed-air "mucking machines" — one bearing a tiny American flag for the occasion — moved up the tracks on both sides of the barrier. They scooped up blasted rock. Soon there was a crawl space.

"Let's go!" a hardrock miner shouted. "Boys, she's open!"

Jubilant men momentarily forgot they were supposed to let Superintendents Frank Kane, from the west side, and H.J. King,

STATE-MENTS

The Lone Eagle aloft
Charles A. Lindbergh had never been to Puget Sound country before Sept. 13, 1927, but he was no stranger — there or anywhere else in the world. Four months earlier, the lanky, curly-haired man they later called "the Lone Eagle" and "Lucky Lindy" took off from Long Island in a little monoplane dubbed the Spirit of St. Louis. Some 33½ hours, five sandwiches and two canteens of water later, he landed at Le Bourget Airfield in Paris — completing the first solo nonstop flight across the Atlantic.

So when Lindbergh flew from Spokane to Seattle's Sand Point Field on the last leg of a triumphant 48-state tour, he was to be the object of no fewer than 500,000 admirers determined to see him before he left. At a jam-packed UW stadium, he made a swing around the track in a car. At Volunteer Park, he greeted thousands of children dismissed from school to see their hero. That night, he spoke at a chamber of commerce banquet, emphasizing the need for more commercial airfields.

Lucky Lindy paid a stiff price for his fame. In 1932, the first-born son of Charles and Anne Morrow Lindbergh was kidnapped and killed. The subsequent trial and execution of Bruno Richard Hauptmann created tremendous tensions for the family. Later, Lindbergh, an outspoken admirer of certain accomplishments in Hitler's Germany, was accused of Nazi sympathies. But his service in the Pacific in World War II and his efforts on behalf of conservation and medical research restored at least some of his luster.

Seattle Times

Great Northern Railway and Washington state VIPs swing open a symbolic gate Jan. 12, 1929, to mark the inauguration of the nation's longest rail tunnel under the Cascades. A more thunderous inaugural ceremony occurred more than half a year earlier, on May 1, 1928, when miners blasted through the last remaining wall of rock separating the tunnel's eastward and westward approaches.

CHRONO-LOG

*Miss Seattle 1926, Leona
Natalie Fengler posed in
flight togs at Sand Point
Field.*

Webster and Stevens Collection,
Museum of History & Industry

from the east, be the first through the opening. They scrambled over the rock, went through the hole and hugged those on the other side.

Measurements later would show they had bored nearly eight miles through granite and been just eight inches shy of a perfect union on the sides, just nine inches off grade on the bottom.

That night, Great Northern officials and the general contractor for the nation's longest (7.79 miles) tunnel — then the fifth-longest in the world — threw a big party for employees at Scenic, at the west end of the tunnel.

The long-awaited breakthrough did not, of course, mean the end of the job. The blast touched off by Coolidge merely had connected the main 2.41-mile tunnel from Berne, on the east side, with a 5.38-mile Pioneer (auxiliary) tunnel from the Scenic side.

It would be seven months before the two main tunnels were connected — straight as a rifle bore, 16 feet wide, 22 feet 10 inches high, walled in concrete. Then tracks were laid.

On Jan. 12, 1929, President-elect Herbert Hoover dedicated the tunnel on a coast-to-coast NBC radio broadcast.

It had required 237 freight cars of dynamite (4.7 million pounds) to blast the main tunnel and all of the auxiliary tunnels. And it had been costly — $14 million, nine lives lost from cave-ins, falling rock and tunnel gas, and one bunkhouse murder. But the reward was a shorter, lower-level haul for freight and passengers, elimination of costly, hard-to-maintain snow sheds and the electrification of a large area between Wenatchee and Skykomish to handle the new electric-powered locomotives.

Most important, the tunnel signaled a virtual end to the ever-present threat of avalanches, such as the Wellington snowslide that had claimed 96 lives almost two decades earlier.

Making history made history at the U

The Pulitzer Prize committee, sitting at Columbia University in New York City, chose May 8 as the day to announce the 1928 awards for literature.

It was a vintage year. Everyone felt certain Eugene O'Neill, America's foremost playwright, would win an award for "Strange Interlude," and that Thornton Wilder virtually was assured an award for his novel, "The Bridge of San Luis Rey." And, of course, Edward Arlington Robinson, long overdue for the poetry award, had published his brilliant narrative poem, "Tristram," the previous year.

As for the coveted award for historical writing, it appeared that Charles Beard had the inside track for his "Rise of American Civilization," with his closest competition coming from Dr. Vernon Louis Parrington, University of Washington English professor and author of the two-volume "Main Currents in American Thought."

Parrington, 55, had told his family not to get its expectations too high, that Beard most likely would win. But that day an official telegram arrived for Parrington with the announcement that he not only had won the history award but his work had been deemed so outstanding by the Pulitzer judges that he was to receive the largest literature prize, $2,000. O'Neill, Wilder and Robinson were to receive $1,000 each.

It was the first Pulitzer for literature to be awarded to a Washingtonian. There have been three since, all for poetry: to Audrey Wurdemann of Seattle in 1935, to UW Professor Theodore Roethke in 1954 and to Carolyn Kizer, identified with both Spokane and Seattle, in 1985.

Parrington, already one of the most beloved professors at the UW and highly respected by scholars throughout the nation, overnight gained international fame. The university promptly renamed its English-department building Parrington Hall in his honor. There was a rush to buy "Main Currents."

Before coming to the UW in 1908, the Illinois native and Harvard graduate briefly played semi-pro baseball. In part because of his athletic prowess, he was hired by the University of Oklahoma not only to teach English and history but also to coach the baseball team and the school's first football team.

Years later, Parrington's son, Vernon, who taught history at Seattle's Lakeside School, said: "Hardly anyone knows this, but Dad's teams had the best won-and-lost record in Oklahoma's football history until Bud Wilkinson came along."

In the spring of '29, Parrington took a leave of absence from the university to finish the third and last volume of his monumental work. The family moved to the little village of Winchcomb, England.

There, less than a year later, Parrington died suddenly at age 58. The book, "The Beginning of Critical Realism in America," was published posthumously.

Some real estate goes for a song

It might offend some first-nighters, but Seattle's fine Opera House could be called — without stretching the facts — "the house that suds built."

Certainly profits from the Gem Saloon, a flourishing Skid Road watering hole, laid the foundation.

It happened this way:

New York-born James Osborne — seafarer, lumberman and religious free-thinker — joined with A.C. Anderson in paying top dollar to Henry Yesler for land around Skid Road — 105 Commercial St., to be exact — on which to build the Gem.

It was, by all accounts, a popular and well-run establishment. When Osborne, a confirmed bachelor, died in 1881, he left modest amounts to his partner's children and $100 to Judge Isaac Hall to preach the funeral oration.

The rest of the money — $20,000, which was then equal to the city's annual budget — was to go for a public hall, provided the city came up with matching funds.

Judge Hall delivered his $100 eulogy to a packed house in the old Pavilion, at the corner of Front and Cherry streets, and Osborne was laid to rest in Lake View Cemetery.

The money went into the bank, where it gathered interest for years. By the time the city finally got around to building a civic auditorium, it had grown to $109,000. The city added another $900,000. The result, in 1928, was the Civic Auditorium.

In 1962, the old Civic Auditorium was transformed into the Opera House, a centerpiece of the Century 21 Exposition.

Sad to say, Osborne — in death — was not always accorded proper respect. Six years after the Civic Auditorium became a reality, there was a minor furor over weeds that had overgrown his grave. The city said it could not legally put up the $200 needed to provide perpetual care. But decency prevailed, and a deal was worked out to maintain the gravesite.

A plaque honoring Osborne — "Seattle citizen and philanthropist" — hung over the door of the lobby of the old Civic for 34 years. But after the Opera House renovation, the plaque wound up in a cubicle that once had been a women's restroom.

There it remained until 1972, when it was placed on the outside west wall of the Opera House.

It doesn't always pay to advertise

James Bassett signed his death warrant when he advertised his new Chrysler roadster for sale in a Seattle newspaper in August 1928.

Bassett, who had just driven out from Maryland and wanted to sell the car before taking a job in the Philippines, was lured to a home in the Richmond Highlands by a strange pair who pretended they wanted to buy the car.

Seattle Times

*Mary Smith and her homicidal son, Decasto Earl
Mayer, meet in the warden's office of the state
penitentiary at Walla Walla in May 1938, a decade
after Mayer chopped James Bassett into little pieces.*

The bogus buyers were Decasto Earl Mayer, a cadaverous-looking ex-convict, and Mayer's elderly mother, Mary Smith, who felt her son's many crimes never disqualified him for sainthood.

Mayer rapped Bassett over the head with a hammer and then dismembered his body in a bathtub while his mother tidied up. The remains were buried in four different places around King County. Mayer and his mother fled but were arrested a month later in Oakland, Calif., driving Bassett's car.

There followed one of the great body hunts in state history. Bloodhounds sniffed the brush. Lakes were scoured. Psychics were called in to tell volunteers where to dig.

But Bassett's remains couldn't be found. Lacking a *corpus delicti*, prosecutors charged the 31-year-old Mayer and his mother only with

A crowd on the shores of Lake Washington greets the arrival of four Soviet fliers and their silver monoplane, Land of the Soviets, at Sand Point Field on Oct. 13, 1929. The visitors, who were on a celebrated but trouble-plagued Moscow-to-New York eastbound flight, took three days' time out to see the sights of Seattle. They didn't make it to New York until Nov. 1.

Seattle Times

grand larceny. Mrs. Smith was sentenced to 10 years, her son to life as a habitual criminal.

Mayer and his mother were almost forgotten when, after nearly a decade, the case once again made the front page. Mrs. Smith began to talk to fellow inmates. One was a convicted swindler, Margaret Fawcett.

Fawcett told the warden what she was hearing, and it was arranged for her to get the lurid details. Those included Mrs. Smith's confession that her poor son was so worn out from butchering Bassett that she had to fix him an eggnog to restore his strength.

But the information wouldn't hold up in court. Authorities had to figure another way to get her to talk. They settled on an inspired, though highly unethical bit of play-acting. They dressed up a policeman in priest's garb and sent him to take her confession so she would rest more easily. She prayed with the pseudo-padre and unburdened her soul.

Using such ill-gotten information in court still posed a problem, so Mayer and his mother were brought to Seattle for further interrogation. Mayer cheated authorities by hanging himself in his cell. Officials, seeing no advantage in putting his mother through more grilling, sent her back to jail until her release at age 86.

If, as the axiom says, the good die young, Mrs. Smith was in no danger of virtue. She passed away peacefully in a Seattle nursing home at the age of 100.

The very model of modern mobility

 On Dec. 2, 1927, millions of Americans headed for auto showrooms to kick tires and admire the lines of Henry Ford's newest creation, the Model A, successor to the legendary Model T that had been introduced 19 years earlier.

The inexpensive Model T had changed the transportation habits of a nation, putting an automobile within reach — or dream — of every American. But other cars, bigger and more expensive, had passed it by. The public wanted color (the T was basic black) and a better ride at the same low price.

In Olympia, a turquoise-blue coupe was enshrined in the center of the lobby of the Hotel Olympian, where its "vibrationless" 40-horsepower engine drew oohs and ahs.

In Seattle, lines began forming two hours before the doors were opened at the Ford Motor Co. showroom adjoining the Ford assembly plant at Lake Union. Among those who queued up to see the six models allotted to Seattle was Mayor Bertha Landes.

Police were called out to keep order as more than 4,000 people went through the showroom in the first two hours.

The automobile came in four colors, cost $385 (for a roadster with a rumble seat) to $570 (for a four-door sedan). It had four-wheel brakes and could attain speeds of 55 to 65 miles an hour.

Washingtonians were obviously not the only ones excited about the Model A. New York City gave the new Ford a welcome that rivaled in enthusiasm the tickertape parade a few months earlier for Charles Lindbergh. Ford fanciers gathered at the city's largest showroom, on Broadway, at 3 a.m., and police had to be called out to keep the crowd from breaking the window.

Production of the Model A was discontinued in late 1931 to make way for Ford's new V-8s. In all, only 5 million Model A's came off the lines. Yet it probably had more lasting impact than any other car in the nation's history. Sixty years after their debut, Model A's survived by the thousands in garages, barns and museums.

Cracks and seams in a bulging economy

The nation — and Washington state — put on a wonderful show of prosperity for most of the 1920s. America's farmers produced second to none. Improved mechanization made the nation's industry the marvel of the world.

But the money increasingly was in the hands of fewer people.

By the early 1920s, those wonderfully productive farmers were losing their farms to foreclosures in record numbers. Before long, wages stagnated for coal miners, railroad workers and the textile industry. Never had they produced so much for so little.

Even as inventories grew, prices stayed up. Families began buying on credit for basic necessities.

From July 1928 to June 1929, more than 500 banks closed their doors. Still, nobody in the nation's capital pushed the panic button, and leaders of business and industry insisted all was well.

If stock prices were to be believed — and they were a major yardstick for gauging the health of the economy — the country had never had it so good. Prices for common stocks more than doubled from 1925 to 1929. Speculators bought heavily on margin, as if there were no tomorrow.

On Oct. 24, 1929, the famous Black Thursday, The Seattle Times reported a dramatic drop in stock prices. But not to worry. President Herbert Hoover wasn't concerned; neither were business leaders.

In the days that followed the initial Thursday crash and the end of the month, it was pretty much business-as-usual in the Puget Sound area.

At Safeway, housewives could buy four pounds of onions for a dime, six pounds of sweet potatoes for a quarter and five pounds

CHRONO-LOG

1928

On a hot August day during Prohibition, moonshine bubbles in a 250-gallon still in a secret room under Falcon Hall in coal-mining town of Ronald in Kittitas County. In the room are 32 barrels of mash, 16 barrels of aging liquor, 23 barrels of "white mule" ready for delivery. Distiller fails to check pressure gauge and there is an explosion. Within minutes, much of Ronald is in flames. Many businesses, 32 homes and 80 acres of forest are destroyed.

Fire rages on Saturday afternoon, Sept. 8, in Olympia's old stone statehouse. Tacoma firemen rush to the capital city to help douse the flames. The structure's most famous adornment, a tower containing eight clocks, is saved from toppling into the street. But the clocks stop forever. When the structure is rebuilt a few years later, the tower is removed.

Spurred by outraged Daughters of the American Revolution, who think it's unpatriotic for people to walk on the bronze seal of George Washington in the floor of the Capitol rotunda, the state Legislature passes a bill authorizing a railing around the seal. However, no money is appropriated.

Cascade railroad tunnel, nation's longest (at 7.79 miles) and world's fifth-longest, is officially blasted through to link east and west shafts.

Civic Auditorium, forerunner of Seattle Opera House, opens.

King County opens its new airport, named Boeing Field in honor of William Boeing, the city's pioneer airplane builder.

1929

City of Tacoma's electrical-power shortage is uniquely solved by berthing the aircraft carrier Lexington at Commencement Bay and hooking up one of its giant generators to supply homes and factories.

Washington State Historical Society

Harvesting on the Carl Anderson farm near Everett in 1928 leaves mounds of hay reminiscent of Old World agriculture.

of apples for 29 cents.

The famous coloratura soprano, Mme. Galli-Curci, was coming to Meany Hall, and the music world was chattering about the latest violin prodigy, a youngster named Yehudi Menuhin.

Out at Husky Stadium, there was a genuine belly laugh when Husky end Larry Westerweller, sidelined after being injured, ran onto the playing field to tackle a University of Oregon halfback running unmolested toward the goal line.

The referee promptly awarded a touchdown to Oregon, and the Ducks went on to post a 14-0 victory.

Still, C.B. Blethen, editor and publisher of The Seattle Times, felt compelled to calm rising fears about the economy by writing a front-page editorial on Sunday, Oct. 27. Seattle, he said, would actually benefit from the crash. Real-estate values in particular would be strengthened.

Despite the soothing words, prices fell sharply again on Monday. The next day — Oct. 29, the infamous "Black Tuesday" — the nation's investors dumped a record 16,410,030 shares on the New York Stock Exchange.

Still, Times readers — like the readers of most newspapers across the country — found a ray of sunshine on their front pages on Black Tuesday.

"Holiday Prospects Bright" was the bold headline. It was followed by three more headlines: "Seattle Merchants Prepare for Rush, Enthusiastic Over Forecast." "Optimism is Expressed by Business Leaders for Good 1929 Season." "It Will Be Active, Is General Opinion of Mercantile Executives Throughout Northwest District as Store Managers Prepare for Sales Armies to Care for Gift Buyers."

So it would be as the nation slid slowly, inexorably into the Great Depression. Some went on as if nothing much had

happened; the vast majority of people in the country tightened their belts, and then tightened them some more.

Plugging into carrier power

As if the growing depression weren't bad enough, a severe drought hit the West in 1929. Western Washington's rivers and reservoirs, usually full in the fall, were almost dry. Skies continued clear and blue throughout November.

Mayor Frank Edwards of Seattle and Mayor James Newbegin of Tacoma declared a state of emergency. Gov. Roland Hartley, Sens. Wesley Jones and C.C. Dill and Rep. Albert Johnson offered to do anything short of hiring a rainmaker.

Seattle drew upon the reserves of small, independent steam plants. Tacoma, which three years earlier had proudly dedicated its new Lake Cushman power dam above Hood Canal, begged the Navy to move the aircraft carrier Lexington from the Puget Sound Naval Shipyard at Bremerton to Tacoma's Commencement Bay.

The Lexington had four giant generators, just one of which could provide enough power to ease Tacoma's shortage with kilowatts to spare.

It was a novel proposal. But moving the Lexington to Tacoma was easier said than done.

Secretary of the Navy Francis Adams branded the idea of powering a city with a warship as patently ridiculous. Besides, he said, all Western states had been hard hit by the long dry spell. Farmers and cattlemen were in serious trouble. San Francisco had barely enough drinking water. The Navy certainly couldn't help them all.

President Hoover declined to get involved, saying the decision was Adams' to make. Adams' response seemed clear enough. He ordered the Lexington to proceed with all haste to California for battle maneuvers. Just as Tacomans were about to give up hope, the Lexington stopped and dropped anchor off Blake Island.

There it stayed for three weeks.

Meanwhile, Seattle and Tacoma initiated "dim-outs." Downtown electrical signs in Seattle were darkened for the first time in memory. In Tacoma, many streetlights as well as electrical signs were turned off. Residents were urged to burn a single light in their homes. Police feared increased crime.

Telegrams were fired off to Washington, D.C., reminding the Navy that King and Pierce counties, now in desperate straits, had been very generous to the military in the past, donating land for Camp Lewis, Sand Point Naval Air Station (officially changed from Sand Point Field in 1926) and Fort Lawton.

The Navy responded that on the slim chance it changed its mind, it would want $60,000 in advance for the use of one generator, free moorage, a good harbor and all power cables laid by Tacoma City Light employees.

Tacoma liked the offer. On Dec. 13, the Lexington was ordered to move to old Baker Dock in Tacoma.

Immediately the great generator of the Lexington began turning the wheels of industry, lighting homes, brightening streets and making Tacoma livable again. Rain and snow arrived in the weeks that followed. Reservoirs filled. Turbines turned at the city's dams.

On Jan. 16, the Lexington left Tacoma for San Pedro, Calif., its job well done.

When the bills were tallied, Tacoma was out about $120,000 — $95,000 to the Navy, another $20,000 for moorage and several thousand dollars for cables and extra piling.

The Seattle Times of Oct. 29, 1929, offered a ray of holiday sunshine along with the bleak stock market news.

RightNow!

STOCKS HIT LOWEST LEVELS IN 16,410,030-SALES DAY!

6 LATEST MARKETS — The Seattle Daily Times

The Seattle Times Has the Largest Net Paid (Full Returns) Circulation in the State of Washington

SEATTLE, WASHINGTON, TUESDAY, OCTOBER 29, 1929.

HOLIDAY PROSPECTS BRIGHT

Seattle Merchants Prepare for Rush, Enthusiastic Over Forecast

PLANE WITH 9 MEN DIE
FIVE ABOARD WHEN LAKE MISSING IN SHIP SINKS WILDERNESS IN STORM

DALADIER FAILS IN EFFORT TO FORM CABINET

OPTIMISM IS EXPRESSED BY BUSINESS LEADERS FOR GOOD 1929 SEASON

Ishbel MacDonald

RECOVERY IS STARTED AS WALL STREET STORM EBBS

5. TOUGHING IT OUT

A SENSE OF TOGETHERNESS
DESPITE THE DEPRESSION

1930 TO 1940

'There won't be any petty graft, because I'll take it all.'

— Vic Meyers, five-time lieutenant governor, two-term secretary of state; spoofing during his campaign for mayor of Seattle

Museum of History & Industry

A resident sits in one of the shelters that passes for a house in Seattle's main Hooverville, the last refuge of jobless men in the '30s. Below, a throng in early 1941 greets the first release of electricity from Grand Coulee Dam, a construction project of the '30s that dominated the state's economy.

During the Great Depression of the 1930s, "Brother, Can You Spare a Dime?" was more than a popular song. It was a fact of life.

More than 5,000 banks collapsed. Unemployment soared to 22 percent in 1933; another 21 percent worked only part time. The Dow Jones average of 30 industrials peaked at about 380 just before the October 1929 crash, then toppled to a low of 38 in the summer of 1932.

Fair or not, a president's name was applied to shantytowns — "Hoovervilles" — that sprung up alongside railroad tracks. In Seattle, they made their appearance somewhere between late 1931 and early '32.

Change was inevitable. In 1932, the nation overwhelmingly elected a Democratic president, Franklin D. Roosevelt, and sang, prematurely, "Happy Days Are Here Again." At the same time Washingtonians were going for

Seattle Times

CHRONO-LOG

1930
*Herbert Crisler,
Seattle photographer and
mountaineer, completes 26-
day journey through
Olympic Peninsula from
Olympic Hot Springs to
Hoquiam. Trek marks first
time — officially, according
to Seattle Times — that a
white man has traversed
that part of state.
Not quite true, however. A
successful expedition in
January 1890, promoted by
the daily Seattle Press,
undertook five-month
exploration led by cowboy-
hunter James Christie. The
party named 49 mountains
and rivers, drew maps, took
photographs, kept diaries
and christened dozens of
peaks after famed editor-
publishers. Many names
didn't stick, but the
expedition did leave behind
some, such as Press Valley,
Mount Ferry (after Gov.
Elisha P. Ferry), Mount
Seattle, Mount Meany (after
Seattle Press editor, later
UW prof Edmond Meany),
Mount Scott (after Chicago
Herald editor James Scott),
Bailey Range (after Seattle
Press publisher William E.
Bailey).*

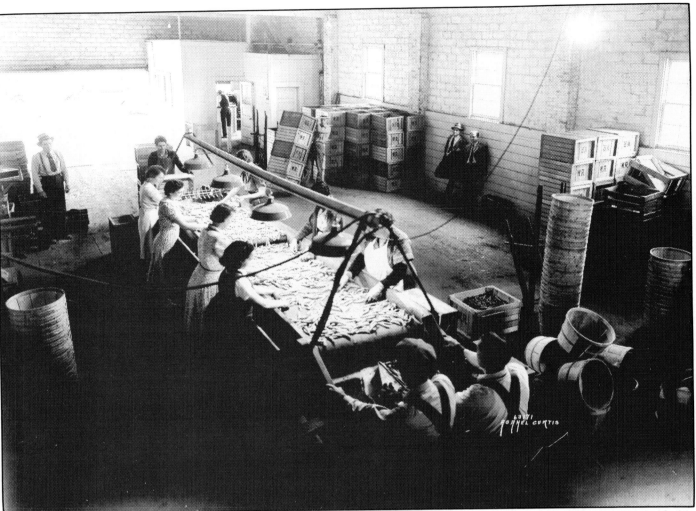

Washington State Historical Society

In the Great Depression year of 1937, men and women sort peas in a packing shed in Raymond, Pacific County.

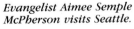
*Evangelist Aimee Semple
McPherson visits Seattle.*

Seattle Times

FDR, they elected a Democratic governor, Clarence D. Martin, for the first time since 1916.

Four years later, this state would face one of the crowded presidential ballot in its history: Roosevelt again, who trounced GOP candidate Alf Landon, 459,579 to 206,892; William Lemke, Union Party (17,463 votes); Norman Thomas, Socialist (with 3,496 votes); Earl Browder, Communist (1,907); William Pelley, Christian (1,598); D. Leigh Colvin, Prohibition (1,041), and John Aiken, Socialist Labor (362).

The '30s saw the flourishing of a particularly offensive — and defenseless — crime, kidnapping. Gangsters John Dillinger, "Machine Gun" Kelly, "Pretty Boy" Floyd and Bonnie Parker and Clyde Barrow became household names. Prohibition ended, phased in by a brief experiment with 3.2 percent beer.

For all the adversity, a remarkable sense of togetherness emerged.

When a long-lost cousin or nephew appeared on the doorstep and asked to be put up in a spare bedroom, few were hard-hearted enough to turn him away. People laughed: "I'm waiting for my ship to come in — but I think it's on the rocks."

The trade-union movement, weakened by a depression that made contract negotiations seem useless and strikes suicidal, gained a powerful new ally: the federal government. The National Recovery Act of 1933 gave employees the right to organize and bargain collectively, and the National Labor Relations Act (the Wagner Act) enacted in 1935 broadened unions' rights and barred unfair labor practices by employers. With a new, more militant federation, the CIO, to supplement the older and more staid AFL, organized labor scored its greatest — and sometimes bloodiest — advances during this decade and boosted the living standard of the American working man for decades to come.

The nation had its first black athletic heroes — Jesse Owens, who dominated track and field at the '36 Olympic Games in Germany, and Joe Louis, who annihilated the German prizefighter Max Schmeling and went on to an illustrious reign as heavyweight boxing champion.

The Golden Age of Radio arrived, making possible the sharing of information, music and ideas in every big city and hamlet in the land. Using his voice like a Stradivarius, FDR reassured the nation with his "fireside chats."

The nation laughed as one with Jack Benny, Bob Hope, Fred Allen, Fibber McGee and Molly, the Great Gildersleeve, Burns and Allen, Edgar Bergen and Charlie McCarthy, Jimmy Durante and Eddie Cantor.

And it became hooked on quiz shows: "Information Please," "Quiz Kids," "Kay Kyser's Kollege of Musical Knowledge," "Dr. I.Q."

Mothers who stayed at home to bake cookies and do housework — and most did — tuned to "Road of Life," "Young Dr. Malone," "Backstage Wife" and Oxydol's own "Ma Perkins," who ran a lumberyard but never seemed to sell any 2-by-4's.

Teen-agers draped themselves around the Atwater Kent or Philco radio on Saturday nights to listen to "Your Hit Parade." Remarkably, youngsters and their grandparents listened to, and liked, the same popular music. And why not? In one decade, more durable tunes arrived on the scene than at any time in the nation's history.

Among them: "Stormy Weather," "Smoke Gets in Your Eyes," "Deep Purple," "All the Things You Are, "Night and Day," "Stardust," "As Time Goes By," "Blue Moon," "Summertime" and "The Way You Look Tonight." Not to overlook such pleasant bits of froth as "The Music Goes 'Round and 'Round," "Three Little Fishes," "The Hut Sut Song" and "Bei Mir Bist Du Schön."

It was a decade in which Kate Smith first sang what has become the unofficial national anthem, "God Bless America," and Margaret Mitchell's epic "Gone With the Wind" became the longest movie produced to that time. Extras died by the thousand in this celluloid Civil War, but what most shocked moviegoers was not the carnage but the utterance of "damn" by Clark Gable.

Dale Carnegie's "How to Win Friends and Influence People" appeared. The Dionne quintuplets were born. In

May 1937 the German zeppelin Hindenburg burned in New Jersey, claiming 36 lives. Half a year earlier, England's King Edward VIII abdicated his throne for "the woman I love," an American divorcée named Wallis Simpson.

And Douglas "Wrong Way" Corrigan flew his $900 Curtiss Robin monoplane from New York to Ireland, thinking all the while, he said with a grin, that he was following his compass to Los Angeles. Only hopeless innocents believed him, but it was great fun.

People dreamed of cashing in on luck on "The Pot o' Gold," or on talent on "Major Bowes' Original Amateur Hour," hosted by Edward Bowes, who left San Francisco after the 1906 earthquake and spent several years as a developer of real estate on Tacoma's west side.

Seattleites fell hard for the 1930s chain-letter fad that promised a bundle of dimes or handkerchiefs or recipes, or whatever the traffic would bear. Even though mathematicians warned of the folly of it all — a chain letter carried to the 12th step would require 181,640,625 unbroken links — Seattle's mail increased by 200,000 envelopes in one two-day period in May 1935, and 50 substitute mail clerks were put to work.

Evidence of zaniness and naiveté were everywhere.

In Milton, Pierce County, a band of Democrats elected a mule with the name of Boston Curtis as GOP precinct committeeman.

The country needed diversions. One had only to turn to The Seattle Times' classified pages to see columns of job-wanted ads and only a handful of jobs available. Typical of the latter: "Woman to live in and care for children and household. Room and board and $1 a week."

At a time when $5 a day provided a comfortable living, one could rent a six-room brick home, with fireplace and view, for $45 a month. Good apartments went for $20. A one-pound can of sockeye salmon cost 11 cents, a one-pound tin of Hills Bros. coffee 29 cents, and any can of Campbell's soup could be bought for 5 cents.

Women transformed flour sacks into undergarments. They paid 19 cents for silk brassieres, 35 cents for silk stockings, 29 cents for bed sheets (9 cents extra for matching pillow cases). Finger waves and marcels cost 10, 25 and 50 cents at Mary Stone's beauty school in Seattle.

If Dad owned a car, he paid $3.49 apiece for gum-dipped Firestone tires; inner tubes 59 cents extra. Used '29 Model A coupés were going for $164; '27 Ford coaches, with wire wheels, cost as little as $65.

Adventurers caught our fancy.

Leslie Melvin, 21, a few years out of Highline High School, mushed with four unmatched dogs from Martin Point, on the Arctic Slope, to Nome in 128 thrill-packed days from October 1931 to February 1932. The distance was 1,500 miles. But Melvin estimated he traveled at least 3,000 miles because of unplanned wrong turns, days of endless circling in blizzards and intentional side trips.

Museum of History & Industry
The Rathskeller, a popular '30s downtown Seattle beer parlor.

Less fortunate was Seattle's Delmar Fadden, the lone-wolf mountaineer. As a 19-year-old in the summer of '32, Fadden spent 28 days hiking — without benefit of trails — from the Pacific Ocean to Hood Canal. Four years later, Fadden undertook a solo ascent of Mount Rainier in the howling blizzards of January. If he succeeded, it would be a first. When Fadden failed to return, rescuers risked death to look for his body. He was found in January 1936, face down, on a glacier at 13,000 feet. He apparently had fallen. That spring, evidence was found at the summit proving that Fadden had reached the top before he died on his return.

Inventive genius flourished.

In 1931, Paul Tutmarc of Seattle and Art Stimpson of Spokane attached a magnetic telephone pickup to Tutmarc's six-string guitar and wired it to a low-powered amplifier. The crude device, assembled in Tutmarc's basement, ranks with the wheel, the internal-combustion engine, television and the airplane in its impact on mankind. The world knows it as the electric guitar.

Youngsters became ingenious at having fun without raiding piggy banks for Indian-head pennies and buffalo nickels.

They made dish gardens by putting salt, Mercurochrome or bluing on lumps of coal and watched the colored crystals grow. They played marbles (for keeps), made stilts out of pieces of scrap lumber, wound notched spools with string and did a rat-a-tat-tat on the neighbor's windows and delighted in the whirring noise created by a button and a piece of string.

When the cover fell off a baseball, it was wrapped in friction tape. Footballs were stuffed with rags when bladders were beyond repair. Basketballs were thrown through barrel hoops nailed to telephone poles.

"Scootmobiles" were fashioned from an apple box, a 2-by-4, the remains of a single roller skate and a couple of jar lids for headlights. One did not buy nails, one pulled them, bent and rusty, from old boards and straightened them with a rock.

The flagpole-sitting, marathon dancing and walkathons begun in the '20s continued through the lean years. Suffering was in.

George McCormick earned notice in 1938 by walking the 48 miles of rocky beach around Vashon Island in 21 hours. Bertha Woodward, the "walking grandmother," four times won first prize in a 52-mile race around Lake Washington. She was 48 in 1938 when she set the women's record of 9 hours 47 minutes, cheered on by her 210-pound truck-driver husband who said he was not "athletically inclined."

There wasn't much to steal in the '30s, but vigilance was needed in bad times as well as good.

The New Order of Cincinnatus was founded in Seattle in 1933 by young Progressive Republicans to joust with entrenched politicians and examine alleged graft and inefficiency in City Hall. One of the more sensational charges (for Seattle, anyway): that dead men and fictitious names had been put on voter-registration rolls.

Everybody had a plan to make things better.

Dr. Francis Townsend, a lean and hungry-looking retired physician, told cheering supporters in Seattle about his tax plan to eliminate poverty, ignorance and disease and give every older person a reasonable pension.

Aimee Semple McPherson, the often calculatedly rapturous evangelist, appeared at one of her Four Square Gospel Churches in Seattle, clad in a flowing blue-and-white robe, to say that "everything happening in this international situation has already been foretold in the Bible . . . including 400-mile-an-hour Nazi airplanes that swarm like locusts."

Father Divine, the balding black evangelist of New York's Harlem, was said to be here in spirit in the storefront and living-room churches that sprung up in his name. A Father Divine cult was begun on an island off Anacortes.

Thousands of Seattle boys walked up the rickety wooden stairs of the Howard Building in Pioneer Square to visit "Doc Evans' Wax Museum," officially known as Museum of Anatomy, Thomas R. Evans, "phys.," proprietor. It was free and contained gaudily painted models of reproductive organs and jars filled with the pickled remains of body parts, all afflicted with what were referred to as "social diseases." Many young men, wide-eyed and with sweaty palms, left vowing a life of celibacy. Handily — and profitably — for those who ran into problems in the future, Doc Evans had a clinic down the hall from his museum.

By decade's end, there were "knock-knock, who's there?" jokes and goldfish gulping. The most publicized gulper, and quite likely the first, was a young Harvard Law School

STATE-MENTS

Hugh Herndon Jr., left, and Clyde Pangborn.

A wing and a prayer
Clyde Pangborn and his flying partner, Hugh Herndon Jr., made history when they completed the first nonstop single-engine flight across the Pacific Oct. 5, 1931, belly-landing Pangborn's dark-red Bellanca monoplane at Wenatchee's Fancher Field after covering 4,600 miles in 41 hours, 13 minutes.

The wheel-less landing was planned. Before leaving Japan's Honshu Island, the two men calculated that the only way they could make the flight, with their limited fuel capacity, was to increase their average cruising speed by 15 miles an hour. They dropped their landing gear when they were airborne to lighten the load and boost their speed. But two of the wheel struts failed to break loose. So, 16 hours out of Japan — 17,000 feet over the Pacific — Pangborn climbed out of the plane and onto a wing in sub-zero temperatures to jerk the rods loose.

It was, Pangborn said later, no great trick. The native of Brewster, Okanogan County, had served in the Army Air Service and then had become a star performer for Gates Flying Circus, walking wings, flying upside down and routinely performing death-defying stunts. Herndon, a wealthy Ivy Leaguer, became his barnstorming partner.

Among those waiting for the fliers on the ground in Wenatchee was a smiling representative of Japan's Asahi Shimbun newspaper. In his hand was a check for $25,000.

Don Duncan

Leo Lassen, "Mr. Baseball" from the 1930s through the '50s, when he was the voice of the Pacific Coast League Seattle Rainiers, calls the plays of a home game in the press box of Sicks' Stadium. When the Rainiers were on the road, Lassen re-created play by play from nothing more than ticker-tape reports.

CHRONO-LOG

student, Irving Clark Jr. of Seattle. Clark, who downed 24 goldfish one afternoon, later became a Seattle attorney, civic activist and radio talk-show host.

Boeing had switched from biplanes to monoplanes. The company developed Model 247 twin-engine transports to compete in the growing commercial-aircraft market, followed by Model 307 Stratoliners. Pan American bought Model 314 Clipper ships for transoceanic flights. The company designed two planes — the B-17 in 1934 and the B-29 in 1938 — that would help win World War II in the following decade.

Seldom a foul from Mr. Baseball

Seattle Times

Fred Hutchinson, who pitched for the Seattle Rainiers in the 1930s and for whom a cancer center is named.

For three decades, starting in 1931, the most recognizable voice in Western Washington was that of Leo Lassen, the man known as "Mr. Baseball."

On hot summer nights, while sprinklers played on lawns, Lassen's voice crackled through thousands of screen doors.

It was impossible to escape it, so everyone listened to what obviously was a love affair between a bespectacled bachelor and a game called baseball.

"It's in the well."

"Hang onto those rocking chairs."

"Mount Rainier is a big ice-cream cone over Franklin High tonight, folks. We give you all the news."

Schoolboys worked up Leo Lassen routines for stunt night, imitating the staccato, slightly sing-song delivery and throwing in a wealth of Lassenisms.

"Uh, next at bat is Dick Gyselman, the darning-needle third baseman" (a reference to Gyselman's slender stature).

"Oh, you could put a Wheaties flake between them," or "He was safe as a Silvertown (tire)."

Lassen also huckstered products unashamedly.

The Seattle Indians, eventually the Rainiers, were the only pro sports show in town as Lassen followed their fortunes from Dugdale Park to Civic Stadium to Sicks' Stadium.

Few realized Lassen did not go on the road with the team, that he re-created half the ball games from a studio booth, embellishing skimpy information provided on a telegraph wire — much as a little-known contemporary, Ronald Reagan, was doing at the time in the Midwest.

When the wire broke down, Lassen would stage mythical rhubarbs between managers and umpires. Jaws wagged. Hats were thrown in the dirt. Fans booed. If the wire still had not resumed its clickety-clack, Lassen would have a nervous pitcher throw repeatedly to first base to keep a runner on the bag.

But mostly it was reliable information. There was no fudging on the things that really counted. Lassen loved and respected the mountain of statistics that are an integral part of the game.

Lassen was talked about in barbershops, where the opinion was widely held that he would be a better manager than any in the league. Men would say, in mock wonderment, "Why, Leo explained the infield-fly rule so that even my wife could understand it."

Lassen was there for all the big events:

■ On July 8, 1937, in old Civic Field, 9,272 paying guests watched and thousands heard on radio the wedding at home plate between the Seattle Indians' premier home-run hitter, Arthur "Mike" Hunt, and Charlotte Axelson. Gov. Clarence D. Martin gave the bride away and the Rev. Mark Matthews, the famous scourge of sin, performed the marriage rites in that great frock coat of his.

Clarence "Snake Eyes" Pickrel, best man at the wedding and starting pitcher that night, not only scattered 10 hits to defeat the Sacramento Solons 3-1, but he hit his first — and last — home run in professional baseball.

■ On Aug. 12, 1938, 16,345 fans filled the stands and overflowed into the outfield of Sicks' Stadium, and thousands more listened to the drama of young Fred Hutchinson — recently of Franklin High School — attempting to pitch his 19th victory on his 19th birthday. "Hutch" recorded a 3-2 win over the San Francisco Seals, but the most memorable moment occurred in the sixth inning when, having given up three walks and a single in succession, he signaled time out, strolled off the mound and up to the dugout.

The stands hummed. Manager Jack Lelivelt nervously inquired, "What's the matter?"

Hutch replied casually, "I'm thirsty. I want a drink of water."

Slaked, he ambled to the mound and shut down the Seals.

(Hutch won 25 and lost 7 that season and went on to pitch for Detroit in the big leagues, then manage Seattle in the Pacific Coast League and the St. Louis Cardinals and Cincinnati Reds in the majors. He died of cancer in November 1964. The Fred Hutchinson Cancer Research Center is named in his honor.)

When Lassen quit the broadcast booth in 1960 after a contract dispute, he went home to attend to his second love, the rose garden. He never again set foot inside a ballpark. That chapter of his life was closed, just like the childhood accident that left Mr. Baseball with a crippled arm and made it impossible for him to play the game he loved so much.

Lassen died in 1975 at the age of 76.

The freestyle reign of Queen Helene

It was a sunny August day in the Los Angeles Coliseum, and the American flag slowly was hoisted as the national anthem was played.

A tall 19-year-old girl with dark, bobbed hair stood on the top step of the victory stand. When the music stopped, she received a standing ovation.

Helene Madison, in a dark-blue swimming suit emblazoned with the red-white-and-blue shield of the United States, had just won the 100-meter freestyle swimming race for women in the 1932 Olympic Games.

Before the week was over, she would stand on the dais two more times — winner of the 400-meter freestyle and anchor-lap swimmer for the 400-meter freestyle relay team.

It was the Summer Olympics at which Mildred "Babe" Didrickson, the irrepressible tomboy, would collect medals in track and field, and Eddie Tolan would reign as the "world's fastest human."

Madison, who had started swimming at Seattle's Green Lake at age 12, won all the freestyle swimming events they had for women in the 10th Olympiad. And everyone agreed the three gold medals could have been a dozen if there had been enough events.

"Queen Helene," as the sportswriters dubbed her, dominated the world of swimming as no one before or since. The year she won in the Olympics, she held all 16 women's world freestyle swimming records and 56 U.S. records. In three years, she had smashed U.S. and world records 117 times.

Every freestyle swimming record from 50 yards to one mile was her personal property. Often she had set them when her coach, Ray Daughters, announced at poolside that there would be timers at various distances and he wanted Helene to swim as far and as fast as she could. It was like asking a sprinter to go out and break world records up to a mile.

When Madison returned to Seattle, a proud city presented her with an automobile, a Navy and police escort through town and the biggest tickertape parade in its history. Two weeks later, with no more swimming worlds to conquer and hoping to cash in on her fame, she turned professional. An exhibition swim for pay in Bitter Lake, at the old Playland Amusement Park, stripped her forever of amateur standing.

The "female Johnny Weismuller" signed a movie contract. Hollywood dyed her hair platinum and put her in a comedy. She bombed. She tried unsuccessfully to make it as a nightclub entertainer. Then she taught swimming and worked as a saleswoman in a sporting-goods store.

When the U.S. Olympic team went to Berlin in 1936, Madison the professional — wishing she had never given up her amateur standing — was left behind, working at a hotdog stand at Green Lake. The greatest swimmer of them all had been denied a job as a Park Department swimming instructor because of a rule against women instructors.

Years later, Madison battled the ravages of diabetes and cancer in a basement apartment across from Green Lake, where it had all begun. Her only companions were a parakeet, Jimmy, and a Siamese cat, Punky. On one wall was a big square of purple velvet, solid with medals. Some had tarnished and turned black.

"They get black if you don't polish them," she said matter-of-factly.

Cancer finally defeated Queen Helene Nov. 26, 1970. A swimming pool in Seattle's North End bears her name.

A different tune

Nicholas Oeconomacos (ee-kono-MAA-kos), a native of the Peloponnesus region of Greece, was a familiar figure on Seattle's streets for several decades. Tall and black-haired, he wore a flowing cape, carried a carved walking stick, puffed black cigars and wore broad-brimmed black hats squarely on his head.

But there was nothing Mephistophelean about the man, who loved church bells and children, believed in brotherhood and sometimes carried his pet canary in a cage on downtown walks.

In his prime, he was the greatest clarinetist of his day — of all time, in the opinion of bandmaster/composer John Philip Sousa. The clarinet won acclaim for Oeconomacos in Europe and in Seattle, where he signed on as first clarinetist for the Seattle Symphony, a prestigious but low-paying job.

Faced with losing his home in 1931 at the onset of the Great Depression, he decided on a dramatic gesture. He, Nicholas Oeconomacos, the world's finest clarinetist, the supreme musician, would play in Seattle's streets to raise money to keep a roof over

Caped clarinetist Nicholas Oeconomacos was a familiar figure on Seattle's streets during the 1930s.

Seattle Times

his head. Solemn and black-robed, he went forth playing on street corners and then holding out his hat to collect pennies, nickels and dimes. And sometimes candy, chewing gum, streetcar tokens and seed for his canary.

In a lesser man, it might have been pathetic. But Oeconomacos played the role with kingly bearing. He would not lower himself to popular musical tastes. The music of Wagner, Bach, Beethoven — his heroes — competed with the roar of traffic and streetcar bells.

Oeconomacos finally was evicted from his home by sheriff's deputies with no taste for their task, and he went to San Francisco to play in orchestra pits and with radio-station ensembles. But he could not stay away.

He returned to set up housekeeping in an ordinary-looking structure at 625 Minor Ave. N. There he created his masterpiece, The House of the Terrestrial Globe. It had three main portals inside a fence studded with gates made from brass bedsteads. Large circles of wood on the house's exterior denoted, he explained, the "areas of the terrestrial globe."

Inside, in disarray, were the busts of composers, framed quotations of musicians, photographs of music teachers, friends and old masters, and numerous yellowed newspaper clippings and posters proclaiming the artistry of Oeconomacos. A huge American flag was draped on a bannister.

It became a house of memories — of his days in French conservatories and French Grand Opera, of his friends, Sousa and Maurice Ravel. Into it he invited real-life students, who made wheezes on clarinets and paid him a few quarters a week.

The clarinetist named the house's areas. The Garden of Golden Memories was a carpet of sawdust in the front yard, the Gate of the Little Flower a patch of rusty screening, the Gate of the Lonely Heart a handsome bedstead.

Oeconomacos built his own Parthenon, a one-man bandstand of fluted columns with peeling paint. He seated himself there, a proud figure, and audiences sat on planks and old chairs and on the edge of a horse trough filled with flowers, near the Gate of the Lonely Heart.

To feed himself, Oeconomacos even played in local beer halls. Classics, of course. And he staged numerous memorial concerts to honor musician friends who had died.

On several occasions, music lovers hired Seattle's Metropolitan Theater and put out posters heralding the one-night stand of "The Great Nicholas Oeconomacos."

In the fall of 1944, Oeconomacos suffered a heart attack. The following February, he died in a local hospital at the age of 81.

Wreckers moved in on the House of the Terrestrial Globe after curiosity seekers had ransacked it, many lured by rumors of $1,500 in cash hidden inside.

Timbers were piled in the sawdust of the Garden of Golden Memories. The only sound was the roar of cars, although some remembered that Homer Hadley, composer and one-time conductor of the Seattle Symphony, had said Oeconomacos played the softest clarinet in the world.

Political funnies with the 'Clown Prince'

In the summer of '32, Victor Aloysius Meyers, a dapper Seattle band leader with a pencil-thin mustache, arrived in Olympia to file for governor. The filing fee was $60. He dug into his wallet, saw he'd be a little short, and said, "What have you got for $20?"

There was lieutenant governor, for $12. And so Meyers paid the fee, filed as a Democrat and easily won in the Roosevelt landslide. He went on to serve five terms as lieutenant governor and twice as

Seattle Times

A contingent of the Civilian Conservation Corps is put through the paces before being sent to work in Snoqualmie National Forest in the summer of 1933.

CHRONO-LOG

secretary of state.

But it was Meyers' wit and flair and his ability to press the flesh, rather than his success at the polls, that made him one of the most engaging figures in the state's political history.

It had all begun as a joke two years earlier. Some Seattle newspapermen, hoping to inject humor into a grim political scene, had talked Meyers into filing for mayor of Seattle. He lost, but he was a laugh-a-minute.

"Two-four time" is better than daylight-saving time, he quipped. "There won't be any petty graft, because I'll take it all."

One day he appeared at a candidates' luncheon in the Olympic Hotel wearing a sheet, like Mahatma Gandhi, and pulling a goat on a rope. When called upon to speak, he played the flute.

He hired a Shakespearean-actor friend to stand in for one of his opponents at a staid women's club luncheon. The sham candidate loudly advocated prostitution and open gambling.

One opponent responded in kind, hiring sound trucks before the primary and sending them out among snoozing Seattleites at 3 a.m. to play loud Sousa marches and exhort over a loudspeaker, "Wake up and vote for Vic Meyers."

As lieutenant governor, Meyers surprised many, becoming a student of parliamentary law and presiding over the Senate with

Seattle Times

Vic Meyers, the consummate politician, never took himself seriously. Here, with a reluctant goat in tow, he clowns his way through a 1932 Seattle municipal election decked out in a "Gandhi business suit."

skill. While other state officials were conspicuous by their absence, he went out among the bonus marchers who descended on Olympia during the Depression, trying to arrange for food and a place for them to pitch their tents. He gave each the benefit of his unfailing greeting: "Hiya, kiddo!"

(The men were part of a veterans' "army" that marched on Washington, D.C., in 1932 to demand that they be allowed to cash in their bonus certificates from World War I. They were violently evicted by a little-known Army chief of staff, Douglas A. MacArthur.)

Meyers steadfastly opposed the sales tax as regressive and hard on the poor. He proposed, to howls of laughter, a Seattle World Fair.

In 1938, when Gov. Clarence D. Martin was out of the state, Meyers called a special session of the Legislature to vote higher old-age assistance funds. Martin raced back to cancel the session. He said afterward he was afraid to leave the state for fear of what Meyers would do.

During World War II, Meyers spoofed reporters with "Habitually I go without a vest so I can't be accused of standing for vested interests." The quip landed in William Safire's book, "The New Language of Politics." It was almost as good as the day Meyers said, "I won't tell any lies about my opponent if he won't tell the truth about me."

After the war, Meyers got the idea of putting a state park in a barren part of Eastern Washington for the then-astronomical sum of $700,000. Opponents called it "Vic's Folly." But Sun Lakes State Park became one of the busiest, and best, in Washington.

Ousted as lieutenant governor in the Eisenhower landslide of '52, Meyers was back in 1956 to bid for the job of secretary of state.

"The last time I talked to you people I asked you to help old Vic out," he would say. "Now I'm asking you to help old Vic back in." The laughter was genuine. So were the votes that put him back in.

Questioned about some of his high-roller expense accounts as secretary of state, Meyers defended a long trip to the East Coast in a state-owned Cadillac by saying, "Why pick on Vic?" The slogan worked for another successful campaign.

It seemed Meyers would go on forever. But something over which he had no control finally soured the voters. State anti-gambling petitions, containing more than 82,000 signatures, were stored in a vault in the secretary of state's office, waiting for validation. One weekend, someone sneaked into the office and stole the petitions.

There were howls of indignation.

Two days after the theft, Meyers was to be the luncheon speaker at a service club in Olympia. Everyone wondered how he would handle the scandal. Meyers stood up, surveyed his audience and said, "I hate to be a name-dropper, but . . ."

The laughter was deafening. But the old magic was wearing thin.

On the eve of his last election in '64, Meyers, a lonely figure in a room in the Olympic Hotel, looked up from an envelope on which he had been scribbling numbers and said, "I'm waiting for the pinochle players' vote to come in." There were not, alas, enough pinochle players.

Meyers, by then known as the "Clown Prince," the "Pagliacci of Politics," delivered an unforgettable valedictory for the TV cameras that night. Hurting inside, he graciously praised his opponent and concluded, "They finally caught up with me."

Conservation's esprit de corps

Born in April 1933 in the deep troughs of the Depression, the Civilian Conservation Corps probably made more lasting friends than any federal job program in the nation's history.

Today, almost half a century after Congress called a halt, parks, forest roads and trails, bridges and telephone lines the CCC built or installed are being used throughout the state and nation. And the millions of seedlings planted by the CCC have added immeasurably to Washington's forest resources.

At its peak, the CCC was nearly four times as large as the regular Army, its "soldiers without uniform" being known by such endearing terms as "tree troopers," "brush marines" and "forest rookies."

Because of its vast timberland, Washington had one of the nation's largest contingents in more than 40 camps on both sides of the Cascades. The state quickly filled its initial quota of 2,500 men — mostly single, aged 18 to 25, with dependent families.

There were poignant scenes outside the King County welfare office when men with hats pulled low over their faces to conceal wrinkles stood in line and tried to pass themselves off as 25. Some men over 60 showed up, begging for jobs.

The "dollar-a-day men" — from whose $30 monthly checks $25

was deducted for their families — were sent to various military establishments for physical training. They were given work denims, olive-drab outfits, shoes, hats and two blankets. Best of all, they received three square meals a day. Many even learned a trade.

One of the legacies of that first year was a million young fir trees planted on Lookout Mountain in the Yacolt Burn, the Clark County scene of one of the nation's most disastrous forest fires more than 30 years earlier.

The CCC concept continued to grow. An all-black unit was cited for top-grade work in Wenatchee National Forest. An Indian contingent worked on reservations. Eventually, an all-Eskimo unit was formed in Alaska.

In this state, the CCC did reclamation work at Grand Coulee Dam and built or refurbished 17 parks. Among them: Gingko Petrified Forest, Deception Pass, Point Defiance, Bogachiel, Lake Wenatchee, Mount Spokane, Lewis and Clark, and Saltwater.

Thanks to the CCC, there is a suspension bridge over the Chehalis River at Rainbow Falls State Park and a stone observation tower on Mount Constitution at Moran State Park, in the San Juans.

Congress turned down FDR's request for a permanent CCC in 1937, but did extend the program to 1940. Another two-year extension was granted that year. But the Depression was largely over and the nation was embroiled in wars on two fronts by the end of 1941. The CCC died a quiet death in the summer of 1942, after having enlisted an estimated 2.5 million young men in some 1,500 camps.

Grand Coulee: never a dam site better

On July 17, 1933, Sen. C.C. Dill and Governor Martin drove stakes and dug shovels into loose dirt at a bend in the Columbia River, at the juncture of Grant, Okanogan, Lincoln and Douglas counties.

Ahead lay the building of Grand Coulee Dam, the greatest construction project undertaken to that time. Lives would be changed, and many — 77 — would be lost.

Nature had been at work there for millions of years, creating the great drainage system that flows south out of Canada and across the eastern half of Washington before turning west to the Pacific. Wind, erosion, lava flows and several ice ages had rounded the hills, flung huge boulders around and carved great ditches called coulees. Deep down, below the basaltic crust, was the bedrock granite upon which men would pour concrete building blocks — week after week, month after month, year after year until the great plug had halted the river's flow.

Eight years later, there would be a 151-mile reservoir, called Lake Roosevelt, backed up almost to the Canadian border. Later there would be a 27-mile-long irrigation lake 283 feet above the dam, named for Frank Banks, project manager for the U.S. Bureau of Reclamation. And there would be earth-filled dams, tunnels, great siphons and several thousand miles of canals, waterways and ditches.

Soon after the dam's two powerhouses began producing electricity in 1941, Grand Coulee became the No. 1 power producer in all the world, and stayed No. 1 until the Soviets completed a dam with more generating capacity in 1955. Grand Coulee would regain the lead in the 1970s when a third powerhouse was brought on line.

Among those witnessing the ground-breaking were Rufus Woods, flamboyant Bull Moose Republican publisher of The Wenatchee World, who had dreamed of that moment for 25 years — ever since Ephrata lawyer Billy Clapp said he had a story that might be the biggest of Woods' life.

Clapp had outlined a scheme for building a dam across the Columbia and diverting some of its water to transform the arid, sparsely populated Columbia Basin from jackrabbit country into a productive Garden of Eden. Woods had poured all his boundless energy, promoter's hype and newspaper resources into convincing the public and the government and into shooting down rival irrigation schemes proposed by private developers.

This day was vindication. And Woods and his buddy, Jim O'Sullivan, who had helped carry the ball against critics at home and abroad, recalled the less kindly things said about the project.

Colliers magazine: "What are they going to do with it?" New York's Rep. Francis Culkin: "The greatest fraud ever perpetrated on the people of the United States." Business Week: "Grand Coulee Dam is typical of those things that won't have any more usefulness than the pyramids of Egypt." Farm Journal: "Of all the outrages on agriculture, we are beginning to think the Columbia Basin Project takes the cake. Who wants it? Nobody."

It was not until President Roosevelt entered the White House, with a pre-election commitment to a project his predecessor, Herbert Hoover, felt was a squandering of public money, that Woods thought the long fight might be nearing its conclusion.

FDR bypassed Congress to allocate $60 million from the federal Energy Relief Administration for a low-level dam to divert water to the basin and generate just enough power to move the water.

Woods and others felt certain that once started, there would be further appropriations so the dam could grow in height and generate power for homes and industry. And they were right. Just 23 months after the ground-breaking, Secretary of the Interior Harold Ickes signed an order providing for a higher dam.

Work on the dam seems never to end.

A $43 million rip-rapping project was undertaken in the riverbed just below the dam in the early '80s.

The irrigation project, which has brought water to 540,000 acres in the Columbia Basin and has the potential for 1 million acres, will not be completed until the middle of the next century — more than 100 years after the ground-breaking.

Grand Coulee Dam's economic and sociological impact in the '30s was enormous. The project attracted land speculators, merchants, prostitutes and men without jobs. It employed 8,800 workers at the peak, and they lived alone or with their families in town or nearby settlements: Grand Coulee, Electric City, Coulee, Coulee City, Elmer City, Grand Coulee Heights, Delano, Osborne, Rim Rock, Basin City, Mason City, Engineer's Town, Government Town and Coulee Dam. Some are still on maps; many are not.

Many workers arrived with their families, pets and all worldly possessions piled high on sputtering jalopies. Women nursed

STATE-MENTS

No orphan this Annie
On a warm July night in 1933, Seattle's Fifth Avenue Theatre played host to the world premiere of Metro-Goldwyn-Mayer's "Tugboat Annie," adapted from the Saturday Evening Post stories of Norman Reilly Raine. It was a premiere worthy of Grauman's Chinese Theater in Hollywood. The event started at noon, when ships and tug whistles blasted on signal. Blank-loaded cannon boomed along a waterfront decorated with 15,000 balloons. Fireworks were shot from the Fifth Avenue's roof.

Puget Sounders took "Annie" to their hearts for a variety of reasons: (1) Raine had invented the character of Tugboat Annie while working as a guest instructor in fiction writing at the University of Washington. (2) Seattleites had lined the shores of Lake Union for one scene in which the tugboat Wallowa (called the Narcissus in the film) belched great clouds of smoke and kicked up a considerable wake while towing the old schooner Commodore. (3) Scenery for the film included Elliott Bay, Queen Anne Hill, the Eastlake District, the Olympic Mountains and the Strait of Juan de Fuca. (4) Everyone wondered which woman connected with Puget Sound tugboating was the role model for the irascible but lovable Annie Brennan, played by Marie Dressler. The film co-starred Wallace Beery.

Raine staunchly maintained the character was fictional, but a reporter wrote some years later that Raine said the character was based very loosely on Thea Foss, of the Foss Tug & Barge Co., who was sweet-natured and quite unlike the movie character.

Ed Walker / Seattle Times

The Pacific Northwest never would have a redevelopment agency equivalent to the '30s Tennessee Valley Authority, but its dams along the Columbia did provide low-cost electricity to industry and homes.

CHRONO-LOG

Seattle Times

Middleweight Al Hostak of Seattle (standing) wins world boxing crown by kayoing titleholder Freddie Steele of Tacoma in the first round as 31,102 fans crowd Seattle's Civic Stadium on July 28, 1938. Ex-champ Jack Dempsey is referee for bout. Hostak loses, regains, then loses title again; works many years as King County sheriff's deputy. Steele quits ring, finds new fame as movie actor, earning acclaim in "GI Joe" and "Hail, the Conquering Hero," and boxing as John L. Sullivan against Errol Flynn (Jim Corbett) in "Gentleman Jim."

1933

Gov. Clarence D. Martin, born in Cheney in 1886, is first native son to become state's chief executive. (Governs until 1941.)

1934

"Wholesale murder" occurs at Erlands Point, near Bremerton, as two women and four men are shot, stabbed or bludgeoned at poker game. Eventually suspect Leo Hall, amateur ice skater, is caught, convicted and hanged. His fatal mistake: tying hands of several victims with ice-skate laces.

1935

Lancelot "Lanny" Ross, Seattle native, is voted most popular male singer in America over such luminaries as Bing Crosby, Rudy Vallee, Gene Austin, Morton Downey and Russ Columbo.

Movie stars Clark Gable, Loretta Young, Jack Oakie arrive at gale-swept Heather Meadows on Mount Baker to begin filming Jack London's classic "Call of the Wild." Forty sled dogs and a crew of 100 precede luminaries.

babies in shacks or tents. Water was carried in pails. Many unmarried construction workers lived in dormitories, two to a room. Outhouses reeked in the summer sun. When the management of a hastily erected hotel bought a new piano for the lobby, a man showed up at the back door to ask for the packing crate. He added gunnysacks and had an instant home.

An enterprising barber set up a shower in the back room of his shop and charged two bits for two minutes of running water. An entrepreneur made a living extricating cars from the mud in Grand Coulee's main street. Women would start across the street in new boots, bog down to their knees and leave their boots behind as they continued on in bare feet.

There was a hunger for entertainment. The Harlem Globetrotters played the House of David. Bob Burns, a popular entertainer, arrived with his "bazooka," a comic horn consisting of two gas pipes and a whiskey funnel. Freddie Steele, the middleweight boxing champion, staged an exhibition.

Taverns and brothels flourished. Grand Coulee's B Street became synonymous with drinking and illicit love. One bar was 100 feet long, made of copper and inset with silver dollars. Many taverns had the swinging bat-doors seen in western movies.

"Taxi dancers" charged 10 cents a dance to women-hungry men, and there were business rooms upstairs with a bed, mattress and wash basin. One construction foreman, unhappy because his favorite brothel was like a furnace in the summer, had his men install a sprinkling system on the roof.

There were a half-dozen movie theaters, and they were jammed on "bank night" when cash prizes were awarded.

During one of his two visits to the site, FDR had a sudden yen for a hamburger. His driver stopped at a stand in Delano, and the proprietor promptly renamed his business "President's Choice."

When work began on the dam, Sam Seaton's cable ferry was the only link between the two sides of the river. In time, a shaky catwalk spanned the river and tested the nerves of those who used it. Then came bridges, to carry cars and trains.

Because of the sheer size of the pour, it was estimated that it would take several decades for the concrete to cool. That wouldn't do. Pipes were installed and cold water was pumped through them to cut the cooling time to a month.

In a world sated with gee-whiz statistics, Grand Coulee's numbers still cause the mind to reel:
- Forty-five million cubic yards of rock and soil were excavated.
- The dam, 550 feet above the lowest bedrock and 5,232 feet across, contains 11.975 million cubic yards of concrete.
- How much is that? Imagine a two-lane highway from Seattle to Miami, then add a 3-foot-wide sidewalk alongside. You'd still have a million cubic yards of concrete left over.

Seattle Times

Katharine Cornell, 1930s "first lady" of the Broadway stage, during a Seattle visit.

The show goes on

The story of Katharine Cornell's Christmas-night opening at Seattle's Metropolitan Theater in 1933 is part of theatrical folklore.

Regal and possessed of a richly husky voice that carried to the upper balcony, Cornell was at the time a legitimate claimant to the title "first lady of the American theater." Her husband, Guthrie McClintic, was a native Seattleite, and that gave even more importance to her appearance.

Cornell was to star in Rudolf Besier's "The Barretts of Wimpole Street" at 8:15 p.m.

But the curtain didn't rise. Instead, theater manager Kent Thomson announced that the train bringing Cornell and the cast had been delayed outside town by a flood and a slide. Would the audience please stand by?

Only a few ticketholders asked for refunds. The rest chose to wait.

Cornell's train finally arrived in town at 11:20. McClintic appeared on stage to announce the curtains would be opened to permit the audience to watch scenery being put in place, lights regulated and period (1855) costumes distributed.

Finally, the show began — at 1:04 a.m. Dec. 26. Cornell responded with an inspired performance as the poetess Elizabeth Barrett, deeply in love with another outstanding poet, Robert Browning. The role of Browning was played by Basil Rathbone, still regarded as Hollywood's definitive Sherlock Holmes.

When the play ended at 3:48 a.m., Cornell received a standing ovation and repeated curtain calls.

Alexander Woollcott, then one of America's premier writers, immortalized the event in a Saturday Evening Post article, "Miss Kitty Takes to the Road," and he buffed the yarn to a high gloss in a book, "Long, Long Ago."

The Seattle Times reviewer noted that an 18-year-old actor in the play showed promise. His name? Orson Welles.

Seattle Times

Newsmen fiddle with awkward tripods and bulky cameras as a young George Weyerhaeuser holds his first press conference in Tacoma shortly after being turned loose June 1, 1935, by his kidnappers, who demanded — and got — a $200,000 ransom.

Kidnapped!

George H. Weyerhaeuser, a curly-haired 9-year-old, was walking home for lunch near Tacoma's Annie Wright Seminary May 24, 1935, when a car drew up alongside him, two men leaped out and young George was carried off.

Kidnapped!

The word struck terror in the hearts of parents everywhere. Still fresh in everyone's mind was the kidnap-slaying three years earlier of pioneer aviator Charles Lindbergh's son.

A $200,000 ransom was asked for Weyerhaeuser, grandson of the Weyerhaeuser Co.'s founder. The boy's parents, Mr. and Mrs. John Philip Weyerhaeuser, paid it in hopes the kidnappers would free their son.

On June 1, young George was turned loose in the middle of the night on a country road near Issaquah. He had been given a blanket for warmth, and a dollar bill was stuffed in his pocket. George made his way to the farmhouse of Louis Bonifas, a woodcutter. He knocked on the door in the wee hours and announced he was the boy everyone was looking for.

Bonifas placed the boy in his rickety car and headed toward Tacoma. Meanwhile, Seattle Times reporters learned of the release and set out to intercept Bonifas and George.

Among those working out of The Times' "kidnap headquarters" in Tacoma's Winthrop Hotel was John Dreher, the newspaper's golf editor. Dreher hired a taxicab and ordered the driver to head toward Issaquah. On a back road, he saw Bonifas' car sputtering down the road. George was in the front seat.

Dreher motioned to Bonifas to stop. Talking fast and pulling bills from his wallet, he persuaded the woodcutter to let him take George to Tacoma in the taxi.

Realizing the road to the Weyerhaeuser home would be crawling with lawmen and reporters, Dreher told George to lie down on the back seat of the taxi and rest. Dreher sat on the floor, out of sight, and conducted the interview.

George said he had been treated reasonably well, although he had some uncomfortable moments. At the outset, he was kept on the floor of the kidnappers' car, with a blanket over him. Later he was placed in the trunk as the car stopped for numerous roadblocks.

For a time, he was chained in a hole in the ground in the Aberdeen area, warmed only by a kerosene lantern. He also was kept in a closet somewhere around Spokane. But his most frightening experience, he said, was being taken into the woods, blindfolded, and being forced to walk on logs over creeks. He was certain his kidnappers intended to drop him in the water.

Shortly after George returned home, police caught the three kidnappers — an ex-convict, William Drainard (alias William Mahan), and Harmon Metz Waley and his 19-year-old wife, Margaret. Mahan was sentenced to 60 years in prison, Waley to 45 and his wife to 20.

George's parents wisely refused to isolate or overprotect their son in the years that followed, and he grew up to head the company that bears his name. Waley wrote to his victim from prison on several occasions, apologizing for his mistake. When he was released, he asked for a job.

In an uncommon demonstration of compassion, Weyerhaeuser found a job for Waley at one of his Oregon plants.

Famous, fatal flight out of Renton

Will Rogers and Wiley Post had an appointment with death when they took off from Renton Airport the morning of Aug. 7, 1935, in Post's new red-and-silver, pontoon-equipped monoplane.

Rogers, 56, with his tousled hair, aw-shucks manner and deft jabs at what then passed for the establishment, was America's most beloved humorist.

Post, 35, whose rakish eye patch and what-the-hell attitude fit his adventurer's image, was the nation's top distance flier, having twice circled the globe alone in his Lockheed monoplane named after his daughter, Winnie Mae.

Post had flown to Seattle from San Francisco five days earlier with his wife, Mae. He wanted to install pontoons at Renton, he said, before flying to Alaska, then crossing the Bering Sea to Siberia, where he expected to hunt tigers. His goal was to touch down in Moscow, he said, and he might take Mae along.

While mechanics struggled with the pontoons, Post fumed at their progress. He went fishing one day off Mission Beach, catching an 18½-pound king salmon. He pronounced himself hooked on fishing.

Rogers, who arrived in Seattle a few days later, was as pleasant with the press as Post was surly. He said he intended to visit Matanuska colony in Alaska, where the government had grubstaked hundreds of dead-broke farmers from the drought-stricken Midwest. He casually chewed gum before takeoff and said

Associated Press

Humorist Will Rogers, left, chats with one-eyed aviator Wiley Post just before both left Renton in August 1935 on their fatal flight over Alaska.

he hoped for a good fish dinner in Alaska.

Mae Post appeared at the airport, kissing her husband goodbye and watching him take off. The flight might be a bit too strenuous for her, she said. She thought she'd go on to California, where her husband could catch up to her later.

Post and Rogers arrived in Juneau eight hours after leaving Renton. Weather was bad. A few days later, they flew on to Fairbanks. On Aug. 15, the pair left for Barrow, became lost in the fog and came down with engine trouble. They landed at Walakpa, an Eskimo hunting camp near the Arctic Ocean, 12 miles southwest of Barrow. They got directions to Barrow from an Eskimo family with whom they shared a meal. Post made repairs to the engine.

Claire Okpeaha, one of the Eskimos, watched the takeoff at 8:15 p.m., three hours after the unscheduled landing. "The plane banked northeast and just went over," he would say later. "It took a back nose dive, right into the creek."

Okpeaha found Rogers and Post dead. He got into his kayak and paddled to Barrow to relay the earthshaking news.

The bodies of Rogers and Post were flown to Seattle. A plaque honors them at the Will Rogers-Wiley Post Memorial Seaplane Base at Renton Airport.

Brief flares in a meteoric career

U.S. Rep. Marion Zioncheck plunged to his death from the fifth-floor window of Seattle's downtown Arctic Building in the late afternoon of Aug. 7, 1936. He was 36.

It was one of the biggest funerals in Seattle's history — hundreds attending because of genuine sorrow over the loss of a politician devoted to the "common man" and hundreds more attending either out of morbid curiosity or hoping to catch a glimpse of Zioncheck's beautiful young widow, Rubye.

There were two Zionchecks:

One, the immigrant Polish boy who rose from the streets to become a two-term congressman.

The other, an erratic personality whose bizarre exploits were chronicled in the nation's newspapers — "Zioncheck Wades in Rockefeller Center Pool," "Zioncheck Delivers Satchel Full of

STATE-MENTS

Bird of passage

In the summer of 1935, a silvery new ferryboat joined Alexander "Cap" Peabody's Puget Sound Navigation Co.'s Black Ball Line in Puget Sound. It was called the Kalakala, or "Flying Bird" in Chinook. As the world's first streamlined ferryboat, it would become one of the most-photographed vessels in America.

The Kalakala began life in 1926 as the unstreamlined Peralta, plying the waters between Oakland and San Francisco until it overturned and burned. Peabody bought the blackened hull and hauled it to the Lake Washington Shipyards, in Kirkland, for extensive remodeling. When the work was finished, the Kalakala — 276 feet long, 97.75 percent metal hull, all-electric welds — looked a lot like a seagoing version of the Airflow Chryslers and DeSotos of that era. On a summer afternoon, when the sun seemed to shower Puget Sound with diamonds, the Kalakala was a breathtaking sight as it headed into Colman Dock.

Being aboard the vessel was equally stimulating, but in a different way. For all her sleek beauty, the Kalakala vibrated, creaked and rattled. Many cures were attempted. Few did any good. She also had a penchant for getting into trouble — ramming boats and barges, wiping out docks and going aground with assorted ailments.

In her heyday, the Kalakala was employed on the Seattle-Bremerton, Seattle-Victoria and Port Angeles-Victoria runs. Later she was kept on standby and in 1967, the once-proud queen of the fleet was sold and taken to Alaska as a seafood-processing plant. She ended her days, a rusting hulk, on the beach at Gibson's Cove near Kodiak.

The aluminum-bodied Kalakala scoots across the Sound in her heyday.

University of Washington

Standing behind coxswain Bob Moch are the Huskies who captured the gold for eight-oared crews in the 1936 Olympics. From left: Don Hume, Joe Rantz, George "Shorty" Hunt, James McMillin, John White, Gordon Adam, Charles Day and Roger Morris. The crew gathered 50 years later to mark their anniversary; only Day was not among the survivors.

CHRONO-LOG

1935

John Nance Garner, vice president, is quoted before sailing from Seattle for Japan and the Philippines: "Boys, I'm deaf, blind and dumb as far as politics is concerned I'm like a soldier — I do what I'm told. When I was in Congress I opened up. But since the day I was elected vice president I've said nothing."

"Cactus Jack," scheduled for an audience with the emperor of Japan, says he's bringing new cotton socks so he doesn't get in the same pickle as presidential candidate William Jennings Bryan, who doffed shoes before His Imperial Highness and discovered holes in his hose.

Four sailing vessels leave Seattle for Alaska's Matanuska Valley, carrying 1,320 adults and children and 4,000 tons of cargo. Most passengers, except for government workers, are farm families from drought-stricken Midwest. Colonists are being relocated as part of government experiment to see if they can make a go of it as homesteaders in the fertile valley near Seward.

Beer Bottles to White House," "Zioncheck Charges Vice President With Kidnapping His Wife."

Born Mantoni Zajaczek, Zioncheck was brought to this country as a small boy and reared on Seattle's tough First Avenue. He sold newspapers in the streets, worked as a logger and sailed on ships to Alaska. After becoming a citizen, he changed his name to something more pronounceable.

Zioncheck was well into his 20s when he earned enough to enter the UW Law School. There, he attacked the fraternity system and student-fund spending. He ran for student-body president as the "poor boy's" candidate, won and was given a dunking in Frosh Pond by those who opposed him.

Once established in private law practice, Zioncheck championed unpopular causes and was a leader in the recall of Mayor Frank Edwards, who, besides appointing his cronies to commissions, committed the unpardonable sin of ousting popular J.D. Ross, superintendent of power and light and father of the city's Skagit hydroelectric project.

At age 31, Zioncheck won the Democratic nomination to Congress, campaigning for massive appropriations for federal works and the five-day workweek. He was swept into office in the Roosevelt landslide of '32.

Bachelor Zioncheck took his mother to Washington, D.C., delivering what was described as a "brilliant, anguished appeal for the working man" in his maiden speech. He set himself the impossible task of analyzing every piece of legislation introduced, word by word.

Re-elected in 1934, Zioncheck returned to the nation's capital without his mother. Speaking out almost daily against "bloated capitalists" and "vested interests," he began to show signs of cracking up. But Rubye Nix, a 21-year-old stenographer, found the antics appealing and telephoned him. They arranged a date and were married the next day. The crack-up continued.

"Zioncheck on Spree in Virgin Islands," "Zioncheck Escapes From Mental Institution."

The cause of Zioncheck's bizarre behavior was never made clear at the time. A latter-day press almost certainly would have consulted experts for a clinical analysis of the apparent breakdown. But that was deemed "private" in those days.

Publicly ridiculed, emotionally and physically drained, Zioncheck returned home to visit his sick mother and to campaign for re-election in '36. He first announced he wouldn't run, then changed his mind.

The end was sudden. Zioncheck drove down to his election headquarters in the Arctic Building with his wife and brother-in-law, William Nadeau. He told them he was going upstairs for a

OLYMPIC GAMES MEDAL WINNERS

⚬⚬⚬ The following medalists were either Washington residents of students at the time they made history. The list includes the place where the Games were held.

1904 (St. Louis)
Charles "Pop" Dvorak, pole vault, 1 gold

1928 (Amsterdam)
Steve Anderson, hurdles, 1 silver
Herman Brix, shotput, 1 silver*

1932 (Los Angeles)
Helene Madison, swimming, 3 gold**

1936 (Berlin)
Jack Medica, swimming, 1 gold, 2 silver
Don Hume, Jim McMillin, John White, Gordon Adam George "Shorty" Hunt, Joe Rantz, Roger Morris, Charles Day, Bob Moch, 8-oared crew, 1 gold

1948 (St. Moritz, winter; London, summer)
Gretchen Fraser, skiing, 1 gold, 1 silver
Warren Westlund, Robert Martin, Robert Will, Gordon Giovanelli, Allen Morgan, 4-oared crew with coxswain, 1 gold

1952 (Oslo, winter; Helsinki, summer)
Karol and Peter Kennedy, pairs ice skating, 1 silver
Carl Lovested Alvin Ulbrickson, Richard Wahlstrom, Fil Leanderson, Albert Rossi, 4-oared crew with coxswain, 1 bronze

1956 (Melbourne)
Peter Rademacher, boxing, 1 gold
A. "Dan" Ayrault, Conn Findlay, Kurt Seiffert, pairs with coxswain, 1 gold
Jim Fifer, pairs without coxswain, 1 gold
Richard Wailes, 8-oared crew, 1 gold

1960 (Rome)
Ted Nash, John Sayre, A. "Dan" Ayrault, Richard Wailes, 4-oared crew without coxswain, 1 gold
Richard Draeger, Conn Findlay, Kent Mitchell, pairs with coxswain, 1 bronze
Quincey Daniels, boxing, 1 bronze

1964 (Tokyo)
Edward Ferry, Conn Findlay, Kent Mitchell, pairs with coxswain, gold
Ted Nash, 4-oared crew without coxswain, 1 bronze

1968 (Mexico City)
Kaye Hall, swimming, 2 gold, 1 bronze
Charles Greene, sprints, 1 gold, 1 bronze

Jack Horsley, swimming, 1 bronze

1972 (Sapporo, winter; Munich, summer)
Susan Corrock, skiing, 1 bronze
Sugar Ray Seales, boxing, 1 gold
Lynn Colella, swimming, 1 silver
John Parker, water polo, 1 bronze

1976 (Montreal)
Leo Randolph, boxing, 1 gold
Rick Colella, swimming, 1 bronze
Conn Findlay, sailing, 1 bronze***
Carol Brown, 8-oared women's crew, 1 bronze

1980 (Lake Placid)
Phil Mahre, skiing, 1 silver

1984 (Sarajevo, winter; Los Angeles, summer)
Debbie Armstrong, skiing, 1 gold
Phil Mahre, skiing, 1 gold
Rosalynn Sumners, ice skating, 1 silver
Steve Mahre, skiing, 1 silver
Tracie Ruiz, synchronized swimming, 2 gold
Candy Costie, synchronized swimming, 1 gold
Mary Wayte, swimming, 1 gold
Matt Dryke, skeetshooting, 1 gold
Bill Buchan, Steve Erickson, sailing, 1 gold
Carl Buchan, Jonathan McKee, sailing, 1 gold
Paul Enquist, rowing pairs, 1 gold
Shyril O'Steen, Betsy Beard, Kristi Norelius, women's 8-oared rowing, 1 gold
Rebecca Twigg, cycling, 1 silver
Doug Burke, water polo, 1 silver
John Stillings and Ed Ives, 4-oared crew with coxswain, 1 silver
Alan Forney, 4-oared crew without coxswain, 1 silver
Charlie Clapp, John Terwilliger, 8-oared crew, 1 silver
Sterling Hinds, track, 1 bronze****
Doug Herland, pairs with coxswain, 1 bronze

1988 (Seoul)
Mary Wayte, swimming, 1 silver, 1 bronze
Tracie Ruiz-Conforto, synchronized swimming, 1 silver
Charlie McKee, yachting, 1 bronze

*Brix was one of four Olympic medalists to play Tarzan in the movies; screen name, Bruce Bennett.
**Madison won the most gold medals – 3 – of any Washingtonian.
***Findlay won the most medals – 3 in crew, 1 in sailing 20 years after he won his first medal.
****Hinds, who attended the UW, ran for Canada.

minute. When considerable time had elapsed, Nadeau went up.

He found Zioncheck seated at his desk writing and asked him to hurry up. Zioncheck put on his coat as if to leave, then suddenly whirled and rushed to the open window and leaped out. His body landed in front of the car in which his wife was waiting.

The note on the desk contained these words: "It was my only purpose in life to improve an unfair economic system which held no promise . . . or even a decent chance to survive, let alone live."

UW keeps its oar in

The 1936 Olympic Games were memorable for the remarkable running and jumping of Jesse Owens and the demagoguery of Adolf Hitler.

But Washington state had plenty to cheer about.

Jack Medica of Seattle, a broad-shouldered All-American swimmer for the University of Washington, was the only American to win a gold medal in swimming, setting a new Olympic record in the 400-meter competition. He also won silver medals in the 1,500-meter freestyle and the 4x200-meter freestyle relay. Medica was the collegiate champion at 220 yards, 440 yards and 1,500 meters. He died in 1985 at age 71.

Starting in the poorest (outside) lane and bucking a strong head wind on the River Dahme, the UW captured the Olympic gold for eight-oared crews, flashing across the finish line a quarter of a length ahead of Italy.

In the 2,000-meter race, Washington — U.S. champion by virtue of victories in the intercollegiate regatta at Poughkeepsie, N.Y., and the Olympic trials at Princeton, N.J. — was in third place at 1,500 meters. The shell named Husky Clipper forged ahead of Italy with 250 meters to go, and appeared to be an easy winner. But Italy put on a spurt that almost caught Washington at the end.

In the post-race victory ceremony, a laurel wreath was draped around coxswain Bob Moch. The gold-medal crew was stroked (first oar) by Don Hume, who was suffering from a severe cold. Other oarsmen: Joe Rantz, George "Shorty" Hunt, James McMillin, John White, Gordon Adam, Roger Morris and Charles Day.

The Huskies almost didn't make it to Berlin. Because the U.S. Olympic Committee was strapped for money, the crew was told it would have to raise $5,000 to pay its own way or be replaced by the country's second-best crew.

The Seattle Times led a fund-raising drive, and money quickly was pledged to send the crew, four substitutes, coach Al Ulbrickson and master shell-builder George Pocock.

A tragedy in Tacoma

Two nights after Christmas 1936, Dr. and Mrs. William Mattson were visiting friends in Tacoma. Alone in the house on the rainy night, drinking root beer and eating popcorn, were their sons, Charles, 10, and Bill, 16; their daughter, Muriel, 14; and Muriel's chum, Virginia Chatfield, 15, of Seattle.

On the spacious lawn outside the residential showplace in the Old Tacoma district were three lighted Christmas trees. Inside was another tree. "Merry Christmas," in big letters, hung from a cord.

Just after 9 p.m., Charles took some glasses to the kitchen. He ran back excitedly to say there was a man with a gun at the window and he was going upstairs to get his BB gun. Laughter.

But the laughter stopped when a man with a white-rag mask over the lower part of his face appeared at two leaded-glass doors, brandishing a weapon. He demanded to be let in, then smashed a door and entered.

Described later as "swarthy," wearing a cap and speaking in a "gruff foreign accent," the man first frisked Bill for money. Then he grabbed young Charles under his arm, saying he had helped pay for the house and was going to get something back.

The kidnapper threw a dirty, much-folded note onto the floor, then took a zigzag path down into the woods behind the house toward Commencement Bay.

Fifteen days later, Gordon Morrow, 19, was chasing a rabbit in the snow near his home south of Everett. He found Charles' unclad, beaten body. The boy had been dead about five days.

The nation reacted with anger, shock and fear. President

Artist's sketch of the never-found kidnapper and killer of Charles Mattson.

Roosevelt expressed his sorrow. A $10,000 reward was offered.

The ransom note, lettered with a child's printing and signed "Tim," had asked $28,000 — a modest sum compared with the $200,000 asked for and paid in the kidnapping of another Tacoma boy, George Weyerhaeuser, just 19 months earlier.

Efforts to contact the kidnapper through "Mabel and Ann" classified ads in The Seattle Times had been fruitless. There were only two solid clues. The mask had slipped for a moment, and the children clearly saw the kidnapper's unshaven face. There was a crudely penciled "Y" as a correction on the ransom note.

Dr. Mattson was not a wealthy man. He had, in fact, lost most of his money in the Great Depression and his home was heavily mortgaged. It was never quite clear why Charles had been selected as the victim. The Mattson family felt the note, obviously old, originally had been intended for someone else.

Despite hundreds of tips, numerous arrests and the assistance of FBI agents, the kidnapper-killer was never found.

The peninsular campaigns

Olympic National Park, the "last wilderness" to some, is a remarkable piece of real estate that includes snow-capped mountains, virgin timber and 6,000 elk and is framed by the Pacific Ocean, Hood Canal and the Strait of Juan de Fuca.

The park that Franklin D. Roosevelt signed into law June 29, 1938, contained 634,000 acres. Equally important, a proviso tacked onto the bill by 1st District Rep. Mon Wallgren permitted the president, by proclamation, to increase the park's size by up to 398,292 acres.

When President Grover Cleveland created Olympic National Forest in 1897, it embraced about half the Olympic Peninsula. President Theodore Roosevelt set aside about 600,000 acres of Olympic National Forest in 1909 and called it "Mount Olympus National Monument."

The centerpiece of the monument was Mount Olympus, 8,982 feet of rock and glacier. But one of the major reasons for establishing the monument was to preserve the *cervus canadensis occidentalis*, better known as the Roosevelt (for Teddy) elk.

Under President Woodrow Wilson, several hundred thousand acres were hacked from the south and west edges of the monument in 1915. The Forest Service managed the monument until 1933, when FDR transferred jurisdiction to the National Park Service. Four years later, he motored around the perimeter of the would-be park, spending a night at Lake Crescent.

Roosevelt was enthusiastic. But the park's biggest booster, along with Wallgren, was Secretary of the Interior Harold Ickes, the acid-tongued curmudgeon of FDR's Cabinet.

Wallgren's proviso to permit presidents to add acreage proved a boon to park lovers. Roosevelt added considerably to the park's size before he died. And in 1953, President Harry Truman added the real prize — a 50-mile ocean strip and the Queets Corridor.

There never was much question that the peninsula was worthy of a national park. The battle from the outset was over its size, with large-park and small-park proponents debating vigorously.

Wallgren, 1st District Rep. Marion Zioncheck and environmentalists of the day were pitted against timber interests, congressmen whose districts depended on logging and a cautious Gov. Clarence D. Martin, who didn't want to commit political suicide.

Long after the park was established, there were continued efforts to nibble away at its fringes to open up more timber for harvest. After leaving the Cabinet, Ickes delivered a memorable indictment of those who continued to push for a smaller park:

"The tree-butchers . . . are again on the march against some of the few remaining stands of America's glorious virgin timber. . . . The gluttons will pass their plates again and again for generous helpings until the despoilers will have sated their greedy appetites on what has, so far, been miraculously saved."

It isn't easy to guess right on the size of national parks. Among those who assailed Wallgren for wanting such a large national park was Asahel Curtis, the famed photographer-conservationist.

Said Curtis, in a speech to the Seattle Bar Association:

"How are you going to get 500,000 tourists into the park in one year as Wallgren claims? Why, how are you going to get even 50,000 tourists a year into that park?"

These days, the park annually draws more than 2 million visitors.

Looking homeward for the last time

On Sept. 6, 1938, a small band of college students gathered in Seattle's downtown Spring Apartment Hotel to pay their respects to a dying giant of American letters.

Thomas Wolfe slowly was pushed through the lobby in a wheelchair, smiling wanly, trying to sign autographs. He was an

A mid-1930s panorama of Seattle's main Hooverville — at nine acres one of the largest in the country — in the area south of where the Kingdome now stands. View is northward.

CHRONO-LOG

1935
Robert Shields of Dayton, Columbia County, begins keeping diary that will give him legitimate claim to title "world's most prolific diarist." Retired schoolteacher and minister writes 4,000 words a day. Gives $100,000 endowment to Washington State University to preserve diaries when he dies.

Will Rogers and Wiley Post take off from Renton Airport Aug. 7, are killed in plane crash more than week later near Barrow, Alaska.

1937
Legislature passes 1,228 pages of statutes, a record. Body is overwhelmingly Democratic — 93 Democrats and six Republicans in House, 41 Democrats and five Republicans in Senate.

1939
John Grant Kelly, publisher of Walla Walla Union Bulletin and also operator of seven Walla Walla Canning Co. outlets, turns out 2,650,000 cases of canned green peas — one sixth of nation's production. Kelly caps depression-era good news by getting Continental Can to establish factory in Walla Walla with sizable payroll.

enormous man (6 feet 5½ inches, 240 pounds), bushy-haired, with a tendency to stutter boyishly when excited.

Eleven days later, Wolfe was dead after brain surgery at a Baltimore hospital. A sprawling chapter in American literature was closed, leaving critics, biographers and readers to assess some of the most compassionate and undisciplined prose ever to pour from the pen of man.

Wolfe's final Seattle days marked the transition of a man with full creative powers to one losing his grip on reality. Alternately lamb and toothless lion, the author was a tragicomic figure. It was as if all his gargantuan appetites, consuming energies, charming egotism and childlike fears had been put under a magnifying glass.

If the death of Wolfe's father in the author's "Look Homeward, Angel" was a monumental separation of man from life, the impending death of his son was no less.

On May 30, Wolfe invited his friends, the James Stevenses (Jim Stevens wrote "Paul Bunyan" stories), to watch a Decoration (Memorial) Day parade from his window in the New Washington Hotel.

Flushed and excited, Wolfe told his guests he had stayed up all night to write and had finished 10,000 words in longhand. It was an awesome output, even for Wolfe. He had never learned to type and wondered where he could have it typed.

Wolfe went on an auto trip through 13 Western states, returning to Seattle in late June. On July 2, he spent the night in a lodge at Mount Rainier, where he scrawled his impressions of the mountain: "the pity, terror, strangeness and magnificence of it all."

They were the last words he wrote, an unintended epitaph to his last desperate days here.

On the Fourth of July, Wolfe took the steamship Princess Kathleen to Vancouver. He caught cold on the windy deck, and returned to the hotel very ill. A few days later, he was examined for possible pneumonia. X-rays indicated tuberculosis was more likely.

Wolfe — who had spit blood from suspected tuberculosis years earlier — was furious and terrorized. He told Stevens, "I don't want to die out here."

Theresa Stevens began charting Wolfe's progress in a daily journal, which later was used liberally by Wolfe's biographers.

Wolfe was admitted to Firlawn Sanitarium, near Kenmore. His family bombarded him with letters and

Thomas Wolfe, in the heyday of his career in the mid-'30s.

telegrams. Maxwell Perkins, his old Charles Scribner's Sons publishing-house friend who had edited many of Wolfe's manuscripts and then had broken with the author, wrote to say their differences were settled and they were friends again. Wolfe was delighted. His brother arrived from the family home in North Carolina. This agitated Wolfe.

Wolfe finally was moved to Providence Hospital. His sister and an old family friend arrived. Wolfe, suffering splitting headaches, began drifting from lucidity to fantasy to torpor.

At his family's request, Wolfe was removed to the Spring Apartment Hotel, which provided a view of Puget Sound and the Olympic Mountains. The headaches continued. Diagnosis: brain tumor or abscess.

Thus it was that on Sept. 6, Wolfe was wheeled out of the lobby and taken to the depot for a train ride to Baltimore. Surgery at Johns Hopkins Hospital there showed massive tuberculosis of the brain. Death came just 18 days before Wolfe's 38th birthday.

Days in the lives of Hoovervillians

In the '30s, a single man in Seattle could buy an abode of sorts for what he now pays for dinner at a fast-food restaurant — if he didn't mind a Hooverville address.

The $5 house was a packing crate, scrap lumber and a roof made of pieces of metal whose joints were caulked with tar scraped from city streets. A little garden out back, a supply of firewood and some decorator touches could boost the price to $30.

Seattle's main Hooverville, one of the largest in the country, was nine acres of shacks on the Charles Street waterfront. At its peak, it had 1,200 male residents, an unelected mayor, a city council and a police chief named Reuben Washington.

Hooverville was the generic term for all shantytowns. Besides *the* Hooverville, there also were "Indian Town," on the Duwamish tideflats; "Hollywood," on Sixth Avenue South, just south of Lander; "Reno," north of Lander; and collections of shanties on Harbor Island and under the bridge to Magnolia Bluff.

The most infamous, because of its tough element, was at the site of the old Washington Iron Works, at Airport Way South and South Connecticut Street, right up against Beacon Hill.

Hoovervilles' legions arrived penniless from lumber camps, fishing fleets, farms and factories whose smokestacks had grown cold. They were not "welfare" cases. They scrounged their own building materials and assembled their own shacks. They made stoves out of oil drums and rigged up lanterns.

Some residents gathered scrap metal, bottles and rags, or bundled up old newspapers for sale. Many haunted Skid Road hiring halls in hopes of finding an occasional job.

Food was cooked in cans. Wholesale bakeries dropped off truckloads of stale bread and pastries. Wizened vegetables were available at produce houses. Often there was stew meat — from somewhere. When in doubt they called it slumgullion. And always there were chickens that seemed to stray outside their pens.

Some of the more enterprising men built makeshift skiffs and fished for salmon in Elliott Bay.

At night, Hooverville residents had a bed and blanket and maybe a pipeful of tobacco. Best of all, "Mayor" Jesse Jackson had a radio in his "executive mansion" and he hooked it to a loudspeaker. The voice of Leo Lassen, Seattle's "Mr. Baseball," rang out over shantytown.

Jackson was a busy man. He settled fights and called ambulances. He met with city officials and played host to visiting sociologists and professors studying how the other half lived.

Ernie Pyle, the newspaperman who became the foot soldier's Boswell during World War II, paid Seattle's Hooverville a visit. So did campaigning Mayor John Dore and City Council candidate Arthur B. Langlie.

Many decried the name "Hooverville," and Mayor Jackson said he personally had nothing against the ex-president. If he had his druthers, he said, he'd name the place after Calvin Coolidge, whom he blamed for the sorry state of the economy.

One survey revealed that the men who answered to such Hooverville handles as Butch, Slim, Shorty and Two-Name Dave Green included two lawyers, a medical doctor (rumored to be on the run from his bossy daughter), barbers, bricklayers, carpenters and a few bank clerks.

Twice the city had Hooverville burned to the ground as a health menace. It rose again. The men — no women allowed — had no place else to go. But by May 1941, the economy had picked up sufficiently for serious "pack-up-and-git" orders to be issued. A new dock was to be built on the site.

On a sunny morning, a bulldozer moved in and shanties began to fall. A huge bonfire was started. "Mayor" George Parish, who had succeeded Jackson two years earlier, calmly puffed his pipe as he watched his city go.

The crowd was small. On that day, everyone was too busy.

6. PAIN AND PATRIOTISM

WITH BOMBS AND BOMBERS, SWEAT AND TEARS,
STATE SHARED THE AGONY OF A WORLD AT WAR

1940 TO 1950

'I saw the Narrows Bridge die today, and only by the grace of God escaped dying with it.'

— Leonard Coatsworth, Tacoma News Tribune copy editor

Museum of History & Industry

Newly discharged troops wave goodbye to World War II as their plane leaves Paine Field for the East Coast in August 1945. Below, an Army corporal helps a Seattle housewife hang the wash while a barrage balloon in the background awaits deployment. The balloons were attached to the ground by cable, then sent aloft to entangle low-flying enemy aircraft.

World War II was the dominant event of the 1940s if not the 20th century, and Washington state was in the thick of it — from the drill fields and rifle ranges of Fort Lewis to the plutonium factory at Hanford, from the around-the-clock welding on warships at Bremerton to the incessant riveting at Boeing on the Duwamish.

War-industry workers and service personnel who flooded in from around the country took such a liking to the state's geography and climate that many put down permanent roots.

Maps were redrawn. Balances of power shifted. The Soviet Union became, briefly — figuratively and

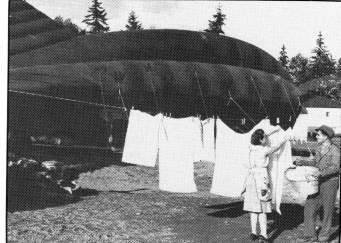

Seattle Times

Martin Moyer

Men and women line up in Seattle to view the 1946 "dream suite," a promise of the postwar boom in home and consumer goods.

CHRONO-LOG

literally — a comrade in arms.

Besides the deaths of young relatives or neighbors, marked by their mothers with a gold star in the window, we also mourned the passing of our most popular band leader, Glenn Miller, whose plane crashed over the English Channel, and the only four-time president in the nation's history, Franklin D. Roosevelt, with whom Seattleites felt a special kinship because his daughter Anna Boettiger lived on Magnolia Bluff.

There were war profiteers and black marketeers. But never before — or since — had the vast majority of Americans been so united.

Old and young shared the same music. "Don't Sit Under the Apple Tree," "The White Cliffs of Dover," "When The Lights Go On Again All Over the World," "A Nightingale Sang in Berkeley Square."

The Bonneville Power Administration, hoping to enhance its image, hired a young folk singer named Woody Guthrie in 1941 to turn out either 30 songs in 30 days or 26 songs in 26 days; the numbers are unclear. Guthrie was paid about $10 each for such songs as "The Grand Coulee Dam" (". . . Cast your eye upon the greatest thing yet built by human hands; on the King Columbia River, it's the big Grand Coulee Dam") and "Roll on Columbia" (". . . Your power is turning our darkness into dawn, so roll on, Columbia, roll on!"). The latter was widely used by Henry Wallace, the Progressive Party's candidate for president in 1948.

Gas rationing limited driving. Having guests for dinner meant weeks of saving blue and red ration points. Victory gardens blossomed behind homes.

Air-raid sirens shrilled during midday tests. Block wardens prowled to enforce blackouts and brownouts. Puget Sound was laced with submarine nets, and Seattle's hills sprouted enormous barrage balloons to foil low-flying enemy aircraft. Boeing was decked out in camouflage.

Once the panic of the war's earliest days subsided, few thought an enemy imminent. But Japan did unleash some balloons armed with incendiary and explosive devices and wafted them across the Pacific. On May 5, 1945, a picnicker tampered with a bomb that had landed near Lakeview, Ore. The resulting explosion claimed six lives, the only casualties from an enemy attack on the U.S. mainland during the war.

It was a time of improvisation.

Many women opted for 55-cent bottles of leg paint from Woolworth's rather than wear baggy rayon hose, imposed by wartime rationing to conserve precious nylon and silk for parachutes.

The Huskies fielded a makeshift team that wound up in the strangest of all Rose Bowls on New Year's Day 1944 — against a team from their own conference, the University of Southern California Trojans. They lost 29-0.

People took their fun when they could find it. "Swing shift" dances started at 1 a.m. in Seattle's tile-and-stucco

Trianon Dance Hall. For $1 a head, war-industry workers, service personnel and young women jitterbugged and fox-trotted far into the night. When couples wearied of dancing, they promenaded on the upstairs viewing balcony and defied the house bouncer by unscrewing light bulbs so they could "neck" in the dark.

But mostly, times were tense. A knock at the door might mean a dreaded telegram from the War Department, announcing still another death. Betraying wartime secrets or troop locations might result in casualties. GIs fretted about receiving "Dear John" letters notifying them that the girl back home had found someone else.

Workers and service personnel from other parts of the country were amused by the state's refusal to allow restaurants to serve liquor by the drink, and local restaurateurs said blue laws doomed the city to second-rate eateries. (That would change when liquor-by-the-drink was adopted in 1948).

Radios were tuned to Gabriel Heatter, H.V. Kaltenborn and The Richfield Reporter for the latest war news. Stories of Allied victories and setbacks dominated the pages of The Times, The Post-Intelligencer and the tabloid-sized Star, which would fold soon after the war ended.

Roosevelt came to Seattle twice during the war. His first visit — to The Boeing Co. in 1942 — was so secret that 30,000 copies of a union newspaper were confiscated because they contained the story. On Aug. 12, 1944, just eight months before his death, Roosevelt arrived in Bremerton to address Puget Sound Naval Shipyard workers and a nationwide radio audience. At the conclusion, he sat next to his chief of staff, Adm. William Leahy, and lit a cigarette in his famous holder. Nearby was his dog, Fala.

To end the war, there was The Bomb, which cast a great mushroom-shaped shadow over the future of the human race. And then there were the war-crimes trials at Nuremberg, where one of Washington's own — Judge William J. Wilkins — helped lay down a moral yardstick for future wars (the right and duty of citizens to defy their leadership when ordered to commit crimes against humanity).

GIs who scrawled "Kilroy was here" from North Africa to New Guinea returned with a fondness for Jeeps and Betty Grable's legs and a dislike of Spam, C-rations, K-rations, crewcuts and taking orders.

Wartime romances and hasty marriages, barely consummated during weekend passes, had to be worked out by couples who discovered they really were strangers.

The University of Washington, where wartime enrollment had been about 11,000 and females outnumbered males 3 to 1, faced an avalanche of mature young men and women attending school on the GI Bill, a federally funded investment in the nation's human resources that still is paying dividends.

Unemployment, which had stood at more than 8 million nationwide in 1940, had shrunk to 670,000 at war's end. Now it loomed again as war industries cut back. Organized labor chafed under wage controls, job freezes and no-strike pledges. (Boeing would be hit by a five-month walkout in 1948.) "Rosie the Riveter," no longer tied to the hearth, wanted the option of working.

The war had cost $350 billion and the debt was worrisome. In 1941, only 3 million Americans earned enough to pay income tax. By war's end, 50 million were paying income tax. And they had to continue paying or the country would be in trouble.

Seattle's population grew from 369,000 in 1940 to 468,000 at the end of the decade; King County's (outside Seattle) grew from 136,000 to 265,000; the state's from 1.7 million to 2.8 million. And the Baby Boom was just about to begin.

Housing was scarce for everybody. Because restrictive covenants and blatant discrimination were not yet illegal, minorities found it almost impossible to rent or buy in some areas. It would be three more years before President Harry Truman desegregated the armed forces and nine before the historic Supreme Court decision outlawing "separate but equal" education.

For those who had savings, a 70-foot-wide waterfront lot at Sheridan Beach cost $600, a three-bedroom Lake Ridge colonial cost $6,250 and a used '38 Buick in "mint condition" could be had for $450.

Wages weren't bad — for then. Boeing was still hiring workers to build B-29s at up to $2.50 an hour. Truck drivers earned about $52 for a 48-hour week. Secretaries who could do it all (type, take dictation, file, answer phones and run errands) earned $7 a day. State legislators were paid $5 a day for 60 days; their "offices" were cardboard files under their desks in the House and Senate.

Men bought double-breasted suits for $29.75 at Penney's, and a wide, flowered tie for $1.49. Fashionable women bought suits for $15 to $20 at I. Magnin. They could add a fancy handkerchief from the Bon Marché for 29 cents.

The United Nations was born of hope in a world weary of war. But the respite from conflict would be brief. Relations turned from cool to chilly between the United States and the Soviet Union, and the Cold War began. In just five years, many veterans of World War II were engaged in another war, in far-off Korea.

Washington state, which had switched from Republican to Democratic in national politics in 1932, went along with the majority of the nation in helping Truman pull off his stunning 1948 presidential victory over Thomas E. Dewey. The campaign was marked by one of Truman's famous "Give 'em hell, Harry" whistlestops in Spokane.

Asked by a young reporter how it felt to be invading Republican territory, Truman replied: "Young man, the Chicago Tribune and the Spokesman-Review are the two worst newspapers in the country." The Spokesman-Review responded editorially with good humor, saying it welcomed the president's visit but felt its honored position, along with the Chicago Tribune, was undeserved.

Although Truman won, his old friend and former West Coast amateur billiards champion, Monrad C. "Mon" Wallgren, a Democrat, failed to win re-election as Washington's governor. He lost to the man he had defeated in 1944, former Gov. Arthur B. Langlie. Langlie would go on to become the state's first three-time governor. Dan Evans, who came later, would serve three consecutive terms.

Meanwhile, young Patrice Munsel of Spokane was making a mark in the world of opera. Munsel, who had early ambitions to become an "artistic whistler" for Disney films, dropped out of Lewis and Clark High School at 15 to study voice in New York. At 17 she became the youngest performer ever signed by the Met. When she was 54, her old high school got around to giving her an honorary diploma.

A blind teen-ager who sang and played the piano came to Seattle in 1948 and formed McSon Trio, a black band that played in private clubs. One night a record-company owner heard him and signed him to record "Confession Blues" and "I Love You, I Love You." The young man who credited Seattle with giving him his start was Ray Charles.

A radio baritone of burnished copper

By 1940, the best-known and most influential American radio broadcaster was a suave, articulate man with a voice like burnished copper whose parents had left North Carolina for the Bellingham area when he was 5.

The young man went on to Washington State College, majoring in political science, speech and international relations, dabbling in dramatics and earning a Phi Beta Kappa key.

He had been born Egbert Roscoe Murrow. The world knew him as Edward R. Murrow.

Murrow worked in the woods of northwest Washington and was a globetrotter on behalf of international education before joining the Columbia Broadcasting System in 1935.

In the late '30s, Murrow began reporting on German troops goose-stepping into vulnerable European countries. When Britain became the focal point, he told an anxious nation of Neville Chamberlain's doomed efforts at the September 1938 Munich conference to get Adolf Hitler to promise he would seek no more conquests.

In 1940, Murrow began coming on the air nightly from the British capital ("This is London"), describing in his calm, assured voice the devastating raids by Hermann Goering's Luftwaffe.

Many bombs fell on CBS' London offices and on those of the British Broadcasting Co. In one broadcast, Murrow said: "I can tell you from personal experience that it's not pleasant to sit in a studio filled with the odor of iodine and antiseptics and talk to you at home while good friends are being carried on stretchers along the corridors outside the studio door."

Murrow wrote several books about his war experiences and later pioneered television documentaries with "See It Now" and celebrity interviews with "Person to Person."

The most celebrated "See It Now" (March 9, 1954) was a scathing, documented attack on Sen. Joseph McCarthy for the senator's bullying witch hunts against those he accused of being communists. When he was presented a Freedom House award for

Seattle Times
Boy and Girl Scouts are enlisted to rally the home troops during a war-bond drive at Victory Square in front of Seattle's old Metropolitan Theater on University Street.

STATE-MENTS

Barbs from the baton
Sir Thomas Beecham, short and stocky with his trademark Vandyke beard and acrobatic baton-waving, was the Peck's Bad Boy of music when the Seattle Symphony Orchestra board hired him in 1941 to come over from England and bring culture to the locals.

Beecham was renowned for introducing new operas, interpreting Mozart and making acid comments. It was the latter that grabbed headlines. Most British audiences, he contended, "are absolutely delightful first-rate jackasses, just as you (Americans) are; this is, of course, the glory of the democratic condition."

Beecham would stop in mid-concert to lecture knitters in the audience to stop clicking their needles, or to extemporize on the idiocy of music critics who presumed to pass judgment on the sounds he was extracting from a bunch of less-than-first-rate musicians. At a dinner meeting in the Washington Athletic Club, Beecham delivered a never-to-be-forgotten assessment of Seattle's cultural state.

"If I were a member of this community," he said, "really I should get weary of being looked upon as a sort of aesthetic dustbin." Taken in its entirety, it probably was not far from the truth. But it was shortened in the retelling and came out: "Did you hear what Beecham called us? A cultural dustbin! Who does he think he is?"

Beecham lasted two full seasons, withdrawing from Seattle's podium in November 1943 for reasons of "ill health." Whether he was ousted or resigned was never really clear.

CHRONO-LOG

Twenty thousand bags of sand — at least a million pounds in all — were used to build this machine-gun nest at what was cautiously described as "a strategic position near Seattle" in 1942.

1942
President Roosevelt orders evacuation in February of all ethnic Japanese from homes and farms on West Coast to prison camps across nation.

Military training bases proliferate to keep up with all-out war demands. Among them: Fairchild Air Force Base near Spokane, Paine Field near Everett and Whidbey Island Naval Air Station.

1943
Part of government's hush-hush Manhattan Project starts taking shape in Hanford, whose "secret city" population swells to 51,000 by year's end in massive endeavor to build plutonium-based atomic bomb.

B-29 Superfortress returning to Boeing Field crashes into Frye packing plant in South Seattle Feb. 18, killing 11 crewmen, one firefighter and 20 plant workers.

1944
Larson Air Force Base in Grant County is named in honor of Yakima-born Maj. Donald Larson, pilot who died earlier in year during bombing run over Germany.

the broadcast, Murrow said:
"There is a false formula for personal security being peddled in our marketplace. It is this, although not so labeled:
"'Don't join anything. Don't associate. Don't write. Don't take a chance on being wrong. Don't espouse unpopular causes. Button your lip and drift with the tide. Seek the ease and luxury of complete equanimity, by refusing to make up your minds about issues that wiser heads will one day decide.'
"This product, if it be bought by enough people, leads to paralysis."
Murrow left CBS in 1961 to become director of the United States Information Agency. The 70-cigarettes-a-day smoker who always ended his broadcasts with "Good night and good luck!" died of lung cancer in 1965.

Slow boat to Alaska

"Satko's Ark."
In the spring of 1940, those words elicited either a laugh or righteous indignation. Paul Satko of Tacoma had built a latter-day Noah's Ark in his backyard and, would you believe it, planned to sail the ark to Alaska with his wife and seven kids.
It was bad enough to try to sail a vessel everyone knew wouldn't stay afloat, critics said, but to jeopardize the lives of defenseless children was pure insanity.
Satko, a welder and pipefitter, was undeterred. He had piled his family in a car and driven out from Virginia two years earlier, hauling a 40-foot-long, welded-steel frame he called a boat. Almost everyone else thought it violated all laws of naval architecture.
Satko settled in Tacoma, got a welding job and invested all his spare time and money in the snub-nosed, high-decked vessel,

Seattle Times
Tacoma pipefitter Paul Satko, right, takes his family on a Puget Sound outing aboard "Satko's Ark" before the clan heads for its Alaskan odyssey in the spring of 1940.

which had a wheelhouse that resembled a chicken coop. The "ark" — Satko's own name for his creation — weighed 15 tons and was powered by a six-cylinder car engine.
So nobody would miss it, Satko slathered the ark with dandelion-yellow paint. A veteran seafaring man, after recovering from shock, termed it a combination "giant bathtub and Dutch clog."
Fascinated by the boat and filled with admiration for the close-knit family, Tacomans threw a dance to raise money for the Satkos' long voyage. An estimated 2,000 gathered at Point Defiance Park to cheer the Satkos when they left.
True to predictions, Satko ran aground off Seattle's Magnolia Bluff. The juvenile court stepped in, taking the younger children into custody. At a hearing, experts testified that Satko's boat was a joke and he didn't know anything about sailing. Undaunted, Satko and his wife sailed the ark to Anacortes. When the children were released from custody, they joined the family.
Figuring he'd be safe from interference by juvenile authorities if he could get outside the United States, Satko left an Anacortes dock under cover of darkness on May 26, 1940. He headed north.
The family was seasick almost constantly. But despite running aground several times and having an engine bearing burn out, the Satkos chugged into Ketchikan 41 days later. Two weeks after that, the ark arrived in Juneau.
Satko homesteaded a 122-acre farm 26 miles from Juneau, calling it "Journey's End." Snows were heavy, ground-clearing hard. Satko managed to grow some vegetables for sale.
In the fall of the family's first year in Alaska, another Satko was born. She was named North Sea Meridian Satko, in honor of the voyage the experts had said was impossible.
Satko gave up the farm and moved his family to Juneau in 1944. Two years later, the Satkos returned to Tacoma, where Satko died in 1957. Many of his descendants reside in the Puget Sound area.

'The durned thing really DOES float!'

On July 2, 1940, Kate Stevens Bates christened a bridge across Lake Washington that was such a radical departure from existing spans that not everyone was sure it would work.
The bridge against which Bates, daughter of Washington's first territorial governor, Isaac Stevens, swung a yellow urn containing water from 58 of the state's lakes and streams, consisted of connected concrete pontoons covered with a roadbed that stretched from Seattle's Mount Baker district to the north end of Mercer Island.
Moments after the ribbons were cut, Gov. Clarence D. Martin climbed into a chauffeured Lincoln convertible and was whisked across the $8.8 million bridge. At the Eastside toll station, his chauffeur paid 45 cents like any other motorist.
The Puget Sound area never would be the same.
Completion of the first floating bridge across Lake Washington marked the beginning of an enormous population growth east of the lake, launched this state's love affair with floating bridges and spelled an immediate end to most ferry travel on the lake. (The Kirkland-Madison Park run continued for a time.)
There are three major pontoon bridges in North America, and all are in Washington state — two across Lake Washington, one across Hood Canal.
The first, whose floating span is 6,561 feet long, officially was named the Lacey V. Murrow Bridge, to honor the state director of highways at the time of its construction. Murrow was the brother of Edward R. Murrow, the broadcaster.
Most people call it the Mercer Island bridge, the Lake Washington bridge, the I-90 bridge, or simply "the floating bridge," to distinguish it from the world's longest floating span (7,578 feet), the Evergreen Point Bridge, completed in 1963 and renamed the Gov. Albert D. Rosellini Evergreen Point Bridge in 1988. The William A. Bugge Hood Canal floating bridge (7,131 feet) was opened in 1961.
Thousands attended opening-day ceremonies for the Mercer Island bridge, purchasing popcorn from wagon vendors and then walking, riding bicycles and driving cars across the span.
Several days before the opening, Clarance B. Blethen, publisher of The Seattle Times and an outspoken critic of the bridge's design, location and possible maintenance costs, drove its length with Murrow and designer Charles Andrew, who also had worked on the Golden Gate Bridge.
Blethen detected no swaying on the span and found the view to be spectacular. With a gracious bow to progress, he wrote a front-page editorial that led off with "... I eat crow" and concluded, "P.S. What sinks me is, the durned thing really DOES float!"

'Gertie' gallops to oblivion

The world listened with disbelief as the news flashed out of Tacoma shortly after 11 o'clock on the morning of Nov. 7, 1940.

The Tacoma Narrows Bridge, then the third-longest suspension bridge in North America, had shaken itself apart in a 42-mile-an-hour wind. The 2,800-foot center span had fallen 190 feet into the swirling waters of the Tacoma Narrows. Approaches hung limply, like wet noodles. Towers tilted comically.

"Galloping Gertie," the nickname hung on the span by motorists who had braved its noticeable undulations in the mildest breeze, had galloped into the pages of history just four months after being opened to traffic.

There was only one fatality, a black spaniel that went down with the car of Leonard Coatsworth, a soft-spoken, scholarly copy editor for The Tacoma News Tribune.

Coatsworth, the last person to attempt a crossing, was cut and bruised when he abandoned his car and crawled to safety. Shortly after the ordeal, he sat at a typewriter and wrote a first-person account that began:

"I saw the Narrows Bridge die today, and only by the grace of God escaped dying with it."

The bridge had collapsed even as engineers at the University of Washington worked on possible cures for the peculiar longitudinal roll that afflicted the span whenever the wind kicked up. Among the suggestions: stabilizing cables, curved wind deflectors on the bridge's sides and holes drilled in the side girders to permit the wind to pass through more easily.

The palliatives became academic when Gertie collapsed.

Pierce County residents for years had dreamed of a bridge to replace the ferryboats that ran across the turbulent Narrows. There was one place, less than a mile across, that seemed ideal for a span from Tacoma to the Kitsap Peninsula on the west.

In 1938, the Washington Toll Bridge Authority obtained $6.4 million in bridge-building loans from the federal Public Works Administration and the Reconstruction Finance Corp. Leon Moisseiff, a New Yorker with excellent credentials, was chosen to design the span.

From the moment the bridge opened, motorists detected a pronounced lurch and roll. Some thought it was a lark. Others worried that it might collapse. Experts said there was nothing to fear.

Winds were a little too brisk for kite-flying the morning of Nov. 7. But the "big kite" across the Narrows couldn't be reeled in.

By 10 a.m., the bridge was rolling so hard that toll takers decided to halt traffic. The last motorist to pass the toll gate was Coatsworth, whose car was piled high with furniture from his summer place on the peninsula. His daughter's dog was in the back seat.

Halfway across the span, the swaying became so violent that Coatsworth's vehicle slammed against the curbing. The bridge seemed to tilt at about a 45-degree angle. Coatsworth leaped from the car, heart pounding, hoping the dog would follow. It didn't, and he began a spine-tingling scamper to safety.

Also on the bridge, just ahead of Coatsworth, was a 25-year-old University of Puget Sound student who, in search of a cheap thrill, had paid a 10-cent toll to walk across the bridge in a high wind.

The younger man made it to safety first. Coatsworth repeatedly was thrown to the pavement as the bridge undulated beneath him. His knees were bleeding. His arms, legs and back were bruised. More than once, he said later, he thought he could not continue.

But continue he did, heartsick about the dog in the car. Behind him, the car slid from side to side, slamming into the curbs.

At about 11 a.m. — a few minutes after Coatsworth reached safety — the bridge began to twist as if it were a toy. Suddenly, a portion of the center span dropped out. When it hit the water, it sent up a geyser almost as high as the bridge's main towers.

Suspension cables attached to the main support cables began to snap like suspenders. There was a loud report as each gave way. Relieved of their tremendous weight, they jerked crazily, like nerve endings. The noise grew louder as metal twisted and chunks of concrete popped into the air like popcorn and plunged into the water.

Then, while onlookers gasped, the remaining portion of the center span broke loose. Coatsworth's automobile slowly turned, end over end, and landed in the water. At almost the same moment, several thousand feet of concrete, steel plates and girders exploded in the Narrows, sending up water from the granddaddy of all bellyflops.

Gertie was dead.

The post-mortems began. There were anguish, wounded professional pride, even macabre humor. Within a few hours, a Tacoma financial institution removed from the Sixth Avenue approach to the bridge a sign that read: "As secure as the Narrows Bridge."

Although the bridge had been insured by 22 different firms to

Seattle Times

The Tacoma Narrows Bridge earns its nickname "Galloping Gertie" in this final and fatal moment of spectacular gyration in steel and cable on Nov. 7, 1940. Bracketed between the second set of lampposts from the right, Leonard Coatsworth's ill-fated car can be seen.

spread the risk, one New York company was stunned to learn it had an $800,000 piece of the action. An agent had written the policy without informing his main office, so certain was he that nothing could happen to the bridge. Another insurance firm had canceled its policy at 9:30 a.m.

Historians discovered that 11 large suspension bridges, including Gertie, had fallen between 1818 and 1940.

Insurance firms paid $4 million. The state also earned some money by selling salvage from the bridge. Engineers returned to drawing board and laboratory, and Tacomans went back to riding ferryboats across the Narrows.

A new bridge model was built at the UW under the direction of Professor F. Burt Farquharson, who had been conducting wind-tunnel tests on a model of the old bridge just before it collapsed. Instead of going to New York for a designer, the state decided to stay in-house, choosing state bridge engineer Charles Andrew, who had a long string of successes to his credit.

Andrew said the new bridge should be much wider (four lanes instead of two), open on the sides, have a roadbed that was open rather than solid, and have considerably more arch in the middle.

The new Tacoma Narrows Bridge was opened to the public in that form Oct. 14, 1950. It was an immediate financial success, and capable of riding the stiffest winds as if they were zephyrs.

It is the fifth-longest suspension span in North America.

History leaves its mark on Hanford

 "Spring can come early to the sand, sage and riverbanks of Hanford. By the end of March, even though trees are still bare, the air often feels soft and the song of the meadowlark makes you stop to listen.

"The air felt that way and the meadowlarks were singing at Hanford in late March just 45 years ago. But the serenity and the usual feeling of spring's rejuvenation inside the big bend of the Columbia River had been shattered. History had arrived at

CHRONO-LOG

Rationing was a fact of life during World War II. As of 1942, stickers like these were required on all vehicles. By March 1944, the basic family-car "A" sticker ration had been cut to two gallons of gasoline a week. The bearer of a "C" card was eligible for much more but had to be a doctor, war-production worker, embalmer, farmer or someone else deemed vital to the Allied effort. Also rationed or controlled were tires, sugar, coffee, meat, canned goods, bicycles, fuel oil, clothing, shoes, typewriters and fats.

Hanford."

Those words were written in 1988 by Times science writer Hill Williams, who grew up in Pasco, 10 miles down the Columbia from Richland. Williams' father, Hill Williams Sr., was editor of the weekly Pasco Herald.

What began that spring of 1943 was the biggest story of the elder Williams' life — and he couldn't write a word of it.

Government men in three-piece suits had arrived in Hanford with briefcases and said they wanted the residents to give up their homes and farms for a project of utmost importance to the nation. Further, they wanted the people to go away quietly and not talk about it.

The plan, they said, was to bring in tens of thousands of people, erect an instant industrial complex from Hanford to nearby White Bluffs, and begin work on the hush-hush project.

Within a few months, Hanford's construction camp had swelled to 51,000 — making it the state's fourth-largest city. Yet, with wartime travel sharply restricted, almost nobody outside the area had the slightest idea it was there.

Security was ultra-tight. Writing about it 45 years later, the younger Williams said the project's chief photographer sometimes would take a picture, develop and print it and deliver it to the requesting agency. The next day, the photographer would be told he needed a special permit to see the photo.

Paydays were wild. A bank set up at Hanford had 23 windows just for cashing Friday paychecks. "Money," a former bank teller told Williams, "was just like baled hay."

Reactors to transform uranium into plutonium for the Manhattan (atomic bomb) Project were completed in just 15 months. The first weapons-grade material — uranium 235 from Oak Ridge, Tenn., and plutonium from Hanford — was delivered to assembly specialists in Los Alamos, N.M., early in 1945. The first test bomb was exploded July 16 of that year near Alamogordo, N.M.

Germany had surrendered a few months earlier, and some project scientists had had second thoughts about proceeding. The Japanese, they reasoned, hadn't been in the atomic-bomb race, so why use it against them?

President Harry Truman sided with those who wanted to end the war quickly and save American lives.

On Aug. 6, 1945, the world learned about the nation's most closely guarded secret when a B-29 Superfortress, christened the Enola Gay and piloted by Lt. Col. Paul Tibbets Jr., dropped the uranium-fission bomb — nicknamed Little Boy — on Hiroshima.

The bomb destroyed 4.7 square miles of the city's most intensively developed area and killed 92,000 people. Others died later as a result of injuries and radiation.

When Japan's warlords hesitated about surrendering, the plutonium bomb — nicknamed Fat Man — was dropped three days later on the Kyushu island city of Nagasaki (40,000 casualties).

All that remained were surrender formalities in September aboard the USS Missouri, which later was brought to Bremerton and opened to the public.

As soon as the first bomb was dropped, The Seattle Times dispatched executive editor Ross Cunningham and reporter Don Magnuson (who was later to become a congressman) to write about the top-secret city in Eastern Washington's sagebrush.

Cunningham and Magnuson quoted workers as saying they knew they were doing something to win the war, but had no idea what they were working on.

Forty-five years after springing to life in the desert at the dawn of the nuclear age, Hanford was notified that its primary nuclear plant was to be closed.

In January 1944, grim-faced Office of Price Administration investigators arrive to inspect gasoline ration books and "ferret out cheats and black marketeers" in the Seattle area.

Seattle Times

When titans walked the state

Washington state could claim two men of uncommon intellect on the national scene in the 1940s: Homer T. Bone of Tacoma, who resigned from the U.S. Senate in 1944 to become a judge of the U.S. Court of Appeals, and William O. Douglas, who moved to Yakima County from Minnesota at age 6 and was named to the U.S. Supreme Court by Franklin Roosevelt in 1939.

Physically, they were as different as two men could be. Bone, whom Time magazine referred to as the Senate's "mightiest atom," stood a bare 5 feet 6 and weighed 135 pounds, and his body was twisted by the ravages of arthritis. Douglas overcame childhood polio to grow into a rugged 6-footer noted for his outdoor adventures, world travels and marriages to women half his age.

Bone — creator of the National Cancer Institute and father of the Bone Power Act that put public utility districts in business — was for many years the acknowledged speed-talking champion of the Senate as he attacked such favorite targets as private power and the "big-dough boys" who profited from armaments. His extemporaneous speeches were legendary.

During an angry floor debate, Bone said of Missouri's Sen. Bennett Clark: "My remarks probably creep into his drab life like a gleam of supernal sunshine. I merely want to elevate him to higher planes of thought."

He put down another adversary with: "He walks around with a load of dignity that would spring the knee joints of an archangel."

Although he campaigned unsuccessfully for various offices under the banner of Socialist, Farmer-Labor and Republican parties, Bone was loyal to the Democrats once elected under their label. He once described the GOP as the party of "Grand Old Promises" and said, "God couldn't be everywhere and He made up the Republican Party to be where He didn't want to be."

When he voted in 1941 for lend-lease aid to Britain, he said, "Gentlemen, let's not call it a loan; let's call it a present. Is there anybody in Washington who believes Great Britain will ever pay us back?"

Early in his career, Bone braved charges of "Bolshevism" to advocate old-age pensions, unemployment insurance and a shorter work week. With remarkable foresight, he warned in 1936 against "undercover government men . . . engaged in a low form of spying and general all-around espionage . . . a most odious form of repression and coercion."

In his long fight for Grand Coulee Dam and against private power, Bone told a National Grange convention: "There is nothing lower on earth than a private power company. . . In my hometown of Tacoma, we pay only one-half cent per kilowatt hour. When you go home, you Eastern delegates, ask your private power companies what they charge you."

Bone delayed leaving the Senate for his judicial post for many months, thwarting Gov. Arthur Langlie's plan to name a Republican successor. Langlie finally agreed to appoint Sen.-elect Warren G. Magnuson 2½ weeks before he was to take office, thus giving Magnuson a small but invaluable seniority edge over a fellow Democrat, Sen. J. William Fulbright of Arkansas.

Douglas was 40 when he surrendered chairmanship of the Securities and Exchange Commission to succeed Louis D. Brandeis on the Supreme Court. He would remain on the bench longer (36 years) than any other justice, write 17 books, marry four times and be considered by both Roosevelt and Truman as a likely presidential running mate.

Douglas used to chuckle and tell how he vanished in the Cascade wilderness in 1948 after Truman got the Democratic nomination, sure that Truman couldn't win and not wanting to be available if Truman telephoned to offer him the No. 2 spot on the ticket.

Douglas made some of his more controversial pronouncements while visiting in the Pacific Northwest. In 1951, while in Seattle, he advocated recognition of the 2-year-old Communist Chinese government, saying, "Unless we are successful in splitting China from Russia, all Southeast Asia will go into the Russian orbit."

In the summer of 1962, Douglas joined the family of Attorney General Robert Kennedy on a camping trip deep in the wilderness of the Olympic Mountains. While Ethel Kennedy, the Kennedy children and family friends rode horses for 16 miles, the determined 63-year-old jurist and the equally determined young attorney general hiked the trail as if they were trying to win a marathon.

Newspapermen stationed 11 miles up the trail saw the two literally running toward their eventual camp at Whiskey Bend. No, they said without breaking stride, they had not stopped to rest. No, they added, they did not intend to stop for any reason until they had finished the entire 16 miles — mostly uphill.

In 1964, the 65-year-old Douglas and his third wife, Joan, 41 years his junior, led a highly publicized hike along the wilderness

Aircraft workers by the thousands gather at camouflaged Boeing Plant 2 in Seattle in April 1945 for ceremonies marking the changeover in bomber production from the B-17, right, to the Superfortress B-29, at left. B-29s carried the first atomic bombs.

Seattle Times

STATE-MENTS

Long, slow rights fight
Gordon Hirabayashi was a 23-year-old University of Washington student when the government imposed a curfew on all ethnic Japanese and began ordering them to internment camps. Hirabayashi refused and was convicted of violating federal orders. The U.S. Supreme Court affirmed his conviction, and he spent five months in jail and three months in a prison camp.

Hirabayashi, who became a professor of sociology at the University of Alberta in Edmonton, Canada, never quit fighting — asking that the courts clear his name and admit that his constitutional rights had been violated. In 1987, 45 years after Hirabayashi's arrest, the 9th Circuit Court of Appeals in San Francisco ruled unanimously that he had been wrongly convicted.

Hirabayashi, then 69, said: "This was a people's case. I was just a cog in the effort to show people that our system and our Constitution work, but we must fight for it."

Postscript: In 1988 — 46 years after the internment began — Congress passed, and President Reagan signed, a bill to provide $20,000 to every Japanese-American whose constitutional rights were violated.

beaches of Olympic National Park to counter rumors that a "scenic road" would be built parallel to the beach, between the Hoh River and Cape Alava.

Douglas said of the hike: "One of the theories of our system of government is to provide a place for all kinds of minorities. . . . We represent the minority that likes to enjoy the woods and beaches undisturbed by roads and cars."

The jurist who branded the Vietnam War unconstitutional and championed from the highest court the right of schoolboys to wear long hair, provided a wealth of memorable quotes:

■ "Certainly he who has a long purse will always have a lawyer, while the indigent will be without one. I know of no more invidious discrimination than that which is based on poverty."

■ "The word 'revolution' has, of course, acquired a subversive connotation in modern times. But it has roots that are eminently respectable in American history. This country is the product of revolution. Our very being emphasizes that when grievances pile high and there are no political remedies, the exercise of sovereign powers reverts to the people."

■ "Running fast-water rivers, or exploring chains of lakes by canoe, hiking ridges, scaling cliffs . . . these are the activities that build character; and they are vital to the American saga."

■ "We must not turn everything into dollars. . . . Let's save something for the spiritual side of man. The great advantage of living at this time in America is that you've seen the wilderness. This may be the last generation to see it."

■ "We invade a park to build a factory, and we call that progress."

In "Of Men and Mountains," a book about his experiences in Washington's Cascades, Douglas wrote what could stand as his epitaph:

"When a man knows how to live dangerously, he is not afraid to die. When he is not afraid to die, he is, strangely, free to live."

Day of infamy, men of fame

Dec. 7, 1941.

The first news flashes from Pearl Harbor were sketchy. Sneak attack. Ships sunk. Many casualties.

That night Americans turned on their radios to hear Walter Winchell's rapid-fire account. Then they switched the dial to Inner Sanctum and Jack Benny. But it was no night for make-believe.

The Pacific Coast, Washington residents were told, was especially vulnerable to a Japanese attack. Window shades must be pulled. There would be no streetlights. Theater marquees would go dark.

The next day, every school, business and home tuned in to hear

President Roosevelt call Dec. 7 "a date which will live in infamy" and to declare that a state of war existed with Japan.

In the schools, Roosevelt's words were broadcast over loudspeakers. Teachers were tense. But young men who were seniors or already 18 years old strutted a bit — anxious to go to war, certain they would return in a short time as heroes.

When the Japanese attacked Pearl Harbor, Donald Ross was a warrant officer and machinist aboard the battleship Nevada, hit by the first wave of dive bombers.

Ross ordered his men out of the forward dynamo room when smoke, steam and heat became unbearable, performing all duties himself until he became blinded and unconscious.

Upon being rescued and revived, Ross stumbled, half-blind, back to the forward dynamo room. Then he went to the aft dynamo room, where he again was overcome by heat and smoke.

He continued to work from memory, unable to see, thinking he was in a room filled with thick smoke. Ordered to a hospital, he learned there was confusion over handling the ship's boats. He asked for a telephone.

For three days and nights, he directed critical supplies to ships preparing to search out the enemy, all the while hiding his blindness from shipmates. He recovered his sight in about three weeks.

For his heroism, Ross was presented the Medal of Honor — this nation's highest decoration for wartime bravery. It was one of 23 such medals earned in the war by men with strong Washington state ties.

Among them:

Gregory "Pappy" Boyington, a Marine flying ace who became the subject of books and a TV series; Maj. Gen. Jonathan "Skinny" Wainwright, born in Walla Walla, captured by the Japanese after Gen. Douglas MacArthur left Corregidor; Robert Galer, a University of Washington basketball star before the war, who shot down 11 enemy airplanes in 29 days in the Solomon Islands.

John Hawk, who positioned himself in front of his troops and acted as a human gunsight, directing his comrades as they fired at German tanks during the Battle of the Bulge; Joe Mann, a paratrooper from Reardan, Lincoln County, who became the most honored American in the Netherlands when he destroyed an enemy ammunition dump, killed six of the enemy advancing toward him and, with his wounded arms bound to his body, threw himself on a live grenade and died to save his comrades; Orville Bloch, an Army first lieutenant who scaled a sheer cliff to enter a small Italian town and wipe out five German machine guns and take 19 prisoners.

Robert Bush, of Pacific County, a 17-year-old hospital apprentice first class, who rescued a wounded officer and then, after being hit repeatedly, picked up a Browning automatic rifle

CHRONO-LOG

MEDAL OF HONOR
WINNERS IN STATE

and fired until he had wiped out 32 of the enemy; Wilburn Ross, an Army private first class who stood in front of his lines on a battlefield in France, taking fresh guns and ammunition brought by his comrades for five straight hours. He accounted for 58 of the enemy, then directed his own unit for 36 more hours.

'This invasion of citizenship rights'

Within 24 hours of the Pearl Harbor attack, 51 people of Japanese ancestry were rounded up and jailed in Seattle "on suspicion." Others were placed under curfews.

A Japanese school in Seattle was ordered closed, the principal jailed.

On Feb. 19, 1942, President Roosevelt signed Executive Order 9066, authorizing the evacuation of all ethnic Japanese from the West Coast. Robert Taft, R-Ohio, was the only senator to strongly object.

The first to be removed from the Puget Sound area were on Bainbridge Island, a short ferry ride from Seattle. By the time the evacuations ended, about 8,000 had been removed from regional homes, farms and businesses.

They were among some 112,000 people of Japanese ancestry (70,000 of them U.S. citizens by birth) scattered in relocation centers across the country — behind barbed wire, in tar-paper barracks, sleeping under the glare of searchlights, guarded by soldiers.

Paradoxically, there was no effort to evacuate the 120,000 ethnic Japanese in the Territory of Hawaii, which was much closer to the fighting. Indeed, it was the site of Pearl Harbor.

In Seattle, there were empty seats in classrooms, empty homes in neighborhoods, empty stalls in the Pike Place Market.

Few discussed the internment. It was simply a fact of life. The government had its reasons: growing public antagonism toward anyone remotely connected to Japan, strong suspicion that they might sabotage industry or guide enemy bombers to our shores; yes, it was too bad that good people were being hurt, but this was war.

But why not those of German and Italian ancestry, too? Simple. The latter resembled most of us; those we now call the "Japanese-Americans" didn't. Then they were simply "Japanese" or "Japs" and somehow responsible for the Pearl Harbor attack.

Often the evacuees were given only a few days' notice to dispose of homes and belongings. It was estimated after the war that they had suffered a financial loss of $400 million, in 1942 dollars.

It cost the government, too — $200 million the first year, $70 million the next.

The families were given identification numbers and crowded into trucks, buses and trains. Most evacuees from the Puget Sound area went first to the Puyallup Fairgrounds, where they awaited assignment.

Camp life bored some and was hard work for others. A few internees moved to the interior, took odd jobs at about 30 cents an hour for a 44-hour week. Children in the camps, usually at the head of their class before the evacuation, attended third-rate schools. Many from the Seattle area wound up in Camp Minidoka, Idaho. Years later, some of them poured their feelings into a book, "The Minidoka Interlude."

From the book: "To us who had faith in the Constitution of the United States, it was a profound shock that our citizenship did not matter and that the rights guaranteed under the Constitution would be so easily taken away from us without due process of law. . .

"But we were determined to accept the order with the full realization of the crisis which threatened the democracy of the world and with the deep sense of responsibility common to all free men."

One of the few voices raised on behalf of the internees in 1942 belonged to Walt Woodward, publisher of the weekly Bainbridge (Island) Review. Some years after the war ended, Woodward described how it was when a "nervous Navy officer, presiding over a radio facility . . . convinced the Army that the first Puget Sound community to have all its Japanese evacuated should be Bainbridge."

A contingent of New Jersey soldiers went from Seattle to Bainbridge by ferry, "rifles at the ready," Woodward wrote. The soldiers moved in formation up the ferry ramp at Winslow. On the pier stood a group of young Nisei (second-generation Japanese).

A Nisei stepped forward and said, "Sir!"

"Yes," the officer replied apprehensively.

"Sir," the Nisei said, "we understand you have evacuation notices to post. We know where they should be placed so that everyone will see them. We are here to point out those places to you."

The young soldiers were dispersed to various command posts throughout the island. The one stationed in the office of Woodward's newspaper made no move to hinder The Review when it went to press with an editorial denouncing "this invasion of citizenship rights."

On evacuation day, Woodward wrote, it was the tough New Jersey soldiers who wept the most as the island's entire population of Japanese took what was to be its last ferry ride to Seattle for a long time.

May Katayama, a high-school junior, registered for herself and the rest of her Bainbridge Island family. She said: "I know it has to be done. I'm not bitter, but I hate to leave the island. I was born here."

Less than a year after the internment began, an all-Nisei fighting unit was approved. It began as the Nisei 100th Infantry Battalion and evolved into the "Go for Broke" 442nd Regimental Combat Team, which fought in Italy and France and became the most decorated unit in U.S. military history.

By war's end, 33,000 Nisei had served in the European, Pacific and China-Burma-India theaters of war.

After V-J Day, many of the internees returned to the communities they had left. Reactions were mixed. In time, however, the evacuees blended into neighborhoods as they never had before. Out of adversity, something good had happened.

In August 1983, Gov. John Spellman went to the Puyallup Fairgrounds to help dedicate a $41,000 memorial to the internees who had been there. The bronze sculpture was created by one of Seattle's most celebrated artist-sculptors, George Tsutakawa, whose own family had been interned while he served in the Army.

Spellman said:

"I've received letters asking if I had forgotten Pearl Harbor, if I had forgotten the mothers of those who gave their lives in defense of this country.

"I haven't forgotten. But all those letters reflect a common confusion: confusing war between Japan and the United States with the mass deprivation of constitutional rights solely because of their race. Their freedom was trampled on for no good reason."

Musical notes on a native son

In the 1940s, the best-known and almost certainly the highest-paid entertainer in the world was Bing Crosby, born Harry Lillis Crosby on May 3, 1903, in Tacoma.

Crosby, grandson of Thurston County pioneer Nathaniel Crosby, spent the first three years of his life in a two-story, Victorian-style home on Tacoma's J Street. Then the family moved to Spokane, where young Crosby acquired his nickname, Bing. He would ask family members to read aloud a youth-oriented page, The Bingville Bugle, in the Spokane Chronicle, crying out, "Read me 'Bing,' read me 'Bing.'"

Crosby attended Catholic schools in Spokane and spent several years at Gonzaga University, where he intended to study law. An entertainment career won out when he began appearing with a young piano player, Al Rinker, whose sister, Mildred Bailey, was a popular singer.

Crosby quit college, and he and Rinker went to California. After a few years of modest success, they joined with Harry Barris to form the Rhythm Boys. Paul Whiteman hired them to sing with his orchestra.

Crosby, noted for his rich "bathtub baritone" and easy singing style, eventually went off on his own — records, radio, movies and, finally, television. He was easy to cartoon. At the height of his popularity, artists had only to sketch a face with jug ears, cover the thinning hair with a hat, tuck a pipe between clenched teeth and add a golf club. Instant recognition!

During World War II, Crosby and the Andrews sisters — singing together or separately — dominated the nation's jukeboxes. Soldiers overseas choked up when Crosby sang "White Christmas" and "I'll Be Home for Christmas." The Germans called him "Der Bingle."

One of their most popular songs in the Pacific Northwest was "The Black Ball Ferry," a tribute to Cap' Peabody's ferry line.

The famous "Road" movies Crosby made with Bob Hope and Dorothy Lamour were the lightweight fare Americans needed in the '40s. After the fighting, the Washington native showed greater depth as an actor than anyone dreamed he possessed.

Crosby paid frequent visits to the Pacific Northwest after becoming famous, usually winding up on a golf course somewhere. A collection of Crosby memorabilia is the centerpiece of the Gallery for Washington State Entertainment in Tacoma, which also honors other natives such as Mary Livingston, Carol Channing, Howard Duff, Frances Farmer, Gypsy Rose Lee, Pat Paulson, Darren McGavin, Janis Paige, Jimi Hendrix and Quincy Jones.

Death from the skies

Edmund T. Allen, 47, director of flight and aerodynamics for The Boeing Co. and one of the world's foremost test pilots, was at the controls of a B-29 Superfortress making a test run and returning to Boeing Field shortly after noon Feb. 18, 1943.

Robert Dansfield, 37, a former United Air Lines pilot, sat in the co-pilot's seat.

Nine others were in the plane, mostly the cream of a crop of young University of Washington engineering graduates hired by Boeing in its all-out effort to provide bombers for World War II.

As the silver-bodied, four-engined aircraft neared downtown Seattle from the north it was laboring and flying dangerously low. Many heard the noise and rushed to windows, shuddering as the bomber barely cleared Harborview County Hospital. Those standing at windows in the Smith Tower could see every detail of the craft, which listed to one side and appeared to be flying with only its right outside engine still firing.

An onlooker at Airport Way South and Maynard Street saw the plane, trailing black smoke, narrowly miss some wires as it flew overhead. Then the engines seemed to pick up and sputter a little.

Several men appeared to leave the plane, presumably hoping to parachute to the ground from less than 100 feet. The plane was headed straight for the Frye & Co. packing plant on Airport Way.

It was lunchtime for many at Frye's. Others were working in the lard room and the hog-killing room. A few workers off for the day had come to pick up paychecks. Elevators were full.

At 12:23 p.m., the B-29 struck power lines in front of the plant, touching off lightning-like flashes and cutting off power over a wide area of the industrial district. Then the craft slammed into Frye's and exploded. Flames shot 200 feet into the air.

Parts of the plane, including a large wing section, clattered into the street below. Human screams and the frantic squealings of trapped hogs could be heard over the roar of the fire.

Firemen and ambulances raced to the scene. A boxing team from an antiaircraft unit bound for a weigh-in at Civic Auditorium stopped at Frye's and the men piled out of a car to give aid. Coastguardsmen were dispatched to help. Inside Frye's, men were trapped and suffocated in elevators. Some were struck by flying plane parts. Others were caught in the flames.

It was a scene of chaos, tragedy and heroics. Ambulances raced off to Harborview with the injured. Pvt. Sam Morris of Tampa, Fla., a heavyweight boxer on the antiaircraft team, fought through the flames and carried out two people. He later showed up at the weigh-in in a badly singed uniform. Five enlisted men, four of them from a black unit, would be awarded Soldiers' Medals for saving lives "with utter disregard for their personal safety."

Firemen toiled valiantly, bringing the main blaze under control within an hour, then mopping up throughout the night. One, Luther Bonner, died.

The final death toll: the 11 Boeing employees in the plane, one firefighter and 20 Frye employees, including August and Fred Hoba, father and son.

Funerals — mass and single — were held throughout the city in the next few days. Boeing briefly halted work on its assembly line five days later in tribute to employees who had lost their lives. A loudspeaker system in the plant carried a bugler's "Taps" from the Masonic Temple, where mourners sat before 11 flag-draped caskets.

The Boeing employees were covered by insurance and other benefits. The majority of the Frye employees had no coverage. Survivors directed their anger at Boeing, the federal government and state workmen's-compensation shortcomings as they waited months for claims to be settled.

Such secrecy shrouded the identity of the ill-fated aircraft that The Times referred to it merely as a "bomber" in early stories.

An airport really takes off

It was obvious by the early '40s that the Puget Sound area needed more than Boeing Field for big-league air travel.

There were two potential sites for an international airport — one between Bellevue and Lake Sammamish, the other at Bow Lake, between Seattle and Tacoma. Bow Lake won in early 1942, because it was closer to major highways and was supposed to have less fog.

Soon afterward, the Seattle Port Commission found itself $100,000 short of the money needed to proceed with what turned out to be an $11 million project. The City of Tacoma, Port of Tacoma and Pierce County agreed to put up the money.

The Port of Seattle could operate the complex; all Tacoma and Pierce County wanted was name recognition.

The Seattle-Tacoma Airport was born, although newspapers continued to call it the Bow Lake Airport up to the day (July 9, 1949) it was formally dedicated by Gov. Arthur B. Langlie. Thereafter it was known, at least in popular reference, simply as Sea-Tac.

It has been said that for $100,000, Tacoma gained millions of

Bainbridge Island Japanese-American Archives

Newly "suspect" Japanese-Americans on Bainbridge Island — Kikuyo and Henry Takayoshi behind their children (from left) Shizue, Mieko, Kiyoko and Takoto — await evacuation to internment camps.

Seattle Times

Part of the tail of a B-29 is visible after the Superfortress crashed into the Frye & Co. packing plant in South Seattle Feb. 18, 1943, while firemen fight the flames and frightened livestock stampede onto the roof.

CHRONO-LOG

1945
Worst school-related accident in state history occurs Nov. 27 when school bus skids off snow-covered road and plunges deep into Lake Chelan, killing 15 pupils and driver. Five youngsters and woman riding to town on business squeeze through windows and reach shore.

1946
Although aircraft, shipbuilding industries continue close to wartime employment levels, other industries are not so fortunate. State employment falls to 754,200 in January, compared with wartime peak of 988,700 in July 1944.

C-46 transport with 32 Marines en route from San Diego to Sand Point Naval Air Station is caught in blizzard Dec. 10, smashes into cliff on Mount Rainier and plummets onto South Tahoma Glacier. Perils of recovery prompt National Park Service to leave bodies sealed in their icy tomb.

dollars in publicity with none of the headaches of operating the airfield or paying for its expansion.

Both cities almost lost their airport identity in September 1983 when the Port of Seattle Commission renamed Sea-Tac as Henry M. Jackson Airport, in honor of the state's recently deceased senator, one of the most powerful in the nation's history.

Few quarreled with honoring Jackson, but many thought there must be a better way to do it. Five months later, port commissioners bowed to public pressure and rechristened the airport Seattle-Tacoma International.

Jackson was not forgotten. Seattle's downtown federal office building was named for him, along with a 50,000-acre pocket of wilderness in the North Cascades.

The egg and us

 A vivacious, slightly buck-toothed redhead — real name Anne Elizabeth, chosen name Betty — whipped together the outline for a book in 1944 at the insistence of her older sister, Mary.

Also at Mary's urging — since she had arranged the appointment — Betty took time off from her job as a clerk for a Seattle construction company to present the rough manuscript to a J.P. Lippincott Co. agent scouting Pacific Northwest writing talent.

The agent read it and laughed — and laughed and laughed.

"Write it," he said. Since the would-be author had been fired for missing work and had nothing better to do, she wrote it and dedicated it to her sister.

In 1945 what she wrote was published under the unlikely title, "The Egg and I." Before the year was out, the name Betty MacDonald was known throughout the country.

The rollicking story about life on an Olympic Peninsula chicken ranch, without electricity or running water, became a piece of Americana. A year after it was published, it passed the 1 million mark in sales. For months Seattleites swapped copies because they sold as fast as they hit the book stores.

The book was snapped up by International Pictures for a movie starring Claudette Colbert and Fred MacMurray. Out of that film came the "Ma and Pa Kettle" sequels, starring Marjorie Main and Percy Kilbride.

MacDonald was feted from coast to coast as the first literary sensation of the war years. Book critics were impressed by her candor and simplicity and the verbal agility that had always been hers, even as a child. Life Magazine photographers visited the Vashon Island "ranch" on which she lived with her husband, Donald.

They were hectic times, and MacDonald would say later, "I think fame is the most appalling thing that can happen to you."

The book was set in the Chimacum area, on the Peninsula, where MacDonald and her first husband, Robert Heskett, had decided to give up white-collar life and try chicken ranching.

MacDonald always had a vivid imagination, and the ranch provided the grist: the neighbors' gossip, the henhouse, the outhouse at night, the bats that flew in the open bedroom windows, the chicken lice, the soggily miserable winters and the glorious summers.

MacDonald followed with "The Plague and I," about her experiences in Seattle's Firland (tuberculosis) Sanatorium, "Onions in the Stew," "Mrs. Piggle Wiggle" and "Anybody Can Do Anything." But nothing ever sold as well as "The Egg and I."

In 1958, the author died of cancer. She was 49. Too young to go, everyone said. But in a brief, skyrocketing career she had done something few have accomplished. Betty MacDonald made people laugh.

The sounds of victory

Harry Truman gathered his Cabinet around him in the White House. Peering through wire-rimmed spectacles at a clock on the wall, he waited until the hands reached 7 p.m. Eastern War Time, Aug. 14, 1945.

Then, in his staccato Missouri twang, he read an announcement awaited by 140 million Americans:

"I have received this afternoon a message from the Japanese government. . . I deem this . . . full acceptance of the Potsdam Declaration . . . the unconditional surrender of Japan."

World War II finally had ended.

It was 4 p.m. in Seattle. Within minutes, downtown was New Year's Eve, the Fourth of July and the Klondike Gold Rush rolled into one.

Office workers threw paper from windows and dashed into the streets. Motorists honked horns nonstop. People cheered and burst into song. Strangers hugged and kissed. Soldiers, sailors and energetic young women jitterbugged on the sidewalks.

When Mrs. Elof H. Soderlund gave birth to twins in Greenwood Maternity Hospital an hour after Truman spoke, she and her husband promptly named them Victoria and Jay (for V-J Day).

The revelry continued far into the night. There were spontaneous block parties. Hoarded liquor flowed. Seattle Mayor Bill Devin and Gov. Mon Wallgren proclaimed a two-day holiday.

Not everyone took to the streets. Some telephoned loved ones long-distance, causing monumental switchboard jams. Others went to churches and synagogues to thank God the war was over and to mourn this country's dead (405,399) and wounded (670,846). Washington state's death toll was 4,147; Seattle-King County's was 2,488. By comparison, only 877 men from the entire state died in World War I.

Many also sought divine guidance to resolve conflicting emotions over the atomic bombs this country had dropped on the Japanese cities of Hiroshima and Nagasaki a few days earlier.

In the next day's Seattle Times, the Bon Marche took out a full-page ad containing a single word, "Hallelujah!" Tucked away on an inside page was an economist's gloomy prediction of massive unemployment by Christmas.

Rationing was suspended immediately on fuel oil, gasoline and all foods except butter and certain meats. Seven million service personnel were to be discharged within 18 months, based on a newly devised military point system.

In Seattle, on the day the surrender was announced, John Wayne was appearing in "Back to Bataan" at the Blue Mouse Theater, Bobby Sherwood's big band was playing at the Trianon, and it cost 15 cents a line at most bowling alleys, although a shortage of help meant many bowlers had to set their own pins.

Horatio Algers in dog tags

With World War II ended, there was relief and a let's-get-on-with-it attitude. New businesses were born overnight. One of the zaniest — and most successful — was The Three GIs, founded by George LaMaine, Don Wallace and Buford Seals Jr., to sell war surplus.

LaMaine had been a captain in an infantry rifle outfit. Wallace had been in the Army. Seals had served with the Coast Guard. What set The Three GIs apart and made them the subject of a five-page spread in Life magazine in December 1947 was a new kind of advertising that spoofed their business.

It didn't start out that way.

Each had raised about $2,000 in 1946. They wangled a bank loan to finance the selling of war-surplus items and moved into an old building in Seattle's Fremont District. They called themselves the Veterans Sales Outlet.

Just before Christmas 1946, on the verge of going under, they approached the Keene & Keene Agency, headed by Jack and Bob Keene, and pleaded with the young advertising team to help them move some merchandise over the holidays.

What they needed, Keene & Keene decided, was a better name and a little humor. The Three GIs were born. Within a year, they were the personification of the American success story, Horatio Alger characters with dog tags.

It seemed for a while that every time Seattleites turned on the radio, they heard "I'm George. I'm Don. I'm Buford," followed by three singing voices that never should have been let out of the shower:

"We're the Three GIs, those happy-go-lucky guys . . ."

Listeners lapped it up. They howled over the merchandise come-ons. Samples:

"Flying gloves, $1.95 a pair. Now you can afford to have something besides time on your hands."

"We've got a large shipment of penetrating oil — more penetrating than a glance from your mother-in-law."

Before long, The Three GIs bought a batch of Army hospital tents in which to sell merchandise. They pitched three in Seattle, two in Tacoma and one in Portland. They built a big warehouse, bought an airplane and a fleet of trucks. They hired ex-GIs who needed jobs. Money poured in.

Every day was Stunt Night at the Bijou. They rode in a surplus jeep up Fourth Avenue. In front of them were a puffing cornetist and a trombonist, garbed in Revolutionary War uniforms, playing "Roll Out the Barrel."

They stood on a downtown street corner and gave away 50 new dollar bills. They told the public, "We don't pay no rents, 'cuz our business is in tents."

The glory days eventually ended as the old gang broke up and some employees left to start their own chain. But one store remained — at 14th Avenue Northwest and Holman Road — where a tent once stood.

Years later, LaMaine was asked about the awful voices on the singing commercial. Were George, Don and Buford really that bad?

"Worse," LaMaine said. "We were so bad they had three other guys do the singing."

A sky suddenly full of saucers

Boise businessman Kenneth Arnold was flying lazy circles around Mount Rainier on June 24, 1947, hoping to sight the wreckage of a light plane believed to have crashed on the snowy slopes the previous winter.

Suddenly he saw what appeared to be nine shiny objects that flew flat, sideways and upside down at "fantastic speeds" he estimated at about 1,700 mph. They were circular, he would say later, and the centers pulsated like fireflies.

When he landed in Pendleton, Ore., Arnold told his story to a United Press reporter, describing the objects as flying erratically "like speedboats on rough water, or as if you skipped a saucer on water." From Arnold's words, the reporter coined the expression "flying saucers."

(In later years, Arnold said the objects were "more like a crescent or half-moon with a slight polliwog tail and a pulsating-type thing in the center" he presumed was their power unit.)

Newspapers containing Arnold's report hardly had hit Pacific Northwest porches when UFO sightings from Tukwila to White Salmon, from Woodland to Bellingham were reported.

A state official in Olympia saw bright objects in the sky "going like the devil." A mother and her young son in Bremerton saw two

Soldiers, sailors and young women overload a Seattle car in the wild euphoria of V-J Day.

Seattle Times

objects, "very shiny, that seemed to be fluttering in the wind." Two Tacoma patrolmen chased "a red-and-silver-colored fleet of flying saucers."

In the next 25 years, according to a Gallup Poll, millions of people around the world would claim to have sighted UFOs, some as pulsating discs, others as cigar-shaped devices with flashing lights. Fifty-one percent of the American public would say they believe UFOs exist.

On the 36th anniversary of his sighting, the one-time University of Minnesota football player and unsuccessful Republican candidate for lieutenant governor and congress in Idaho, told The Seattle Times he was tired of having UFO-sighters treated as if they had lost their senses.

Since his original sighting, he said, he had seen UFOs seven more times. Twice he took in-flight movies of them. Each time, he said, he noted similarities: a center spot in the UFOs that gave off pulsations, "as if it were alive;" the incredible speeds (1,000 miles an hour or more), and the swift and erratic maneuverings.

But the most remarkable thing about the UFOS he saw, Arnold said, was their apparent ability to change density at will, like jellyfish in the sea. While photographing them over Lassen Peak, he said, "a pine tree on the ground shows right through one of them." And yet, he added, moments later they all appeared to have solidified.

Finally, Arnold said, all the flying saucers he saw were in groups — the largest, 23 or 24 in a string, resembled a flight of birds. Unlike regular military aircraft formations, the "leader" always was higher and the others followed in a descending pattern.

Arnold never claimed to have seen any little men on the UFOs — "I leave that to others." Nor did he believe that he was the first to sight them, saying they were mentioned in the Bible (Ezekiel) and that the logs of English sea captains hundreds of years ago contained detailed notations and even drawings of UFOs.

Hour of the inquisitors

The 1947 state Legislature authorized a Legislative Fact-Finding Committee on Un-American Activities, to be headed by Albert Canwell, a freshman Republican legislator from Spokane.

In the late spring of 1948, what became known as the Canwell Committee set up operations at the 146th Field Artillery Armory in Seattle and began a probe of alleged active and former communists and "fellow travelers" at the University of Washington and the Seattle Repertory Playhouse (no connection to the present Seattle Repertory Theater).

One day there was a knock at the door of Melvin Rader, a shambling, soft-spoken philosophy professor at the UW. Two men confronted Rader, saying they were investigating subversion on the campus. Based on their information, they said, Rader was "in the center of the communist conspiracy."

The Walla Walla native was stunned. The public record showed he was a lifelong liberal — active in the American Civil Liberties Union, defender of the Loyalists in the Spanish Civil War, outspokenly in favor of prison reform and the leader of an unsuccessful attempt to unionize the university's faculty in the 1930s. But the professor vigorously denied membership in the Communist Party or any allegiance to it.

Before long, Rader was enmeshed in the peculiar nature of such committees, which flourished in the postwar era. Many people presumed that being called before a committee investigating subversion was, in itself, proof of guilt. There was no opportunity to call witnesses or to challenge damaging statements.

Seattle Times

A crumpled Oldsmobile-turned-instant-convertible at Second Avenue and Yesler Way squats in mute testimony to the rain of masonry triggered by the "Big Quake of '49."

CHRONO-LOG

1948

Columbia River rampages on Memorial Day, slamming into Vanport, Ore., built to house 50,000 wartime workers at Kaiser Shipyards in nearby Portland. Flood kills 15 people, leaves thousands homeless.

1949

Jan. 2

Pilot of DC-3 carrying 27 Yale students back to Connecticut after holidays ignores warnings from tower, and takes off from icy Boeing Field runway in fog, veering into experimental hangar. Plane and building burst into flames; 11 students, all three crew members die.

July 19

Right engine of nonscheduled C-46 converted cargo plane fails on takeoff from Boeing Field, smashes into seven Georgetown homes and on apartment. Eight killed, 30 injured, including four city firemen burned when one of the plane's fuel tanks explodes three hours after crash.

First politically divided Legislature in state history is seated. House is controlled by Democrats, 67-32; Senate by Republicans, 27-19.

Washingtonians defeat measure that would have restricted sale of beer and wine to state liquor stores.

Asked to justify his refusal to permit those appearing before his committee to speak on their behalf, Canwell told a reporter: "I am all for free speech, but I object to providing the forum for communists."

Rader was not alone. At least a dozen other university professors also were subpoenaed by the committee. Some admitted to having been party members in the past, but denied present membership. Some informed on other faculty members who had attended meetings. A few refused to answer any committee questions and were cited for contempt. Jobs were lost.

But Rader was different. He would not inform, he said, because there was nothing to inform about. He would not take the Fifth Amendment, he said, because he was not a communist and never had been one. Fellow professors also said they didn't think Rader was a communist.

That wasn't good enough for the committee. Its star witness against Rader was a former communist, George Hewitt, touring the country as a paid informant for various un-American activities committees. Hewitt said he knew Rader as a highly placed communist, so big that most other communists couldn't have known about him. And he said he could place Rader at a special communist school in Kingston, N.Y., on a specific date in the late 1930s.

Rader replied that Hewitt was dead wrong. At the time he was supposed to be attending the Red school, he said, he was vacationing with his family at Cougar Creek Lodge in Snohomish.

The Seattle Times assigned a reporter, Ed Guthman, to investigate the critical issue of Rader's whereabouts when he was supposed to be attending the school.

In the end, to the satisfaction of The Times and most involved in the case, Rader was cleared. Headlines proclaimed his innocence. Canwell said he never had been convinced Rader really was a communist, but didn't say why his committee investigators knowingly had hung onto a page from a lodge register that would have cleared Rader months before.

For his work on the Rader story, Guthman earned a Pulitzer Prize for local news reporting — the first Pulitzer won by The Times.

Canwell was defeated at the polls after one term. He ran for various offices over the years, but never won election again.

In a bizarre twist to the hearings here, the Legislature decided in 1955 to turn over to the FBI all Canwell committee records. Three safes believed to hold the records were opened in Olympia. The results were stunning: Two safes contained only a few dusty papers and books. The third was empty.

Asked to explain what had happened to the records, Canwell said he had destroyed many of them so they wouldn't fall into the wrong hands. He said he had microfilmed others and put them in the hands of an agency "whose business is not public." He never

did turn them over.

As a result of the Canwell-committee hearings, a UW faculty committee investigated six faculty members accused of Communist ties. When the deliberations were concluded, Raymond B. Allen, president of the university, dismissed three faculty members: Ralph Gundlach, a psychologist, who moved to another state to work; Herbert J. Phillips, a philosopher, who became a ship's scaler on the Seattle waterfront, and Joseph Butterworth, a physically disabled English professor, who never was employed again.

When Rader died in 1981, at age 77, Guthman, then editor of the Philadelphia Inquirer, said of the Canwell episode:

"It is a chapter (in America's history) that should never be repeated. But I'm afraid it will be."

The day the earth didn't stand still

It was springlike in Puget Sound country on Wednesday, April 13, 1949. Trees coming into leaf. Daffodils and tulips blooming. Lawns high enough to mow. It was a workday. But schoolchildren were on spring vacation.

A few minutes before lunchtime there was a violent upheaval along a fault line deep beneath the earth's crust near Olympia. The ground shuddered and pitched, rippling like ocean waves.

The first shock reached the University of Washington's seismograph at 11:55:54 a.m., knocking both needles off the drum. Eighteen seconds later, there was a second shock of almost equal force.

It was the worst recorded earthquake in the state's history, an 8 on the modified Mercalli scale of temblor intensity, a 7.1 on the Richter scale of ground motion — thus putting it in the "major earthquake" category.

Eight died from falling debris or heart attacks. Many more were injured, seriously or superficially. More than 1,100 homes were damaged. Millions of dollars in damage was done to schools, public buildings and private businesses.

The seismic upheaval dwarfed the state's previous record-holder — a 6 on the Mercalli on Feb. 14, 1946.

People reacted sensibly and foolishly.

Professor Glenn Hughes, head of the UW School of Drama, was speaking on "Naturalism in the Russian Theater" in rickety old Denny Hall. With typical urbanity, Hughes interrupted his discourse to say:

"I don't care for this at all. I think we all had better leave at once. So, ladies and gentlemen, walk, but do not run, from the building. But do it now."

Twenty-five Cub Scouts 287 feet above the ground in the Capitol dome in Olympia held hands, choked down fears and stayed put until a state trooper came up later to lead them down. A frightened elderly woman ran from her home and leaped from a bank into the water beneath the Duwamish River Bridge. A neighbor saw her leap and pulled her out.

Delegates to a church conference in Tacoma were viewing a reissue of the old film, "King of Kings," at the Roxy Theater. The crucifixion of Christ had begun, with its accompanying thunder and earthquake, at the very moment the theater began to vibrate for real.

Filmgoers in Tacoma's Blue Mouse Theater were watching "The Last Days of Pompeii," and a few patrons raced up the aisles fearing the last days of Tacoma.

The death toll could have been much higher.

Tons of brick and mortar fell from three gables atop West Seattle's three-story Lafayette Elementary School. Because of Easter vacation, no children were inside.

A 23-ton saddle fell from a tower of the Tacoma Narrows Bridge, being rebuilt after its spectacular 1940 collapse. It hurtled through a barge below, injuring two workmen.

Cracks opened in the earth near Seattle's Green Lake. Fissures formed in the Husky football team's practice field. A 100-foot piece of steel fell from the top of the 576-foot KJR transmitting tower near the West Waterway of the Duwamish.

The car of the mayor of Chehalis was buried under tons of rubble. He was not inside. Water tanks burst. Plaster showered from ceilings. Almost the entire stock of books fell from shelves on the fourth floor of Seattle's Main Library.

Fire escapes were ripped from their moorings. Water mains burst. Church towers swayed. Chimneys toppled. A skylight in the State Capitol building shattered, littering unoccupied House and Senate desks with shards of glass.

Killed by falling debris were a worker in an Olympia veneer plant, a young man outside a Castle Rock school, an 11-year-old boy outside a Tacoma elementary school, a 70-year-old man outside a Chehalis store. Heart attacks claimed four more.

The actual quake lasted only 20 seconds or so. But the mopping up continued for days, and repairs went on for years.

7. BACK TO WORK

BLAND WAS IN — BUT SO WAS
RED-BAITING AND RAMPANT CONSUMERISM

**1950 TO
1960**

*'Give me one
of those damn
pills. I need it
worse than
you do.'*

**— Boeing head Bill
Allen, on watching a
test pilot execute a
stunt maneuver with a
brand-new 707.**

Seattle Times

*The Barclay Girls, a Seattle dance troupe, give 3,000 returning Korean War vets a high-kicking
welcome along the docks of Seattle in the summer of '52. Below, Scott MacDonald, left, and
Bobby Israel of Seattle reflect the early '50s toy craze in plastic, Buck Rogers-style space zappers.*

Washingtonians, like most Americans, were weary of depressions and
wars and wanted to catch their breath and get on with their families
and careers in the 1950s.

Dwight D. Eisenhower,
the father figure and World
War II hero who ascended to the White
House, was ideally suited to the national
mood. When Ike chose golf over heavy-
duty managing, he was doing what others
wanted to do.

And when Sen. Joseph McCarthy and
his charges of communism in high places
got out of hand, those who disagreed with
the hysteria found it safer to speak softly
among selected friends than to stand up

Seattle Times

Chrysler Corp.

Detroit's tail fins reached their extravagant apogee in 1959, and then virtually disappeared. Pictured here is a Dodge Lancer.

CHRONO-LOG

1950

Northgate, largest shopping center on continent, opens in 40-acre clearing north of Seattle city limits.

Gary Larson, creator of offbeat cartoon The Far Side, is born in Tacoma. Originally titled "Nature's Way," cartoons appear in Seattle Times in late '70s. After being syndicated in 1980, one-panel funnies catch nation's fancy, appearing in more than 800 newspapers by '88.

Hydro racer Stan Sayres' Slo-Mo-Shun IV, with Ted Jones at the wheel, wins Gold Cup race in Detroit, opening way for Seattle to host "World Series of hydroplaning" for first time, in 1951.

"Great Blizzard of '50" dumps total of 25 inches on Puget Sound beginning Jan. 13. While nowhere near Seattle snowfall of 64 inches in January 1880 blizzard, storm is responsible for four deaths.

1951

State ferry system begins with purchase of aging Black Ball fleet from Alexander "Cap" Peabody.

Eleven people die when Boeing B-50 on test flight crashes into Lester Apartments in South Seattle near Boeing Field.

Henry "Hank" Ketcham, '38 graduate of Seattle's Queen Anne High School, launches comic strip starring mischievous 4-year-old. Strip, titled "Dennis the Menace," is instant success, appearing in hundreds of newspapers around the world.

publicly and risk the label of "pinko" or "comsymp" (communist sympathizer).

As the decade began, we fast became involved in hostilities in Korea. But as if to deny its bloodshed, it continued officially to be labeled a "conflict" rather than a full-fledged war. It became that in common usage, however.

Nobody could say Seattle didn't give Korean War GIs a memorable sendoff and welcome home at Pier 91. The Barclay Can-Can Girls (from the George Barclay Dance Studio) were trotted out for each departure and return, along with Jackie Souders' band.

In all, more than 200 women wore the Barclay get-up and danced to "Hinky Dinky Parlez Vous" and Offenbach's famous can-can number. The young ladies frequently wept as wounded servicemen, close to their own age, left the ships — missing arms and legs and, in some cases, eyesight.

At the start of the decade, there wasn't much one could buy with a penny. At the end, there wasn't much one could buy with a nickel.

Marilyn Monroe was the up-and-coming star. Bogey and Hepburn packed them in with "The African Queen." Gene Kelly was dynamite in "Singin' in the Rain."

Elizabeth II ascended the British throne. Vice President Richard Nixon appeared on TV with his dog, Checkers, to explain a campaign slush fund, and during a visit to Seattle there were unfounded rumors that someone tried to poison him.

But the operative word was bland.

Homes built for those who qualified for GI loans (4.5 percent interest) were mostly unadorned, one-story boxes.

Seattle Times

President Dwight D. Eisenhower, flanked by his wife, Mamie, shakes hands with a welcome-to-Seattle contingent of "Ike Girls" at Boeing Field amid the presidential campaign of 1956.

Much of the popular music had become saccharine ("How Much is That Doggie in the Window?"). One of the top platters on jukeboxes featured an operatic tenor, Mario Lanza, singing "Be My Love." Gretchen Christopher, Barbara Ellis and Gary Troxel, fresh out of Olympia High School and calling themselves The Fleetwoods (after their telephone prefix), went to the top of the charts with "Come Softly to Me" and "Mr. Blue."

Change was inevitable. Before the decade ended, it took the form of a musical revolution known as rock 'n' roll.

Early in the decade, the Dodgers were still in Brooklyn, the Giants at the Polo Grounds. A youngster named George Harrison attended school in Liverpool, England, while his fellow Beatle-to-be, Paul McCartney, lived half a British isle away. Comic-strip readers wondered if Daisy Mae ever would get L'il Abner to the altar. Roger Bannister had yet to run the "unattainable" four-minute mile.

Power mowers were a rich man's toy, automatic dishwashers uncommon, transistor radios a new-fangled gimmick. Crowds flocked to the Paramount Theater to see Cinerama, which employed three cameras and three projectors. Cars grew bloated and adopted large fins until they looked like beached whales. One of suburbia's status symbols was the block-long station wagon, to accommodate growing families. Developers started building two-car garages. Grocery stores began stocking frozen foods. And millions of Americans turned to filtered cigarettes and calorie-counting.

Fed up with "white sidewall" haircuts, ex-GIs let their hair grow longer and fuller on the sides. They discovered (rediscovered) narrow ties, part of the wide-narrow-wide-narrow tie cycle that is as inevitable as economic ups and downs.

Women rushed to climb into "the sack." Not to worry. It was only a dress — of especially unflattering design. But anything to be stylish.

Seattle's Metropolitan and Liberty theaters were torn down.

On April 21, 1950, the largest shopping center in North America up to that time was opened in a 40-acre clearing north of the Seattle city limits. It was called Northgate and it spawned copycats across the country.

There was a statewide scare in 1951 when Defense Mobilizer Charles E. Wilson suggested that major aluminum producers consider moving their plants out of the Northwest because of a power shortage.

The state's most devastating modern-day forest fire occurred in September 1951 on the Olympic Peninsula. It became known as the Forks Fire. Although most of the town of Forks was spared, flames destroyed several dozen homes, a sawmill, barns and an estimated 25,000 acres of timber.

On Dec. 4, 1952, Washington housewives and cooks bought yellow-colored oleomargarine in stores for the first time — the result of a landslide vote in favor of doing away with tiny packets of dye that for years had been used to color ersatz butter.

As a promotion stunt, Yellow Cabs rushed colored oleo to small stores in Seattle, Spokane and Tacoma.

In the spirit of the times, University of Washington President Dr. Henry Schmitz decided in 1954 to deny a request that Dr. J. Robert Oppenheimer, "father of the atomic bomb," be named as Walker-Ames lecturer at the UW. The Atomic Energy Commission, citing problems with Oppenheimer's "character and associations," recently had voted 4-1 to deny the physicist access to the atomic secrets he had helped discover. Schmitz's stand was widely applauded by some and condemned by others.

But the Oppenheimer affair would have nowhere near the lasting impact of a May 1954 U.S. Supreme Court decision (Brown vs. Board of Education) that outlawed segregation in public schools.

A three-month strike paralyzed the state's lumber industry in 1955. It hurt, but aircraft-making was supplanting timber as the prime generator of paychecks.

A man Washington state could claim as its own shared the Nobel Prize for physics in 1956 for helping invent the transistor nine years before. Walter Brattain was born in China but grew up in Spokane and on a homestead near Tonasket.

Brattain made us feel good. But our certainty that America always would be first in science was jarred when the Russians launched Sputnik in the fall of '57. The most convenient whipping boy was the schools, which had supposedly fallen down in teaching physics, chemistry and math. The old math soon gave way to the "new math" and a generation of confused parents.

Meanwhile, the Russians also were beginning to show muscle in sports. The Leningrad Trud Rowing Club's eight-oared shell — the most powerful in the world — scored a 1½-length victory over the UW at England's Henley Royal Regatta in the summer of 1958. When the Husky crew was invited a month later to become the first American sports team to compete in the Soviet Union after the war, many viewed it as a clumsy Russian attempt to rub in their superiority over the Yanks.

GI's leaving the Seattle docks for Korea in January 1952 are directed through the snow by a microphone-wielding military policeman.

Seattle Times

But the Al Ulbrickson-coached Huskies accepted the challenge. And in one of the greatest upsets in modern sports history, the Huskies scored a 1½-length victory over the Trud crew in a 2,000-meter race on the Khimkinskoe Reservoir, 20 miles from Moscow.

The university continued to make news the following year (May 4, 1959) when University Hospital (320 beds) was opened on what had been a nine-hole golf course. The hospital would become renowned in the region for its pain clinic, spinal-cord injury center, the cyclotron in its cancer-radiation center, an intensive-care unit for premature babies, kidney dialysis and pioneer work on bone-marrow transplants.

But more people would note that a young basketball player, Elgin Baylor, transferred from the College of Idaho to Seattle University and immediately made the Madison Street school a national power.

The snows of yesteryear, Chap. III

Midwest-type blizzards are so rare in the Puget Sound country that they are identified by year and invariably prefaced with the superlative "great," as in the Great 13-Day Snow of 1893 and the Great Blizzard of 1916.

The Great Blizzard of 1950 even has a date — Jan. 13.

The new decade began with snow flurries and bitter cold that lasted for two weeks. On the 13th, a genuine blizzard howled across the state, sending temperatures to near-zero in Western Washington and 20- and 30-below across the mountains, thus earning the state an unaccustomed label, "icebox of the nation."

Snow was driven by winds up to 60 miles an hour. Traffic stalled. In Grays Harbor County, men described as "walking icicles" watched helplessly as a fishing vessel sank in the harbor. Reconstruction of the Tacoma Narrows Bridge was halted when workers were blinded by snow.

Sanding crews couldn't keep up. Merchants sold out chains and sawdust tires (the earliest snow tire, the treads of which were impregnated with sawdust) and begged suppliers for more. Boeing sent everyone home at 2 p.m. the day of the great blizzard. Courts closed an hour later. Air traffic stopped. Shipping came to a standstill. Downtown Seattle hotels were filled to overflowing. Sheriff's deputies fought through snowdrifts on Vashon Island to deliver milk to an 8-month-old baby.

Four people died.

Seattle Times reporter Lenny Anderson described Jan. 13 as "a hands-in-the-pockets, hat-over-the-ears, turned-up-collar and rolled-up cuffs kind of night." Anderson continued:

"The city last midnight was a ghost town, weird and white, and full of wind and snow, but of travelers virtually empty. Spitting pellets of ice that hit like buckshot sped along on a raging wind that pursued itself through the lonely streets..."

Although the howling winds subsided the next day, fresh snow continued to fall intermittently for almost another week, and before it was over 25 inches had accumulated. By Jan. 20, the thaw had begun.

Getting up to speed on the water

For years unlimited-class speedboat racing was a cozy little party on the Detroit River, where bandleader Guy Lombardo and Gar Wood took turns winning the Gold Cup. Great Britain's Sir Malcolm Campbell, who had the proper gentleman's credentials, occasionally took his Bluebird II out on the water to set a new speed record.

Then Seattle car dealer Stan Sayres, designer Ted Jones and builder Anchor Jensen got together and set the speedboating world on its ear, ushering in an entirely new way of traveling on water at rapid speeds. Why not, they said, glide over the water instead of plowing through it. Hydroplaning, if you will.

At 7:10 on the morning of June 26, 1950, Sayres slipped behind the wheel of a shiny-hulled, new, unlimited-class powerboat named Slo-mo-shun IV at Sand Point Naval Air Station on Lake Washington. Jones was his crew.

Sayres was determined to erase from the record books:

Campbell's world speedboat mark of 141.74 miles an hour set in 1939 on England's Lake Coniston, Harold Wilson's North American standard of 138.50 mph set in Miss Canada IV in 1949, and the U.S. record of 127 mph set by Jack Shafer and Dan Arena in Such Crust I on Gull Lake, Mich.

For four days the previous week, Sayres had been stymied first by rough water and then by a broken propeller during a trial run. Referee Kent Hitchcock of California, technical adviser to the president of the American Powerboat Association, granted a four-day extension to the sanctioned record attempt.

Stan Sayres sits at the wheel of his world record-holding powerboat Slo-mo-shun IV. To Sayres' right is Ted Jones, the boat's designer; to the rear is Anchor Jensen, its builder.

CHRONO-LOG

1952

Sen. Joseph McCarthy, Communist-hunter, campaigns here for Republican incumbent U.S. Sen. Harry Cain in race against Democrat Henry "Scoop" Jackson. Wisconsin Republican leaves in huff after local TV station tells him part of his speech has to be deleted as potentially libelous. Jackson overcomes Eisenhower landslide in November to defeat Cain, and stays in office until death in 1983.

Thirty-seven people are killed when military transport crashes in South Tacoma fog moments after pilot abandons plans to land at fog-shrouded McChord and decides to try for Great Falls, Mont.

Eighty-seven military personnel on way home for Christmas holidays die when Air Force C-124 Globemaster crashes, burns on takeoff from Moses Lake air base.

Construction begins on The Dalles Dam on Columbia. (Dam is completed in 1958.) Year also marks beginning of first large-scale irrigation by water from Grand Coulee Dam.

This time the water was perfect. Just a light chop. Sayres, who had exceeded the record in practice runs, roared off to the measured-mile course. He would be allowed three sets of north and south runs, and the average time of the best two-way runs would constitute his speed.

Sayres headed out toward Juanita, turned south and opened the throttle on the 1,500-horsepower Allison engine. Slo-mo-shun IV roared and raised a roostertail as it headed for the starting line. But Sayres was slightly off course. False start.

Sayres continued south, made a wide swing and opened the throttle again, heading north. He finished the mile in 21.98 seconds, at a speed of 163.785 mph.

After refueling, Sayres took off again. This time he completed the north-to-south run. Time: 22.95 seconds, or 157.2 mph.

The two runs were averaged. Slo-mo-shun IV, Seattle-designed and Seattle-built, had brought the world's speedboat record to Lake Washington. It was an eye-popping 160.3235 mph — more than 18 miles an hour faster than Campbell's old mark.

A jubilant Sayres said, "The boat was not extended." He lauded Jones and Jensen and the five mechanics, Elmer Linenschmidt, Mike Welch, Joe Schobert, Jerry Barker and Bob Swanson, all of Seattle, and he praised Don Spencer of Western Gear Works, which manufactured the boat's step-up gear.

Now for the real test. The boat obviously could tear up a straight course. But skeptics wondered if a craft of such radical design could negotiate turns and win races.

Sayres decided to answer his critics at the 43rd running of the Gold Cup race on the Detroit River, a competition begun in 1904 and never held

west of Detroit.

With Jones at the wheel, Slo-mo-shun IV won the 90-mile race called the "World Series of American speedboat racing." He took all three heats, setting a new race record of 78.217 mph and a new 30-mile heat mark of 80.151. Lombardo took second.

Sayres promptly elected to exercise the winner's prerogative and bring the 1951 Gold Cup race to Lake Washington, a decision that would cause great anguish among powerboating's close-knit fraternity and launch a Detroit-Seattle rivalry that in the next few years reached almost hysterical proportions.

But Sayres still had one more race to win that year, the International Harmsworth Trophy, again on the Detroit River. After Jones hurt his hand when he hit a wake during a trial run, Lou Fageol was installed as the driver. Fageol won handily, setting a new five-mile mark of 102.676 mph.

Honors were heaped on Sayres: Seattle's "Man of the Year" in sports; election, with Jones and Fageol, to motorboat racing's Hall of Fame; a medal of honor from the Union of International Motorboating for the top achievement in the sport in 1950.

The Gold Cup was placed lovingly in the trophy case at the Seattle Yacht Club.

Seattle, which did not have big-league sports of any kind in 1950, was on the threshold of a giddy era of hydroplaning which, for sheer emotion and crowd size (300,000 fans), probably has not been equaled in this country.

Words like sponson, quillshaft and cavitation became a part of the working vocabulary of many Seattleites. Youngsters towed wooden hydroplanes behind their bicycles and employed the long-lost skills of horse-traders to collect hydroplane buttons.

The brave men who donned coveralls and helmets and skittered across the water at breakneck speeds were lionized. When they were severely injured or died in pursuit of victory, the tragedies were deeply felt.

The first of a string of memorable fatalities occurred during the third heat of a Gold Cup race on Aug. 6, 1951, in full view of a quarter-million spectators. The Quicksilver, out of Portland, exploded and sank in the southwest turn, north of Seward Park. Orth Mathiot, 56, the driver, and T/Sgt. Thompson Whitaker, 27, the mechanic, were killed.

Slo-mo V went on to win the race that day. In fact, the IV and V won five straight Gold Cups for Sayres, with Fageol, Stanley Dollar and Joe Taggart taking turns at the wheel. Sayres personally boosted the speed record to 178.497 mph.

Then the unthinkable happened. Joe Schoenith's Gale V won the 1955 Gold Cup, and Seattleites, with heavy hearts, saw the trophy carted back to the Detroit Yacht Club.

Hydroplane races, including the Gold Cup, would return to Lake Washington. But emotions never again reached quite the frenzied pitch of those early years.

Keeping a score on conductors

 It was regarded as a coup when in the spring of 1951, the board of the Seattle Symphony Orchestra signed conductor Manuel Rosenthal of France to a two-year contract.

Rosenthal was a noted composer and had conducted orchestras all over the world, including acclaimed guest appearances with the Seattle Symphony. Furthermore, the woman he introduced either as Mrs. Rosenthal or by her concert-singing name, Claudine Verneuil, had been warmly embraced locally for both her charm and culinary talents.

Unlike Britain's testy Sir Thomas Beecham, who had hurled insults with abandon when he conducted the Seattle orchestra, Rosenthal only once had put down the local community. Upset that a Beethoven festival had to be canceled when just 200 tickets were sold, he had asked, more in sorrow than anger, "Why must Seattle be a beautiful body without a brain?"

In fact, the city was so forgiving and apparently so lacking in short-term memory that when the maestro flew into Seattle-Tacoma Airport from Paris a few months later, he was greeted by a band of symphony supporters that included a scantily clad drum majorette, an accordion player and a chorus singing:

"Hoop de doo, hoop de doo,

"Here's Manuel Rosenthal, our troubles are through . . ."

The conductor, according to newspaper accounts, was rendered speechless.

In October 1951, while music lovers eagerly awaited the return of Rosenthal and his wife from a concert tour in South America, a moral crisis arose.

The couple were detained by immigration authorities at New York's Ellis Island. The reason: Rosenthal was alleged to have committed "moral turpitude" by claiming on entry papers that the woman with whom he was traveling was his legal wife. In fact, the authorities said, the real Mrs. Rosenthal, whom the musician had

It was how he conducted himself, not the Seattle Symphony Orchestra, that caused trouble for maestro Manuel Rosenthal.

married 22 years earlier, was in Paris with their 18-year-old son.

Although the lawfully wedded Mrs. Rosenthal said she forgave her husband's indiscretion "because he is a great artist," the symphony board assembled in emergency session and showed a less forgiving nature.

Rosenthal's contract was canceled, and the season's first concert delayed.

High & low crimes and misdemeanors

The state Legislative Council's Crime Investigating Committee began prowling the state in search of crime and vice in high and low places in the fall of 1951.

Like the House un-American Activities Committee of the late '40s, which took on the name of its chairman, Albert Canwell, the eight-member crime committee also became closely identified with its chairman, state Sen. Albert D. Rosellini.

The Rosellini Crime Committee, also called the "Little Kefauver Committee" (after U.S. Sen. Estes Kefauver's national crime-investigating panel), delved into bingo parlors, cardrooms, backroom bookie joints, prostitution and police payoffs in what at times resembled a three-ring circus.

It was good theater. But not everyone enjoyed the spotlight.

In Vancouver, Clark County Prosecutor R. DeWitt Jones accused the committee of McCarthyism for feeding on rumors and invading "a man's sacred right to privacy." In Tacoma, which had named no fewer than three police chiefs in 1951, the Rev. Harold Long branded the committee's investigation as worthless. "It shows a lot of dirty linen," he snapped, "but it doesn't wash it."

The crime hearings became the biggest TV draw in Northwest history to that time. Viewers heard Pierce County Prosecutor John J. O'Connell testify that Tacoma law-enforcement officers had received $20,000 in payoffs the previous year to allow brothels to operate. Tacoma Police Commissioner James Kerr said Fort Lewis officials asked him to leave a few bordellos open for GIs.

There was testimony about bootleg establishments operated by "Screwy Louise" and "Peanuts." And "Amanda Truelove" and "Ann Thompson" were said to be operating bottle clubs and other things which could not be mentioned in polite society.

At one point in the Tacoma hearings, chairman Rosellini, saying he feared for the morals of the young, excluded from the room everyone under age 18. He also urged mothers to keep their children away from TV sets when the testimony was especially seamy.

Seattle's hearings, which were to have followed immediately, were delayed until spring. By that time, the state Supreme Court had narrowed the field of inquiry by saying witnesses need testify only about "crimes" with statewide impact.

The spectacle suffered. There wasn't much excitement in the revelation that a former toll taker had allowed a relative to cross the Longview Toll Bridge without paying.

In Seattle, the high point was the appearance of a 20-year-old ex-narcotics addict who wore a white hood pierced with eyeholes and told how years of "slavery to dope" had ruined his life.

In May 1952, state Sen. William Goodloe forsook his role as attorney for one of the witnesses and attacked Rosellini: "I would like to know, from the viewpoint of a Republican, whether you are running for governor and . . ."

Rosellini rapped his gavel. When Goodloe persisted — asking questions about the cost of the committee and its purpose — he was led forcibly from the hearing room.

(Rosellini eventually did run for governor, and win, in 1956. Goodloe became a King County Superior Court judge and after several unsuccessful tries was elected to the state Supreme Court in 1984. He retired in 1988.)

Meanwhile, the crime hearings ran out of steam. Yakima and Wenatchee were pronounced "clean" by Rosellini, and Everett — later to figure in a major prostitution scandal — was hailed as the "cleanest in the state in its population class."

The rearing of kidvid

Back in the '50s when television was the new baby-sitter on the block, every station worth its call letters had kids'-show personalities and a studio filled with props.

They came on live, first in black-and-white and then in color, these clowns, cowboys and salty characters from the sea. They became as much a part of growing up as Little Orphan Annie and Jack Armstrong had been for earlier generations.

Tube regulars could sing the theme songs years later.

"Zero dackus, mucho cracus,
"hallaballooza bub;
"That's the secret password that we
"use down at the club."

That signaled the arrival of Seattle's Stan Boreson, on KING-

Roy Scully / Seattle Times

In a rare show of 1950s kidvid inter-station togetherness are Channel 7's J.P. Patches in his flivver surrounded, from left, by Channel 11's Miss Elaine, Channel 5's Stan Boreson, Channel 4's Carol Lee Smith, Channel 7's Miss Virginia and Channel 5's Wunda Wunda.

TV's Clubhouse, playing his accordion and singing in a lutefisk-flavored voice.

"Wunda Wunda is my name;
"Boys and girls, I'm glad you came.
"We'll have fun as I explain
"How we play our Wunda games."

And that was Ruth Prins, another KING-TV star, known to preschoolers as Wunda Wunda.

Besides Boreson and Prins there were Sheriff Tex (Texas Jim Lewis), KING; Captain Puget (Don McCune), KOMO; Brakeman Bill (Bill McLain), Tacoma's KTNT, and J.P. Patches (Chris Wedes), who had the longest run of all — almost 23 years — as a funny-faced, baggy-pants clown for KIRO.

A ham on the clam circuit

"No longer the slave of ambition,
I laugh at the world and its shams
And I think of my happy condition,
Surrounded by acres of clams."
— From "The Old Settler," by Francis D. Henry, 1902

Sung in a bathtub baritone to guitar accompaniment, those words were the unmistakable trademark of Ivar Haglund, as much a part of Seattle as its waterfront, Smith Tower and seafood. In short, a living, breathing legend.

Ivar grew up in West Seattle, attended the University of Washington and opened his first restaurant, Ivar's Acres of Clams, in 1946. What set him apart was a genius for promotion. Let others be slick. He would be homespun Ivar, short-legged, mustached, wearing a seafaring cap, strumming a guitar and singing ditties that smelled of seaweed. He counted authentic folk singers Pete Seeger and Woody Guthrie as friends.

Ivar joked about his product: "Keep clam." "Only one cup of clam nectar without special permission from your wife." (The latter a sly reference to the nectar's reputed aphrodisiac qualities.)

Ivar staged an underwater fight between an octopus and prizefighter "Two-Ton" Tony Galento. When a train's tank car spilled 1,000 gallons of syrup near his restaurant he went out and cooked up pancakes while photographers recorded the scene.

STATE-MENTS

Piper Cub high
Lt. John Hodgkin startled the world April 12, 1951, by landing his ski-equipped Piper Cub on the top of 14,410-foot-high Mount Rainier — and then not having enough fuel to get it off again.

The McChord AFB officer stayed with the plane as gale winds raked the summit during the night. The next morning, as rescuers worked their way up the mountain, Hodgkin pushed his 'Cub off the top and glided without power down to Lake Mowich, in the national park. There he made another smooth landing. After McChord's Air Rescue Squadron dropped him fuel, Hodgkin took off again, amazing old-time pilots with his soft landing, on skis, on a grassy spot at Spanaway Airfield.

Almost everyone thought it a wonderful stunt. Two who did not were the Air Force, which restricted Hodgkin to barracks, and the National Park Service, which charged the flyer with breaking the law by landing a plane in a national park. A U.S. commissioner levied a $350 fine but waived jail time. Hodgkin, an aerial photographer in civilian life, said he undertook the flight to prove light planes have an important role in alpine warfare and rescue work.

In June 1952, Hodgkin, unrepentant, landed a light plane atop Washington's 12,307-foot Mount Adams. He did it, he said, to prove the feasibility of flying mining engineers to mountain tops for exploratory work. He repeated the Mount Adams feat two days later with a passenger. Both times he had enough fuel to fly off.

CHRONO-LOG

Associated Press

*In 1952, President Harry Truman visits in Spokane with
Warren Magnuson, center, and Henry Jackson, who would
represent Washington as Democratic powers in the Senate.*

Ivar added more restaurants. He ran for a seat on the Port
Commission 1983, had second thoughts and tried to back out. The
public said no way and elected him by a landslide.

In later life, Ivar realized two of his fondest boyhood dreams —
purchasing the 42-story Smith Tower he had watched being built
when he was a youngster, and putting on an annual Fourth of July
fireworks show that dazzled the whole town. He died in 1985, just
short of his 80th birthday.

The fireworks show continued, in his name.

Awash in a new ferry system

In 1951, when the state finally purchased the aging Black Ball
ferryboat fleet and set up its own state-run ferry system, a jubilant
Gov. Arthur B. Langlie hailed a "new era of Puget Sound
transportation."

There would be no more strikes, said Langlie; toll bridges
would be built and paid off quickly. And in time there would be
fare-free, cross-Sound transportation emanating from Seattle. It
sounded great.

It didn't happen.

The man from whom the state bought its ferry system was
Alexander "Cap" Peabody, born in Port Townsend with sailing
blood in his veins. His great-great-grandfather had helped found
the New York-to-Liverpool Black Ball Line in 1816.

Cap's father, Charles Peabody, launched the Alaska Steamship
Co. before the Klondike gold rush. He then founded the Puget
Sound Navigation Co., wisely foreseeing the end of the little
"mosquito fleet" boats that plied the Sound, and converting his
trim-lined fleet to snub-nosed ferryboats.

In 1929, Cap Peabody assumed the presidency of the Puget
Sound Navigation Co. from Joshua Green, who had started as a
purser with the mosquito fleet and was to become one of Seattle's
foremost bankers.

Peabody's reign was marked by success and strife because, as
the state later learned, it was impossible to satisfy everyone in the
ferry business and still make a profit.

In the '40s, Peabody proposed to end money-losing routes,
personally pay for building a bridge across Agate Pass from
Bainbridge Island to the Kitsap Peninsula and add a short Hood
Canal crossing at Lofall to connect with the Olympic Peninsula.

Other governors had gone along with Peabody's plans. Langlie
vowed he would not.

Langlie wanted the state to acquire the ferry system and was
willing to fight. To halt Peabody's Lofall terminal, Langlie denied
him access to state highways.

Peabody responded by buying private property and
constructing his own highway link. Langlie got the state Public
Service Commission to deny Peabody's application to shut down
the Seattle-Suquamish run. The pressure continued.

With great reluctance, Peabody finally agreed to sell out to the
state for nearly $6 million. But when the state Supreme Court

ruled the state had no business getting into the ferry business,
Peabody described himself as the happiest man in the world.

Langlie persisted, pushing the Legislature to pass a ferry-
control bill permitting the state to set rates in state waters.

That did it. In 1951, facing an order to reduce fares by 30
percent while costs were rising, Peabody succumbed — selling out
for $4.5 million. He moved his offices from Colman Dock next
door to Pier 53 and continued to operate a Seattle-British
Columbia Service, under the Black Ball flag.

Having finally acquired its own ferry system, the state
proceeded to do exactly what Peabody had advocated all along —
trimming unprofitable runs, building an Agate Pass bridge and
operating a Lofall ferry (replaced in time with the Hood Canal
Floating Bridge).

The year Peabody sold out, he was honored by the Puget Sound
Maritime Society, which concluded a tribute by playing for the
first time in Seattle the Bing Crosby-Andrews Sisters' "Black Ball
Ferry" recording, featuring lyrics by Dixie Thompson of Kent and
music by John Rarig, a Roosevelt High School grad who had gone
to Hollywood.

Peabody threw back his head and roared with laughter when
he heard:

*"Every GOP and Democrat-o
"Hears the whistles go,
"As the ferryboats keep chuggin' right along."*

Peabody died in 1980 at the age of 85.

The powerhouse boys in Congress

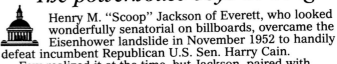

Henry M. "Scoop" Jackson of Everett, who looked
wonderfully senatorial on billboards, overcame the
Eisenhower landslide in November 1952 to handily
defeat incumbent Republican U.S. Sen. Harry Cain.

Few realized it at the time, but Jackson, paired with
Democratic Sen. Warren G. "Maggie" Magnuson, would establish
Washington state as having the most powerful one-two punch in
the Senate in the 20th century.

In a Ralph Nader poll of senatorial aides, Jackson rated No. 1
in effectiveness. Magnuson finished second. On the surface, the
two were not a bit alike.

Magnuson, in office since 1944, worked hard and played hard,
especially during his bachelor days when his romances with
beautiful women were legend. That all ended when he married
Jermaine Peralta in 1964 (Lyndon Johnson was best man), and she
became his confidante and best friend as well.

The more serious Jackson — also a longtime bachelor until he
married Helen Hardin in 1961 — simply worked hard. He liked to
refer to himself as "a work horse, not a show horse," noting that
he rarely missed more than a handful of the Senate's more than
1,200 annual roll calls.

Maggie smoked cigars, regularly bent an elbow with the boys,
spun a good yarn, was a big spender and paid little attention to his
personal well-being. In later years, he joked that if he had known
he would live so long he would have taken better care of himself.
He seldom forgot a face, but couldn't always put a name to it.

Jackson was a physical-fitness buff, temperate and tightfisted.
(His staff, however, was higher paid than Magnuson's, and he
never kept a penny he earned from speeches, giving it all to
scholarships in the name of his deceased sister.)

Unlike Magnuson, Jackson not only remembered faces but
could put names to thousands of them.

Despite their differences, Magnuson and Jackson worked
together like the mechanism of a fine watch. And if Jackson
tended to be more conservative in foreign policy, neither ever
forgot his liberal origins when it came to social legislation.

Of the two, Magnuson had the tougher childhood. Orphaned at
three weeks, he grew up in a Norwegian immigrant family in
Moorhead, Minn., and in North Dakota. After attending the
University of North Dakota and North Dakota State, he rode
freight trains West to finish his undergraduate degree and study
law at the University of Washington.

He served in the Legislature, as King County prosecutor and as
a U.S. representative before moving into the Senate. After heading
the Senate Commerce Committee for many years, he realized his
fondest dream — chairmanship of the powerful Appropriations
Committee.

In that job, Magnuson was at his best, sleeves rolled up,
wheedling, cajoling, building a new coalition every day on a
different issue. It was no accident that in 1976 Washington state
received $2,176 in per capita federal spending, trailing only New
York's $2,228.

Magnuson pushed through important legislation on health and
consumer-protection issues. He brought in much-needed money
for cancer research.

But he wasn't afraid to go against the folks back home on

principle. Over the protests of some, he successfully fought to ban supertankers from Puget Sound. And despite representing a state heavily dependent on military installations and defense contracts, he supported a measure to limit U.S. involvement in Southeast Asia.

Even though he had his fervent supporters, "good old Maggie" had some close calls at the ballot box. The Republicans always found him a bit too liberal, with none of Jackson's military and global clout, and there weren't always enough Democrats around to make his elections easy.

He almost lost in 1962 to a political neophyte, a 32-year-old Lutheran pastor from Edmonds, Richard Christensen. The cleric campaigned against an empty rocking chair he said Magnuson occupied in the Senate.

Jackson, who picked up his nickname from a comic-strip character named "Scoop" in his hometown (Everett) newspaper, earned a law degree from the UW, spending one summer as a social worker. He said it made him forever sensitive to the needs of have-nots.

After serving a two-year term as Snohomish County prosecutor, Jackson was elected to Congress in 1940. Twelve years later, he was a senator.

Jackson's accomplishments were the stuff of legends. He combined with Maine Democratic Sen. Ed Muskie to write an Environmental Protection Act hailed by some as the most important piece of legislation in the century.

He also was credited with:

■ The third Grand Coulee Dam powerhouse (in concert with Magnuson); promoting the second Bacon Siphon to expand the Columbia Basin's irrigated land, the North Cascades wilderness area and park, and federal money to help local communities deal with the new Trident submarine base at Bangor.

■ The so-called Fort Lawton Bill, setting a precedent for states to have first crack at surplus federal property; legislation to prevent timber companies from "getting their hands on Olympic National Park," and rivers-and-harbors bills that touch every county in the state with a shoreline.

The state's junior senator became one of the nation's foremost experts on military and foreign affairs, one of Israel's staunchest backers and a bona fide presidential contender.

John F. Kennedy wanted Jackson as his running mate in 1960, but opted for Texas Sen. Lyndon Johnson because the latter might bring in votes from the heavily populated Lone Star State. Richard Nixon offered Jackson his choice of secretary of defense or secretary of state. He declined both.

Never mind that some called Scoop a saber-rattler because of his fondness for military might, or the "senator from Boeing" because of what was perceived as his unfailing backing of Boeing's projects (TFX, SST and assorted space hardware).

Republicans liked him, and liberal Democrats, who sometimes acted disenchanted, had no place else to go in general elections. The senator from Everett always won overwhelmingly. In fact, he was so certain to win that when the GOP ran relatively unknown Charles Elicker against him in a "laugher," Jackson good-naturedly introduced his opponent around the room when they appeared together at political functions.

Almost as important as Jackson's legislative record was his bearing. He invariably looked and acted liked a statesman during televised Senate hearings (Army-McCarthy, TFX).

Many political experts felt that Jackson, despite a lack of charisma, would make an outstanding president. He tried for the Oval Office twice — in 1972 and 1976, winning the Massachusetts primary in '76 before his campaign ran out of steam and money.

Many Washingtonians selfishly heaved a sigh of relief. They still had Maggie and Jackson in the Senate. But four years later, in the fall of 1980, the unthinkable happened. Magnuson, aging and in failing health, lost to Slade Gorton, a Republican.

Half of the one-two punch was gone.

And on Sept. 1, 1983, the other half went. Jackson, always the picture of health, died of a massive heart attack. He was replaced by former three-time Gov. Dan Evans, a Republican, who then won the office outright in a race against Rep. Mike Lowry.

Magnuson maintained a mostly quiet life of retirement in Seattle until his death May 20, 1989, but mourners who came to say a last goodbye filled every corner of St. Mark's Cathedral.

Good men would represent Washington state in the future. But the era of Maggie and Jackson would not soon be duplicated.

A lot of hoop-la between the two U's

Although the University of Washington and Seattle University are only a few miles apart as the seagull flies, their basketball teams have been separated by a gulf wider than the English Channel.

On March 13, 1953 — more than halfway into the 20th century

— the two teams finally could avoid each other no longer. They were brought together in the regional playoffs of the National Collegiate Athletic Association's basketball tournament. The site: Gill Coliseum in Corvallis, Ore.

Seattle had two-fifths of the Associated Press All-American basketball team that year. From the Seattle U Chieftains, a 5-9, 160-pound master of feint and jump shot, Johnny O'Brien, also known as "Johnny O" and "Super Chief." From the UW Huskies, a 6-foot-7-inch, 210-pounder named Bob Houbregs, the premier hook-shot artist of the continent.

William Harrison "Tippy" Dye masterminded the Huskies. Horace Albert "Al" Brightman called the shots for the Chieftains.

Puget Sounders, delirious over having the two teams meet at last, billed it as the basketball game of the century. The debate over which was the better team had raged for months. Now it would be settled.

The Huskies drew a bye for the first game in Corvallis and waited to see if Seattle U could hurdle Idaho State in a preliminary. Super Chief O'Brien had a hot hand, and his nifty twin brother, Eddie, fed him as one born to the task. The Chiefs won 88-77.

The big game was televised. Not everyone had a TV set in those days, so they got friendly with neighbors who did. By tipoff time, both teams were like fiddle strings tightened to the snapping point. Coaches paced.

The Huskies took the court. Fabled names: Mike McCutcheon, Doug McClary, Joe Cipriano, Charles Koon, the great Houbregs. Ditto the Chiefs: the O'Brien twins, Stan Glowaski, Ray Moscatel, Wayne Sanford.

While 10,214 fans screamed insanely, the basketball was thrown into the air. And the Huskies were off like a racehorse loaded with amphetamines. Swish. Swish. Swish.

The Huskies led 24-11 at the end of the first quarter, 47-33 at halftime. Cipriano, McCutcheon and McClary wove a cocoon around Johnny O.

By the end of the third quarter, the Huskies led 68-47. With three minutes left in the game and the Huskies ahead 90-57, Dye mercifully inserted his second-stringers. The final score was 92-70. It could have been worse if Dye had wished.

Houbregs smashed the single-game playoff record with 45 points. His 20 field goals were another playoff record. Although O'Brien had been double- and triple-teamed, he scored 25 points.

The Huskies went on to take third place in the NCAA tournament, after dropping a game to Kansas. The Chieftains, rebounding from the loss, easily defeated Wyoming the next night, 80-64.

Although Husky fans did most of the gloating, O'Brien set a three-game regional scoring mark (97 points) and a new

Seattle Times

It's the pits for Westlake Avenue North auto dealer A.W. Hauck — and a number of other people — in April 1954 as windshields came down with a mysterious case of acne.

CHRONO-LOG

Museum of History & Industry
With this typical television set of the 1950s, a Capehart, you got a lot of cabinet but not the big picture — TV screen measured only 6 by 8½ inches. The wooden doors were for closing over the tube when not in use.

1955

Robert Clendenin boards passenger jet at Sea-Tac Nov. 22 and fatally shoots stewardess Sally Shedd, who he feels has spurned him for another man, then kills himself. Clendenin has written letter to Shedd's father, saying if he and she die together he wants them buried in same coffin. Father makes sure killer's last wish is not granted.

Twenty-seven people, including 25 soldiers flying home for Thanksgiving, die when nonscheduled DC-4 pancakes into snow-covered field shortly after takeoff south of Boeing Field. Forty-seven passengers survive.

In what is called "The Great Experiment," Bob Fesler, Seattle-bred softball pitcher of national acclaim, signs contract to pitch for Seattle Rainiers. Great as he is, Fesler never masters longer throwing distance (46 ft. vs. 60 feet for baseball).

1956

Jack Kerouac, author of "On the Road" and an originator of term "Beat Generation," spends summer as fire lookout on Desolation Peak in North Cascades.

Five people die as Northwest Orient Airlines plane carrying 37 crash-lands off Vashon Island shortly after takeoff from Seattle-Tacoma Airport.

tournament free-throw record (39). Houbregs, playing in four games — regional and final — set a tournament record for field goals (57).

O'Brien went on to become a King County commissioner, Houbregs to serve for a time as general manager of the Seattle SuperSonics basketball team.

It's the pits: mini-hysteria of an era

On March 25, 1954, Bellingham police logged about 300 complaints from motorists who said their car windshields had been pitted, apparently by hoodlums firing pellet guns. Three weeks later there were similar reports in Burlington, south of Bellingham.

By mid-April the entire Puget Sound region was in the grip of what became known as the "great windshield pitting mystery." Police in Seattle and Tacoma fielded thousands of reports, prompting Seattle Police Chief J.H. Lawrence to say it would take 200 armed youngsters, roaming full time, to inflict all the windshield damage being reported.

Stories were wild.

People reported seeing pits form before their eyes when they attempted to remove black particles from their windshields.

Not so, said others. The pits were created by bubbles that formed within the glass and expanded to the bursting point. An automobile-glass repairman blamed "gray or black balls" that ate into glass. Still others attributed the damage to fallout from hydrogen-bomb tests or an alien substance raining down on Earth.

Two King County sheriff's deputies radioed that pits were breaking out on the windshield of a private car while they watched. If that weren't bad enough, they radioed in a few minutes later to announce that the mysterious pitting agent had attacked their own squad car.

Motorists who had to leave their cars outside began putting canvas, cardboard and newspaper on their windshields as protection. Reports subsided almost as quickly as they had begun, leaving the mystery to scientists and scholars.

After a lengthy study, University of Washington scientists discounted the whole affair. The pits, they said, were normal and appeared to have been caused by gravel and other objects striking windshields. Older cars, they noted, had more windshield pits than new ones, as would be expected.

Psychologists wondered if the pits hadn't been on windshields

Seattle Times
This is how the Pioneer Safe Deposit Vaults looked the morning after they were looted of up to $500,000 on a February 1954 weekend. The case remains unsolved.

all the time and were merely being noticed as the publicity grew. They hinted at mass hysteria.

The day after the pitting stopped in the Northwest, there were reports of an outbreak in Canton, Ohio, followed by windshield pitting in Wisconsin and Illinois. True believers said this proved the pitting agent was being carried on fast-moving, high-level winds that had passed over the Pacific Northwest.

No BB-shooting vandals were ever found.

End of hysteria in the Northwest? Not quite. In March 1962, secretaries all over Seattle reported back from their lunch breaks with their nylon stockings in tatters, or so they believed.

Runs that hadn't been there in the morning suddenly made them look like bag ladies, the secretaries complained. The reports caused thousands of women to look more carefully at their legs. And many saw runs they couldn't explain.

The culprit? Some blamed heavy rains. Others fingered nuclear fallout.

But weather experts said it had been raining heavily for several days, and it seemed strange that a substance in the rain would suddenly start eating into stockings. Furthermore, there had been no significant radioactive fallout for months. Still, there were experts who said that a heavy concentration of acid in rain could zap stocking threads.

The stocking-running mystery did not begin in the Northwest. It had first been reported in Washington, D.C., in 1940. And there had been brief outbreaks in Southern California, Pennsylvania and New Jersey, along with a small-scale episode in Seattle in 1958.

Like the windshield-pitting mystery, it didn't seem to cause any lasting damage.

Holiday heist on First Avenue

While Seattleites enjoyed a long Washington's Birthday weekend in 1954, three cracksmen broke into Pioneer Safe Deposit Vaults, in the basement of a building at 701 First Ave., just two blocks from police headquarters.

They hadn't needed to worry too much about police, however. On the rainy Saturday night that they broke in, most of the lawmen and their wives were attending the 60th annual policemen's ball.

With professional skill, the intruders entered a back door on Post Street, sealing the cracks so sound, light and odors wouldn't escape. Then they took acetylene torches to the thin steel doors of the vault office.

Easy so far. The hard work was ahead. They had to get through an 8-inch-thick brick wall, using picks, sledgehammers and air guns. Then they had to torch through a steel wall nearly 2 inches thick.

It took hours. But they had lots of time.

Finally, they broke through, to be faced with 1,640 safe-deposit boxes. They began chiseling open the boxes, rifling over 400 of them for jewels, raw gold, negotiable bonds and cash.

One of the men, police learned later from stool pigeons, was so high on narcotics he kept pounding on vaults and singing "Hi ho, ho ho, it's off to work we go!" Just like in Snow White. Only this was for real.

Presumably it was the dope addict's racket that finally caused the three to flee before cracking all the boxes. They left behind enough burglar tools to stock a small hardware store, a common practice for pros who didn't want to get caught with tools in their possession.

Pandemonium reigned when the vaults were opened Tuesday. Within a few hours the vault's anteroom was jammed with anxious customers, many of whom didn't want to say how much or what had been in their strongboxes for fear of getting into trouble with the Bureau of Internal Revenue. Estimates ranged from $200,000 to $500,000.

The heist was never solved. The only clue was a single bond that showed up in Nevada.

Ride 'em no more, cowboy

 It was sometime in 1954 when cowboys cornered a 29-year-old horse in a corral at Loomis, Okanogan County, so a veterinarian could repair the animal's teeth. The horse's heart gave out, and he rolled over and died.

Gone was Badger Mountain, one of the two most famous bucking horses in rodeo history, the other being the fabled Wyoming terror, Midnight.

Badger Mountain was three times national Bucking Horse of the Year — 1,200 pounds of smoke-colored, sunfishing fury in the rodeo arena; fabled from Baton Rouge to Pendleton. Those who saw him come boiling out of a chute, a wild-eyed cowboy on his back, never forgot the sight.

Boeing Airplane Co.

Alvin "Tex" Johnston, Boeing's chief of flight testing, poses in the cockpit of a 707 jetliner prototype — called the Dash 80 at that stage — in August 1955.

Badger had a trick. Just out of the chute, he would hit hard on his hind feet and poke his nose into the sky. He would do a little ballet dance, stretched full length, while the cowboy loosened his grip. Then the horse would spin away and kick straight at the moon, and that irritant on his back would come unglued, flying into space and sprawling in the dirt.

But beneath that mean exterior, Badger had a gentle streak. His task completed, he always jumped sideways, breaking his stride, to avoid trampling the fallen cowboy.

For 17 years Badger Mountain threw every cowboy who drew his number. Every one, that is, except a cowboy named Nick Knight. Three times Knight climbed aboard Badger. And three times he lasted 10 seconds. Knight, who left the rodeo arena to become a Nevada businessman, never told his secret.

Tim Bernard, who had a horse ranch in Loomis, acquired Badger Mountain in Waterville, Douglas County, when Badger was 6 years old.

"First time I saw him, I knew he was so great," Bernard used to say. "He had this unpredictable head movement. It went every which way. And he just loved to unseat cowboys."

When Badger wasn't on the rodeo circuit, he scampered on Bernard's range. He was retired from the circuit at age 27 and lived the good life as horses go. Even when Badger was old and his teeth were going bad, Bernard never tried to ride him — partly out of sentiment and because "I guess the Badger could have thrown me about 100 straight times if he wanted."

When Badger died, a grieving Bernard and some ranch hands dug a big hole out behind the barn, bared their heads and covered the bucking horse with dirt.

Boeing leads the Jet Set

The Boeing Co. gambled money, prestige and corporate existence during the early '50s on the Dash 80, prototype of the 707, in a race to become the first aircraft manufacturer to usher in the Jet Age.

Boeing, of course, won.

The man at the helm was William Allen, native of Lolo, Mont.

(pop. 200), a lawyer for Boeing for 20 years before being named in 1945 to succeed the late Philip Johnson as company president.

They were not the best of times. Wartime contracts were being phased out, laying off thousands of production workers. Buses and trains were still favored by most long-distance travelers.

Allen never claimed engineering know-how or even a schoolboy's yearning to take the controls of a cockpit. But when it came time for Boeing to take a chance, he was a riverboat gambler.

In later years, he said he bet the farm on the 707 because he had complete faith in the engineers who thought jetliners economically feasible. He also was convinced the flying public would throw its business to the fastest and most comfortable plane.

On Aug. 7, 1955, while a quarter-million spectators gathered on the shores of Lake Washington for a Gold Cup hydroplane race, Alvin "Tex" Johnston, Boeing's chief test pilot, decided to take the Dash 80 up for a spin. He headed for the Gold Cup course, where his boss, Bill Allen, and other spectators were relaxing between heats under a powder-blue sky.

As the jet flew over, Johnston put it into a slow roll — a stunt maneuver. In case anyone missed the first roll, he repeated it.

Although Allen was relatively unflappable, he was unable to talk about the incident for years. When he finally broke his silence he told a reporter:

"I guess you could say that when he did it I was surprised. That's a mild word. I was completely startled. I was naive enough to believe it was not his intention, that he had turned too quickly and was forced to roll. Then he came back and did it again."

Allen said he had been standing beside Larry Bell of Bell Aircraft Co., who had been dipping into a small bottle and taking pills he said were for his heart.

"After Tex did his second roll," Allen said, "I had the presence of mind to say to Larry, 'Give me one of those damn pills. I need it worse than you do.' "

Johnston was called into Allen's office the next morning for an explanation. Allen said Johnston told him:

"Well . . .I had an audience of 300,000 — I just couldn't help it."

Metro

Swimming in Lake Washington was a no-no by the late 1950s, when a civic group formed to restore its purity. The result was Metro (Municipality of Metropolitan Seattle). This '58 photo was used in advertising campaigns to win support for the cleanup agency.

CHRONO-LOG

1957

One of state's more original town names, George, Wash., is dreamed up by Philip Nalder, Columbia Basin Irrigation Project manager, and Charles Brown. Town founded by Brown officially incorporated April Fool's Day 1962.

Sixteen public utility districts form Washington Public Power Supply System. (Twenty-three years later WPPSS will haunt stockholders and public officials due to massive default over financing nuclear power plants.)

Teamsters head Dave Beck appears before Senate Rackets Committee in Washington, D.C., invokes Fifth Amendment repeatedly to charges he has misused more than $300,000 in union funds. Televised hearings mark beginning of end in labor career of Beck, but he survives into 1980s as grand old statesman of labor-management, political issues.

Bucking the tide at Ediz Hook

Bert Thomas had been in the 46-degree water nearly 11 hours, his 275-pound body coated with grease, his balding head covered with a rubber cap, his tree-trunk-sized arms laboring in what with characteristic bravado he termed "the most powerful sidestroke the world has ever known." He also had said, "If you are a betting man, bet on me."

This was his moment of truth.

At 5:55 p.m. the previous day, Thomas had stepped into the Strait of Juan de Fuca at Ediz Hook, a spit jutting out from Port Angeles, for his fifth attempt to become the first human to swim the 18.3 miles of swells and tidal rips separating Vancouver Island and Washington state.

Sixteen times the Strait had turned back swimmers since the previous August when Florence Chadwick, conquerer of the English Channel, had been dragged from the water almost incoherent after 5½ hours.

Thomas, who viewed Chadwick's failure on television and had announced to his wife, Marion, "I could do that," had been stopped by cramps once and by tides three times since his boast. But all of those attempts had been on a Victoria-Port Angeles course. This time he had reversed the direction.

Traveling behind a tender from which he took nourishment through tubes and listened to loudspeaker-beamed military marches and battle songs that stirred his ex-Marine soul, Thomas continued to stroke. He smiled as his daughter, Sharon, repeatedly shouted: "Go, Daddy, go!"

Already he had passed the treacherous Race Rocks that had defeated so many swimmers. Lifting his head from the water, he could see beach fires ahead and lights blazing in houses on the banks above Esquimalt, just outside Victoria.

Now he was close enough to hear the cheers of 1,500 people who had gathered on the shore. Only another quarter mile . . .

Suddenly the tide had turned and Thomas was bucking it, going nowhere. His arms continued to move, in slow motion.

Twenty-five yards from shore, Thomas put everything into a final sprint. His feet touched bottom. He staggered onto the shore and lurched into the waiting arms of his wife.

It was 5:05 a.m., July 8, 1955. Eleven hours and 10 minutes had elapsed since Thomas left Ediz Hook. The former Marine frogman, ex-logger and football player out of tiny Morton, in the Cascade foothills, had proved conclusively that his critics were wrong. He was not a fake. He had made good on his biggest boast.

In May 1956, Thomas became the first person to swim from Seattle to Tacoma (15 hours, 23 minutes). In August 1958, he attempted to swim the English Channel both ways, nonstop. He

completed the France-to-England swim, but failed to make it back.

Thomas died of a heart attack in 1972 at age 46. There is a plaque at Ediz Hook marking the spot where he stepped into the water for his historic swim.

Home for Christmas the hard way

It was Dec. 18, 1955, and a storm was boiling down out of the Arctic when a C-45 cargo plane, en route from Moses Lake's Larson Air Force Base to an air station at Blaine, Whatcom County, went into a flat spin over the Cascades.

It fell to about 10,000 feet before the pilot, Maj. Glen Pebles, commander of the Blaine air station, brought it under control.

When the plane continued to lose altitude, Pebles ordered his two crewmen and a military hitchhiker to don parachutes. The hitchhiker was Sgt. John Horan, 25, a paratrooper who had been bumming rides from Fort Bragg, N.C., to Fort Lewis, to join his Japanese war bride and their three small children.

His family was arriving by ship in Seattle, Horan said, and he was going to spend Christmas with them.

Hoping to lighten the load on the struggling plane, Pebles ordered Horan to jump about 15 miles west of Ellensburg. No sooner had Horan left the craft than it began to stabilize. Pebles continued on toward Blaine with the two crewmen. They would not have to jump.

It was 1:30 p.m. when Horan's parachute opened and he found himself in a blizzard, falling toward trees and a thick snowpack. He wore a GI jacket, a winter uniform and paratrooper's boots. In his pocket was his wife's Christmas present, a necklace. Horan's chances of survival were next to zero. His only hope seemed to be that he might land near a highway.

The sergeant came down in a small clearing on Keechelus Ridge. Bundling up his 'chute, he began scrambling through eight-feet-deep snow, sinking almost to his hips with every step. He floundered on for hours, perspiring despite the cold, hoping to find a sign of civilization.

As darkness fell, he spied a cabin and struggled toward it, legs aching, feet numb, very hungry. Smashing a window, Horan crawled inside, finding matches for a fire and some cocoa. He melted snow and made hot cocoa, feeling stronger as he thawed out. He thought he could hear the roar of trucks in the distance.

By morning, searchers were looking for the lost sergeant — about 20 miles from where he had landed. Meanwhile, Horan had left the cabin on snowshoes fashioned from shingles ripped from the cabin's roof. He had gone about 500 feet when the shingles broke under his weight. He returned to the cabin with a heavy heart.

The next day his luck was no better.

Back in Seattle, the Navy transport Frederick Funston docked and Teruko Horan was met by a chaplain instead of her husband.

"I don't know, I don't know," was all she could repeat after hearing the news. She and the three children were taken to Fort Lawton's Hostess House to wait. They held out little hope.

On the third day, Horan figured he'd make one more try. Desperately searching the cabin, Horan's eyes lit on the small wire shelves in the refrigerator. Wrapping his feet in pieces of parachute and tying on the shelves with straps, he started out again.

All afternoon and night he floundered through the snow. With the makeshift snowshoes, he sank only about 18 inches. It wasn't fast, but he was moving.

An icy rain drenched his wool clothing. His lungs burned. But to rest was out of the question.

The morning of Dec. 22 was more of the same. Then about midday, he began hearing truck noises. The rain fell harder than ever and he was numb with the cold, but his spirits were buoyed. There was no way he was going to quit with the noise that close.

He dropped over the rim of a hill, hearing cars on the Snoqualmie Pass highway and human voices. He slid down a snow bank onto the highway, rounded a bend and hobbled into Rustic Inn, near Easton. Everyone there, it seemed, had heard about the lost parachutist.

As Horan sipped soup and hot tea and removed the soaked parachute bindings from his painfully frostbitten feet, he asked about his wife and the men in the

Associated Press

Army Sgt. John Horan recuperates after his December 1955 ordeal.

disabled C-45. His wife had arrived and the men had landed safely, he was told.

It was 4 p.m. Dec. 22. A depressed Mrs. Horan had been invited along with her children to attend a Christmas party at Fort Lawton. As she sat looking at a Christmas tree, the auxiliary chaplain walked up to her and with a smile said:

"This is your first Christmas in America, Mrs. Horan. We have the most wonderful present for you. Your husband is safe."

Shortly afterward, Horan was on the phone to his wife. He was sorry, he said, but he had lost her Christmas present during his ordeal. All he could bring was himself.

Horan spent weeks in the hospital and lost all his toes to frostbite. He settled down in Stowe, Vt., where he became the town's postmaster. The couple also had another child.

Years later he said that every Christmas he put the refrigerator shelves under the tree and waited for one of his children to say:

"Dad, tell us about your Christmas adventure a long time ago."

The hostage season

The "Big House" at Walla Walla had always been a place where inmates were put in cells and the public could forget them. Maybe that was the problem.

In the summer of 1955, prisoners armed with homemade knives, axes and baseball bats twice took guards as hostages to bargain for better conditions.

In early July, the inmates grabbed nine hostages and staged a 26-hour revolt. It ended when Dr. Thomas Harris, state director of institutions, agreed to a variety of reforms.

Six weeks later, a dozen convicts grabbed 14 hostages for six hours to force Warden Lawrence Delmore Jr., to grant them personal interviews in which to air further complaints. He agreed.

After the riots, legislators and lawmen criticized Harris as being too lenient. But he claimed he had made the best possible deal under the circumstances.

Besides, it was pointed out, no one was injured.

Public and private moments with Elvis

A sideburned young man in tight-fitting black pants, a black shirt unbuttoned to the breastbone and a sequined gold jacket leaped onto a stage in Tacoma's Lincoln Bowl on Sept. 1, 1957, and ran his fingers across the strings of a guitar slung over his shoulder.

The result was pandemonium among the 6,000 screaming spectators, about 80 percent of them teen-age girls, who had gathered in folding chairs and bleacher seats for Elvis Presley's first appearance in the Pacific Northwest.

Presley, 22, fresh from a shot on the Ed Sullivan show in which he had been photographed only from the waist up because of his gyrations, flashed that familiar pouty smile and launched into "Don' be cruel to a heart that's true . . ."

As he sang, he began a slow rhythmic movement of his pelvic region, his legs vibrated, his upper torso caught up the movement and alternately swayed and shimmied. Each new movement was greeted by fresh screams.

The baritone voice was charged with electricity. Presley's celebrated movements, along with his caressing of the microphone, oozed s-e-x appeal at a time when that three-letter word rarely was spoken in polite society.

Elvis sang at least a dozen songs — "Heartbreak Hotel," "Teddy Bear," "Blue Suede Shoes," "Love Me Tender" — before climaxing the show with a frenetic, whirling-dervish rendition of what he called "The Elvis Presley National Anthem":

"Hew hain't nuthin' but a houn' dog, cry-hy-in' all the time . . ."

He strutted like a duck, hands dangling loosely in front of him. He went to his knees in an attitude of prayer, taking the slender mike with him. And he finished with a burst of shimmying that left him limp, his thick black hair hanging over his eyes, perspiration pouring down his pancake makeup.

Elvis did a Tarzanlike leap from the stage, raced to a waiting limousine and was whisked away in a cloud of dust.

Girls, dragging unwilling boys by the hand, rushed to the spot where Elvis had vaulted into the car. They scooped up the dirt, kissed it and poured it into pockets and purses. Then they tore off to the stands, these wives and mothers of tomorrow, to where hucksters were doing a brisk business in Presley buttons.

Earlier, Col. Tom Parker, the man who gave the nation the alcohol-based elixir Hadacol before becoming Elvis' agent, introduced his meal ticket to the assembled press.

Elvis, polite and boyish-looking, wore a straw hat, an expensive-looking blue-and-white sweater and loafers. Prefacing every answer with "Suh," he said he had four Cadillacs, a Messerschmidt, a Lincoln, a Mark II and two motorcycles, and was trying to save his money.

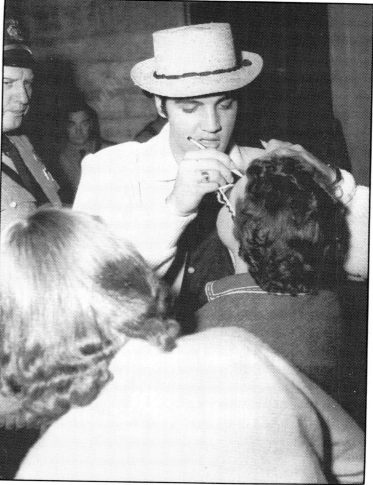
Elvis Presley autographs a fan's forehead during an appearance — the rock 'n' roll idol's first in the Pacific Northwest — at Tacoma's Lincoln Bowl on Sept. 1, 1957.

Wayne Zimmerman

He didn't consider his gyrations immoral ("Suh, I'd never do anything to shame my mutha.") And he was ready to go into the service if drafted (he was; he did).

Presley made his second appearance that night in Sicks' Stadium in Seattle, attracting more than 16,000 shrieking fans.

He would appear several more times in the Northwest, including an extended stay in 1962 to film "Take Me to the Fair" at the Century 21 Exposition, and a performance in April 1976, when he was a bloated parody of what he had been 19 years earlier. He died Aug. 16, 1977, at the age of 42.

There were Presley fan clubs all over the world at the apex of the singer's fame. But Patricia Maude Patterson, who headed one of the clubs, had more reason than most for her devotion. The Seattle woman had first met Presley when he was 10, "very poor, wearing patched jeans and living in a small house" in Mississippi.

One of the fondest memories of Patterson's life was the night Presley called her when he was filming "Take Me to the Fair" and asked if he could come to her Queen Anne home and relax. He sang to her that night, while she — 70 years old, a link with his past — played the piano.

The rise, fall and rise of Dave Beck

Dave Beck, who grew up in Seattle's Belltown and rose from laundry-truck driver to labor organizer to president of the powerful International Brotherhood of Teamsters, had been a household name around Puget Sound for years when he suddenly became unofficial Public Enemy No. 1.

The occasion was the televised Senate Rackets Committee hearings in Washington, D.C., in 1957. Although many had read about him for years, it was the first time they had seen the blue-eyed, cherub-cheeked Beck close up and personal.

Under intense questioning by the committee chairman, Sen. John McClellan, D-Ark., and the committee's no-holds-barred counsel, tousle-haired Robert F. Kennedy, Beck repeatedly invoked the Fifth Amendment against self-incrimination when asked about Teamsters money, including a flat-out charge that he had misused more than $300,000 in union funds.

It was sensational stuff, and it marked the beginning of the end of the labor career of the man who had succeeded Dan Tobin as

Roy Scully / Seattle Times

Heavyweight amateur champion Pete Rademacher, center figure in the Sicks' Stadium ring, squares off in the opening round against his professional counterpart, Floyd Patterson, the night of Aug. 22, 1957.

CHRONO-LOG

1958

U.S. Department of Justice settles last "official" claims of Japanese-Americans for property losses during World War II internment on West Coast. (In 1988, however, Congress passes and President Reagan signs bill providing $20,000 to each internee on grounds that constitutional rights have been violated.)

Husky rowing crew scores 1½-length victory over Leningrad Trud Rowing Club's eight-oared shell in 2,000-meter race on Khimkinskoe Reservoir. Event marks first American sports team to compete in Soviet Union after war. Defeat is so unexpected Russians have to delay awards ceremony as they search for suitable trophy.

1959

Boeing 707 transport makes first nonstop flight from London to Seattle.

Legislature makes first appropriation for Seattle World's Fair — "Century 21" Exposition — which will be held in 1962.

head of the Teamsters.

Beck wound up in court, where the federal government found him guilty of two counts of filing false income-tax returns for a union council and the state found him guilty of misusing $1,900 from the sale of a union-owned Cadillac.

Beck went to federal prison on McNeil Island in 1962, where he served half of a 5½-year sentence (the sentences were served concurrently).

It was quite a comedown for Beck: friend of the nation's mighty; asked by Franklin D. Roosevelt to join his Cabinet as secretary of labor; the only person to serve as a University of Washington regent without graduating from high school.

But Beck fooled a lot of people. He emerged from prison the eternal optimist, expressing faith in the growth potential of the Puget Sound area, saying the enforced vacation had given him a chance to exercise, sleep without worry and improve his diet.

He was fond of saying that it would be good for his embattled successor, Jimmy Hoffa, to go to prison, "because I came out in much better shape than when I went in."

Instead of hiding from the public, Beck returned to Seattle to walk the streets, head high, and greet old friends. He made himself available to college students who wanted to ask questions of a real-life labor legend. He spoke on the creamed-peas-and-chicken luncheon circuit, singing a song that was music to businessmen's ears — strong on anti-communism, all-out for cooperation between labor and management.

Governor Rosellini granted Beck a state pardon in 1964. President Gerald Ford followed with a federal pardon in 1975.

The man who, in his labor-organizing days, had been accused of putting goon squads into the streets to bring bosses to heel, suddenly found himself far more popular than if he had stayed on top.

Beck continued to enjoy good health and a sharp memory into his 90s, working out real-estate deals and untangling tax problems that continued to dog him. The only person he could never bring himself to forgive, he said, was Bobby Kennedy, for the way he had treated him during the rackets hearings.

Lords of the ring

It was pure P.T. Barnum. Audacious, preposterous, incredible. Step right up, folks.

Curiosity whetted, the folks did — paying $10 for general-admission tickets to Sicks' Stadium the night of Aug. 22, 1957, to witness the first-ever heavyweight title bout between the

professional and amateur champions of the world.

At 9:30 p.m., the balding, articulate amateur champion, the Melbourne Olympic Games heavyweight gold medalist, Pete Rademacher — out of Grandview, Yakima County — walked to the center of an 18-foot ring constructed over the stadium's pitcher's mound. The 28-year-old Rademacher stood opposite the somber, gentlemanly king of the world's professional heavyweights, 22-year-old Floyd Patterson.

The referee and sole arbiter of the conflict was Tommy Loughran, himself a former light-heavyweight champion of dancing-master skills.

At ringside, to report on what some termed "the greatest mismatch since the Christians fought the lions," were such heralded members of the sports-writing fraternity as Red Smith of the New York Herald Tribune, John Lardner of Newsweek, Jimmy Cannon of the New York Post, Martin Kane of Sports Illustrated and Nate Fleischer of Ring magazine.

In the top-dollar seats were Bing Crosby, Phil Harris, Ralph Edwards, Art Linkletter and other luminaries. They were among 16,961 fans who paid a total of $243,000 — "the largest gate of modern times in the West" — to see if a 202-pound bull could catch up with a 187-pound matador.

Lurking in the wings, counting the house, keeping out would-be gate-crashers, was the gaunt undertakerish figure of "Deacon" Jack Hurley, who, having missed the opportunity to foist the Piltdown Man on a gullible world, had conjured up this midsummer night's dream.

With the flair of a true impresario, Hurley literally had staged the fight out of the Olympic Hotel room that served as his sleeping quarters, ticket office and matchmaking headquarters. He put money in one pocket and sold tickets out of the other.

The pain in his ulcerated stomach was nothing compared to the stab in his heart at having to charge admission for this spectacular event, Hurley had said with straightforward gaze. But when the UW regents denied him the use of Husky Stadium, and he had to stage the bout in the smaller Sicks', he had been "forced" to charge admission so the real connoisseurs could attend.

Whatever happened once the bell rang, Hurley couldn't lose. A covey of well-heeled marks from Columbus, Ga., calling themselves Youth Unlimited, Inc., and backing Rademacher, had anted a $250,000 guarantee to Patterson.

Never mind that the New York Boxing Association had demanded that its Washington State counterpart be expelled from the national association for sanctioning the fight. Never mind that Rep. Hugh Scott of Pennsylvania had sent Washington's Gov. Albert Rosellini an impassioned telegram imploring him to halt this "preplanned slaughter."

The bell rang on schedule.

Rademacher pursued, clumsily. Patterson, in his peek-a-boo style, retreated. It was a dull first round. The experts favored Patterson. Loughran, the only one whose vote counted, gave the round to Rademacher.

The second round forever will be engraved in the memories of those who witnessed it. David threw his rock and found Goliath.

Rademacher landed two hard rights to Patterson's head, then uncorked another right and Patterson went down. The champion of the world was off his feet for the count of four and there was bedlam. Although Loughran ruled it a slip, it was not. Patterson said so later.

Not really hurt, Patterson wore that faintly bemused expression that was to become so familiar in the years that followed. He bounced up and deftly dodged as Rademacher pursued with wild, misdirected blows. Rademacher's round again.

The third saw Patterson hit Rademacher hard very early. Rademacher eventually went down for a nine count.

There should have been no fourth round. The experts had said so. But there was. And Rademacher, although repeatedly beaten to the punch, gamely kept swinging.

Skill showed in the fifth. Patterson's skill. The commercial champion knocked down the amateur pretender four times with right hands, for counts of five, seven, nine and nine.

In the sixth, Patterson decked Rademacher for a nine-count early in the going and finished him off with a hard right near the end. Loughran might not have tolled a legitimate "10," but Rademacher's trainer, George Chemeres, was hollering: "That's it!" That's IT!"

When the nation's sportswriters and broadcasters balloted at the end of 1957 for the sports oddity of the year, the Rademacher-Patterson fight won in a walk. Hal Wood, United Press sportswriter in San Francisco, called it flat-out "the top sports event of 1957." Wood wrote:

"Never in the history of prize fights has there been such a ridiculous and successful promotion as this one."

Deacon Hurley, whose nickname derived from his somber dress and mournful look, continued to hold court in the lobby of the Olympic until his death in 1972.

8. CHALLENGE AND CHANGE

A TIME OF FALLEN HEROES, CIVIL RIGHTS, CAMPUS UNREST AND A WAR THAT WON'T GO AWAY

**1960 TO
1970**

'I thought: It's a disaster, a total failure; we're doomed.'

— City Councilman Al Rochester, originator of 1962 Seattle World's Fair, upon first visiting it

Richard S. Heyza / Seattle Times

Bedraggled concertgoers build campfires and take shelter under makeshift tents at the first Sky River Rock Festival and Lighter Than Air Fair in September 1968 near Sultan. Below, the shaft of a partly finished Space Needle soars starkly skyward on the Denny Regrade in October 1961.

Unlike the generally laid back '50s, whose major dislocations were McCarthyism and a brutal war in Korea, the Soaring '60s were marked by dramatic social change, national heartache and challenges to the "system."

At the beginning of the decade, "Put on a Happy Face" and "Itsy Bitsy Teenie Weenie Yellow Polka Dot Bikini" blared from our radios. But "Never on Sunday" was more representative of a growing tell-it-like-it-is mood. And soon we heard "Where Have All the Flowers Gone" and "Blowin' in the Wind" and "Little Boxes."

Movie patrons lined up for "Exodus," "Ben Hur" (a remake of the 1926 silent spectacle), "Inherit the Wind," "Easy Rider" and "The Apartment," but stayed away in

Seattle Times

CHRONO-LOG

1960

UW Huskies chalk up first Rose Bowl victory by beating Wisconsin 44-8. Big heroes: quarterback Bob Schloredt, halfback George Fleming. Game also marks first time Huskies score points in Pasadena since 1926.

Jo Anne Gunderson of Kirkland wins both women's national amateur golf title and women's collegiate golf title.

The Brothers Four, folk-singing group formed at UW chapter of Phi Gamma Delta (Fiji) fraternity, is invited to appear on Ed Sullivan Show. For next decade, singers Mike Kirkland, John Paine, Dick Foley and Bob Flick tour nation's campuses singing "Greenfields," "Green Leaves of Summer," "Michael, Row Your Boat Ashore," "Try to Remember," "This Land is Your Land." Kirkland later replaced by Bob Haworth; Foley becomes KOMO-TV talk-show personality in '70s and '80s.

Gail Cogdill, former Washington State University pass-catcher, is named 1960s Rookie of the Year in National Football League for performance with Detroit Lions. Meanwhile, WSU end Hugh Campbell sets national collegiate record for receptions and yards gained.

In 1969, "the Rev." Fred W. DeMara, the hard-working new pastor of San Juan Baptist church in Friday Harbor, turned out to be none other than Ferdinand Waldo DeMara, "The Great Imposter," famed for posing in the past as a psychology professor, a Trappist monk, an assistant warden in a Texas prison and a surgeon with the Royal Canadian Navy.

droves from the $37 million bust, "Cleopatra," starring Liz Taylor and Richard Burton. Stay-at-homes viewed "Wyatt Earp," "Peter Gunn," "Maverick," "Father Knows Best," "77 Sunset Strip" and "The Untouchables," which told it the way the sponsors said it was.

Among the cultural oddities: The Frug. The Watusi. The Monkey. Go-go boots. Fishnet stockings. The mini-skirt, and its logical flip-side, the maxi-skirt, as well as the forgettable Nehru jacket.

And maybe not so odd in a decade that saw the introduction of The Pill, to stop conception, and the sexual revolution, to make it easier, the big Northeast Blackout of Nov. 9, 1965, affected 30 million people and nine months later resulted in a dramatic increase in the birth rate.

In May 1960 Francis Gary Powers was shot down over the Soviet Union in his U-2 spy plane, and Ike got caught in a national fib.

Robert Welch was beginning to promote the ultra-conservative John Birch Society, and everyone wanted to know what Tonight Show host Jack Paar was really like.

Adlai Stevenson verbalized brilliantly. Judy Garland sang about rainbows and other hard-to-catch things. Clark Gable, Marilyn Monroe, Gary Cooper and Robert Taylor epitomized Hollywood's star system. And none would survive the decade.

When a freckled redhead, John Glenn, the prototype all-American boy, orbited the earth three times Feb. 20, 1962, he captured

Greg Gilbert / Seattle Times

In a ceremony typical of the hippie '60s, Joyce McClain and Robert Fuller marry in Golden Gardens Park. Officiating, at center, is Monty West, a former visiting assistant professor of anthropology at the UW.

the public's fancy as no one since Charles Lindbergh became the first to fly alone across the Atlantic.

Americans held their breath in October 1962 wondering who would blink first — President John F. Kennedy or Soviet Premier Nikita Khrushchev — in the Cuban missile crisis. They were shocked that same year to learn that the drug thalidomide had caused thousands of babies to be born deformed.

It was a decade of fallen heroes. Lee Harvey Oswald ended Kennedy's quest for Camelot Nov. 22, 1963 in Dallas and plunged the nation into numbing grief, inescapable because the shocking visuals could be played and replayed, hour after hour, on TV. James Earl Ray gunned down Martin Luther King Jr. April 4, 1968 on a Memphis motel balcony and we wrung our hands and said, "When will it end?" The question was answered "not yet" when, on June 5, 1968 in Los Angeles, Sirhan Sirhan halted Robert Kennedy's bid to succeed his fallen brother.

In time, our leaders quit referring to the troops in Vietnam as "advisers." They were there, they said, to prevent fulfillment of the "domino theory" (if Indochina topples, other nations in Southeast Asia and the Pacific Rim will fall).

Each month brought a dramatic increase in the body bags being flown out of Dak To. Lyndon Johnson, who succeeded Kennedy and pushed through massive social legislation to further the Great Society, would be driven from the office by a war whose momentum he had increased with the 1964 Gulf of Tonkin incident and then could not stop.

Before the decade ended, teachers would picket, Indians would stage fish-ins and college presidents would engage in — and often

lose — arguments with the Black Student Union and Students for a Democratic Society.

Blacks who began the decade literally as Ralph Ellison's "Invisible Man" ended it on newspaper front pages and as featured players on the evening news. There was the violence of sit-ins, Bull Connors sending police dogs after civil rights marchers in Birmingham, Ala., the Selma, Ga., march, and King's "I Have a Dream" speech on the Washington Mall.

Although the Civil Rights Act of 1964 and the Voting Rights Act of '65 were the most significant human-rights laws since the Emancipation Proclamation a century earlier, they increased expectations rather than bringing an end to the struggle. The inner cities of Detroit, Newark and Los Angeles went up in flames as violence erupted in the ghettos. In Seattle, luckier than most, the upheaval was limited to rock-throwing, name-calling and sit-ins.

Riots in the streets during Chicago's Democratic Convention of '68 gave a black eye to Chicago police and the city's "Boss," Mayor Richard Daley, and upstaged what was going on inside the convention hall. The Democratic nominee, Hubert Humphrey, paid the price by losing a close election to Richard Nixon, even though he carried Washington state, the only state in the West outside of Hawaii to vote Democratic.

Scandal tore at the last vestiges of our innocence. The last Kennedy, Ted,

inheritor of the name and the mystique, blew what seemed an automatic bid for the presidency when his car plunged off a bridge July 18, 1969, and campaign worker Mary Jo Kopechne was drowned at a place called Chappaquiddick — the same week that we celebrated one of our nation's most glorious accomplishments, the moon landing. West Point, bastion of honor, dismissed 105 cadets for cheating. And in far-off Vietnam, American GIs ostensibly sent to bring about democracy were murdering civilians in what became known as the My Lai massacre.

The '60s brought us books that heightened our concerns about auto safety (Ralph Nader's "Unsafe at Any Speed") and the environment (Rachel Carson's indictment of pesticides, "Silent Spring") and marked the introduction ('63) of The Seattle Times Troubleshooter to answer the questions of an increasingly sophisticated consumer-oriented society.

Statistics (we loved numbers) showed that Jonas Salk's polio vaccine, introduced in 1954, was really working. Polio cases dropped from 35,592 in 1953 to fewer than 100 in '64.

Outdoorsy Washingtonians cheered the creation of a 400,000-acre North Cascades National Park. The more sedentary were happy to see completion of the North Cross-State Highway.

Construction began on the $390 million third powerhouse to make Grand Coulee Dam once again the world's largest hydroelectric-power producer (9 million kilowatts).

There were dramatic changes.

Sunday liquor was approved for lounges and taverns. And motorists, for the first time since 1926, had to get used to long stretches of highway without the benefit of Burma-Shave signs when Philip Morris took over the shaving-cream company and

Richard S. Heyza / Seattle Times

Actor Marlon Brando gestures to an Olympia audience while speaking on behalf of Indian fishing rights in March 1964 — a full 10 years before the famed Boldt decision. Behind Brando sits Gov. Albert Rosellini.

decided on up-tempo advertising. But those who motored in Washington and other states during the signs' heyday would never forget such commercial poetry as:

Paul V. Thomas / Seattle Times

The brash, outdoorsy, take-charge vim of Bobby Kennedy, left, shown here on an Olympic Peninsula hike with Supreme Court Justice William O. Douglas, typified the early '60s.

Within this vale of toil and sin
your head grows bald but not your chin.

— Burma Shave

Dan Evans bucked a Democratic tide in 1964 to capture the governor's office from two-time Gov. Albert D. Rosellini. Evans would become the state's first governor to win election three straight times, a feat that was especially noteworthy because: He campaigned for a state income tax the voters wouldn't approve, denounced the John Birch Society in defiance of his party's right wing, and openly supported Nelson Rockefeller over Richard Nixon when Evans was the keynote speaker at the 1968 Republican convention.

The state's population increased by 560,030 in the '60s (from 2,853,214 to 3,413,244). But the growth no longer was in the big cities. Seattle's population fell by more than 26,000 (from 557,087 to 530,831), a decline that would continue through the '70s.

On Good Friday, March 27, 1964, much of south central Alaska was devastated by the most violent earthquake officially recorded in North America. It registered between 8.3 and 8.5 on the Richter scale (25 times stronger than Washington's '49 quake) and claimed 113 lives.

It also unleashed an enormous tsunami, or seismic sea wave, that swept southward, killing four campers on the Oregon coast and more than a dozen people in Crescent City, Calif. Several bridges along the Washington coast were washed out. A year later, scientists determined that the initial shock, plus the 12,000 aftershocks that occurred in the next 69 days, contained 500,000 times the energy yield of the atomic bomb set off over Hiroshima in 1945.

We had our share of mysteries:

■ Eight-year-old Ann Marie Burr vanished from her Tacoma home on a Sunday morning in August 1961. Although her parents never gave up hope and police refused to close the file, no trace of the youngster would be found.

■ A thunderous explosion, followed by fire, ripped through half a city block in North Spokane in March 1962. Twenty-nine people were hurt, four buildings demolished and power lines downed. There was speculation that it was caused by a natural-gas leak. But the source was never found.

Former President Harry Truman wounded Washington's civic

CHRONO-LOG

1961
*Eighteen servicemen die
May 24 as C-124
Globemaster crashes three
miles south of McCbord Air
Force Base.*

*Bob Twitchell,
former Snohomish County
sheriff, three others
convicted in federal court
of conspiracy to permit a
prostitution ring to operate.*

*Anne Marie Burr, 8,
vanishes from parents'
home in Tacoma during
night of Aug. 31. She is never
found.*

1962
*Explosion, fire rip
through North Spokane in
March, injuring 29. Cause is
never found.*

*Century 21 Exposition,
known as Seattle World's
Fair, opens April 21. In its
six-month run, it draws 9.6
million visitors; even turns
profit.*

*Dave Beck, former head
of Teamsters union, enters
McNeil Island federal prison
June 20 to begin serving
five-year sentence for
preparing fraudulent union
income-tax return.*

*Boeing loses
multibillion-dollar TFX
contract to General
Dynamics, headquartered
in Fort Worth. Feeling is
that Boeing bid lost because
Vice President Lyndon
Johnson wanted contract
for his home state.*

*A brief sign of the times
was this neon emblem of
the Seattle Pilots baseball
team at Sicks' Stadium.
The team lasted there all of
the 1969 season.*

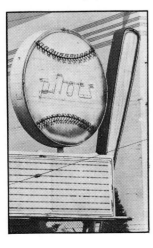

Greg Gilbert / Seattle Times

*Makeshift clubs are swung in April 1969 when a melee erupts outside the University of Washington's Loew Hall.
Demonstrating Students for a Democratic Society (SDS) were trying to halt job-placement interviews with private
companies and government agencies the protesters felt were fueling the Vietnam War.*

pride in 1963 when he said Eisenhower's 1954 decision to mothball the battleship Missouri at the Bremerton Naval Shipyard was equivalent to putting the vessel in a closet because so few people could see it there. Personally, said feisty Harry, he preferred Brooklyn, San Francisco or Norfolk, Va., as a showcase for the historic battlewagon on which the Japanese officially surrendered to end World War II.

Truman's comment prompted King County Commissioner Ed Munro to send Bremerton Mayor H.O. Domstad a letter, addressed to the mayor of Closet, Wash. It was delivered without a hitch.

Truman notwithstanding, the Mighty Mo continued to attract nearly 300,000 visitors a year to Bremerton before it was moved to Long Beach, Calif., in 1984 for a $500 million overhaul and a return to active duty.

The 1965 Legislature spun its wheels for 47 days while politicians bickered over the state's first legislative redistricting in 64 years. The compromise measure finally signed by Governor Evans was designed to fulfill the Supreme Court's "one-man, one-vote" mandate.

On New Year's Eve 1966, Boeing was named as winner of the supersonic-transport design competition. There was much cheering. But an American-built SST proved an elusive dream.

An event of far greater importance to Boeing and the Pacific Northwest occurred in 1968 when the world's largest commercial jetliner, the 747, roared off an Everett airfield and launched a new era in air travel.

Fluoridation of Seattle's water supply finally won voter approval on the third try in November 1968. An attempt to turn back the clock was overwhelmingly rejected five years later.

The first of the Baby Boom generation went off to college in the late '60s, and life would never be the same. Most had

been reared according to Dr. Benjamin Spock and had the best baby-sitters, including the electronic box in the living room. Many had been given private lessons in everything from tennis to yoga.

They were the biggest, healthiest and, presumably, least likely generation in the nation's history to engage in protest. But that is exactly what they did.

They grew their hair long, donned ragged clothes, strummed guitars, burned draft cards as well as incense and coined slogans — "Stop and smell the flowers," "Make love, not war," "Do your own thing" — which made at least as much sense as mainstream society's new catchwords: relevant, viable and meaningful.

Many gathered in the northwest corner of the University of Washington campus, dubbed "Hippie Hill," to get high on pot, acid, speed and crystal and stay out of the way of the police they called pigs.

While parents fretted about the new drugs, young adults pointed to their parents' dependence on an old one, alcohol. It was the start of street kids, co-ed dormitories and "pads" shared by scores of young people.

Richard S. Heyza / Seattle Times

*Jimi Hendrix's beadstone in Greenwood Memorial Park in
Renton.*

The 1968 Sky River Rock Festival and Lighter Than Air Fair at Sultan made history of a sort in Snohomish County when it rained and the place turned into a quagmire and everyone had a marvelous time wallowing in the mud. The second annual festival and fair went off peacefully, in a cloud of pot smoke, near Tenino.

The Seattle native who may best have captured the spirit of the troubled late '60s was Jimi Hendrix, a rock guitarist — some called him the best ever — who dropped out of Garfield High School and never seemed overly enamored of his hometown.

Hendrix who affected an enormous Afro, beads, feathers and colorful costumes and played with lightning fingers and wrote Bob Dylan-like lyrics, found fame in London and New York and other places far from his roots. During a concert tour in Seattle in 1968, he agreed to address the student body of Garfield. Asked by a student how long ago he had left the school, Hendrix replied, "Oh, about 90 million years ago."

In terms of how far he was removed from the city, in terms of interests, fame and fortune, the hyperbole may have been justified. Hendrix died in September 1970, presumably of a drug overdose, leaving a legacy of music and a style still revered by rock aficionados. He was a featured performer in the documentary film "Woodstock," along with Joe Cocker, Joan Baez, Sly & the Family Stone, and Country Joe and the Fish.

Hendrix is buried in Renton's Greenwood Cemetery, under a headstone marked by a guitar and the words: "Forever in Our Hearts. James M. 'Jimi' Hendrix, 1942-1970."

Rock fans raised $30,000 to establish a memorial viewpoint to Hendrix in the African savanna area of Woodland Park Zoo. It was dedicated in the summer of '83.

"Will I live tomorrow? Well, I just can't say. But I know for sure I don't live today."

— From Hendrix's "I Don't Live Today"

The '60s left some indelible memories:

■ Two Washingtonians wrote best-sellers. Mary McCarthy, born in Seattle, won critical acclaim for "The Group," a novel about young women graduating from Vassar College and entering the world of the 1930s.

Frank Herbert, of Tacoma, persevered through rejections by 20 publishers and finally saw the publication of his science-fiction "Dune" trilogy, which became a cult classic and was translated into 14 languages. A $40 million film version of the novel, produced in 1984, starred former Seattle actor Kyle MacLachlan.

■ An automobile-insurance firm canceled a Seattle man's policy because of "pornographic art" in his home, then reinstated it when the "porno" was determined to be a copy of a statue by Michelangelo and two Picasso prints.

■ Helen Hubner accidentally tossed into her garbage three tissue-wrapped rings valued at $5,000 and spent four days burrowing in refuse at Seattle's South Park transfer center to retrieve them.

■ Seven members of the far-right Minutemen — arrested by the FBI and charged with conspiring to rob four Seattle-area banks, blow up the Redmond police station and dynamite a Redmond power plant — labeled themselves, James Bond-style, from 001 to 007.

■ When Jim Owens' UW Huskies received a bid to the 1964 Rose Bowl with a lowly 6-4 record, former Husky coach Howie Odell wisecracked:

"How times change. I remember when we were 7-3 — and I got fired."

■ Henry Broderick, Seattle's best-known realtor, quipped to 99-year-old Joshua Green, Seattle's best-known financier, when Green was named Seattle's Man of the Century: "You've lived so long you're a curiosity."

Green, noted for his high celluloid collars and Southern charm, died in January 1975 at the age of 105.

UW life is a bowl of roses

On the first day of the new decade, a one-eyed quarterback named Bob Schloredt and a versatile halfback/field-goal kicker named George Fleming led the University of Washington Huskies to a stunning 44-8 victory over Wisconsin in the Rose Bowl.

Local fans took to the streets at game's end, honking car horns, shouting themselves hoarse and shooting off fireworks. Head man Jim Owens, a master at developing hard-nosed young men to play both offense and defense, was hailed as the savior of Husky football. The day after the game he could have run for any public office in the state and won in a walk.

The outcome on New Year's Day strained credulity.

It was not only the Huskies' first Rose Bowl victory, but the first time they had scored any points in Pasadena since 1926. The Big Ten had defeated Pacific Coast Conference teams in 12 of the past 13 Rose Bowl games.

Schloredt, already named to the Associated Press All-American team, shared honors with Fleming as the game's Most Valuable Player. (Fleming would eventually serve several terms in the Legislature and be a candidate for lieutenant governor in 1988.) But almost any fan on the street could name other Husky stars: Lee Folkins. Kurt Gegner. Chuck Allen. Tim Bullard. John Meyers. Roy McCasson. Bill Kinnune. Don McKeta. Ray Jackson. Joe Jones. Don Millich.

The margin of victory looked like a typographical error.

The Huskies scored six touchdowns and one field goal, a 44-yarder by Fleming. Fleming also returned a punt for a 55-yard

touchdown and kicked five extra points. Schloredt ran for one touchdown, passed for another and accounted for 95 yards running and 102 yards passing.

An encore was impossible. But the Huskies gave it a good try the following year when they found themselves in their second-straight Rose Bowl, this time against heavily favored Minnesota, ranked No. 1 in all the polls.

Washington won, 17-7, and claimed the national title.

It wasn't easy. The Huskies scored all their points in the first half, then held off the much larger Minnesota team in the third and fourth quarters. Sportswriter Red Smith described it as a game of whippets (the Huskies) vs. mastiffs (the Golden Gophers).

Schloredt, star of the 1960 Rose Bowl, had suffered a broken collarbone 10 weeks before the game and been supplanted at quarterback by Bob Hivner. But he got into the '61 game early and came up with his second straight MVP performance.

Among the stars: Fleming, who kicked a long field goal; elusive running back Charlie Mitchell, and lineman Roy McCasson, who dominated the Gophers' All-American Tom Brown.

Halftime activities were marked by one of the most unusual occurrences in Rose Bowl history. A group of Cal Tech students had pilfered Husky card stunts and reworked them through the night. Fans in the stands and millions tuned in on national TV saw the substituted version:

"Cal Tech" popped up instead of "Washington." The head of the Cal Tech mascot, a beaver, supplanted that of a Husky dog. And when a slow spellout of H-u-s-k-i-e-s was called for, it came out "S-e-i-k-s-u-h."

Enough was enough. Amid howls of laughter, Husky cheerleaders suspended the remaining card stunts.

With two straight victories over the Big 10, Pacific Coast Conference teams took heart and turned the tables on their former tormentors. In fact, one of the rare Pacific Coast Conference losses in the next quarter of a century occurred on New Year's Day, 1964, when the Huskies lost to Illinois, 17-7.

The pioneers of kidney treatment

While the Huskies were defeating Wisconsin in the 1960 Rose Bowl, Dr. Belding Scribner, 38-year-old professor of medicine at the University of Washington, was fighting a battle of a far different kind.

Distressed by the deaths of several patients with kidney failure, Scribner was determined to find a way to keep others alive. The answer, he was certain, lay in being able to repeatedly hook up a kidney-dialysis machine at the same point of entry in a patient's forearm.

As it was, the artery and vein used for dialysis had to be closed after each treatment. After one or two treatments, dialysis usually was abandoned.

Scribner awoke in the middle of the night with an idea that would make medical history. Why not, he asked himself, put one tube, or cannula, in an artery and another in a vein and hook the two together with a U-shaped shunt, which could be connected to the dialysis machine. After impurities had been cleansed from the blood, the shunt could be reconnected to maintain normal blood flow.

Scribner refined the idea with the help of Dr. David Dillard, a 36-year-old surgeon and associate professor in the university's medical school, and Wayne Quinton, a 39-year-old engineer employed by the medical school.

For their first guinea pig they chose Clyde Shields, a 39-year-old machinist with kidney failure. The operation to insert the

Greg Gilbert / Seattle Times
Helmeted police line a sidewalk not far from a UW campus construction project where black contractors were protesting the lack of minority jobs in September 1969 — and had pushed a bulldozer down an embankment to make their point.

CHRONO-LOG

1962

State Rep. John Goldmark of Okanogan, three-term legislator and leader of House liberal wing, is defeated in primary after being bitterly attacked by John Birch Society and other far-right forces. Goldmark files $225,000 libel suit against four individuals and two publishing companies. He wins, but case is set aside by U.S. Supreme Court.

Forty-four servicemen die Sept. 10 as Strategic Air Command jet tanker plows into ravine 20 miles northeast of Spokane.

Columbus Day Storm wreaks havoc around Puget Sound, killing seven people and damaging countless homes.

Richard Christensen, 32-year-old Lutheran pastor from Edmonds running on GOP ticket, comes within 45,000 votes of defeating longtime Democratic Sen. Warren Magnuson and pulling off major political upset.

cannulae and tie them together with a Teflon shunt was performed March 9, 1960, at University Hospital.

Shields, who almost certainly would have died in a short time without the treatment, became the first person in history to have his life sustained indefinitely by an artificial kidney. He would return to work and enjoy grandchildren until he died 11 years later of a heart attack unrelated to his treatment.

Within a few weeks, the devices were inserted in the arms of two other patients.

Then a problem arose. Now that medical science had the know-how to keep patients alive, who would provide the treatment and where would they get enough dialysis machines?

Swedish Hospital was selected as the site of the world's first kidney center. It was opened in 1961 as the Seattle Artificial Kidney Center (now the Northwest Kidney Center).

Unfortunately, the center had the capacity to handle just a dozen of the many patients facing death from kidney failure. To decide which of the many applicants would receive treatment, a seven-member committee was formed to perform the awesome task of playing God. The committee consisted of a minister, a banker, a labor leader, a physician, a housewife, a lawyer and a government official. They served without pay and remained anonymous.

Faced with a dozen applicants for a single opening, the committee would choose the patient with the highest potential for service to society.

What was needed was a home-dialysis machine that would make treatment available to far more people. Scribner posed the problem to Dr. Albert Babb, chairman of the university's department of nuclear engineering who, along with his staff, already had made numerous improvements in early versions of the kidney machine.

A note of urgency in his voice, Scribner told Babb he had the ideal patient for home dialysis — Carolyn Helm, a 16-year-old honor student at Franklin High School. She was too young to be accepted for treatment at the kidney center and almost certainly would die within a few months without treatment.

Babb gathered his staff around him the next day to ask for their help. The response was enthusiastic. The first home unit was built at the university's nuclear reactor building and was ready for use by Helm four months after Scribner called Babb. The machine had a built-in alarm system to awaken Helm if there was a malfunction.

Thousands of copies of that first home-dialysis machine are now in use around the world. Helm was a student at the university when she died of a stroke three years after going on the machine.

Both Scribner and Babb were widely honored for their pioneer work on behalf of patients with kidney failure. Babb also played a leading role in research for new ways to treat sickle-cell anemia.

Legson Kayira at the University of Washington.

Out of Africa

Wearing an oversized overcoat given him by an assistant secretary of state in Washington, D.C., a beaming young African, Legson Kayira, arrived in Seattle in December 1960 to fulfill a vow to obtain a college education in America.

Legson, who said his age was between 18 and 22 as near as he could tell, had set out barefoot from his small village in Nyasaland (now Malawi) two years earlier in hopes of "walking to America." On his khaki shirt was a badge bearing the words "I Will Try," which inspired him to keep going.

He slept by the side of the road. He earned money for food by carrying bricks (at two-fifths of a cent each) on construction jobs.

At a U.S. Information Service library in Uganda, he found a directory to American colleges. The first one that caught his eye was Skagit Valley Junior College in Mount Vernon, Wash., which sounded as if it might be near Washington, D.C. Legson sent a letter to the college requesting admission. Two weeks later he received a reply, saying he would be admitted on a full scholarship.

Legson renewed his trek again, battling loneliness, hunger, thirst, heat and the constant fear that he would be set upon by hostile tribes. He caught a ride to Khartoum, Sudan, on a Nile steamer. There he was told he could not be granted a visa to the United States because he had no money, no medical certificate and no papers from Skagit Valley College.

The college was notified. Dr. George Hodson, dean of students at Skagit Valley, enlisted student help to raise more than $1,000 to buy clothing and pay Legson's air fare. The William Atwood family of Bayview, near the college, offered him a place to live.

Legson tried hard, despite problems with the language. He completed two years at Skagit Valley and then earned a bachelor's degree at the University of Washington.

In the summer of 1964, The Seattle Times sent reporter Lane Smith and Legson on a 12,000-mile journey back to Legson's village, to celebrate Nyasaland's emergence as the new nation of Malawi.

Legson was reunited with his mother, brother and sister and the villagers he had known as a boy. But everyone knew he was not the same young man who had left six years earlier.

Legson went on to earn a master's degree in history at Cambridge University in England. He wrote a book about his experiences and titled it, "I Will Try." He followed with four more books.

No hall for Hall

Gus Hall, general secretary of the U.S. Communist Party, came to the Pacific Northwest in February 1962 to address students on college campuses.

One after another, the doors of five state-supported colleges were closed to Hall. A variety of reasons were given, but there was a common theme: State-supported facilities should not be used to promote a "system of government alien to the American way."

Barred from colleges, Hall's backers lined up an auditorium in a downtown Seattle office building. A few days before the scheduled lecture, those doors also were closed "because of a conflict in booking."

Hall was a man without a hall.

Newspapers were flooded with letters to the editor, supporting or opposing Hall's right to speak. Campus opinion was divided. Some faculty members at the University of Washington, citing academic freedom, said students should have an opportunity to hear Hall, especially since he was clearly labeled as a Communist and his message was obviously "left-wing propaganda."

Hall finally found his forum — Eagleson Hall, operated by the University YMCA-YWCA.

At the appointed hour, the hall, across from the UW campus, was jammed with college students who wanted to hear what the fuss was all about. They expected dynamite and were treated to a soggy firecracker.

Hall's message — telling students how they were being exploited by capitalism — had little relevance for those who had never known want. Some of his comments were greeted with derisive laughter.

Drs. John Caner, Rachit Buri and Belding Scribner test artificial-kidney equipment used in a low-temperature technique they developed at the University of Washington School of Medicine.

Opening-day ceremonies at the Seattle World's Fair in April 1962 included a water-skiing exhibition at Memorial Stadium.

When tempers had cooled on both sides, Ross Cunningham, executive editor of The Seattle Times, remarked editorially that instead of giving Hall loads of publicity and a chance to question the nation's belief in freedom of speech, the city should make available to Hall and others with a message the old "free speech corner" that operated in Seattle's early days at Occidental Avenue and Washington Street.

From the turn of the century to the 1930s, Cunningham said, partisans for a variety of viewpoints — arch-conservative, radical left and religious — mounted soapboxes there to have their say. People could listen, applaud, boo, shout questions or walk away.

Many thought it made good sense. But nothing ever came of it.

More than fair enough

 At noon April 21, 1962, President John F. Kennedy sat at a desk far from the Northwest and officially opened the Century 21 Exposition — Seattle's second World's Fair in this century.

As he spoke the words, "Let the fair begin," Kennedy depressed the same Klondike-gold telegraph key with which President William Howard Taft had opened Seattle's Alaska-Yukon-Pacific Exposition in 1909.

Joe Gandy, Ewen Dingwall, William Street and Edward Carlson — key fair officials — stood under overcast skies in the World's Fair Stadium as Metropolitan Opera diva Mary Costa sang the national anthem, Broadway star John Raitt sang "Meet Me at the Needle, Nellie" and Hollywood luminary Danny Kaye read the fair's credo, pledging a quest for peace and understanding in the 21st century.

Minutes later, an F-102 Air Force jet fighter flying over Seattle to salute the fair's opening crashed into a Mountlake Terrace neighborhood, killing Mr. and Mrs. Raymond Smith in their home and damaging at least six other houses. The pilot parachuted safely into Lake Washington.

Things could only get better, and they did.

Before the day was over, attendance at the 74-acre fairgrounds reached 50,000. In the next six months, the Seattle World's Fair — a dizzying array of high-tech exhibits, famous visitors and exotic foods — dominated life around Puget Sound. The fair was featured in national magazines and on network TV, drew 9.6 million

visitors and turned a profit.

Most important, it left behind a legacy that included the Space Needle, Science Center, Coliseum, Opera House, Playhouse, Arena, Monorail terminal, International Fountain, Fun Forest and assorted sculpture and artworks.

It was an audacious venture. The first world's fair in this country in 22 years should by rights have been staged in New York or Chicago or Los Angeles. Instead, it was put on in the far northwest corner of the country.

In its early stages, it sometimes resembled one of those old Judy Garland-Mickey Rooney movies in which the kids renovated a barn, assembled some acts and brought in a big-time Broadway producer for opening night. But that was part of its charm.

The idea was spawned in the early 1950s by Seattle City Councilman Al Rochester, who thought it would be a nice idea for Seattle to put on a little world's fair in 1959 to mark the 50th anniversary of the Alaska-Yukon-Pacific Exposition.

Rochester discussed it over lunch with Ross Cunningham, who headed the editorial page for The Seattle Times; Denney Givens, director of public affairs for the Seattle Chamber of Commerce, and Don Follett, manager of the chamber.

Nobody laughed. Encouraged, Rochester talked the City Council into signing a memorial to the Legislature asking for an appropriation to study the idea. Olympia obliged with $5,000. By 1957, the lawmakers had appropriated $7.5 million for a fair and formed a World's Fair Commission that included Carlson, attorney William Goodloe and legislator/editor Ray Olsen. Seattle's voters already had approved $7.5 million for a civic center and fair-backers began thinking of combining the two.

But where? The eventual winner was the old Civic Auditorium site on Mercer Street, not ideal for traffic (it still isn't) but with the right amount of space and a goodly number of turn-of-the-century buildings ready for the wrecking ball.

In time, the federal government opened its checkbook and promised a pavilion, and the international body that approves world's fairs and expositions set the date: six months in 1962.

Watching a fairgrounds take shape is the ultimate experience for sidewalk superintendents. All of Seattle looked on. Families prowled the grounds on weekends, laughing while children scampered up the Coliseum's supports and slid down on their backsides.

The whole town got a crick in its neck from watching the Space

CHRONO-LOG

Needle rise to its full 605 feet. They marveled that a tiny electric motor, with the proper gearing, would be able to turn the Needle restaurant one revolution every hour. After the 609-foot-tall SeaFirst Building was completed in 1969, Seattleites called it "the box the Space Needle came in."

Not that there weren't problems. Elderly dwellers complained about being ousted from their apartments so owners could capitalize on fair visitors. Experts predicted traffic jams from Seattle to Olympia. Buttons appeared with the message, "Don't Gouge Me, I'm a Seattleite."

At about 10 a.m. on the day the fair opened, Rochester — the man who had spawned the idea more than a decade before — went up the Space Needle with his wife and civic leader Ned Skinner and his wife. As he told it later:

"We looked out and saw acres and acres of empty parking spots. There were even empty spots right on the street. I couldn't believe it. I thought, 'It's a disaster, a total failure; we're doomed."

Time proved him wrong.

U.S. Attorney General and presidential brother Bobby Kennedy lunched at the Space Needle with his very large family. Diminutive (5-foot 4-inch) Soviet Cosmonaut Gherman Titov, who had circled the earth 17 times in the spacecraft Vostok II, sat on a Japanese motorcycle and grinned. Evangelist Billy Graham prayed in — and for — a throng in the stadium. Count Basie and his 16-piece band played "Take the 'A' Train" in the arena. Carl Sandburg read poetry in the playhouse.

Roy Rogers and Dale Evans came. So did John Wayne and his wife, Pilar. Jack Lemmon, Victor Borge and Maurice Chevalier put in appearances. Elvis Presley stopped traffic on the Monorail while making the movie "Take Me to the Fair."

Britain's Prince Philip toured the fair and later that evening addressed the English Speaking Union on a subject dear to the hearts of Brits and Seattleites:

"Let cats and lizards rejoice in basking in everlasting sunshine, but mists and drizzles and even occasional light rains make sunshine all the more welcome and constitute the proper environment of man.

"They prevent the dreaded dehydration which shrivels the brain, makes sluggish the blood and dims the moist and flashing eye. And, of course, provide an endless subject for conversation."

To initiate the new Opera House, designed by architects James Chiarelli and B. Marcus Priteca, Van Cliburn played Rachmaninoff's Third Piano Concerto and Igor Stravinsky directed his "Firebird Suite."

Everybody talked about:

■ Belgian waffles. The Bubbleator that whisked patrons high up in the Coliseum to the World of Tomorrow. The clever way music and water patterns had been coordinated at the

International Fountain. Heart-of-gold Gracie Hansen, decked out in rhinestones and feathers, riding herd on the showgirls at the Paradise International.

■ Thai food. The Boeing Spacearium. Circus Berlin's high-wire aerialists. Throwing pennies in the pools at the Science Center. Riding the giant ferris wheel at the Gayway (remember, this was 1962). And the unchallenged No. 1 hit show on the fairgrounds, the remarkable precision of men and horses in the Canadian Tattoo.

■ New citizens being naturalized under a sea of flapping flags in the Plaza of the States. Conductor Jackie Souders strutting at the head of the official fair band as it roamed the grounds.

One of the most imaginative promotions was to fly in 20-year-old Sal Durante, the Brooklyn truck driver who had made a bare-handed catch of Roger Maris' historic 61st home run (the one that broke Babe Ruth's record) in Yankee Stadium.

At first, promoters wanted Durante to catch a baseball thrown from the top of the Space Needle by Tracy Stallard, who had tossed the record-breaking ball to Maris and was now pitching for the Seattle Rainiers. When experts pointed out that a ball thrown from that height might kill a fairgoer or deprive Durante of his front teeth, plans were changed.

Stallard, it was decided, would hurl the baseball off the 100-feet-high giant ferris wheel. If Durante caught it, he would pocket $1,000. If he dropped it, tough luck, kid.

In practice, Durante was a whiz with the glove, catching balls behind his back, slyly winking at onlookers, mentally counting the thousand bucks he would take home to his pregnant wife.

Came the money throw, and Durante was stricken with stage fright. His glove suddenly was as hard as a brick. The $1,000 ball hit his mitt and trickled off onto the concrete.

The crowd groaned. Durante, shoulders slumped, walked away.

Years later the truth came out. The promoters handed Durante an envelope before he returned to Brooklyn. Inside was a check for $1,000.

It figured. No fair that could inspire the song lyrics "Meet me in Seattle . . . that's where I'll be at'll" could be hard-hearted.

At 5:11 p.m. (sunset) on Oct. 21, 1962, the fair came to a close in the World's Fair Stadium where it all began. There were marching musicians, songs by Spokane-born opera singer Patrice Munsel and a fireworks display depicting Mount Rainier, the fair's man-in-space symbol, flags of the United Nations, a rocket blasting off, a satellite in orbit and an 80-foot-high Space Needle.

When the ceremony ended, fairgoers made a final tour of the grounds, paying their respects to an old friend before the lights winked off for the last time.

'But he that filches . . . my good name'

Three-time State Rep. John Goldmark of Okanogan was defeated in 1962 after a nasty campaign in which he was made to appear to have Communist leanings because of his membership in the American Civil Liberties Union and his wife Sally's tenuous connections with the Communist Party when she was a girl in New York during the Depression.

Other politicians who had been ousted after being labeled Red or pink had slipped away quietly. But not Goldmark. The lawyer, cattle rancher and World War II Navy officer filed a landmark libel suit against his detractors: The Tonasket Tribune and its editor, Ashley Holden; Loris Gillespie, Okanogan County businessman and former publisher of The Okanogan Independent; former state Sen. Albert Canwell of Spokane (of 1950s Canwell Committee fame), and Don Caron of Okanogan, state organizer for the right-wing John Birch Society.

William Dwyer, a bright young Seattle lawyer who was to become a federal judge 24 years later, argued Goldmark's case in the Okanogan County Courthouse in the winter of 1963. The trial lasted several months and received national attention. In the end, a jury found that Goldmark had indeed been libeled and was entitled to monetary damages. (The verdict eventually would be set aside by a Supreme Court decision that permitted much broader criticism of public officials.)

But Sally and John Goldmarks' lives were never the same. They moved to Seattle, where John practiced law. He died of cancer in 1978. Sally died of a respiratory ailment in the fall of 1985.

The final tragic chapter was written a few months later on Christmas Eve.

David Lewis Rice, a disturbed 27-year-old with far-right leanings and a touch of the bizarre (his attorneys would later argue that Rice believed extraterrestrial beings gave him guidance) set out to kill "the top communist" and "leading Jew" in Washington state. Rice selected as his victim Charles Goldmark, a Seattle lawyer, the son of John Goldmark who had filed the long-ago libel suit.

In his fuzzy thinking, aided by hate literature and whatever he

Seattle Times

A float plane leans drunkenly against a Lake Union dockside flying business the morning after the great Columbus Day storm of 1962.

Johnny Closs / Seattle Times

John and Sally Goldmark at their Okanogan County ranch in October 1962, during the dark days between Goldmark's loss in the legislative primaries and the historic libel trial.

may have heard about the case of 23 years earlier, Rice linked the name Goldmark with communism. And, to him, it sounded Jewish — although the Goldmarks' roots were really Presbyterian.

Rice knocked on the door of the Goldmarks' home in the Madrona district, pretending to deliver a Christmas package. Inside the home, he brandished a fake handgun, then handcuffed and chloroformed Goldmark, his wife, Annie, and their two sons, Derek, 12, and Colin, 10.

The Goldmarks were savagely attacked with a steam iron and other household implements. Annie died immediately. All eventually would die. Rice, arrested days later, was convicted of aggravated first-degree murder and sentenced to death.

But the Goldmark saga had still another aftermath. One of the most vehement opponents to Dwyer's nomination to the federal judgeship in 1987 was then-91-year-old Ashley Holden, who mounted a Bellevue letter-writing campaign.

His charge? That Dwyer was "too liberal."

Gone with the Columbus Day wind

 Three forces came together out in the Pacific on Oct. 12, 1962, to spawn the most savage storm in the recorded history of the West Coast.

It raged from British Columbia to San Francisco Bay and became known as the Columbus Day Storm.

The ingredients:

■ Typhoon Frieda, which originated in Asia, swept across the Pacific and created a low-pressure area when it blew itself out about 900 miles south of Alaska's Dutch Harbor.

■ West of San Francisco, unusually warm and moist air collided with a stream of very cold air from the Gulf of Alaska, causing some powerful storms along the coast Oct. 10 and 11.

■ When the low-pressure area from Frieda moved south and joined the mix, the result was explosive. Scientists officially labeled it an "extra-tropical cyclone."

Fifty-three thousand homes were damaged on the West Coast. Forty-six people died — 35 in Oregon, seven in Washington, three elsewhere.

In Washington, the sky turned yellow-gray. Howling winds reached 83 miles an hour at the Coast Guard's West Point Light

station, 88 in Tacoma, 100 in Renton and, the fiercest gust of all, 160 mph at the Naselle radar site in Pacific County.

Windows were smashed. Roofs were clawed off houses. Power poles were jerked out of the ground. Log booms scattered. Shingles flew through the air like Frisbees. An estimated 1.5 billion board feet of timber blew down.

In Spanaway, Pierce County, a pet lion escaped its pen and attacked three people before it was killed. A 10-car ferry, the Chief Kivina, sank at its Lummi Island pier. Small planes were smashed. Thousands of chickens and more than 100 cattle died.

The worst previous storm in the Puget Sound area occurred Oct. 31, 1934.

(That disturbance, packing winds up to 83 miles an hour, ripped the trans-Pacific liner President Madison loose from her moorings at Seattle's Pier 41 and drove her into the moored sternwheeler Harvester, sinking the latter. The seiner Agnes sank off Port Townsend, drowning five crewmen. A wall of Seattle's Alki Hotel blew down, killing one person. Four planes were crushed when supports gave way at a Boeing Field hangar.)

Although damage was much less widespread, a freak tornado that swept across Lake Washington Sept. 28, 1962 — shortly before the Columbus Day storm — had a center whose wind speeds were higher than any previously recorded here.

The tornado dropped from the sky as a black cloud, cutting a narrow swath through a four-block area of Seattle's View Ridge. It boiled across Lake Washington to Juanita, then turned north to Snohomish County, expiring almost as suddenly as it had kicked up.

The tornado peeled off several roofs, picked up a one-ton front porch and deposited it 70 feet behind a house, snapped trees like matchsticks and briefly lifted schoolchildren off the ground. Fortunately, though, nobody was hurt.

A saga of persistence

Perennial loser "Persistent Payson" Peterson.

Payson Peterson was his name. But they took to calling him "Persistent Payson," because that's what he was.

Tall and husky, a graduate of Cornell University and a veteran of World War I and the French Foreign Legion, the affable Peterson came out to Washington and won election to the Legislature in 1927 from tiny Alpine, near Stevens Pass. At 28, he was the state's youngest legislator.

Everyone predicted a remarkable political career for Peterson, who soon moved to the town of Snohomish.

Remarkable, yes. But in an unexpected way.

Peterson, a Republican, made a bid in 1930 to unseat the incumbent 2nd District congressman, Lindley Hadley, who had been in office 28 years and was chairman of the powerful House Ways and Means Committee. Peterson lost by only 156 votes, an amazing showing.

Came 1932, Peterson ran again — and lost. Ditto in 1934, 1936, 1938, 1940, 1942, 1944, 1946, 1948 and 1950.

Enough was enough, said Peterson in 1952. He'd been called a "liberal" Republican. Then, by golly, he would switch to the Democrats and run for Congress under that label.

Of all the years to switch, Peterson had picked one of the worst. Popular Dwight Eisenhower was the Republican standard-bearer for president. The 2nd District went Republican for the first time in 20 years.

In 1954, his 13th try, Peterson announced that 13 was his lucky number. It wasn't. Neither were numbers 14, 15, 16, 17, 18 and 19, although Peterson twice won the Democratic nomination, to go with his seven nominations as a Republican.

Between the 16th and 17th defeats, Peterson was given a $10,000-a-year job as a civil-defense consultant. He probably could have held it for life, but quit the sinecure in 1962 to run again for Congress. He also ran in 1964 and 1966, switching to the 1st Congressional District for the latter campaign.

Peterson's 19 straight defeats as a congressional candidate was a state record and possibly a national record — certainly worth a footnote in history books.

What exasperated his friends is that Peterson refused to settle for anything but a national office. They noted that even though he always lost he never failed to carry his hometown of Snohomish, where people knew and liked him.

At his friends' urging, a reluctant Peterson agreed to run for

STATE-MENTS

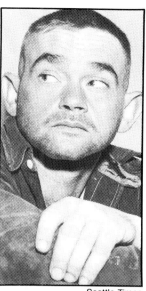

Seattle Times

Joseph Chester Self was hanged for less than a fistful of dollars.

Repentance

On the evening of June 19, 1963, Joseph Chester Self ate a dinner of Cornish game hen, pizza and tossed salad. He then accompanied the Rev. George McCabe to a small nearby room, where they knelt in prayer and took communion. At 12:01 a.m. June 20, Self dropped through the trapdoor of the gallows at the state penitentiary at Walla Walla.

Many others would wind up on Death Row. But Self, the 73rd person to be executed in Washington, was to be the last for at least the next quarter of a century — the longest period in state history in which the death penalty was not carried out.

Self was hanged for killing Seattle taxicab driver Ralph Gemmill Jr. during a $15 robbery in Pierce County in March 1960. Gemmill's body was found with two bullet wounds, one in the back of the head. Three days after the killing, Self phoned the sheriff's office and said he wanted to surrender. He told officers he had shot Gemmill during a struggle over the gun. Self was 29 at the time of the murder, a wiry, jumpy, self-admitted "foul ball" who had lost both parents by age 11 and been dishonorably discharged from the Army. He had spent time in prison for burglary and grand theft.

Before his execution, though, he appeared to have undergone a profound transformation. He admitted there had been no struggle when he killed Gemmill, converted to Roman Catholicism under McCabe's guidance and arranged to donate his corneas to an eye bank.

CHRONO-LOG

*Seattleite Jim Whittaker on
the Top of the World in
1963.*

REI

mayor of Snohomish in 1967. But, he said, he would not make a single speech or spend a penny on advertising.

And so after 37 lean years, Peterson, gray and 68, handily won the only office he never campaigned for. Contacted on the eve of his victory, Peterson was asked if it meant he was through running for Congress.

"Of course not," Persistent Payson persisted. "This was just a side issue."

As good as his word, Mayor Peterson tried again in 1968, returning to the 2nd District and changing his label back to Republican. As usual, he lost.

Peterson sat out the 1970 election, the first time he did so in 40 years. And when Snohomish switched to the city-manager system of government in 1971 and abolished the job of mayor, Peterson lost the job for which he hadn't campaigned.

Peterson wasn't around to see who won the next congressional election. He died Sept. 30, 1972.

The Whittaker ascendancy

In the spring of 1963, lanky, 6-foot-5-inch Jim Whittaker, who grew up in Seattle and cut his climbing teeth on the slopes of Mount Rainier, was with an American expedition attempting to scale the world's highest mountain, 29,028-foot Mount Everest in the Himalayas.

Both Whittaker and twin brother Lou had been invited. Jim, sales manager for Recreational Equipment, Inc. (REI), figured he could spare the time. Lou, who had just launched his own outdoor-equipment business in Tacoma, decided he could not.

The Everest expedition had been above 20,000 feet for days, socked in by high winds and blowing snow. Whittaker, party leader Norman Dyhrenfurth and two Nepalese guides were at Camp 6, at 27,300 feet. Supplies and oxygen were running low. Four other strong American climbers were high up on another part of the mountain.

Very early on the morning of May 1, Whittaker and Dyhrenfurth decided to go for it, a now-or-never bid to become the first Americans to reach the summit.

They left camp at 6 a.m. in what Whittaker later recalled as "a hell of a day" — howling winds, driving snow, the temperature at 35 below. An hour later, Dyhrenfurth no longer could keep up. He and one guide turned back. It was up to Whittaker and a wiry little Nepalese, Nawang Gombu.

The two climbers pressed on, each breath an effort, each step like pulling a ball and chain. Whittaker's cheek was frostbitten through his face mask, one eye nearly swollen shut. The weather broke slightly and the two climbers could see the ridge that led to the main summit.

Whittaker and Gombu, tiny black dots in the snow, kept putting one foot in front of the other because, as Whittaker said later, "You feel you have to get it, you don't even think about turning around."

Seven hours after leaving camp, Whittaker and Gombu — the American "giant" and the little Nepalese — stood atop Mount Everest. Twenty years later, Whittaker said he could not recall his thoughts when he set foot on the summit. There certainly was no feeling of conquest. Relief, maybe. The exultation would come later.

The two stayed on top just 20 minutes, taking the obligatory pictures as they planted an American flag, aware their oxygen was running low. They spent the night high up on the mountain. Word was flashed around the world the next day that an American finally had reached the summit. (Sir Edmund Hillary of Britain was the first, in 1953.)

But party leader Dyhrenfurth would not divulge the triumphant mountaineer's name. A week later, Whittaker was identified as

Bob Peterson

University of Washington and NCAA pole-vault champ Brian Sternberg heads over the bar.

the man.

Dyhrenfurth's temporary silence was due more to diplomacy than taciturnity. He didn't want to detract from the accomplishments, a few days later, of four other Northwest members of the expedition who also attained the summit. Thomas Hornbein and Willi Unsoeld went up the previously unclimbed West Ridge and came down Whittaker's route on the South Col. Lute Jerstad and Barry Bishop also went up the South Col.

Their feats were every bit as remarkable as Whittaker's. But because Whittaker (with Gombu) was this nation's first, he became an instant American hero, the friend of presidents, adviser to editors of the National Geographic, a member of the National Parks Board. He took his place in history books alongside John Glenn, first American astronaut to circle the Earth while in outer space, and Charles Lindbergh, the first pilot to fly alone across the Atlantic.

After his brother had become famous, Lou Whittaker was asked "what if both of you had made the summit assault together?"

Lou thought for a moment and then said, "Fifty feet from the top, we'd have wrestled there in the snow to see who'd be the first up." But the twin brother who didn't go to Everest may be best known for his reply to that old question, "Why do you climb a mountain?" The most common response is, "because it is there." Whittaker replied: "If you have to ask, you wouldn't understand if I told you."

In 1975, a Jim Whittaker-led expedition failed to reach the summit of K2, the world's second-highest peak. But he came back three years later and his party put four climbers on the top. He was not among them. He had had, he said, his moment of glory and it was now time for others.

'It's not courage, but patience'

Brian Sternberg first attempted to pole-vault with a wooden stick in the backyard. He recalled later that it broke. Sternberg graduated to bamboo, then metal and finally to the fiberglass pole that catapulted him to world prominence.

The University of Washington student already was the National Collegiate Athletic Association pole-vault champion when he soared a world record 16 feet 8 inches at the Compton, Calif., relays June 7, 1963. Tall (6-2), strong, limber and fast, Sternberg seemed almost certain to push the record higher. Nobody was prepared to say what his limit might be.

Twenty-five days later, while working out on the trampoline at the university in preparation for a world-class track meet in the Soviet Union, Sternberg miscalculated during the second revolution of a mid-air spin. He fell, head first, from high above the trampoline, landing hard and shoving his head forward on his chest. Nothing was broken, but two vertebrae were dislocated.

Sternberg lay flat, in terrible pain, unable to move. He was paralyzed from the neck down.

Although he eventually regained partial control of his arms, Sternberg never walked again. He did, however, throw himself into the Fellowship of Christian Athletes with the same dedication he had brought to the pole vault, delivering inspirational messages to clubs, church groups and schools. He also served on the State Athletic Commission and attended the '68 Olympic Games in Mexico City.

Sternberg sent letters and made phone calls to other young men and women who suddenly found themselves paraplegics. But he and his parents, Harold and Helen Sternberg, never gave up hope that someday he would get out of his wheelchair. As a family they promoted funding for research into spinal-cord damage.

Once, when he was lauded for his courage, Sternberg replied, "I call it patience. You don't really have a choice."

Although Sternberg was unable to compete in that 1963 track meet in the Soviet Union, the host country did not forget him. At the end of the meet, Sternberg was sent the same medal given to all winners.

In 1980, he was elected to the Washington State Sports Hall of Fame.

Beatlemania on the waterfront

Pandemonium reigned outside the Edgewater Inn, along Seattle's waterfront, on Aug. 21, 1964. Hundreds of teen-agers massed against barricades erected by police outside the entrance. A patrol boat cruised on the Elliott Bay side of the hotel.

The inn manager received word on his walkie-talkie that three girls had been found hiding under a bed in Room 318; two more had been found under a bed in Room 231.

A young man held up an autographed poster of Elvis Presley and proclaimed defiantly that Elvis would always be his favorite. Other young men grabbed it from him and tore it to pieces. The young man wept.

At 4:02 a.m., a black limousine came into view and edged toward the inn's entrance. Screeching girls descended on the car, some flinging themselves across the hood, others banging on the windows. The crowd surged in dangerous waves.

Eventually, the car broke through. Its occupants scurried up the stairs to Suite 272 as private detectives struggled to hold back the mob.

John Lennon, Paul McCartney, George Harrison and Ringo

Richard S. Heyza / Seattle Times

In her sign, a lone protester at Seattle Center rails against the Beatles as "false gods."

Starr had arrived in Seattle.

The Beatles performed that night before 14,300 fans in the Coliseum, against a backdrop of non-stop shrieking and thousands of flash photographs. They sang "I Want to Hold Your Hand," "A Hard Day's Night," "Long Tall Sally," "Twist and Shout," "Roll Over Beethoven" and other favorites.

After the concert, teen-agers climbed all over a Cadillac in which they thought the Beatles would be riding, caving in the roof and trunk and ripping off mirrors. Police finally backed an ambulance up to a Coliseum door and the Fab Four piled in. Sirens sounded as the young singers were taken back to the Edgewater.

The Beatles escaped the next morning and flew to British Columbia for a concert.

Having a whale of a time with Namu

In June 1965, an 8,000-pound killer whale was captured by two Canadian gillnetters near Namu, B.C.

Ted Griffin, director of the Seattle Marine Aquarium at Pier 56, purchased the black-and-white whale for $8,000 and named it Namu (meaning "many winds" in Bella Bella Indian language).

Bob Hardwick, a KVI Radio personality, agreed to tow Namu and his floating pen 400 miles to Seattle with his little tugboat, the Robert E. Lee.

It was the stuff of soap operas. The little tug huffed and puffed. But the holding pen was too heavy. The 65-foot-long Iver Foss came to the rescue and threw out a line.

The 19-day odyssey made front-page headlines, and Namu and Griffin were genuine celebrities by the time they arrived in Seattle.

A bitter debate soon broke out over Griffin's efforts to capture

George Carkonen / Seattle Times

A limousine carrying the Fab Four inches its way through a gaggle of teen fans during the Beatles' Seattle visit.

STATE-MENTS

Associated Press

Gerry Lindgren, left, passes a startled Leonid Ivanov.

See how they run

In the summer of 1964, David met Goliath at a track meet in the Los Angeles Coliseum. "David" was Gerry Lindgren (5-5, 120 pounds), a squeaky-voiced 18-year-old fresh out of Spokane's Rogers High School. His mission: Run 10,000 meters against powerfully built Leonid Ivanov, 25, the Soviet champion at that distance, and Ivanov's running mate, barrel-chested Nikolai Dutov, 26. Both were regarded as legitimate contenders for an Olympic gold medal in Tokyo later that summer.

When they lined up to run, the young man they called the "Spokane Sparrow" looked hopelessly mismatched. Sure, he was the best long-distance runner Washington state had ever produced (prep state-meet mile record of 4:06, national high-school two-mile indoor record of 8:40, the prep three-mile outdoor record of 13:17). But this was reality. The Soviets, after sizing up Lindgren, echoed the prevailing sentiment through an interpreter. Lindgren, they said, was "too young" for a long race.

The gun sounded. But Lindgren, not one of the Russians, bolted to the lead. And he held on, fighting off challenges, lap after lap, even widening the gap. As he headed toward the tape on the final lap, Lindgren was 120 yards in front of the struggling Ivanov. Less than two months later, Lindgren romped to victory in the 10,000-meter run in this country's Olympic trials, finishing 45 yards ahead of runner-up Billy Mills, who had never gotten a wing up on the Sparrow.

But in Tokyo two days before the 10,000-meter race, Lindgren injured his ankle. He finished ninth. The gold medalist was Billy Mills.

CHRONO-LOG

*Bobo was the star of
Woodland Park Zoo life in
the 1960s.*

Seattle Times

more killer whales, including a mate for Namu. Griffin, who had established a solid rapport with Namu by going into the water with him, said his studies increased public awareness of the beauty and importance of killer whales to the ecological chain.

Save-the-whale groups countered that pods of whales were being broken up and families disrupted by Griffin's whale hunts. The whales, they said, should be swimming wild and free. There were highly publicized threats that someone would go into the water with wire cutters to set Namu free.

Namu wintered in Rich Cove, on the Kitsap Peninsula, during which he was filmed endlessly for a movie, "Namu, the Killer Whale." A new pen was built for his return to the waterfront in the spring.

Meanwhile, Griffin's efforts to find a mate for Namu resulted in two tragedies that bolstered the case for leaving whales alone. One female died from being harpooned; another female died when it was given too much tranquilizer.

Namu returned to Pier 56 in April 1966. On July 10, he did a power dive into the stainless-steel netting of his new pen. He smashed a hole, became entangled and, being an air-breathing mammal, drowned. He was widely mourned, especially by children. The movie in which Namu starred premiered in Seattle three weeks after his death.

In 1972, the Legislature enacted a law restricting the whale-catching business.

Associated Press

*Seattle Marine Aquarium director Ted Griffin brashly rides
Namu the killer whale during an exhibition in June 1966.*

Zoo story

His table manners were terrible, his head came to a point and he swatted his girlfriend around. But Woodland Park Zoo-goers took to their hearts a 535-pound male gorilla named Bobo. From the day he came to the zoo in June 1953, Bobo was its number No. 1 attraction.

When schoolchildren came they almost ran over each other to be the first to Bobo's cage. They marveled at his size, his macho chest-thumping and the famous Bobo stare, a cross between a glower and a look of great wisdom.

When Bobo charged the zoo's impact-resistant glass, the children would scream and recoil.

Bobo's birthdays were special. A candle-laden cake always was set in his favorite tire. Hundreds would gather to see the inevitable: Bobo glowering at the cake, taking a run at it and batting it into the

air, against the wall, with one sweep of his great hairy arm. Bobo then would dismantle the gooey remains.

A female gorilla named Fifi was installed in Bobo's cage in hopes he would father a bunch of little apes. It was not a marriage made in heaven. Bobo patently ignored his mate most of the time. His greatest show of affection was to unloose a haymaker and knock Fifi across the cage.

Bobo was born in French Equatorial Africa and abandoned by his mother when he was a few weeks old. He was found by a big-game hunter and turned over to the Raymond Lowmans of Anacortes. The Lowmans nursed Bobo as if he were a human baby, feeding him formula and baby food and dressing him in diapers and sweaters.

When Bobo was 22 months old, the Lowmans decided he had outgrown their home and needed to be in a zoo. He was taken to Woodland Park.

Bobo died in his sleep Feb. 21, 1968, a few months shy of 17. Many said the zoo would never be the same. A taxidermist worked his magic and, looking very lifelike and fierce, Bobo was given a place of prominence in the Museum of History and Industry.

He now resides in an Anacortes museum, not far from the home where he spent his infancy.

A King is dead . . .

An unusual thing happened on April 7, 1968.

Little streams of humanity that began moving toward the Seattle Center Arena grew into rivers. They merged at Boren Avenue and Denny Way, filling two street lanes for 10 blocks, and followed the man at the front of the march, the Rev. Dr. John Adams.

Adams had been a close friend of the Rev. Dr. Martin Luther King Jr. King had been killed by an assassin's bullet three days before.

The march Adams led was heading for a city-wide memorial service honoring the slain civil-rights leader.

The arena would hold slightly more than 4,200 people. Everyone hoped it would be filled. But by the time the marchers got there it was already full. The scheduled 2 p.m. program was delayed 55 minutes while everyone moved to the 14,000-seat High School Memorial Stadium.

Don Hannula, reporting that day for The Seattle Times, wrote:

"As the people poured into the stadium, Sam Smith, Seattle's first black councilman, looked over the faces of whites, blacks, Indians, Japanese, Chinese, Protestant, Catholic and Jewish clergy, the governor, the mayor, the working man and even some released from jail for the service.

"With a hand resting on a shoulder of his son, Stephen, 11, Smith said:

"This is the essence of a country."

Gov. Dan Evans told the gathering that violence was the way of the coward, nonviolence the way of the hero, and he asked, "Does it always take martyrdom to cause concern?"

Adams drew a standing ovation when he called for passage of an enforceable open-housing ordinance in Seattle as a memorial to King. Five thousand petitions were passed out to the mourners. (Eight days later, Seattle Mayor Dorm Braman signed an open-housing ordinance.)

In the 1980s, Empire Way — a major north-south thoroughfare in Seattle — was renamed in King's honor.

A bare-bones subject

Two Washington State University scientists appeared one day in the Washington, D.C., office of Sen. Warren Magnuson. Their purpose? To announce discovery of human bones in Eastern Washington.

What was so different about that? The bones could be up to 13,000 years old, Roald Fryxell and Richard Daughterty said, which would make them the oldest ever found in this region of the Western Hemisphere.

The find, publicly announced on April 29, 1968, consisted of charred and split bones and parts of a human skull that had been unearthed by WSU archaeologists and graduate students on the banks of the Palouse River.

They were called Marmes Man (Roland Marmes owned the ranch at which the ancient bones were found), and the site eventually became known as Marmes Rockshelter.

The first bones had been found at the site four years earlier, but it was not until shortly before the press conference in Magnuson's office that they were scientifically dated as having come from an era approximately 10 centuries before the birth of Christ.

The charring and splitting, scientists said, indicated that

Bruce McKim / Seattle Times

Seattle marchers throng Denny Way on April 8, 1968, in a tribute to Dr. Martin Luther King Jr., assassinated four days earlier in Memphis.

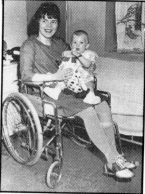

Seattle Times

Karla Little and daughter Laurie after their survival course.

Survival course

When a helicopter pilot sighted the wreckage of a light plane on the side of Mount St. Helens in late June 1966, there seemed little chance of survivors. The plane, piloted by Grant Erickson, a Sioux Falls, S.D., businessman, had slammed into the mountain several days earlier, carrying Erickson's wife, Dolly; his grown daughter, Karla Little of Seattle, and Little's 2-month-old daughter, Laurie. They were bound for a family reunion in California.

When rescuers reached the wreckage they found the Ericksons dead. But Karla Little was alive, with a broken back, and in her arms, uninjured, was her infant daughter. When Little's husband, Loren, was notified, he could only exclaim, "It's a miracle."

Karla Little was pinned in the wreckage, a bag containing milk and baby food tantalizingly out of reach. She breast-fed Laurie for two days. To keep out the freezing wind, she managed to put a blanket over a broken window. She cuddled Laurie to her breast to keep her warm.

Although paralyzed from the waist down for many months, Karla Little eventually walked again. Years later, a brace on her leg was the only reminder of the accident. Laurie enjoyed a lively, healthy childhood. The father, who learned about miracles firsthand, became an ophthalmologist.

Marmes Man (or woman) may have been eaten by other humans. The size of the bones further indicated that Marmes Man was young, maybe no more than a teen-ager.

Along with the announcement came jarring news. The site, which contained enough material to keep archaeologists busy for years, was to be flooded in December by waters backed up from Lower Monumental Dam on the Snake River, 20 miles downstream from the Marmes site. To protect the site, a levee would have to be built. Otherwise, all would be lost.

In the weeks and months that followed, the Marmes site was a hive of activity. More bone fragments were found by WSU faculty and students working with dental picks, trowels and brushes.

Flooding was delayed as a $1.5 million cofferdam was rushed to completion. When it was finished, everyone heaved a sigh of relief. The joy was shortlived. As the floodwaters began to back up, the cofferdam began to leak. Pumps couldn't keep up.

In February 1969, the excavation was covered with plastic sheeting and buried under nearly 8,000 cubic yards of sand, in hopes that the site could be reopened at some future date.

It is now covered by water.

Whistle blows on a tolerance policy

With the tacit approval of City Hall, Seattle police slid into what was called the tolerance policy in the 1950s. It meant that certain offenses — such as gambling and sins of the flesh — would be tolerated if they kept a very low profile and toed a line laid down by police.

The rationale made a certain amount of sense. Since the beginning of recorded history, there had been drinking and gambling. And the world's oldest profession wasn't called that for nothing. Prohibition had been tried and found wanting. There were better uses for police than tying them up enforcing the unenforceable.

Besides, it wasn't good politics to crack down on high-stakes gambling in Chinatown. It would never do to outlaw bingo in church parlors. If cardroom patrons wanted to exceed the unofficial $2 tolerance limit, it wouldn't hurt to look the other way just this once.

Seattle's tolerance policy began to unravel after an unauthorized police raid on Sept. 24, 1969, on Charles Berger's Lifeline Club on First Avenue.

The club was filled with bingo players. Police made arrests and confiscated records indicating the club had made contributions to a great number of politicians, including several in law enforcement. Records also showed the club was connected with several other bingo parlors.

The skeleton was out of the closet.

Police began talking. They named higher-ups and said they'd received favors in exchange for permitting gambling operations to exceed the unwritten limits of the tolerance policy, and to permit prostitution to operate under the covers, so to speak, in controlled areas.

Two weeks after the raid, Police Chief Frank Ramon announced his retirement.

In 1970, M.E. "Buzz" Cook, senior assistant police chief, was indicted for perjury by a federal grand jury, which said he had lied about payoffs that gamblers made to police. Cook swore his innocence, saying he had spent most of his working life in traffic control. But several officers testified against him, and he was found guilty and sentenced to three years in prison. (His conviction was overturned by one appeals court, then reinstated by another.)

Cook's federal-court trial produced days of testimony about a system of shakedowns and payoffs that benefited police and other government officials. It led to a 1971 grand-jury probe that resulted in the indictment of 19 public officials on charges of being part of a conspiracy to share proceeds from illegal activities permitted under the tolerance policy.

Many of the big names in the original indictment — including former Prosecutor Charles O. Carroll and former Chief Ramon — eventually were excluded. But the tolerance policy had been discredited.

Boeing's men on the moon

The Boeing Co. continued a move into space technology that had begun in the late '40s with research on the Bomarc interceptor missile.

The research had gained impetus with the company's Minuteman ballistic-missile assignment for the Air Force in 1958 and its role in the Air Force Dyna-Soar manned space-glider

CHRONO-LOG

1967

Olympia selected
as site for new four-year
college, The Evergreen State.

For first time,
black city councilmen are
elected in Seattle (Sam
Smith) and Pasco (Art
Fletcher). Following year,
Republicans name Fletcher
to run for lieutenant
governor — first black
nominated for Washington
state office. He loses to
incumbent John Cherberg
by 55,000 votes.

Seattleite David Stern
develops for University
Federal Savings & Loan
what becomes one of most
recognizable symbols in the
world: "Happy Face"
button.

Eight Puget Sound-area
pulp and paper mills are
ordered to reduce water
pollution by treating sulfite
waste discharges and
installing deep outfall lines.
Estimated cost: $90,000.

1968

First Boeing 747,
world's largest commercial
jet, roars off Everett airfield,
launching new era in air
travel.

Water fluoridation
wins Seattle voter approval
finally despite some
opponents' claim it's
Communist plot.

Bobo the gorilla,
No. 1 attraction of
Woodland Park Zoo for 15
years, dies in his sleep.

program, even though the
latter subsequently was
canceled.

The breakthrough came
in December 1961, when the
National Aeronautics and
Space Administration
selected Boeing to develop
the first stage of the
Advanced Saturn launch
vehicle, the Saturn V. More
space assignments followed
until, in the spring of 1967 —
five months after three
astronauts died in a fire
aboard the Apollo 1 —
Boeing was named to
integrate the entire Saturn V-
Apollo launch vehicle-
spacecraft combination.

The giant aircraft builder
did its job well. In November
1967, a Saturn-Apollo test
launch at Cape Kennedy was
so picture-perfect that
Richard Nelson, Boeing's
launch-systems branch
manager, said jubilantly, "I
don't imagine the wave-off
for Columbus could have
been any greater than this."

But there was something
even better in the future.

Early on the morning of
July 16, 1969, about 50 miles
from where Jules Verne had
launched a storybook rocket
to the moon a century
earlier, the years of
preparation paid off.

The Apollo 11 mission,
carrying Neil Armstrong,
Edwin "Buzz" Aldrin and
Michael Collins, blasted off
from Cape Kennedy on a
148,500-mile journey to the
moon.

*A phalanx of marchers moves through downtown Seattle in
November 1969 after gathering in front of the Federal Courthouse
to vent their protest against the Vietnam War.*

The launch was flawless. When the trio reached the moon,
Collins staying behind with the command ship Columbia, while
Armstrong and Aldrin headed for the Sea of Tranquility on the
east side of the moon in the lunar module Eagle.

Armstrong's first words when he stepped onto the moon:
"That's one small step for a man, one giant leap for mankind."

The mission returned safely to earth, splashing down 912 miles
southwest of Hawaii on July 24, eight days after leaving the cape.

Apollos 12, 14 and 15 also would land on the moon. The latter,
in the summer of 1971, saw astronauts James Irwin and David
Scott land at the foot of the moon's Apennine Mountains and go
exploring in a Boeing-designed and -built lunar rover.

A freeway unites, but also divides

Construction continued
throughout the 1960s on a
freeway to replace the
narrow, twisting "Old
Highway 99" as Western
Washington's main north-
south arterial. The newcomer
would be known as Interstate
5.

There were hassles over
whether "the ditch" should
cut through Seattle, which
has a narrow midriff, or go
east of Lake Washington.
When a mid-city route was
selected there were more
arguments over whether
there should be a lid over the
roadway.

(Although the lid was
turned down, a reasonable
facsimile would be built
piecemeal in the decades
that followed).

Freeways, it turned out,
posed psychological as well
as physical barriers. People
who once thought of
themselves as neighbors,
separated by a few blocks,
suddenly found themselves
separated by an enormous
gulf as houses were removed
for I-5's right-of-way.

One of the major links,
the Freeway Bridge, was
completed in June 1961. But
it was another 4½ years —
Feb. 3, 1965 — before the
ribbon was cut on the 19-
mile Seattle-to-Everett
portion of I-5. And it was
another two years after that
— Jan. 31, 1967 — before the last remaining section, from Olive
Way in Seattle south to Midway, was completed, making it
possible to travel from Everett to Tacoma by freeway for the first
time.

Building a freeway in Western Washington was not like laying
one across the nation's flatlands. Among the memorable statistics
for the 17.2-mile piece of road from Olive Way to Midway:

■ 1,350 acres of right-of-way, 85 on-and-off ramps, 128,170 feet
of guard rails, 448 signs from Dearborn Street to Midway, 100
electric pumps in little concrete pillboxes at the Tukwila
interchange, to drain hillsides of nearly 2 million gallons of water
a day.

■ 18 million cubic yards of dirt moved (far more than was
moved for the Denny Regrade); 684,192 cubic yards of concrete
for assorted pilings and spans, and another 183,000 cubic yards
for paving.

A Domesday report

A grown-up Seattle wanted to be big-time in sports. The
success of Houston's Astrodome, coupled with the
Emerald City's fabled rain, made it logical to consider a
domed stadium as the best way to attract big-league professional
teams.

But getting voter approval for a domed stadium and then
deciding where to build it would take years.

Voters turned down a $15 million bond issue for a domed
stadium in November 1960. In September 1966, a $38 million bond
issue failed to get the necessary 60 percent approval.

Sometime after the '66 turndown, promoters tried a new
approach. Instead of trying to sell a stadium exclusively for
professional sports, they broadened the appeal. It would be an all-
purpose facility, usable for tractor pulls, rock concerts, Billy
Graham revivals, home shows and whatever professional sports
were available.

In November 1968, 62.3 percent of the voters said yes to a $40

*Apollo 15 astronaut Jim Irwin strides away from his born-in-Kent lunar rover and across the
moon's sands in July 1971.*

million bond issue.

Now the question was: Where to build it?

Among the sites suggested: Riverton, Northup Way, Seattle Center, South Park, Yesler Way (King Street).

In May 1970, the voters made one thing perfectly clear — by a majority of 60.71 percent, they agreed with Frank Ruano's crusade against locating a stadium at the hard-to-get-to Seattle Center. In the fall of 1971, a committee selected King Street, down by the railroad tracks and close to where the city was born almost 120 years earlier.

The stadium, officially named the Kingdome in 1975, has the world's largest thin-shell concrete dome. It contains 52,000 cubic yards of concrete and 440 tons of structural steel and is designed to support a snow load of 4,600 tons.

It was officially dedicated March 27, 1976. The multi-purpose idea paid off. Billy Graham set a total-attendance record of 434,100 for a crusade May 9-16, 1967.

New kid on the NBA block

While Seattle eyed baseball as the true mark of big-league status, another franchise sneaked into town in December 1966.

Walter Kennedy, czar of the National Basketball Association, announced the league would admit Seattle the following year. Games would be played in the 14,000-seat Seattle Center Coliseum.

Co-owners Sam Schulman and Gene Klein paid $1.7 million for the franchise. They named Don Richman as general manager, Dick Vertlieb as business manager, and Al Bianchi, an assistant coach of the Chicago Bulls, as head coach.

The expansion franchise, after much debate, was named the SuperSonics. Seattle — as a new kid on the NBA block — was allowed to pick expendable players from established teams in a special draft.

The Sonics, opening on the road during their first season in 1967, lost to the San Francisco Warriors. Despite an enormous amount of civic boosting, only 4,473 fans turned out for the first home game in the Coliseum Oct. 20 against another expansion team, the San Diego Rockets. The Sonics lost, 121-114.

On Oct. 21, in their third game, the Sonics, led by Walt Hazzard's 27 points, finally broke into the win column, defeating the Rockets 117-110 in overtime. There were 4,562 spectators — 90 less than the turnout the same night for a hockey game played by the Seattle Totems of the Western Hockey League.

Besides the high-scoring Hazzard, mainstays of that first Sonics team were Tom Meschery, Rod Thorn, Bob Rule, Dorie Murrey, Bob Weiss, Al Tucker and Tommy Kron.

Crowds grew enormously in the years that followed, until Seattle became the best draw in the league. The team's record showed a similar improvement. Coaches came and went. There was a brisk turnover in players.

But one thing never changed. Bob Blackburn, who came up from Oregon after 18 years as the voice of the Portland Beavers baseball team, broadcast the very first game. He was still going strong in the '80s.

In 1978, the Lenny Wilkens-coached Sonics barely lost the NBA championship playoffs to the Washington Bullets. The next year, the Sonics and the Bullets tangled again for the title in a series made famous by Bullets' coach Dick Motta's line, "It isn't over until the fat lady sings."

Richard S. Heyza / Seattle Times

Interstate 5's ribbons of unfinished concrete wind south past downtown in this view of October 1965, when the tallest object on the downtown Seattle skyline was the Smith Tower, at top.

The fat lady rang down the curtain in the fifth game, won by the Sonics, 97-93. Seattle had taken the world title four games to one.

With their first modern major-league sports championship in hand, Seattleites went on a binge. They poured into the streets, honking horns, unfurling makeshift banners and holding up forefingers and shouting "We're No. 1." There were tailgate parties. Alki Beach was jammed with traffic.

When the Sonics came home, an estimated 300,000 people lined Fourth Avenue or hung from ledges, lampposts and windowsills to shout themselves hoarse at the heroes of the hour, who rode in open cars to a ceremony in Victory Square, north of the Olympic Hotel.

Some predicted a basketball dynasty in the Pacific Northwest. But it was not to be. The team fell on hard times, was slowly dismantled and spent the '80s fighting to regain its magic.

Struggling to stay in the big leagues

"Take me out to the ball game . . . buy me some peanuts and Crackerjack . . ."

Sometimes it seemed it would never happen.

But it finally did.

Seattle acquired an expansion-team franchise in 1968, with the promise that a domed stadium would be built. The first team, the Pilots (a name chosen from among 21,252 entries), walked out on the field of Sicks' Stadium in Rainier Valley on the beautiful spring day of April 11, 1969, climaxing years of dreams.

Critics laughed at the little crackerbox stadium. But it was filled with memories of the Seattle Rainiers. And, as oldtime sportscaster Leo Lassen would have said, the grass was green, the sky was real and on clear days Mount Rainier was a giant ice-cream sundae peeking over Franklin High School.

Purists chuckled at the assemblage of castoffs wearing the Pilots uniform. No matter. It was great to be big-league, and some fine players came to the little stadium at the foot of McClellan Hill, even if they were wearing the uniforms of the opposition.

On that historic opening day, the place smelled of fresh paint, and some of the early arrivals among the 15,014 fans had to wait until carpenters finished nailing down their seats. Lacking a flagpole, the Stars and Stripes were hung from a light standard.

The pre-game ceremony consisted of Rod Belcher singing "Go, Go, You Pilots." Sen. Warren Magnuson stood well in front of the pitcher's mound to shotput three pitches in the general direction of the state's junior senator, Henry Jackson. And Bob McGrath once again proved the national anthem is not unsingable — if you have the voice for it.

In the broadcast booth, trying to make old-timers forget the revered Lassen, were Bill Schonley and Jimmy Dudley.

The game went off as scheduled and was a reasonable facsimile of the one envisioned by Abner Doubleday. With Gary "Ding Dong" Bell on the mound for the Pilots and a non-expansion big-league team, the Chicago White Sox, in the visitor's dugout, a minor miracle occurred — the Pilots won, 7-0.

Having split a pair of games with the Los Angeles Angels before the home-opener, the Pilots found themselves atop the American League West, with two wins and one loss. It was, of course, an unnatural position. The team soon reverted to type.

First baseman Don Mincher hit the first major-league home run

CHRONO-LOG

It's $200-pickup at the Rainier Food Giant in Seattle after the April 29, 1965 earthquake, which registered between 6.5 and 7 on the Richter scale and killed eight people from either falling debris or heart attacks.

1968

King County voters OK bonds for domed stadium; construction is completed seven years later.

Under prompting by Harry Edwards, San Jose State College instructor, black athletes at UW "whitelist" athletic director Jim Owens and staff on discrimination charges. They win several concessions, including suspension of trainer, appointment of black faculty member as counselor and hiring of black assistant coach, former Husky player Carver Gayton.

1969

In conflict over meaning of "patriotism" so symbolic of '60s, Seattle police confiscate young woman's red-white-and-blue dress on grounds she's desecrating flag. When going to retrieve it she finds, true to manual, it has been burned.

in Sicks,' a Ruthian shot over the right field fence. Tommy Harper stole the first of 73 bases he would pilfer that year, a "modern" one-season record for an American League player.

But the biggest cheer was reserved for the weak-hitting shortstop, Ray Oyler, who stroked a single and was on his way to being immortalized by the Ray Oyler Fan Club.

Crowds dwindled during the long, hot summer, and at season's end the unthinkable happened. The Pilots slipped into bankruptcy and were moved to Milwaukee (to become the Brewers). Seattle, with a domed stadium approved by the voters the previous year, was without a team and justifiably angry.

State, county and city went to court — to demand money for being shortchanged by major-league baseball and to ask that another team be sent to the city as quickly as possible.

Seven years later, Seattle acquired another baseball team. It was the first time a big-league franchise had been awarded in a courtroom.

On April 7, 1977, Seattle's second team, the Mariners, opened in the Kingdome against the Los Angeles Angels. This time there were 57,762 fans. Bowie Kuhn was on hand again. Senator Jackson threw out the first ball.

Although the final score was a duplicate of the one in 1969 (7-0), the M's were on the short end this time.

Two years later, on a warm July night, 58,905 fans from all over the country jammed the Kingdome to see the annual All-Star game, won 7-6 by the National League when the winning run was walked across the plate in the ninth inning.

With an eye to Sasquatches

The Pacific Northwest has been a happy hunting ground for the fabled Sasquatch or Big Foot — a towering man/ape that walks on two legs.

Sasquatch-hunting boomed after Roger Patterson, a one-time rodeo rider from Yakima, showed a 1967 film clip purporting to be a female Sasquatch walking along a creek bed about 100 miles northeast of Eureka, Calif.

The cynics said it could have been a human wearing a monkey suit. Those who believed in Sasquatches knew better.

In July 1969, a Grays Harbor County deputy sheriff reported sighting an 8-foot-tall creature alongside a road in the woods near Hoquiam. His evidence consisted of a Polaroid photograph of trampled grass and a few strands of hair. A few weeks later, two teen-agers reported being chased half a mile by three creatures almost 11 feet tall about 25 miles east of Darrington in Snohomish County.

In November 1970, Stevens County hunting guide Ivan Marx displayed casts of what he said were Sasquatch footprints.

The search shifted to Stevens County in December 1969 when more than 1,000 large, almost-human tracks reportedly were found in fresh snow near the shore of Roosevelt Lake, behind Grand Coulee Dam.

Moved by humanitarian concerns, Skamania County commissioners said, they passed a law in November 1970 to protect the Sasquatch from hunters in the Mount St. Helens area. To kill one could result in a $10,000 fine and five years in jail.

It may have been the first time an animal was "saved" before it was discovered.

Among those who have refused to dismiss the Sasquatch as a figment of the imagination is Dr. Grover Krantz, of the Washington State University anthropology department, who said plaster casts of outsized footprints he had examined were consistent with the size and weight of a giant hominid.

Like the search for UFOs and for the sea serpent Ogopogo in British Columbia's Lake Okanagan, the Sasquatch hunt goes on.

Twitting 'em at the polls

 One of those refreshingly zany chapters in the state's political history was written in 1968. Lorenzo Milam, a fun-loving writer-broadcaster, talked Richard Greene, a professor of Greek and Latin at the University of Hawaii, into filing as a Republican for Washington state land commissioner against incumbent Bert Cole, a Democrat.

After defeating four other Republican candidates in the primary for the right to face Cole in the general election, Greene — who had once taught at the University of Washington — announced he would remain in Hawaii during the campaign. That left it up to his campaign committee to battle Cole through a series of memorable press releases.

Greene, through his committee, started out by saying he wanted the state of Idaho to annex a large part of Eastern Washington, especially Spokane, which he called "a trackless waste contributing nothing to the Evergreen State but rattlesnakes and nitwits."

Greene's platform, written by Dr. Jon Gallant, a professor of genetics at the UW, was the hit of the state-issued voter's pamphlet. Sample promises:

"Land Use: Land should be used gently but firmly."

"State Parks: I envision a wilderness area on the site of The Boeing Company."

If elected land commissioner, Greene said, he would "go out fearlessly and commission the land."

Asked what he considered the main issue in the campaign, Greene replied, "Dirt."

The Washington Post, the Wall Street Journal and other Eastern media produced stories on the pleasantly different land-commissioner race in Washington.

On election eve, lagging far behind Cole, Greene expressed confidence that "we can widen the gap." To no one's surprise, he lost overwhelmingly.

Post-election, the man who provided so many laughs turned serious. He had won in the primary election, Greene said, because people didn't know or care what he stood for. They merely had picked a name that had appeared frequently in the news. He also said he wasn't enamored of the idea that voters, however uninformed, should be yanked from their beds or TV sets and encouraged to go to the polling booth.

"Somehow," he said, "we have the misguided idea that quantity is important to democracy. I disagree."

Green was fun for a while. But then he hit too close to home.

Put-on candidate Richard Greene lolls in the waters of Hawaii while "campaigning" for Washington state land commissioner in 1968.

9. END OF INNOCENCE

AMID SCANDAL IN HIGH PLACES, REFORM; AMIDST PLENTY, A WORLD BECOMES FINITE

1970 TO 🌿 1980

'Judge, you did the right thing. A deal's a deal.'

— 10-year-old Charlie Wilkins, on the Boldt fishing decision

Greg Gilbert / Seattle Times

An officer in riot helmet and gas mask peers through the shattered pane of a U.S. Courthouse window in February 1970 after a protest by anti-Vietnam War demonstrators. Below, people gather at Seattle City Hall in 1971 to receive free food from Neighbors in Need.

On April 29, 1975, the last U.S. troops left Saigon and Americans heaved a collective, painful sigh of relief. Although the emotional trauma of the war was far from over, Tony Orlando and Dawn singing "Tie a Yellow Ribbon 'Round the Old Oak Tree" began to have a nicer ring.

The undeclared war had divided the nation and taken a terrible toll of lives — 58,014 Americans, 1,112 from Washington state; not to mention about 1.5 million Vietnamese.

If there was any innocence left in the country at the start of the decade, it soon left as the war and scandals in high places inflicted serious, if not mortal, wounds on the national psyche.

Larry Dion / Seattle Times

Larry Dion / Seattle Times

Federal agents examine the damage done by a bomb blast in October 1970 to the UW's Clark Hall, which housed military reserve officer training classes.

CHRONO-LOG

1970

Seattle's Medic One begins its lifesaving mission as "hospital on wheels," pioneering emergency medical care in Northwest.

Year of unrest begins at St. Thomas the Apostle Seminary in Kenmore as seminarians boycott classes to protest suspension of student who went to Ballard tavern to recruit dancer for rock show at state reformatory. Protesters picket home of Archbishop Thomas Connolly.

Seattle's Ozark Hotel fire, set by unknown arsonist, kills 20 people.

Washington voters approve Referendum 20, legalizing abortions, after bitter and emotional campaign. Is nation's first election on question.

1971

Tacomans mourn death of Joe Jordan, possible model for Sam the piano player in Bogart classic "Casablanca." Jordan is best known for "Lovey Joe," composed for Fanny Brice in Ziegfeld Follies of 1910.

A sitting vice president, Spiro Agnew, resigned to avoid prosecution. Many of President Richard Nixon's most trusted lieutenants, including former Seattle attorney John Ehrlichman, went to prison as a result of the Watergate scandal. Finally, the president himself — a loser to Hubert Humphrey in Washington state in 1968, an overwhelming choice over George McGovern here in 1972 — left office in disgrace.

We had a few scandals of our own.

Joseph Alioto, former San Francisco mayor and a skilled attorney, was hailed as a hero for winning a $16 million judgment for the state in a complex antitrust case against electrical-equipment manufacturers. But the cheers turned to questions when it was learned that Alioto had kicked back $800,000 of his $2.3 million fee to the man who hired him, state Attorney General John J. O'Connell. Alioto and O'Connell survived two lawsuits by the state aimed at recovering all the money paid to Alioto.

Robert Perry, a longtime state House representative from Seattle's 32nd District, fled to Costa Rica in late 1977 to escape federal charges of tax evasion and extortion related to the scandal-ridden West Seattle Bridge project. When a repentant Perry returned 18 months later, he promised to tell all — about kickbacks and regular checks sent to him while he was a legislator. Besides Perry, only one person — a lobbyist for the Washington Water Power Co. — was convicted.

After Watergate, there was a new mood for public accountability. Washington's voters passed Initiative 276, requiring financial disclosure for elected officials. It survived court tests and became law.

Blue-collar workers strike, professionals don't. Everybody knew that. Or thought they did.

Aberdeen's public-

Dale Blindheim / Seattle Times

Lucille Taillon, a Hare Krishna devotee, at work in downtown Seattle in July 1977.

school teachers staged Washington's first-ever teacher's strike in 1972. Before the decade ended, teachers also struck in Federal Way, Edmonds, Tacoma and Seattle. Surgeries had to be put on hold as 1,800 nurses walked out for 10 weeks in 15 Seattle-area hospitals in 1976.

A lot of traditional economic wisdom became suspect. Unchecked inflation and recessions ran side by side. As interest rates rose, borrowing increased. Houses that had cost $15,000 in the Puget Sound area in the 1950s were resold for five times that amount, and more, in the late '70s.

The slumping economy touched the lives of disbelieving white-collar workers with homes in suburbia, two cars and a boat and, suddenly, no job. Concern about hunger was widespread.

As battles raged over food-stamp regulations and the release of surplus commodities from warehouses, Democratic Sen. Warren Magnuson took the Senate floor to express his "total humiliation" that citizens of Kobe, Japan — not of the United States — were donating rice and canned goods to feed Seattle's new poor.

In what Seattle Times religion writer Ray Ruppert called "truly the churches' finest hour," mainstream churches and synagogues responded with what became known as Neighbors in Need. Millions of dollars worth of food were collected and distributed, no questions asked.

But, as Washingtonians learned, a growing number of young people were attracted to religious sects far removed from Neighbors in Need. Many took to the streets to proclaim their particular brand of born-again Christianity. A new type of bumper sticker began showing up, with the words, "I Found It" and "Honk If You Love Jesus."

Although relieved that errant offspring had turned away from drugs, many parents worried about "brainwashing" as the sects moved in increasing numbers to the Pacific Northwest.

The worst fears of the critics were realized in 1978 when more than 900 followers of California cult leader Jim Jones committed mass suicide by drinking poison in Jonestown, Guyana.

In politics, change was in the wind.

After being elected governor for the third straight time in 1972, Dan Evans decided it was time to move on. He did not run for a fourth term in 1976, and wound up as president of The Evergreen State College, the state's first new institution of higher learning in 72 years. As if to prove they took seriously the college's mandate to approach education in innovative ways, students selected the geoduck as their mascot.

Rather than seek a seventh term, U.S. Rep. Brock Adams joined President Jimmy Carter's administration as secretary of transportation. Two years later, he left during a Cabinet reorganization, only to make a political comeback in the '80s that landed him in the U.S. Senate.

On March 22, 1973, the Legislature ratified the Equal Rights Amendment to the U.S. Constitution. But not enough states followed suit to make the ERA law.

More successful was the Legislature-passed "Costigan Bill," to permit University of Washington professors to teach beyond age 70. It was inspired by Giovanni Costigan, a white-haired history professor who spoke in reasoned tones about world-shaking events and had appeared on countless "outstanding professor" lists at the university.

In November 1978, Seattleites bucked a national trend promoted by singer Anita Bryant, decisively defeating Initiative 13, which would have repealed an ordinance banning discrimination based on sexual orientation.

Many people quit eating lettuce, and statewide fasts supported Cesar Chavez' United Farm Workers union as organizers pressed Yakima Valley growers to improve conditions for migrants.

We also had our share of violence and close calls:

■ Silas Trim Bissell, a sometime poet related to the carpet-sweeper Bissells, and his wife, Judith, placed a bomb — that didn't go off — under the Air Force ROTC building at the UW in January 1970. The Bissells fled — and separated — after posting $50,000 bond. Judith stayed in the underground movement until she went to prison for trying to blow up the office of a California state senator; Bissell moved to Eugene, Ore., where he changed his name, became a physical therapist and remained free for 17 years. But someone finally recognized him and he was brought back to Seattle to stand trial for the long-ago bombing.

■ Six men and a woman, known as "the Seattle Seven," were charged with conspiracy to damage federal property after paint bombs were lobbed and windows smashed at Seattle's Federal Courthouse Feb. 17, 1970. Their trial in

Jerry Gay / Seattle Times

Long-suffering patrons in Ballard queue up to make an appointment to buy gasoline in the oil-embargo, gas-shortage days of early February 1974.

STATE-MENTS

Dick Balch prepares for a bash.

A smash hit
Federal Way Chevrolet dealer Dick Balch burst on the scene in the summer of 1970 with an advertising gimmick so improbable, so totally outrageous that it made people laugh and wince at the same time. It succeeded in propelling Balch from anonymity to celebrity status almost overnight. And in the process he became one of the top car-sellers in the country.

What Balch did defied all tradition and logic. He appeared on camera, grinning behind a Fu Manchu moustache, picked up a sledgehammer and, taking careful aim at a spanking-new automobile, proceeded to bash in the hood, fender, grille or windshield. Then, with a cackle that was a little like scraping fingernails on a blackboard, Balch would cry out, "If you can't trust your car dealer, who can you trust?"

One of Balch's zaniest stunts was to appear with a car radio in his hand and say, "Hi, I'm Dick Balch; buy a car from me, and I'll throw the car-radio in." With that, he would throw the radio through a new windshield. Insane laughter followed. Such antics elevated him to the status of folk hero, a modern-day version of the frontier flimflam man selling Kickapoo Joy Juice.

Balch became so wealthy he built a playboy-type pad and drove around in a customized van. He married several times. But 11 years after he started, he laid off his 60 employees and went out of business — victim of a temporary slump in the economy. He now divides his time between the Pacific Northwest and Hawaii.

Tacoma at times bordered on a three-ring circus. But the system the seven deplored set them free when a mistrial was declared and the government closed the case.

■ Ricky Anthony Young, upset at an upcoming probation-revocation hearing before Benton-Franklin County Superior Court Judge James Lawless, sent a pipe bomb to the judge's chambers. Lawless died in the explosion June 3, 1974.

■ Carl Harp, the "Bellevue sniper," fired a rifle randomly at motorists on Interstate 405 on March 14, 1975, killing Abraham Saltzman, 54, of Bellevue and seriously wounding John Roger Mott, 22, of Seattle.

■ The George Jackson Brigade, named for a slain California prison radical and headed by John Sherman, claimed responsibility for a string of bombings and bank robberies in Western Washington and Oregon in the summer of 1975. Sherman, a master of disguise who twice escaped after being captured, finally was collared in Denver late in 1981 and sent back to federal prison to serve a 40-year sentence.

■ Three-year-old David Weilbacher of Yakima was beaten to death in the summer of 1976 by his mother, Debbie, and four members of a fundamentalist cult bent on ridding the child of evil spirits. On the witness stand, Weilbacher told the court "God's gonna raise him still, and bring him back."

Average citizens became increasingly interested in power of another sort — the kind needed to run the engines of modern life.

Our automobiles, which seemed destined to grow to battleship proportions, found a reason to slim down. We called it "the energy crisis of '74," and it had us fuming in long service-station lines and vowing to wreak vengeance on "those responsible." Nobody ever quite figured out who was to blame. But the crisis put a damper on gas-guzzlers and ushered in the 55-mile-an-hour speed limit.

To help ensure the nation against future fuel crises, Alaska began laying a controversial 798-mile-long oil pipeline. Soon Washingtonians were in a battle to halt two oil-moving proposals: a pipeline across some of the state's most fragile areas to carry oil to refineries in "northern tier" states, and the arrival of supertankers in Puget Sound to unload oil at Anacortes for shipment to the northern tier. It took 10 years to defeat the pipeline. Sen. Magnuson scuttled the supertanker proposal by deftly attaching it to the Marine Mammals Act.

Nuclear power, once hailed as the logical successor to a dwindling world fossil-fuel supply, began posing more questions than answers in the '70s. Worries grew over what to do with the huge quantities of radioactive waste generated by the plants. The accident at the Three Mile Island plant in Pennsylvania heightened already grave concerns about safety. And the Washington Public Power Supply System's grandiose scheme to build five nuclear-power plants became the target of increased suspicion as projected costs (up from $4.1 billion to nearly $12 billion) began to resemble the national debt of earlier times.

The one nuclear plant that went into operation in the Pacific Northwest during the decade was in Rainier, Ore., across the Columbia River from Washington.

While the drive to harness the atom for peaceful purposes faltered, efforts to apply atomic theory to military hardware blossomed.

Bangor, a little Navy ammunition depot on the Kitsap Peninsula, was selected as the site for a $750 million Trident nuclear-submarine base. Land sales boomed, and peace activists were arrested regularly for scaling the base's wire fence.

Even as Bangor was being developed, new uses were being found for military bases geared to the past.

Several hundred Indian activists, joined by actress Jane Fonda, staged a campout at the gates of abandoned Fort Lawton in March 1970 to dramatize their claim to a portion of the land before it could be turned into Seattle's Discovery Park. The Indians were given 17 acres, part of which was used for the Daybreak Star Cultural Arts Center.

Sand Point Naval Air Station shrunk in size and mission, sharing space with the National Oceanic and Atmospheric Administration. NOAA vessels continued to be berthed in Lake Union, however.

As big-time sports flooded the Puget Sound area and the media paid daily homage to football, baseball and basketball, the Washington state athlete who appeared most often on national television was an unassuming, crewcut lefthander out of Tacoma. His name: Earl Anthony. His game: bowling.

But college football provided the single biggest sports thrill as Husky coach Don James, in just his third year since arriving from Kent State University, masterminded one of the greatest upsets in Rose Bowl history, a 27-20 victory over

CHRONO-LOG

Jerry Gay / Seattle Times
Alice Ray-Keil of the Seattle-based Pacific Life Community tries to cut a barbed-wire fence at the Trident submarine base at Bangor as an act of protest against the policy of basing subs there armed with nuclear missiles.

1971

High point of Boeing cutback reached in April, when local employment drops below 40,000 — from a high of 95,000 in '68. Some 8,800 workers are laid off just from January through September.

"D.B. Cooper" hijacks Northwest Airlines Boeing 727 on Thanksgiving Eve, getting away with $200,000. After bailing out over southwestern Washington, he is never seen again and passes into Northwest folklore.

1972

Sugar Ray Seales, Tacoma middleweight, is only U.S. boxer to win gold medal in Munich Olympics.

1973

Legislature ratifies Equal Rights Amendment to U.S. Constitution. But not enough states follow suit to make ERA law.

Worst electricity shortage hits state since emergence of hydroelectric power in region. Unusually light snowfall the previous winter is blamed.

State voters reject proposal to reduce legal drinking age to 19.

Michigan, Jan. 2, 1978.

Sports weren't the only source of entertainment. Fads flourished. Young people shed their clothes and "streaked" in the buff at public events, usually one jump ahead of pursuing police. People began dancing again, in discos. And despite its grim themes, the movie "Deliverance" started a run on banjos.

The in-words were "communicate" (for normal folks) and "interface" (for those with a smattering of computer smarts). Communicate with the kids, with the boss, with the spouse, with the next-door neighbor.

Hair got shorter, clothes neater. The Beatles broke up, but Bob Dylan and the Rolling Stones kept going. Bruce Springsteen emerged. The Osmonds and Neil Diamond offered slick, sanitized rock.

Medic One to the rescue

On Feb. 20, 1970, the Seattle Fire Department took delivery of a cumbersome-looking 22-foot-long mobile-home body atop an Oldsmobile Toronado frame. Its interior was stuffed with emergency medical equipment.

The unit — billed as a mobile coronary-care unit or "a hospital on wheels" — had cost $28,000 to build. It was a gift from the Washington-Alaska Regional Medical Program.

Dr. Leonard Cobb, chief of cardiology at Harborview Medical Center, was ecstatic. He had requested the unit after noting that most people who died of cardiac arrest did so outside of a hospital. Valuable minutes that could save lives were being lost between the onset of a heart attack or a traumatic injury and competent medical treatment.

Fire Chief Gordon Vickery told Cobb his firefighters could be trained to operate the life-saving equipment. It was a radical idea.

A few weeks after the unit arrived, paramedics raced to their first call. Although the patient was too far gone, the system had worked. Somebody had called in, and the unit had responded promptly.

Within a short time, the hospital on wheels had recorded its first success story. The victim lived another five years.

It was the start of Medic One, an around-the-clock life-saving concept that began almost simultaneously in Miami and Los Angeles as well. Seattle's became a national showpiece. Before long, the city was hailed as "the best place in the country in which to have a heart attack."

This was something the public could understand and support. When money for the initial experiment ran out, public subscriptions kept it going until it could become tax-supported and be expanded throughout King County.

Today, virtually every city of any size in the country is served by something similar to Medic One. And tens of thousands of people — victims of heart attacks, choking, stabbings and assorted accidents — are living productive lives rather than taking up space in a cemetery.

(In time, it became clear that if the prompt response of Medic One paramedics could save lives, then having thousands of ordinary citizens trained to administer cardiopulmonary resuscitation (CPR) might save even more lives. The result was Medic II. By the late '80s, almost 400,000 people had been trained in CPR in and around Seattle.)

If Seattle is the best place to have a heart attack, the Pacific Northwest also is well prepared to treat traumatic burns.

In 1974, the nation's largest Regional Burn Center was established at Harborview.

Nowhere to hide

At 2:30 a.m. March 20, 1970, fires set by an arsonist swept up two stairways of Seattle's five-story Ozark Hotel, at Westlake Avenue and Lenora Street, turning it into a giant torch that lit the downtown skyline.

By the time fire engines got there, windows had blown out, the interior glowed red and many residents frantically clung to window ledges.

Tragic stories abounded. One man, in tears, told of trying to hold a woman by the hand after she missed a jump to the fire escape. Her weight was too much for him, and she fell to the pavement and died.

There were stories of courage, too. A policeman pulled a paralyzed woman from her room and held her against a fire escape until firefighters could reach them with a ladder. A 60-year old man clung for what seemed an eternity to a window ledge, while flames licked at his hands and face. He survived.

Fourteen men and six women died. Ten more were hospitalized with serious injuries. It was the worst fire since 31 died when a B-

29 slammed into a Georgetown meat-packing plant in 1943.

Ironically, firefighters — concerned about Seattle's old buildings — had paid a visit to the Ozark the previous day, noting paper-thin doors and transoms that could break and act as a funnel for smoke and flames. A fire marshal who examined the charred remains of the hotel said all 20 lives might have been saved if the owners had spent just $182.40 — the cost of a sheet of plasterboard for each of the hotel's 60 rooms.

As a result of the tragedy, the city enacted stringent new fire-safety codes. The arsonist was never caught.

War on the home front

🚫 In the spring of 1970, students all across the United States joined in protests against the sending of U.S. troops into Cambodia and the shooting deaths of four Kent State University students by national guardsmen in Ohio.

On May 5, an estimated 7,000 students and non-students gathered on the UW campus before noon for a rally at which they voiced loud support for a long list of demands that included impeachment of President Nixon, official university condemnation of the Kent State killings, a pledge by the university's president never to use National Guard troops on the UW campus and an end to the Reserve Officers Training Corps, as well as to military recruiting and war-related research on campus.

In the early afternoon, UW President Charles Odegaard addressed the rally with a bullhorn, reading a wire he had sent to Nixon as a private citizen, abhorring the Kent State deaths and urging Nixon to more fully explain his Cambodia policy.

But the cheers turned to boos when Odegaard declined to pledge never to use National Guardsmen on campus. Nor, he said, did he have any intention of changing existing policies on ROTC, military recruiting and war-related research.

By a voice vote, the protesters decided to march through the University District. Sentiment grew for blocking the Seattle Freeway with a tidal wave of humanity, bound for the federal courthouse downtown.

Shortly before 2 p.m., about 5,000 demonstrators entered the Northeast 45th Street ramp into the southbound lanes of Interstate 5. Traffic slowed, then came to a halt. The marchers proceeded over the University Bridge to the Boylston Avenue-Roanoke Street exit, where many walked off the freeway. But more than half stayed on I-5, sitting or talking with motorists about their opposition to the war and the Kent State killings. Some drivers listened patiently. Others became angry.

Riot-equipped state troopers were called out to confront the freeway-sitters. Some clubs were swung.

At the courthouse, other young demonstrators sat along Fifth Avenue, blocking traffic and listening to speeches. The loudest applause was for an elderly observer, Dr. Souren Tashian, who told the protesters, in a quivering voice:

"To us old folks, you are the hope of the United States. Keep it up until the end comes to this catastrophic and shameful war."

The next day, UW students went on strike. Roving bands, chanting "Join us; join us!" entered campus buildings and disrupted classes. In the late afternoon, strikers joined a demonstration of about 10,000 people outside City Hall. When the rally ended, about 2,000 moved to the freeway, blocking all downtown lanes at the height of rush-hour traffic.

It was not as peaceful as the previous day's freeway march. This time police, deputy sheriffs and state troopers met the marchers with tear gas and riot clubs. Some students were injured when they leaped from the freeway. Rocks were thrown. Four troopers were hurt.

Odegaard canceled classes the following day, to allow tempers to cool and permit students to attend memorials to the four killed at Kent State.

Tomb of the unknown concert-goer

"Here lies a young man known but to God. He surely is loved and missed by someone, somewhere."

That inscription on a headstone in Puyallup's Woodbine Cemetery marks the final resting place of a celebrator who died July 3, 1970, when he fell 75 feet over a waterfall and landed on rocks at "Buffalo" Don Murphy's Flying M Ranch in Eatonville.

The victim — about 21, 5 feet 8 inches tall, 160 pounds, sandy hair — had joined about 10,000 other people at what was billed as a Buffalo Party Convention and Pig Roast, although authorities called it a thinly disguised excuse for a rock festival.

Nobody at the convention seemed to know the young man. And in the weeks, months and years that followed, no one ever came forward to identify him. Fingerprints sent to the FBI, the armed services and Canadian authorities failed to provide any clues. There was speculation he might be Australian, one of a growing

Greg Gilbert / Seattle Times

Thousands of protesters tie up traffic on the Seattle Freeway in May 1970 as they head back to the University of Washington after a mass gathering at City Hall to denounce the U.S. military incursion into Cambodia.

STATE-MENTS

Warner Brothers

Bruce Lee in "Enter the Dragon."

Magnet for mourners

Lake View Cemetery on Capitol Hill is billed as Seattle's historical burial ground, the resting place of scores of pioneers whose names live on in streets and buildings and history books. But the most visited grave since 1973 is that of film star Bruce Lee. Born in San Francisco and reared in Hong Kong, Lee came to the University of Washington in the early 1960s, studying philosophy, teaching martial-arts classes and marrying Seattleite Linda McCulloch. He went on to international moviedom fame by employing a razzle-dazzle of hands and feet, known as kung fu, in battling evildoers.

Lee's red-marble headstone, inset with a Hong Kong-made ceramic portrait, is a magnet for mourners from all over the world. After paying a visit to the grave, some Danish seamen left money to provide flowers at regular intervals. Cards addressed to "Mr. Bruce Lee" have been arriving from foreign countries for years. After being first placed on the grave, the cards are bundled up and given to the actor's widow.

Lee was laid to rest in Lake View on July 30, 1973. Two of Hollywood's best-known stars, Steve McQueen and James Coburn, helped bear the $5,000 bronze coffin to the gravesite. Lee had died of a brain trauma 10 days earlier in Hong Kong. He was 32. The precise cause was never determined. An estimated 12,000 mourners, many of them weeping teen-age girls, had jammed police barricades at the Hong Kong funeral services. In contrast, the Seattle services were quiet, for family and close friends only, with eulogies by Seattle grocer Taky Kimura and Warner Bros. President Ted Ashley.

number of the world's young nomads.

Twenty-four days after he died, the anonymous festival-goer was buried at state expense. Eight people who had attended the convention-rock concert showed up for the graveside rites. One said, "Somebody just had to be there to say goodbye."

The grave was unmarked. But a few days after the burial, Mr. and Mrs. Don Wahlstrom of Tacoma decided to buy a headstone after reading newspaper accounts of the death. A physician donated a bronze flower container.

Wahlstrom said he continued to visit the grave over the years, wondering about the parents — somewhere — who might still be waiting for their son to return. The words he put on the headstone, Wahlstrom said, "just bubbled up."

Vanishing point

At 9:30 p.m. April 14, 1971, a blue-hulled, 22-foot sailboat — unnamed except for the number 192 on its mainsail — left Mojean's Public Dock in Tacoma. It was a Wednesday night. Small-craft warnings issued earlier in the day had been canceled. Swells had subsided to "relatively moderate."

Seven high-spirited college students had scampered aboard the boat, owned by Lyle Williams, a Tacoma carpet-layer and father of one of the amateur sailors, Brian.

They planned an hour-and-a-half cruise, they said, as a break from an Intercollegiate Knights convention at the University of Washington. As they sailed off into the darkness, nobody guessed that they, the sailboat and, by the elder Williams' reckoning, "39

or 40 floatable items," would simply vanish.

When they didn't return, five Coast Guard vessels, 35 auxiliary boats and several low-flying planes combed the waters around Commencement Bay and Vashon Island, venturing as far north as the Strait of Juan de Fuca. They found nothing — no bodies, no lifejackets, not the smallest piece of the sailboat's hull.

Parents of the missing students offered a $1,000 reward that triggered about 300 reports, a few from obvious charlatans. Jeane Dixon, the psychic, offered her services.

The closest thing to a break in the case occurred in January 1980. The seiner Albany, out of Gig Harbor, was bottom-fishing in about 200 feet of water in Colvos Passage when one of its cables snagged what apparently was a boat. When the nets were pulled up, the snagged craft almost made it to the surface. Onlookers thought they saw a sailboat under the water before it broke loose and returned to the bottom.

Although a minesweeper spent a day dragging the bottom where the Albany reported its strange catch, the sailboat didn't turn up.

Still missing and presumed dead besides Brian Williams: Gary Oman, Pullman; James Dickinson, Albion, Whitman County; Dennis Newton, Potlatch, Idaho; Brian Wilson, Loon Lake, Stevens County; Robert Sherwood, Toppenish, Yakima County, and Barbara Komorek, Seattle.

The 'bad humor' men

Humor, like romance, depends on mood, time and place. At the height of the Boeing cutback in April 1971 — when local

A true sign of the times greets motorists on Pacific Highway South at the height of the Boeing layoffs and high unemployment in April 1971.

Associated Press

CHRONO-LOG

employment dropped below 40,000 from a high of 95,000 in 1968 — Bob McDonald and Jim Youngren had what seemed like a great idea for a gag.

The two, employees of the realty firm of Henry Broderick, Inc. put up $160 to rent space on a billboard near Sea-Tac airport, across from a cemetery.

On it were printed these words: "Will the last person leaving Seattle — turn out the lights."

It was an overnight sensation.

For a day or two, McDonald and Youngren were hailed as two very funny men. Then the mood changed. Reporters sampled public opinion. Editorialists viewed with alarm. A radio station demanded the billboard's removal.

McDonald and Youngren stopped taking bows. People avoided them on elevators. There were mumblings about "sick humor." Suddenly, said McDonald, they were regarded as subversive.

When a billboard sprouted in Spokane ("The lights are still burning brightly here") and horror stories about Seattle's unemployment and financial woes appeared in The Wall Street Journal, Christian Science Monitor and Time magazine, there were those who thought the city had suffered irreparable damage nationally.

The company that had rented the space to McDonald and Youngren removed the sign, refunding half the money.

About a year later, a chastened McDonald explained the motivation for putting up the sign. He and Youngren frequently met out-of-state investors at the airport and drove them into town.

"They were amazed that Seattle wasn't a ghost town with weeds growing in the streets," said McDonald. "We wanted to counteract that attitude with a little humor.

"We are not hard-hearted or insensitive. We knew there was desperate unemployment and far too many vacant homes, particularly in the suburbs. These were no laughing matter. But we also felt that although Seattle was down, it certainly wasn't dead.

"The ridiculous idea that there ever would be a last man leaving town and turning out the lights seemed to us a spoof on all the doom-and-gloom talk."

No, the two did not put up any more billboards.

Postscript: When Congress killed the supersonic-transport project in March 1971, The Boeing Co. laid off 7,000 employees to keep its head above water. One year later, the company's SST mockup — developed as part of a $1 billion program — was sold to a promoter for $31,119. It was put on display at a roadside museum in Florida.

A wing and no prayer — and $200,000

On Thanksgiving Eve, Nov. 24, 1971, a slender man wearing sunglasses, a dark suit, a narrow tie and carrying a dark raincoat and briefcase, boarded Northwest Airlines Flight 305 at Portland, bound for Seattle.

He had signed in as "Dan Cooper."

As the Boeing 727 rolled onto the runway for takeoff at 2:53

p.m., the man passed the stewardess a handwritten note announcing there was a bomb in his briefcase. To add credibility, he briefly opened the lid so the woman could glimpse two red cylinders and some wiring.

While the stewardess was telling the pilot, 20-year veteran Bill Scott, the man with the briefcase nervously chain-smoked filter-tip cigarettes. As the jet winged its way north, the man known as Cooper issued a demand for four parachutes and $200,000 in $20 bills.

Scott notified airline officials by radio. Law-enforcement agencies were alerted. It took several hours to assemble the cash and parachutes. To kill time, the pilot circled Seattle-Tacoma International Airport for nearly two hours, telling passengers he had minor mechanical problems and wanted to use up fuel.

"Cooper" was unhappy with the delay. When the jet landed at 5:46 p.m., it taxied to a remote but well-lighted area — on the hijacker's orders.

All the passengers got off, except for Cooper. He examined the money and parachutes when they were delivered, then indicated he wanted a stewardess, Tina Mucklow, to remain with the plane, along with pilot Scott, co-pilot Bob Rataczak and flight engineer H.E. Anderson.

After the refueling, which took so long that Cooper snapped, "Let's get this circus on the road," the pilot was ordered to take off again — destination Mexico.

Told that a flight of that distance would require another refueling stop, Cooper directed the pilot to head for Reno, flying at about 10,000 feet and slightly less than 200 miles an hour.

Mucklow was ordered back to the cockpit, but soon was summoned to help Cooper open the door under the rear of the fuselage and let down a ramp. Frigid air rushed in. The stewardess was ordered back to the cockpit.

Meanwhile, the 727 — now code-named Victor 23 — was being followed by two F-106 fighters from McChord Air Force Base. In Portland, an Army National Guard helicopter took off at about the time the 727 would be flying overhead. None of the three tails located Victor 23 in the darkness.

At 8:11 p.m., the four people in the cockpit felt a slight bump as the jetliner flew over LaCenter, about 25 miles northeast of the Columbia. There was no further word from Cooper. Messages radioed back to the cabin went unanswered.

The vastly reconfigured Flight 305 landed in Reno 3½ hours after leaving Sea-Tac, damaging the ramp hanging below the plane. Cooper was gone. So was the money. Two of the four parachutes had been left behind.

Thus began one of the most intensive manhunts in Pacific Northwest history. There were hundreds of tips and leads, but no clues. The man who had signed himself Dan Cooper became known to the public as "D.B. Cooper" when someone misread the register.

Cooper became the stuff of legends, a Robin Hood of the skies, the first and only person to successfully hijack a passenger jet for ransom. He was hailed in song. At the Ariel Store and Tavern in Cowlitz County, near where Cooper might have landed if he survived, a party has been held each year on the anniversary of the jump.

There always are delicious rumors that D.B. himself shows up, in disguise, to join in a round of drinks.

The FBI dismisses the folklore. The man called Cooper, agents say, was poorly equipped for the bailout. Furthermore, one of the parachutes he took with him was faulty. He almost certainly died in the jump.

Their belief was bolstered in February 1980, when 8-year-old Brian Ingram of Vancouver found three rotting packets of the D.B. Cooper hijack money on the north beach of the Columbia, five miles from the Interstate Bridge between Vancouver and Portland. In all, $5,800 was found.

Proof?

The legend-weavers remain unconvinced. Old D.B. planted that money, they say, expecting it to be found. He's off somewhere, his feet up, hoisting a tall cool one and laughing about the stunt he pulled off on a long-ago Thanksgiving Eve.

A police sketch of the mysterious and elusive hijacker "D.B. Cooper."

Mountains of mound theory

Despite the efforts of scientific gumshoes, a classic whodunnit in Washington state was no closer to a universally accepted solution in the 1970s than it was a century earlier.

What or who was responsible for those neatly rounded, precisely laid out earthen spheres that pimple the prairies on both sides of the Cascades?

Similar bumps can be found in the country of Kenya and in 27 Western states from Canada to Mexico. But the most studied examples are the Mima (MY-muh) Mounds near Thurston County's Offut Lake, Little Rock and Tenino.

Farmers' plows, grazing cattle and sand-and-gravel miners have destroyed many of the estimated 900,000 Mima Mounds that once existed on more than 30,000 acres. But thousands still can be seen on a drive down old Highway 99, even though the open vistas of 30 years ago have been invaded by an increasing number of Douglas firs.

About 4,000 prize examples — 10 to 40 feet in diameter and up to 7 feet tall — have been saved for posterity in the 446-acre Mima Mounds Natural Area Preserve near Little Rock.

Capt. Charles Wilkes and his U.S. Exploring Expedition first reported on the Thurston County mounds in 1841. Wilkes wrote in his diary:

"They are evidently of old formation by a bygone race as they have the marks of savage labour... They are certainly not places of burial and not provided by accidental causes."

The Wilkes party dug into three mounds, finding mostly clay, sand and pebbles on a bed of coarse gravel. Scores of scientists and thousands of shovel-wielding amateur treasure hunters who have followed Wilkes have turned up nothing more.

Many theories have been advanced and found wanting. The mounds are not Indian burial grounds, the residue of great Indian shellfish feasts, the work of ants or sucker fish, buffalo wallows or the result of volcanic upheavals.

The two explanations that have survived are given equal weight by the Department of Natural Resources at the Mima Mounds preserve. And yet they are about as conclusive as arguments over which came first, the chicken or the egg.

"Officially," the mounds were formed by glacial action or frost, or by families of gophers.

Glacier and frost theories are based on unarguable geological fact. Great sheets of ice did extend as far south as Washington state's mounds during the last Ice Age, about 13,500 years ago.

While most scientists were expressing satisfaction with one of the glacier or frost theories, the proverbial monkey wrench was thrown into the mix in 1941 by Walter Dalquest, a geology and mammalogy student at the UW, and Victor Scheffer, a biologist for the Fish and Wildlife Service. The mounds, they said, had been made by *thomomys mazama* or the pocket gopher.

Nobody laughed. Scheffer was the author of highly acclaimed books on natural history; in 1977 he received the UW's Distinguished Alumnus Award.

Scheffer-Dalquest theorized that ordinary gophers — not some super-race of rodents — came after the Ice Age and made the mounds over a period of years. A family of 10 gophers in one area, they said, can move four to five tons of earth a year. Furthermore, gophers are anti-social, and the spacing of the mounds "indicates they set up territories to build their enormous nests."

On the other hand, Gordon Alcorn, a biologist and ornithologist at the University of Puget Sound, favored the glacier theory.

Alcorn says he and his wife were driving near the top of Canada's Rogers Pass when they saw mounds of silt atop a glacier and said simultaneously, "That's it."

The most recent theory, advanced in 1989 by A. Lincoln Washburn, a UW geology professor emeritus, credits the mounds to erosion-resistant root systems of vegetation that formed on silt-and-gravel deposits following the last ice age.

But some prefer the Paul Bunyan theory. It goes like this:

The legendary woodsman, wanting to build a Great Wall of China out West, hired a bunch of Irishmen to do the job. They dug a hole that later filled with water — the Pacific Ocean. They piled up the dirt to form the Cascades.

And one day, before walking off the job and returning to Ireland, they all overturned their wheelbarrows — creating the Mima Mounds.

Taking the initiative

For a time in 1973, a 32-year-old furniture salesman named Bruce Helm was an authentic folk hero throughout the state, chased after for quotes by the media, mentioned on TV by Walter Cronkite, profiled in The Wall Street Journal and cited in the pages of Reader's Digest as a model of what citizen activism is all about.

Helm's fame was based on Initiative 282, a petition drive he promoted to roll back the salaries of state officials.

Not only did Helm pull off the impossible, getting nearly 700,000 signatures in 18 days, but he succeeded in getting under the skin of the usually unflappable Gov. Dan Evans.

Asked for a comment when it became apparent that Helm had gathered enough signatures to put his initiative on the ballot, Evans snappishly referred to Helm as "that Lynnwood furniture salesman." Actually, Helm lived in the Lynnwood area but worked in the family furniture store in Ballard.

Helm was just another citizen — married, two young sons, UW graduate in speech — when he heard on the evening news that state legislators had just raised the salaries of elected officials by 197 percent and put an emergency clause on the pay raise.

A nationwide salary freeze at the time limited pay increases to 5.5 percent. Helm was incensed at both the amount of the raise voted in Olympia and the manner in which it was done — "clandestinely and with the emergency clause."

After doing a slow burn over the weekend, Helm drove to Olympia and asked what was required to halt the pay increase. What he wanted to do would be impossible, he was told, because of the emergency clause. But he could fight the clause in the courts or he could attempt to get an initiative on the ballot. Of course, the latter also would be impossible, because he would need 117,000 signatures and the deadline for filing was less than three weeks away.

Helm accepted the challenge, filing a lawsuit to remove the emergency clause and drawing up initiative petitions.

Victor B. Scheffer

Looking like great earthen welts, the Mima Mounds mysteriously corrugate the landscape in parts of Thurston County, as seen in this aerial view taken in 1977.

As word of his one-man fight spread, it resulted in one of the greatest outpourings of citizen support in state history. Printers offered their services. Stationers supplied free paper. Hundreds called to volunteer as signature-gatherers. Space was donated for a campaign headquarters.

So much money poured in, unsolicited, that Helm began sending it back.

A caravan was formed to deliver the petitions to Olympia. A State Patrol escort, sirens whining, guided Helm and friends up to the Statehouse. Old-timers in Olympia called it "the darndest thing" they had ever seen.

Put on the ballot, the measure was approved by voters, 4 to 1.

Helm resisted efforts to run for office afterward, saying he was happy selling furniture. When Evans, who had once made the cutting remark about Helm, ran for the U.S. Senate against Mike Lowry in 1982, Helm was asked how he had voted.

"Evans," he replied softly.

CHRONO-LOG

'Ted' leaves a long trail of death

Theodore "Ted" Bundy showed bright promise in the early '70s — good-looking, articulate, a better-than-average student in subjects that interested him, a volunteer at the Seattle Crisis Clinic and a hard worker on several Republican political campaigns.

He drove a tan Volkswagen.

■ On Feb. 1, 1974, Lynda Ann Healy, 21, who did ski reports for a Seattle radio station, disappeared from her basement bedroom in the University District.

■ On March 12, Donna Gail Manson, 19, disappeared from the campus of The Evergreen State College in Olympia.

■ On April 17, Susan Rancourt, 18, disappeared from the campus of Central Washington State University in Ellensburg.

■ On May 6, Roberta Kathleen Parks, 22, disappeared from the campus of Oregon State University in Corvallis.

■ On June 1, Brenda Ball, 22, was last seen leaving a tavern in Burien.

■ On June 11, Georgann Hawkins, 18, disappeared from behind her sorority house at the University of Washington.

■ On July 14, Janice Ott, 23, and Denise Naslund, 19, disappeared from Lake Sammamish State Park. They had been seen talking with a tanned, good-looking young man with his arm in a sling. He had called himself Ted, and he drove a brown or tan Volkswagen.

■ Carol Valenzuela, 20, disappeared Aug. 2 in Vancouver, Wash.

Associated Press
Ted Bundy makes a point at his murder trial in Miami in June 1979.

The remains of Manson and Hawkins were never identified. Those of the others were found in the Cascade foothills. They were presumed to have died from strangulation or bludgeoning.

Ted Bundy left Seattle for Utah to enter law school in the late summer of 1974. During his time in Utah, at least six women disappeared. One, Carol DaRonch, 19, escaped from her attacker, a man in a tan Volkswagen. She later identified him as Bundy.

Bundy made several trips to Colorado. He passed through Snomass and a nurse, Caryn Campbell, was murdered. He bought gas in Grand Junction and Denise Oliverson disappeared on her bicycle. He passed through Vail and Julie Cunningham disappeared.

Bundy served time in Utah for the attempted kidnapping of DaRonch, and then was taken to Colorado to stand trial for the murder of Campbell. He twice made spectacular escapes in Colorado, once leaping from a courthouse window, another time dieting for weeks until he was slender enough to escape through his jail cell's false ceiling.

After his last escape, he remained free until he was captured in Florida, where he had lived next door to Florida State's Chi Omega sorority house in Tallahassee. Margaret Bowman, 21, and Lisa Levy, 20, were clubbed to death in the sorority house, two other students were battered and a fifth woman was savagely beaten in her nearby apartment.

Bundy drove a stolen vehicle to Lake City, Fla., where 12-year-old Kimberly Dianne Leach disappeared from her junior high school. Her body later was found, the victim, as police put it, of "homicidal violence."

Bundy was captured and convicted of first-degree murder in the deaths of Leach, Bowman and Levy. In a bizarre courtroom scene in Orlando in 1980, Bundy, who often acted as his own attorney, was permitted to question his girlfriend, Carole Boone, on the witness stand. He asked if she would marry him. She replied that she would and Bundy replied, "I do hereby marry you." Boone had arranged for a notary public to be present in the courtroom, and officials later said the marriage was legal. Boone later gave birth to a daughter she said was Bundy's.

Such antics, coupled with his All-American-boy looks and escapes, made Bundy one of the nation's most publicized serial killers, the subject of five books and a TV movie.

Bundy was a resident of Florida's death row for nine years and five months until his electrocution Jan. 24, 1989, in Florida State prison's "Old Sparky." His trials and appeals cost the state more than $16 million.

Shortly before his execution, Bundy confessed to eight so-called "Ted" killings in Washington, but denied involvement in Valenzuela's murder, even though it bore the "Ted" imprint. He also admitted to several other murders in Washington, two in Oregon and two in Utah in which he had not been a suspect. Investigators believed he committed at least three dozen murders and possibly more than 100.

Spokane: Fair game at last

Spokane, the state's second-largest city, proved in 1974 that it, too, could stage a world's fair.

Expo '74 dealt with one of the most important themes of the last half of the 20th century — the fragile environment. The 184-day fair drew 5,187,826 patrons, highlighted by an attendance of 85,000 for opening-day ceremonies featuring President Nixon.

Because of the Watergate scandal, Nixon wasn't around when the fair closed. President Ford did the honors with a taped message in which he said: "This is only the beginning of what lies ahead. This is a past that has no ending. It is a challenge to every man and woman to refrain from waste and destruction so that the land we love may be preserved for future generations."

Governor Evans called Expo's close the end of Act I and said the job of Act II would be to "prove that what Expo was all about can come true."

Traditionally, world's fairs lose money. Expo '74 was the third straight Washington state exposition to turn a profit.

Spokane's fair left a legacy in the form of Riverfront Park in the shadow of the business district. The park rests on two islands and both banks of the Spokane River, which surges through the heart of the city over a spectacular twin-tiered falls. That portion of the river had been obscured for years by railroad property.

President Carter — governor of Georgia when the fair opened — officially dedicated the park in May 1978.

Indian fishing: the scales of justice

 In April 1974, U.S. District Judge George Boldt of Tacoma issued a fishing-rights ruling that was one of the most important and controversial in the nation's history.

After hearing months of testimony and grappling with the issues and with his own conscience, Boldt ruled that treaties drawn up in the 19th century granting Native Americans the right to fish "in common with" other citizens entitled them to 50 percent of the harvestable salmon and steelhead from traditional Indian fishing waters.

Many commercial fishermen and ordinary citizens were incensed. Indians — who had been clubbed, maced and jailed for doing what Boldt now said was their right — felt it was long overdue justice at the hands of the white man.

Boldt said he didn't make the law, he just interpreted it. "If I'm wrong," he added, "the higher courts will tell me."

They didn't. The decision was upheld by the Ninth Circuit Court of Appeals and then, 6 to 3, by the U.S. Supreme Court. Thus far, all efforts to overturn it have failed.

Boldt was an unlikely person to deliver what some regarded as a radical opinion. A native Montanan and son of a Swedish-Danish immigrant, he was small in stature and dapper in dress, favoring bow ties long after they were out of fashion. He was unfailingly polite and precise in his speech. His politics were strongly conservative. He was recommended for the federal bench by a three-time Republican governor, Arthur B. Langlie, and appointed by a Republican president, Dwight Eisenhower.

As a traveling judge, Boldt put behind bars such notorious underworld figures as Frankie Carbo, Blinky Palermo and Mickey Cohen. He had thrown the book at ex-Teamster president Dave Beck. Fortune magazine had named him one of the six outstanding federal judges in the country.

When Boldt took on the fishing-rights case, he tried to put himself back to 1854 when Territorial Gov. Isaac Stevens gathered with some 630 lower Puget Sound Indians on the Nisqually Flats, near a small stream that whites called Medicine Creek.

Stevens made certain promises to the Indians on behalf of their conquerors. Among them, that the Indians could fish "in common with" other citizens of the territory. According to dictionaries of the time, Boldt decided, that meant a 50-50 split.

Usually, federal decisions take on the name of the plaintiffs or defendants in a case. The fishing-rights decision was different. It became known far and wide as the "Boldt decision."

Among the reporters covering the lengthy hearings that led to Boldt's decision was Jack Wilkins. After the ruling came down on Lincoln's Birthday in 1974, Wilkins explained to his 10-year-old son, Charlie, what the judge had decided about treaty promises. Then he asked the boy how he felt.

When Wilkins heard the response, he asked his son to send a note to Boldt.

They say that Boldt, who died of Alzheimer's disease at the age of 80, always treasured Charlie's note, which read:

"Judge, you did the right thing. A deal's a deal."

Matt McVay / Seattle Times

Purse seiners and gillnetters crowd and block the ferry Kaleetan at Friday Harbor in September 1978 in protest of the Boldt decision on Indian fishing rights four years earlier.

Fatal attractions

There were numerous reminders in the '70s that although the state's mountains are beautiful to look at, they can be deadly.

■ Twenty-nine students and instructors from a University of Puget Sound mountain-climbing class were camped about 500 feet above the parking lot at Timberline, on the north slope of Mount St. Helens, the evening of April 26, 1975.

At about 8:25 p.m., while several people watched from the parking lot, there was a roar above the camp. Someone yelled "avalanche." In moments, a great white mass thundered down on the campers.

Five died under the snow: Philip Burdick, Eatonville; Eric Spurrell, Denver; Richard Pfeifer, Federal Way; Nina Engebretsen, Tacoma; and Karen Moniot, Tacoma.

■ Internationally famous mountain climber Willi Unsoeld, who had reached the summit of Mount Everest in 1963, died in an avalanche on Mount Rainier March 4, 1979, along with an Evergreen State College student, Janie Diepenbrock.

Unsoeld had taken 19 students with him in an attempt to climb the mountain in winter. They made a base camp above the 11,000-foot level and began an assault on the 14,411-foot summit. At about 12,800 feet, a storm forced the party to retreat in zero visibility. They were descending the mountain from their base camp, by way of Cadaver Gap — a route deemed the safest —

when an avalanche swept over Unsoeld, Diepenbrock and two men on the lead rope.

All were buried, Unsoeld and Diepenbrock the deepest. By the time the veteran climber and the college student were found, they had been under the snow for nearly an hour. Both were dead.

The saddened climbers returned to 10,000-foot Camp Muir to wait out the storm. There they held a memorial service later described as "a time of soul-searching, of sharing, of singing, and of really getting to know ourselves."

Lou Whittaker, the premier Mount Rainier guide, was one of four guides who went up to help the climbers down. As they returned to Paradise Lodge — 10 days after beginning their adventure — the climbers could be heard singing, bravely and perhaps a bit defiantly:

"You can't kill the spirit;
"It's like the mountain;
"Old and strong,
"It goes on and on."

One of the climbers, Eric Kessler of New Jersey, summed up their feeling: "Willi said to us, 'Death is not too great a price to pay for a life lived to the fullest,' and we believe that."

Postscript: It was not the first mountain tragedy for the Unsoelds. Nanda Devi, daughter of Willi and Jolene Unsoeld, had died in the arms of her father Sept. 8, 1976, on the slopes of the Himalayan mountain after which she had been named. In the fall of 1982, after his father's death, Krag Unsoeld fell 18 feet and struck his head on a rock while engaged in a difficult two-man climb in Wyoming's Grand Tetons. It was touch-and-go for a while but Krag, 26, survived.

Asked if she thought her family should quit climbing, Jolene Unsoeld said: "I haven't quit climbing, so I don't know why they should."

Unsoeld, active in Democratic politics as well, scaled a personal mountain in 1988 when she scored a razor-thin victory in the 3rd District congressional race.

A soaring of 'Hawks

The world may little know or little care what happened in Seattle Sept. 12, 1976, but you could never tell that to the 58,441 fans who jammed the Kingdome for the first official NFL game played by the Seahawks.

What matter that the Jack Patera-coached Seahawks dropped a 30-24 thriller to the St. Louis Cardinals? The important thing was that Jim Zorn, the Seahawks' free-agent quarterback, threw for 292 yards and two touchdowns, both to wide receiver Sam McCullum. And a slender, boyish-looking wide receiver named Steve Largent caught five passes as easily as if he had been playing catch with Zorn in a sandlot game.

The 'Hawks, everyone agreed, were a team of the future. No less than NFL Commissioner Pete Rozelle was on hand for the opener.

In time, Zorn-to-Largent would become one of the most productive, and feared, passing-and-receiving combinations in the NFL and provide the town with its first professional football heroes.

Seven years after that inaugural game, the Seahawks made the NFL playoffs as a wild card for the first time. There was a different coach, Chuck Knox, and a different quarterback, Dave Krieg. But Largent, en route to the Pro Football Hall of Fame, was still catching footballs.

Seattle won two playoff games — 31-7 over Denver and 27-20 over heavily favored Miami — before losing, 30-14, to Oakland in the game that decided the AFC championship and a berth in the 1984 Super Bowl.

Getting a pro football team had been a lot easier than getting,

STATE-MENTS

Seattle Opera Association
Janice Yoes as Brünnhilde in Seattle Opera's "Die Walküre."

Seattle: Ringleader

Seattle Opera launched the most ambitious artistic undertaking in Pacific Northwest history in July 1975 when it staged Richard Wagner's monumental four-opera "Der Ring des Nibelungen," or the Ring of the Nibelung, in the original German and in English.

It marked the first time any opera company had attempted to perform The Ring in both languages. The reason: Each cycle of four operas lasts 18 hours over four days and involves 34 soloists, 60 choral singers and 86 orchestral musicians. Seattle did it not once but twice in less than two weeks.

Glynn Ross, general director of Seattle Opera, beamed from the wings as the first Pacific Northwest Festival drew near-capacity crowds and earned critical acclaim for Das Rheingold, Die Walkure, Siegfried and Gotterdammerung. It was Ross's dream to put Seattle on the international music map, and he had succeeded.

Once was not enough. Seattle kept doing it, year after year. The word spread quickly. Opera buffs soon were flying into Sea-Tac each summer from all over the world to renew acquaintances with the gods, dwarfs and dragons who make up Wagner's complicated music-drama.

There was no Ring in 1988, and some feared it might be lost forever. But Ross's successor, Speight Jenkins, hinted at a renewal in the future — if not every year, then perhaps every other year.

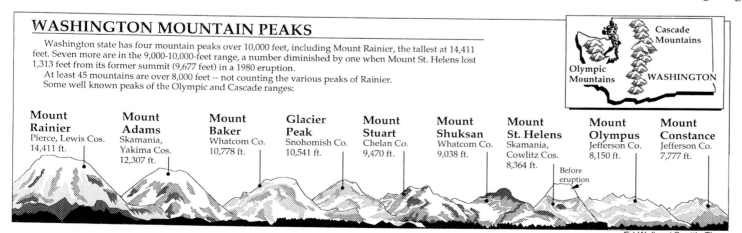

WASHINGTON MOUNTAIN PEAKS

Washington state has four mountain peaks over 10,000 feet, including Mount Rainier, the tallest at 14,411 feet. Seven more are in the 9,000-10,000-feet range, a number diminished by one when Mount St. Helens lost 1,313 feet from its former summit (9,677 feet) in a 1980 eruption.

At least 45 mountains are over 8,000 feet -- not counting the various peaks of Rainier.

Some well known peaks of the Olympic and Cascade ranges:

Cascade Mountains
Olympic Mountains WASHINGTON

Mount Rainier
Pierce, Lewis Cos.
14,411 ft.

Mount Adams
Skamania, Yakima Cos.
12,307 ft.

Mount Baker
Whatcom Co.
10,778 ft.

Glacier Peak
Snohomish Co.
10,541 ft.

Mount Stuart
Chelan Co.
9,470 ft.

Mount Shuksan
Whatcom Co.
9,038 ft.

Mount St. Helens
Skamania, Cowlitz Cos.
8,364 ft.
Before eruption

Mount Olympus
Jefferson Co.
8,150 ft.

Mount Constance
Jefferson Co.
7,777 ft.

Ed Walker / Seattle Times

CHRONO-LOG

Seattle Times

In 1974, Karen and Mickey Taylor paid $17,000 for a thoroughbred they named Seattle Slew because one of his feet sort of "slewed in." As a 3-year-old in 1977, he won the Triple Crown. After earning $1.2 million from racing, Slew was retired to stud, siring numerous major-stakes winners and earning millions (40 shares at $3.5 million a share) for the Taylors who, pre-Slew, had run a small lumber operation in the Columbia River town of White Salmon. Slew flew in a private jet to Seattle-Tacoma Airport in the summer of 1977 and made two exhibition "golden gallops" at Longacres Race Track.

1976

Sen. Henry M. Jackson seems to have good shot at Democratic presidential nomination, winning Massachusetts and New York. By late March, folksy approach of Jimmy Carter, outsider from Georgia, begins to draw crowds; appeal of Jackson, insider from Senate, begins to pale. When Pennsylvania primary votes are counted in late April, "Scoop's" bid for White House is essentially over.

Seattle Seahawks play their first official National Football League game to 58,441 fans in Kingdome. 'Hawks lose anyway, 30-24, to St. Louis Cardinals.

1978

Sales tax eliminated from food July 1 in accordance with initiative approved by Washington's voters the previous year.

King Tutankhamen exhibit packs more than 500,000 visitors into Seattle Center to see treasures from tomb of 14th century B.C. Egyptian monarch.

and keeping, a big-league baseball team.

Tampa Bay and Seattle were selected in June 1974 to become the 27th and 28th members of the NFL. The franchise was awarded to a group of local businessmen organized by D.E. "Ned" Skinner and including Lloyd Nordstrom, Herman Sarkowsky, M. Lamont Bean, Howard S. Wright and Lynn Himmelman. Nordstrom, representing eight members of the Nordstrom family, became the majority shareholder (51 percent).

More than 10,000 names were suggested by the public for the No-Name team. Seahawks was the choice of 151 entries. Nordstrom & Co. paid $16 million for the franchise.

Fourteen years earlier, the American Football League (which later merged with the NFL) had offered a Seattle businessman a franchise for $25,000. He wasn't interested.

The Nordstrom family eventually became the sole owner of the franchise, which they sold for $80 million in 1988 to California land developers Kenneth Behring and Ken Hofmann.

For some, a sting Ray

Dixy Lee Ray, running as a Democrat, was elected as the state's first woman governor in the fall of 1976 — outpolling Republican John Spellman by almost 130,000 votes in the race to determine who would succeed the long-ensconced Dan Evans.

The victory of Ray, who grew up in Pierce County and had climbed to the top of Mount Rainier as a teen-ager, made national headlines. She was seen by many as the forerunner of a new breed of politician, the scientist-manager.

She had taught zoology at the University of Washington, directed the Pacific Science Center and been both a member and chairman of the Atomic Energy Commission. The latter position made her the most powerful woman in the Nixon administration.

When the AEC was abolished in 1974, Ray became assistant secretary of state for Oceans, International Environment and

Seattle Times

Seattle Seahawks quarterback Jim Zorn readies for a pass during a November 1979 game in the Kingdome.

Scientific Matters. She resigned soon after being confirmed.

A high IQ, however, didn't translate into long-lasting popularity for Ray. She got into running feuds with party leaders and the media (she named the pigs on her Fox Island farm after newsmen she disliked), and she was given to schoolmarmish lectures when questioned about atomic energy or environmental concerns.

Typical Ray comments:
■ Chemical explosions such as one at Hanford are "such a common occurrence that it scarcely warrants or merits front-page reporting."
■ "From now on we'll send them a Kleenex at the time they are fired if they're going to be a crybaby." (Commenting on the sudden firing of state officials.)
■ Of an oil spill: "Clearly its major effect is on birds . . . and that is not happy. I hate to say this, but birds die every day. In every major oil spill, marine life has recovered in a year."
■ "There is no evidence that survivors of the Hiroshima bombing have suffered any more cancer than anyone else . . . including the second generation."
■ "The problems facing the nuclear industry are largely raised by fears of the public, but we all know that fear requires ignorance."

Ray accused President Carter of being "frightened in his mother's womb" for dragging his feet on a plutonium nuclear-reactor plant at Clinch River, Tenn., and she called the state's senior senator, Warren Magnuson, a "dictator" for his concerns about Cherry Point as an oil-port site.

Four years after her popular victory, Ray failed to survive the Democratic primary, losing to Jim McDermott, who then lost a close race to Spellman in the general election.

The bumpy road to busing

Ever since the U.S. Supreme Court's historic school-desegregation decision in 1954, it was inevitable that Seattle, like all large cities, would have to desegregate voluntarily or watch the courts step in.

On Sept. 29, 1978, Seattle became the largest city in America to desegregate its schools without a court order.

A cause for cheering? Not quite. Two months later, residents went to the polls and passed anti-busing Initiative 350.

U.S. District Judge Donald Voorhees promptly declared the initiative unconstitutional, and by the time the U.S. Supreme Court ruled two years later that Voorhees was correct, busing had become as much a part of the school system as fall football.

The road to busing had been bumpy.

In 1963, what became known as the Voluntary Racial Transfer Program was instituted in hopes that blacks would transfer to predominantly white schools and vice versa. What began with high hopes soon foundered on reality. Only 90 of a hoped-for 1,600 students applied for transfers.

Greg Gilbert / Seattle Times

Dixy Lee Ray enjoys some moments of tranquillity at her Puget Sound retreat on Fox Island in early November 1976 — just two days before she was elected Washington's first woman governor.

In 1966, a federal lawsuit was filed on behalf of 30 black students to force the district to draw up a comprehensive desegregation plan. When the district promised to work toward that end, the suit was dropped.

Progress continued to be painfully slow. When a plan to require mandatory busing for middle-schoolers was proposed in 1967, it touched off a lawsuit by Citizens Against Mandatory Busing (CAMB) and an attempted recall of the Seattle School Board.

The suit was successful at the outset. King County Superior Court Judge William Wilkins issued a permanent injunction against the middle-school proposal. But Wilkins' ruling was overturned by the state Supreme Court in 1972.

The board survived the recall. But Superintendent Forbes Bottomly, a driving force behind desegregation, resigned, feeling he had outlived his usefulness.

Meanwhile, the voluntary-transfer program had been gaining momentum — except that blacks noted they were bearing a disproportionate burden. Of 2,400 transfer students in 1969, 2,000 were black. The district continued to nibble at the problem, passing a resolution to desegregate Garfield High by 1975, then pulling back.

In December 1977, the board, with the blessing of Superintendent David Moberly, adopted the "fixed assignment" desegregation plan that went into effect in the fall of 1978.

A teacher's strike at the beginning of the fall term delayed desegregation by three weeks. But on the first day of classes, 20,500 of the district's 55,000 students boarded buses, 12,500 of them as part of the "Seattle plan" for desegregation.

Despite some pickets with homemade signs ("Boycott Busing") and 80 police officers assigned to keep the peace, it went smoothly.

A decade later, busing's merits were still being debated. The school district's population had shrunk from 55,000 to 45,000 — the result, many said, of "white flight" to the suburbs. Furthermore, more than half of those enrolled in public schools were minorities, causing many to wonder if busing were still necessary.

But all, pro or con, could look back with some pride to 1978. In Boston and Little Rock, the citizenry had fought bitterly to halt school desegregation. In Seattle, they had limited their weapons to words and ballots. And in the end had bowed to the inevitable.

Down and dirty in Pierce County

Pierce County residents were shocked, angry — perhaps disbelieving more than anything else — when what became known as the racketeering scandal broke on a quiet afternoon in November 1978.

Word was flashed that the county's popular 50-year-old sheriff, George Janovich, had been arrested by federal agents outside a supermarket. Fourteen others were being rounded up, including the reputed "Mr. Big," bail bondsman, tavern owner and used-car dealer John Carbone. It sounded like Chicago or New York, not Tacoma.

Government lawyers put all their cards on the table from the outset. They had, they said, broken up "the Enterprise," headed by Carbone and including lieutenants, enforcers, torchers and a protector — Janovich — who had accepted a $1,300 bribe from a federal agent posing as a racketeer.

The group's goal, said the feds, was to control Pierce County's tavern industry through firebombings (16 in two years), beatings, shootings, extortion and bribes. On the side, The Enterprise dabbled in illegal gambling.

The bulky federal document read like a chapter of "The Godfather." The talk in supporting documents was straight out of Mickey Spillane. Pierce County was dazed. Most of all, it felt betrayed by Janovich, a career law-enforcement officer who had just been re-elected in a landslide.

There had been a series of seemingly unrelated incidents hinting that all was not perfect. Taverns had been burned with almost monthly regularity. Some, like the Back Forty, had been torched repeatedly. A no-nonsense state Liquor Control Board inspector, Mel Journey, was shot and nearly killed outside his home one morning. The landmark Top of the Ocean restaurant was burned to the waterline. The Gig Harbor home of Carbone was set afire while he was vacationing on his yacht.

Taken separately, the fires and the muscle didn't mean much. Taken all together, as part of an "enterprise," they formed the key ingredients in the federal case.

Once the racketeering story broke, relationships among the principals began to fall into place. It was like taking a peek at the last page of a mystery novel, knowing whodunnit and then clearly understanding all the clues the author drops along the way.

The trial was held in San Francisco in the summer of 1979. A jury of six men and six women deliberated for a week before finding Janovich, Carbone and five others guilty of a total of 45

Cole Porter / Seattle Times

Seattle schoolchildren wait for their morning transportation a few days after the city implemented its busing desegregation plan.

counts of racketeering. Six others had pleaded guilty earlier.

Janovich was sentenced to 12 years in prison, Carbone to 25.

Liquor inspector Journey and two tavern owners, who charged that Janovich and others had tried to deny them their civil rights, were paid $3.7 million by the county.

Tilting at Puget Sound windmills

All cities that grow and prosper are blessed, at various times in their history, with the few who manage to transform impossible dreams into reality.

In Seattle the most visible and tireless dreamer-doer for a quarter of a century has been a rather ordinary-looking bond counselor who lugs a bulging brown briefcase wherever he goes. Most citizens wouldn't recognize him if he passed them on the street. But virtually all would know his name: Jim Ellis.

James Reed Ellis grew up in the Rainier Valley and was the first Franklin High School graduate to attend Yale University; where he debated and, at 150 pounds, played football. After World War II, he attended the University of Washington Law School.

In time, Ellis would be president of the UW Board of Regents, president of the Municipal League, a member of the National Water Commission and the prime mover behind just about every "impossible" project in King County.

In the early 1950s, Ellis joined and then led the charge to restore Lake Washington, Lake Union and Puget Sound to the purity that existed before hordes began using them for commerce and as garbage dumps.

The result was Metro (Municipality of Metropolitan Seattle), which made the waters purer than anyone thought possible and, in the late '70s, became a countywide agency empowered to work on solutions to a broad range of problems, including transportation.

In 1965, Ellis delivered a speech to the Seattle Rotary Club challenging the city's leaders to embark on a golden age of development, a sort of "forward thrust" for Seattle and King County.

It led to Forward Thrust, an $819 million dream that included parks, fire stations, swimming pools, a domed stadium, low-income housing, rail rapid-transit, improved streets and storm sewers.

It, too, was deemed impossible (a union publication dubbed it "Forward Bust"). But in 1968 the voters said yes to $339.9 million worth of proposals. The major loser was the rail system. For his work on Forward Thrust, Ellis was praised by Time magazine.

In the late '70s, Ellis threw himself into farmland preservation. All the while, he was promoting still another impossible dream — the construction of a mighty convention and trade center that would be flung across Interstate 5 in downtown Seattle.

It would, said Ellis, attract people from all over the world, swell the public coffers and make Seattle one of the great international

The west span of the Hood Canal Floating Bridge — or what was left of it — became a climbing attraction after the Big Blow of mid-February 1979.

Kathy Andrisevic / Seattle Times

CHRONO-LOG

1978

Pierce County scandal involving arson, extortion and attempted murder breaks wide open with arrest of Sheriff George Janovich, 14 others on charges of racketeering.

Bucking national trend promoted by singer Anita Bryant, Seattleites decisively defeat Initiative 13, which would have repealed ordinance banning discrimination against homosexuals.

1979

Deng Xiaoping, Chinese vice premier, visits Seattle at end of historic nine-day tour of U.S. Deng works crowds like seasoned politician and tours Boeing 747 plant in Everett.

Washington voters, who turned down nickel deposit on bottles and cans in 1970, show no change of heart when measure appears on ballot again. Beverage, container and grocery industries, which spend $200,000 to defeat 1970 initiative, lay out nearly $1 million to assure defeat in 1979.

cities. The cost to the state: $99 million or so; less if there was private participation.

It was not smooth sailing.

Advocates of low-income housing, including the Church Council of Greater Seattle, demanded that the poor and elderly displaced by the center be provided with replacement housing. Costs rose to $150 million, and when private money promised by the backers didn't materialize, the Legislature — angry that King County always had its hand out — had to bail out the project.

But through it all, Ellis, seemingly undaunted, continued to speak of the convention and trade center as a cash cow, to be milked for the public good.

It was typical Ellis talk, eternally optimistic and public-spirited. When Forward Thrust money built Freeway Park, adjacent to the convention center, Ellis stayed true to that style. Of his success in getting the park, he said matter-of-factly: "The freeway cut a gash. What we did was cover that gash much like you sew up a wound."

That sinking feeling

Until 1979, the lives of Western Washington residents were guided by two articles of faith: The weather consists of occasional dry spells interspersed between long periods of rain; floating bridges don't sink.

Scratch the latter.

Winds gusting up to 100 miles an hour, combined with a strong outgoing tide, accomplished what engineers said could never happen when shortly before 7 a.m. Feb. 13, the western half of the

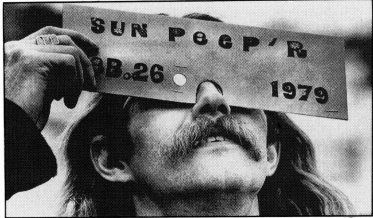

Associated Press

Tim Donovan of Seattle demonstrates a $1 method of protecting the eyes with the "sunglasses" he was selling during the solar eclipse of Feb. 26, 1979 at Goldendale.

1.3-mile Hood Canal (William A. Bugge) Floating Bridge broke into three sections.

Two pieces sank almost immediately. The third floated about a quarter of a mile to the north and then joined the others in more than 300 feet of water. In all, the three pieces contained 13 pontoons, each 360 feet long and weighing 500 tons.

Besides a great chunk of the bridge, two pickup trucks, a private car, a compressor, generator and a small crane also went to the bottom. But nobody perished.

Traffic had been halted and the bridge's drawspan opened at 11:30 the previous night to ease pressure from the onslaught of winds and tide. It was opened briefly at 2 the following morning to permit two power-company employees to drive across and check on a powerline failure.

Shortly before it sank, Red Taylor of Tacoma attempted to drive his tractor-trailer rig across from the west side. When he realized the bridge was starting to break up, he backed off.

From the beginning, the bridge had been plagued with problems. Two pontoons sank in the Duwamish River while they were being built. A storm damaged other pontoons during construction in 1960. Two years after the bridge opened in 1961, it was damaged by a storm and traffic had to be moved by ferryboat during repairs. There were ongoing difficulties with the cables that anchored the span to the bottom of the canal.

Except for slowing down travelers to and from the Olympic Peninsula, the sinking of the Hood Canal Bridge could have been worse. The $26.7 million span was insured and repairs were quickly begun.

Blaring car horns, cheers and heavy traffic signaled the reopening of the rebuilt bridge Oct. 23, 1982. The first "official" vehicle across the bridge that day was Red Taylor's tractor-trailer rig — completing the journey begun nearly four years before.

Empire of the sun — sort of

The last total eclipse of the sun in the United States until August 2017 occurred Feb. 26, 1979. And perhaps the best viewing place in the country was Goldendale, a little farming community of 3,400 people in Klickitat County.

By a lucky roll of the celestial dice, Goldendale, where old car bodies rust in the outback, had found itself in the path of a solar eclipse for the second time this century (the first was 1918).

Professional astronomers and thousands of skywatchers gathered for the event, along with a motley band from Berkeley, Calif., who called themselves the New Reformed Druids of North America and set up camp in Sam Hill's replica of Stonehenge, on the banks of the Columbia.

Well aware of its unique place in the world of astronomy, Goldendale had obtained federal help to build an observatory on a 150-acre site north of town in 1973, after inheriting a 24-inch reflecting telescope built for Portland's Clark College. Experts had said there was too much air pollution to locate in Portland.

Astronomers came from as far away as Germany and France to jam the observatory's limited space during the eclipse. Hucksters on the streets sold shoulder patches, stamp cachets and T-shirts ("Biggest Coverup in 70 years," "Where The Sun Don't Shine Every 70 Years"). The hottest item was a pennant, "Where in Hell is Goldendale?"

Some visitors stopped to listen to a man who billed himself as the "Lay Ombudsman of the Impossible Fact." His display — the only one that wasn't selling something — consisted of a styrofoam ball, cardboard stuck in a mop bucket and readerboards that were a montage of headlines and photographs snipped from magazines.

By 7:30 a.m., as the hills grew black with spectators and vehicles, a light rain was falling on Goldendale's parade. The sky was dark with clouds and there was no hint of sun.

The ranks of the Druids down in Stonehenge had been swollen by representatives of the Church of All Worlds, Covenant of the Goddess, Evergreen Grove (Zen Druidism) of Olympia, Holy Order of Mother Earth and the Association for the Advancement of Aquarian Age Awareness. The would-be sorcerers performed dances, offered up sacrifices of meats and grains and chanted and prayed — to dispel the clouds and bring out the sun.

Cynics laughed, because the sky was really socked in. Even the Druids seemed unsure.

But at about 8:10 — five minutes before the scheduled eclipse — a patch of clear sky appeared. It grew and grew, until the sun was revealed as a huge orange wafer in a sea of blue. Then everything became still as the sun slowly winked behind the moon's eyelid.

Within moments, Goldendale was as dark as night. Roosters crowed. Cattle made lowing noises.

The eclipse lasted for only a few eerie minutes. Then the sun reappeared, to be quickly blotted out by heavy black clouds.

The Druids smiled.

10. PROMISES TO KEEP

ACHIEVEMENTS BEYOND DREAMS,
BUT BRUTE FORCES STILL UNTAMED

1980 TO ❧ 1989

*'We did a lot
of praying, too.
A lot of it.'*

**— Camper Sue Ruff,
recalling touch-and-go
survival as Mount St.
Helens erupted.**

Greg Gilbert / Seattle Times

Big buildings shot up all over downtown Seattle in the '80s, altering the skyline and dwarfing the Smith Tower, right, for years the tallest skyscraper downtown. Growth was so fast that some citizens began pushing for a cap on heights. Below, Mount St. Helens fumes after its eruption May 18, 1980.

If those who lived in the Washington of 1889 could return during its centennial year, they would view with disbelief the hordes of people, buildings that dwarf the tallest Douglas fir, factories that turn out jetliners longer than wagon trains, and sagebrush and jackrabbit land that, with irrigation, produces enough apples and wheat to feed millions.

They would marvel at concrete bridges that float on water, superferries that haul cars and people around Puget Sound, giant domed stadiums built for our entertainment, and thousands of miles of roadways.

They would see great medical centers, where hearts are transplanted and cancer cells surgically removed or bombarded with chemicals and radiation; and they would be happy to know that inoculations now ward off many once-fatal or disfiguring diseases.

But they would be less pleased to find dwindling timber and fish resources, air that sometimes smells bad and makes the eyes smart, littered roadsides, automobiles that at rush hour move more slowly than horses, the homeless begging on the same streets

Rick Perry / Seattle Times

Dressed in mourning, an abortion opponent takes part in a 1985 protest at the Federal Courthouse in Seattle.

Craig Fujii / Seattle Times

CHRONO-LOG

1980
Mount St. Helens erupts, blasting more than 8 billion cubic yards of mountaintop into stratosphere and claiming 57 lives.

1981
Drawspan bulge of Mercer Island Floating Bridge is removed, ending decades-long sore point with cross-Lake Washington motorists.

***Boeing gives birth** to new generation of jetliners — the 767, unveiled at Everett Aug. 5. Its running mate, the 757, rolls out at Renton Feb. 19, a year later.*

1982
Don Bennett, 52-year-old Seattle businessman, does one-legged hop up and down Mount Rainier. All-around athlete Bennett had lost right leg above knee in boat-propeller accident 10 years earlier.

trod by the well-to-do, and a new plague, acquired immune deficiency syndrome.

They would discover that Mount St. Helens has lost its beautiful cone-shaped top and that as a result of dams, the once-swift-flowing Columbia River now is more like a long chain of lakes.

Washington voters, once on the liberal side, twice in the '80s overwhelmingly endorsed the Ronald Reagan presidency, with its supply-side economics, high-priced defense posture and adventures in Libya, Grenada, the Persian Gulf and Central America. Booth Gardner, the Democrat they elected as governor, probably would have been viewed as a Republican in earlier times.

The '80s saw the passing of what may have been the greatest one-two punch in the U.S. Senate's history with the defeat of "Maggie" and the death of "Scoop."

The decade contained many surprises in the financial world besides the 508-point decline in the stock market on Black Monday (Oct. 19, 1987) and insider-trading scandals. Our state's largest bank, Seattle First National, staggered when millions of dollars in energy loans went sour; savings and loans struggled, and a state nuclear-power consortium defaulted on billions of dollars worth of bonds. The Legislature hastily passed a law to protect the state's No. 1 employer, Boeing, amid rumors that corporate raider T. Boone Pickens contemplated a takeover attempt.

While many prospered, unemployment reached 25 percent or more in rural communities. Logging was especially hard-hit. As streets filled with the homeless and tougher commitment laws made it increasingly difficult to institutionalize those with mental problems, panhandling rose in larger cities; Seattle enacted tough laws against it. The state's low minimum wage spurred angry debate.

Housing prices, stabilized at the beginning of the decade after runaway inflation during much of the '70s, took off again near the end of the decade. Buyers sought bargains, costing "only" $100,000.

Seattle's two major daily newspapers, The Times and The Post-Intelligencer, came under a Joint Operating Agreement May 23, 1983, in a marriage — critics called it unholy wedlock — designed to save the money-losing P-I from financial collapse. Under terms of the 50-year JOA, the two newspapers would maintain separate editorial departments, publish a joint Sunday newspaper, the vast majority of which was produced by Times staffers, and share the profits. The Times handled circulation, production, advertising and business-office functions for both newspapers.

Activists won a few and lost a few. Smoking was banned in many public and work areas, and there was growing speculation that alcohol would be the next target. An arsonist burned an Everett abortion clinic and went to jail.

U.S. District Judge Jack Tanner of Tacoma issued two landmark decisions: ruling in 1980 that living conditions in the

state penitentiary at Walla Walla constituted cruel and unusual punishment for inmates and violated their constitutional rights; and ruling in 1983 that the state of Washington had been guilty of "direct, overt and institutionalized discrimination" against women state employees by paying them less than it paid men for comparable work.

The word Yuppie (young urban professionals) entered our vocabularies. The prototype Yuppie had an MBA, carried a briefcase, played the stock market, drove a BMW and lived in suburbia or in upscale apartments and condos close to the inner city.

Boeing won cruise-missile and other major defense contracts and introduced to the world its new generation of jetliners — the 767 at Everett in 1981 and the 757 at Renton the following year. There was no rush to buy them at the outset, and some wondered if they were the wrong airplanes for the '80s and '90s. But time proved kind. In head-to-head competition with the world's best planes, Boeing emerged with billions of dollars in orders ($20 billion in 1988 alone) that assured a busy work force well into the next century.

Below-normal rainfall for several years introduced to Western Washington an unaccustomed word: drought. Warnings that the earth was warming up and that traditional weather patterns were likely to change everywhere left us wondering what the future might hold.

Interstate 90, the cross-country highway that ended abruptly at Bellevue, continued its decade-long, snail's-pace crossing of Mercer Island and Lake Washington to Seattle, at a cost of billions. Those "connections to nowhere" that for years had ended in the sky suddenly were being tied into I-5. On Labor Day weekend 1981, the drawspan bulge was removed from the Mercer Island Floating Bridge. In the 41 years of its existence, the bulge had been blamed for more than 300 accidents and nine deaths.

Strong opposition arose when the Navy selected Everett as the site for a new carrier task force. Protesters in rubber boats tried to block the first Trident nuclear submarine, the Ohio, on its journey to the Navy base at Bangor in Kitsap County, and Buddhist monks quietly built a peace pagoda outside the Bangor gates.

There was widespread outrage when the Hanford Nuclear Reservation in Eastern Washington became a finalist as a repository for the nation's atomic waste. And when the N Reactor at Hanford was shut down in 1988, there was far more concern for

Mark Harrison / Seattle Times

William Freeburg, who made a quilt panel as part of Seattle's contribution to the huge quilt that is a national memorial to those who died of AIDS, hugs a friend at a 1988 exhibition.

Bruce McKim / Seattle Times

A protest boat, at lower right, speeds past the Ohio, the first Trident submarine to arrive at the Bangor naval base, as the huge vessel enters Hood Canal in 1982.

the people who would lose their jobs than for the loss of an industry producing weapons-grade plutonium.

Nor were many tears shed in April 1982 when Gov. John Spellman formally rejected Northern Tier's application to pipe Alaskan oil across Washington to the Midwest.

Members of two infamous Los Angeles street gangs, the Crips and the Bloods, muscled their way into the Puget Sound area to deal drugs and wage guerrilla war on the streets. Police and schools undertook programs to keep vulnerable youngsters from falling prey to the lure of big money and deadly weapons.

Developers, along with workers building a $430 million bus tunnel, tore up downtown Seattle so it frequently resembled war-ravaged Beirut. In the suburbs, any acreage covered with trees was fair game for another shopping mall.

Old public schools were closed and new ones built as living patterns changed. Seattle University dropped basketball, a sport in which it had been a national power in the '50s.

Sports, once limited to the playing field, moved to the drug-testing laboratory, the picket line, the courtroom and the corporate boardroom. If enough inducements were offered, would George (Argyros) keep the Mariners in Seattle, would Barry (Ackerly) build a new stadium for the SuperSonics basketball team, would players who had signed contracts agree to take the field?

The Mariners, perennial losers, signed aging Gaylord Perry long enough for him to pitch his 300th victory and assure eventual entry into the Hall of Fame.

Brian Bosworth — The Boz — parlayed a modified Mohawk haircut, gold earrings and a knack for self-

Jimi Lott / Seattle Times

An oily sea bird is picked up at Dungeness Spit after an oil spill in December 1985.

promotion into an $11 million contract to play linebacker for the Seahawks a year after being barred from the Orange Bowl for using forbidden steroids. Bosworth, at age 23, thought it was time to write (with help) his autobiography. Astonishingly, people lined up to buy it and newspapers serialized it.

Marv Harshman closed out his basketball-coaching career at the University of Washington as the winningest active college coach, and the Huskies' Don James established himself as one of the premier football coaches in the country by stringing together consecutive appearances in bowl games.

The underdog Washington State Cougars twice denied their cross-state rival a seemingly certain Rose Bowl trip, edging the Huskies 24-20 in 1982 and trouncing them 17-6 in 1983. And in 1988, it was the Cougars who earned a bowl bid (Aloha), while the so-so Huskies stayed at home.

On April 21, 1983, Tacoma unveiled the $44 million, wooden-roofed Tacoma Dome that many found more attractive than Seattle's larger Kingdome. The T-Dome played host to rock concerts, tractor pulls, football games and its prime tenant, the Tacoma Stars of the Major Indoor Soccer League.

Soccer, the most popular game in the world outside the United States, had a brief but sensational moment in the sports sun in the early '80s with the Seattle Sounders.

Rosalynn Sumners of Edmonds, world-champion figure skater in 1983, had to settle for a silver medal in her specialty at the '84 Winter Olympics.

Religion, in various forms, became front-page news.

Catholic Archbishop Raymond Hunthausen, an outspoken peace activist, found himself under fire from

CHRONO-LOG

Rajneeshpuram press office

The Bhagwan Shree Rajneesh, who headed the Oregon commune of Rajneeshpuram in the early '80s and whose devotees bought him a Rolls Royce every birthday — and any other special occasion; he had 93 — exhorts his followers during a meditation session. Several dozen Washingtonians joined the commune, but the Bhagwan was eventually ousted from the country by immigration authorities, and he moved to India.

1982
Body of first five victims of Green River killer are found, marking beginning of nation's biggest known serial-murder case and eventually resulting in discovery of 48 presumed victims, all women.

State inaugurates million-dollar-jackpot lottery. Jana Dee Page is first winner.

1983
Kettle Falls, Ferry County, begins electing official town "grouch" to serve one-year term. Sign outside town proclaims: "Home of 1,240 Friendly People — and 1 Grouch."

A road sign with a prophetic ring to it stands in front of a cooling tower at Satsop, Grays Harbor County, where two of the WPPSS nuclear power plants were built.

Chris Johns / Seattle Times

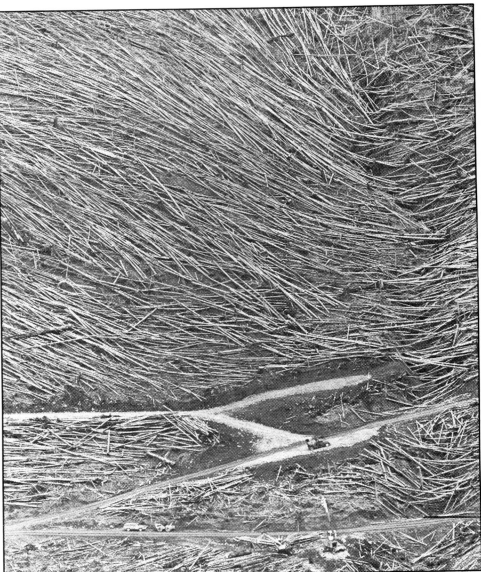

Chris Johns / Seattle Times

As if lost in a forest of giant porcupine quills, a vehicle sits amid a wasteland of denuded timber blown down by the eruption of Mount St. Helens.

home-front critics for alleged liberalism and from Rome for his permissive administrative style. The Vatican stripped him of his powers for a time and kept him under a watchful eye.

Fundamentalism moved out of the church and into the political arena as backers of evangelist Pat Robertson flooded Washington's Republican caucuses in 1988, giving Robertson his only state victory in the nation over eventual party standard-bearer George Bush.

Washington voters continued to show their independence, however, by giving their electoral votes to loser Michael Dukakis.

Dick Scobee, who was born in Cle Elum and grew up in Auburn, was one of the astronauts aboard the spacecraft Challenger when it exploded catastrophically Jan. 28, 1986.

Pinnacle of power, beauty and death

As the decade began, Mount St. Helens was an almost symmetrical snow-capped cone rising 9,677 feet above sea level at the southern end of great Cascade spine that runs through Washington state. Spirit Lake, on the volcano's northwest slope, was one of the region's most breathtaking sights, reflecting the mountain in its mirrorlike alpine blue.

St. Helens was a must for climbers bent on recording ascents of major peaks, a long slog that taxed endurance more than mountaineering skills, but could turn nasty at times. Persistent rumors that the mountain harbored evil spirits added to its appeal.

Although St. Helens had been the last of Washington's active volcanoes to erupt (more than 120 years earlier), it seemed far more likely in the late '70s that Mount Baker, showing little flurries of activity, would be the next.

All that changed in March 1980, when St. Helens suddenly came to life with internal rumblings, steam plumes and spurts of ash. Scientists came running; so did sightseers and thrill-seekers.

In May, geologists no longer wondered if it would erupt, only when and in what form. A bulge appeared on the northwest flank, growing like a water-filled blister.

Zones were drawn. Red meant high danger. Blue meant be alert.

May 18 dawned sunny and clear. The mountain, which had been shuddering with small earthquakes, was uncommonly quiet. Inside, forces almost beyond imagination were building.

At 8:32 a.m., they exploded with a power equal to 30 million tons of TNT. The explosion pulverized 2,400 feet of mountaintop, containing about 8.8 billion cubic yards of rock, dirt and ice.

Shock waves rattled windows as far away as Vancouver, B.C. But those close to the volcano were under a sound umbrella. There was no noise — only the unforgettable sight. Within seconds of the blast, searing winds of unmeasurable velocity raked the hills, snapping limbs from giant trees and toppling them like matchsticks over 150 square miles.

A black, ash-laden cloud boiled to a height of 75,000 feet — nearly three times as high as Mount Everest — mushrooming at the top. Winds carried the talcum-like ash northeast across the state, depositing it on fields, roads and rooftops. It fell like powder snow, blinding and choking everyone in its path, forcing travelers to take refuge for up to three days in schoolhouses, churches and restaurants. The ash eventually made its way around the world.

Superheated glaciers rolled down the mountain and into the Toutle River, picking up debris and dirt, swallowing roads, scattering bridges and trapping livestock. The surge spilled muddy water over I-5 and deposited millions of cubic yards of silt and debris into the Cowlitz River, which choked and gagged and carried what it could down to the mighty Columbia.

The eruption claimed 57 dead or missing.

Among them:

■ Reid Blackburn, a 27-year-old photographer for The Vancouver Columbian, who was on a photo assignment.

■John Killian, 29, and his wife, Christy, 20, who had driven their pickup truck to Fawn Lake to spend the weekend fishing. Although the couple presumably were buried under a mountain of pulverized rock and ash, John's father, Ralph, regularly visited the site afterward, digging for clues.

Myths grew up around at least two who died that day on St. Helens:

■Irascible 83-year-old Harry Truman reportedly had vowed never to leave his beloved Spirit Lake Lodge, saying to himself, "You old bastard, I stuck it out 54 years and I can stick it out another 54 years." Truman, immortalized in Stuff & Company's "Ode to Mount St. Helens," told reporters he had a secret cave to hide in if the mountain blew. But subsequent information has indicated Truman actually had a secret deal with the county police to remove him by helicopter at the last minute. Neither helicopter nor cave could save him when the mountain blew.

■David Johnson, a 30-year-old U.S. Geological Survey geologist manning an observation post on Coldwater Ridge, five miles from the volcano, was supposed to have sent a dramatic last-second radio message: "Vancouver! Vancouver! This is it! Is the transmitter working?" The truth is, no one — including the USGS and all the ham radio operators listening to those final moments — ever heard Johnson say anything.

In a way, what happened May 18 was only the beginning.

There were poignant survivor stories, fast-buck souvenir schemes, a multimillion-dollar cleanup and diking jobs in the rivers, lawsuits charging lack of warning and the inevitable fictionalized film, "St. Helens," starring Art Carney.

The mountain continued to shake with small quakes — scientists called them harmonic tremors — for the next half-dozen years. Even as mapmakers reduced the mountain's elevation to 7,300 feet, the cone blown off in the eruption began rebuilding. At the present rate, scientists estimate it will take two centuries to restore what was lost. And while it has taken years and cost millions to heal the battered land, the human devastation has lingered.

One year later, Bruce Nelson and Sue Ruff recalled in vivid detail the eruption that changed their lives.

Nelson and Ruff, along with Terry Crall and Karen Verner, and Brian Thomas and Ben Balch were camped in three tents along the Green River, 14 miles from the volcano, presuming themselves safe in the Blue Zone.

At about 8:30 on the morning of May 18: Sue sat in front of a tent. Bruce was gathering wood for a cooking fire. Terry was

changing his fishing gear in hopes of catching a big steelhead he'd just seen. Karen was in her sleeping bag. Brian had just rolled out of his tent in longjohns. Ben was dressed, except for shoes.

The only sounds were from the river and the birds. A gentle wind was stirring in the trees.

"All of a sudden I looked up and saw the sky just being engulfed by this black cloud," Bruce said. "I shouted, 'She's blown.' It was just magnificent. I was excited. We were behind a hill. There was no sound at all.

"Seconds later, the wind started up. It was awesome. Trees started to bend and crack. Ash and pumice started to rain down on us."

Through the darkness and the ash, Bruce saw a tree fall on the tent with Karen inside. He and Sue ran toward a small hole in the ground. They crouched as trees toppled above them.

"Because it was so dark, you couldn't see anything," Bruce said. "You just heard it — a whole forest coming down all at once."

When the trees stopped falling, Bruce and Sue worked their way out of the hole. The two tents nearby were buried under trees.

Brian and Ben were hurt, Brian with a broken hip and Ben with third-degree burns on his neck, legs and arms. Neither could walk.

None of the four could see or hear Terry or Karen.

Bruce and Sue would have to go for help.

There was only one way out — back over the road by which they had come. It led toward the mountain, and Bruce and Sue felt certain they were walking into disaster, that the mountain would erupt again. They moved out reluctantly as the ground heaved and shook.

Ash was hot and suffocating. Around them, everywhere, were pumice and large chunks of ice blown from the mountain's glaciers. Mile after mile, they trudged on. They desperately wanted a sip of water.

When Sue became tired, they would sit and talk seriously — about Terry and Karen, about how much all of them meant to each other, about "what we'd have to tell our grandchildren someday, if we survived."

"We did a lot of praying, too," Sue said. "A lot of it."

It was mid-afternoon when they heard a helicopter. They guessed they had walked 20 miles. The sky had cleared. They boarded the chopper and showed the pilot where he could later pick up Brian and Bruce. Back in Kelso, they faced the parents of their dead friends, Terry and Karen, feeling strangely guilty that they had survived.

Rick Perry / Seattle Times

Two months before Mount St. Helens erupted, crusty 83-year-old Harry Truman, who had lived in the peak's shadow 54 years, was photographed beside a painting of the mountain and tranquil Spirit Lake. He died when the mountain blew.

Steve Titus' rape conviction was overturned because of a reporter who wouldn't give up.

Mike Siegel / Seattle Times

CHRONO-LOG

United Press International

Charles Rodman Campbell, on work release from a 1974 conviction of sodomy and assault in Snohomish County, returned in 1982 to the scene of the crime and slashed the throats of Renae Wicklund, her daughter, Shannah, and neighbor, Barbara Hendrickson. Relatives of the victims accused state prison officials of gross negligence for freeing Campbell early and for putting him on work-release a short drive from the women's homes. Campbell is back in prison now — on death row in the state penitentiary at Walla Walla.

1983
Dr. Barney Clark of Burien, world's first recipient of artificial heart, dies after 112 days of extra life on it.

1984
Sarah Doherty, 24-year-old Seattle occupational therapist, becomes first woman to climb Mount Rainier on one leg. Doherty, who lost right leg and part of pelvis when hit by a car 11 years before, keeps balance with specially designed crutches.

The wrong man

In mid-April 1981, Steve Titus took the advice of a friend and placed a telephone call to Paul Henderson, a Seattle Times reporter.

Titus was desperate. He had been convicted of the 1980 rape of a 17-year-old hitchhiker on a secluded road in South King County. He faced 10 years in prison for a crime he insisted he didn't commit. Attorneys and a private investigator hadn't been able to help him. Would Henderson try?

Henderson, known to mix compassion with a reporter's ingrained cynicism, agreed to meet Titus two days later. The two sat at Titus' kitchen table, with a 4-inch-thick stack of police documents and a sixpack of beer.

Titus led Henderson through the case step by step, pointing out the circumstantial evidence, the flimsy identification made by a distraught young woman. He said he had spent every waking hour the past few months trying to defend himself from a miscarriage of justice so he could get on with his life and marry his fianceé.

Five hours later, Henderson arose from the table, convinced Titus had not had a fair trial and might even be innocent. What impressed him most was Titus himself. It was not in character, he thought, for a guilty man to spend his last days of freedom trying to prove his innocence.

Henderson became consumed by the story. He tested every bit of evidence — tire tracks, alibis and photographs used to help the victim identify her rapist. He visited the crime scene with a stopwatch and timed the known movements of Titus and the victim the night of the rape.

In the end, he determined it would have been virtually impossible for Titus to have committed the crime.

Henderson began writing a series detailing discrepancies in the police version of what had happened. One of the big breaks was in learning that another rape had been reported a short time earlier in the same place Titus was supposed to have committed his

crime. Furthermore, the methods used in that other rape were identical to those in "the Titus case."

Henderson's articles prompted Superior Court Judge Charles Johnson to throw out Titus' conviction and order a new trial.

There were still skeptics who wondered if Titus might not, after all, be guilty. But they were silenced when the prosecutor officially dropped the charge against him and accused a Titus look-alike, 29-year-old Edward Lee King, who drove a car similar to that of Titus.

Police said the rape victim, when shown a picture of King, blurted out: "Oh my God, what have I done to Mr. Titus?"

King eventually confessed to a string of rapes in King and Snohomish counties, including the one for which Titus was scheduled to go to prison.

Henderson's work on the case was honored with numerous awards, the most prestigious coming in April 1982, when it was announced that Paul Henderson, the reporter who wouldn't quit, had won the Pulitzer Prize for local investigative reporting.

Even though Titus was exonerated, he lost a high-paying job. His family said he never regained his former easy-going ways. He parted with his fiancée. Obsessed with confronting his former accusers in court, he filed a $20 million civil suit against the Port of Seattle, alleging false arrest and violation of his civil rights. Stress and high blood pressure became constant companions.

Titus suffered a massive heart attack Jan. 30, 1985, and remained in a coma until he died nine days later. He was 35.

Henderson left newspapering to become a private investigator.

'Just a tremendous volume of ice'

A 29-member mountaineering party stopped to rest in the sun at the base of Disappointment Cleaver on the southeast face of Mount Rainier at 6 a.m. June 21, 1981. The climbers were at about 11,500 feet.

The climb had been routine, starting a few hours earlier at Camp Muir (10,000 feet), under a clear sky and a shining moon. The party had taken the most popular route — across Cowlitz Glacier, Cathedral Rock and Ingraham Flats to the base of the Cleaver.

Suddenly, chunks of glacial ice broke loose from above and thundered down on the climbers. There was little time to move.

One of the climbers, 40-year-old Cordell Berge of Eugene, Ore., later would describe what happened:

Everyone seemed to cry "Avalanche!" at the same time.

"Where do you go?" he said. "You get up and run. We did, toward the ridge, to get out of the path. Your feet seem to move in slow motion, sinking six inches to a foot in the snow. You are

Chris Johns / Seattle Times

Wearing his artificial left leg, Charles Leonard O'Brien stands on the slopes of Mount Rainier during the 1981 Project Pelion, an ascent by nine handicapped climbers.

roped, and there is no way to go faster."

Berge said he felt compelled to turn his head to see what was coming.

"It was unbelievable — just a tremendous volume of ice. I thought about that for maybe a second or two, and then I was in it — going down, covered briefly.

"It seemed like an eternity. I guess I was under it for maybe two or three seconds. Our group was closest to the ridge, and the stuff just swept over us, and we were all stretched out in the clear — close to a crevasse."

Berge looked around for the two other roped parties that had been next to him. He saw only snow and ice.

"It was astounding," he said. "They had simply vanished."

Ten climbers and one guide were dead in the worst mountaineering disaster in the nation's history.

The 18 survivors included five guides. Among the latter was Peter Whittaker, son of Lou Whittaker, co-owner of the national park's guide service, and nephew of Jim Whittaker, first American to climb Mount Everest.

Berge's wife, Jo, had driven with him to the mountain, staying at Paradise Inn and getting acquainted with the wife of another climber, Ira Liedman of Hatfield, Pa. When word was flashed down the mountain that the climbing party had been hit by an icefall, that there were some dead and some survivors, the two wives clung to each other, neither knowing what the verdict would be.

They were that way, holding each other, when Berge walked out. Liedman didn't.

Bad weather set in soon after the icefall. Rescuers braved falling ice, snow and high winds but found no trace of the climbers other than a few pieces of gear and clothing.

Later in the summer, five bodies were seen in the ice. But it was decided that removing them would be too difficult; all would remain where they were. Eerily, the same decision had been made at almost the same spot 35 years before, when 32 servicemen lost their lives after a transport plane hit the Cleaver.

Disabled? Not really

Two weeks after the lethal icefall, the mountain was bathed in sunshine and blessed with perfect climbing conditions on the Fourth of July as Jim Whittaker led one of the strangest parties to scale Mount Rainier.

It was called Project Pelion, named after the mountain in Greece, and it included five blind climbers, two deaf ones, an amputee and an epileptic.

The climbers formed a line and walked abreast the last quarter of a mile to Rainier's true summit. Among them were Whittaker, his wife, Diane Roberts, and Phil Bartow, director of the Institute for Outdoor Awareness in Swarthmore, Pa., who had conceived the idea of the climb as the centerpiece of the nation's participation in the International Year of the Disabled.

Seattle newspapermen Svein Gilje and Tim Egan were permitted to climb to the top with the party.

At the summit, the climbers signed their names in the official log of mountaineers who make the top — a number estimated at about 1,500 a year — and then unfurled U.S. and United Nations flags sent from the White House.

Charles Leonard O'Brien, an attorney from Carlisle, Pa., who had lost a leg as an Army Ranger when he stepped on a mine in Vietnam, had been notified during the early-morning hours of the ascent that his wife had given birth to twins. He got on the party's radio to learn the vital statistics of the girl (7 pounds 6 ounces) and boy (6 pounds 7 ounces), whom the couple decided to name Megan Dianne Tahoma (an Indian name for the mountain) and Mathew James Rainier.

Attaining the summit besides O'Brien were: Richard Rose, Vancouver, Wash., epileptic; Alec Haiman, New York, deaf; Sheila Holzworth, Des Moines, Iowa, blind; Fred Noesner, Glenside, Pa., blind; Justin McDevitt, Rosemont, Pa., blind; Kirk Adams, Snohomish, blind; Paul Stefurak, Federal Way, deaf, and Doug Wakefield, Arlington, Va., blind.

'Big Daddy' came in the final heat

In the days when hydroplaning was king in Seattle every summer, the crown belonged to brash, curly-haired Bill Muncey, who moved to Seattle from Detroit in the mid-1950s.

Muncey talked a great race and then delivered by driving the

Matt McVay / Seattle Times
A victorious Bill Muncey after an unlimited hydroplane race.

Ted Jones-designed Thriftways to national honors.

Things happened to Muncey:

In 1958, he rammed and sank a 40-foot-long Coast Guard cutter after the rudder broke on Miss Thriftway. He set a straightaway-mile record of 192 miles an hour in 1960 and later called it the most frightening experience of his life. In 1962, he went to court to win the Gold Cup by proving he did not strike a buoy. In the 1970s, he won a record nine-in-a-row and 24 of 32 races in the Atlas, affectionately known as "the Blue Blaster."

Muncey's talents were not limited to hydroplanes.

For a time, he was a Seattle disk jockey. He played the saxophone in a benefit performance with the Seattle Symphony. In 1968, he ran for lieutenant governor as a Republican, losing in the primary.

Muncey once arrived at the scene of a head-on collision near Everett, jumped from his car and sprinted up the highway with warning flares. He directed traffic, commandeered a blanket for a woman believed to be suffering from shock and took charge until a trooper arrived. Then he took one last look around, climbed into his car without identifying himself and drove on to Seattle.

Muncey also was the prototype family man. He called his parents after every race. And few who saw it ever forgot the sight of Muncey hugging his 9-year-old son Edward on the bow of the Atlas after winning a 1980 hydroplane race in Seattle.

Muncey, the consummate racing tactician, won more heats, more races (62), more Gold Cups (8), more national championships (7) than any other driver. He also suffered numerous injuries and once joked he had more bruises than daredevil motorcyclist Evel Knievel.

As he aged and people urged him to quit driving, Muncey replied with a grin, "If the equipment is still performing well, I can still get to the bank on Monday morning." But fully aware the sport had claimed many of his friends, he said to fellow driver Chuck Hickling, "When the Big Daddy comes and taps you on the shoulder, it's time to go, whether it's on the race course or stepping off a curb."

Big Daddy came Oct. 18, 1981. Muncey was driving the first lap of the final heat of a $175,000 championship race in Atlas Van Lines at Laguna de Coyuca, north of Acapulco, Mexico. His powerboat had taken the lead from the Budweiser and Pay'N Pak when it flipped over backward at 170 miles an hour.

Muncey was one month shy of his 53rd birthday.

Scott Pierce of Oh Boy Oberto, in one of the powerboats behind Muncey, said, "We've lost him right where he belonged, out there in first place, going for it all the way."

Just the ticket

⑤ Jana Dee Page, a 30-year-old former rodeo princess and registered nurse, became the first million-dollar winner in Washington's new lottery on Dec. 17, 1982.

Page lived with her husband, Bob, and two children in Walla Walla. Among the things she hoped to do with her money, she said, was get her favorite horse back from an aunt and uncle who had been boarding it the past five years.

The lottery had arrived with amazing suddenness.

Earlier in the year, State Reps. Carol Monohon (D-Raymond) and Gene Struthers (R-Walla Walla) proposed a state lottery as a way of balancing the budget. Substitute House Bill 1251, which did it, was approved in a special legislative session and signed into law July 16 by Gov. John Spellman.

A new state agency was hastily formed to operate the lottery and establish a network of ticket outlets. The first tickets went on sale Nov. 15. In the first week, more than 9.6 million were sold and more than $4.3 million paid out in prizes to players.

Madison Avenue-slick ads promoting the game of chance were soon appearing on radio, TV and in newspapers. Gambling not only was institutionalized; it was now patriotic. It was quite a switch for Washington.

The Territorial Legislature had given King County commissioners permission to issue lottery licenses to "responsible persons" in 1875, but the experiment had left such a bad taste in everyone's mouth that lotteries were expressly forbidden when the new state adopted its first constitution in 1889.

Among those granted a territorial lottery license was Henry Yesler, the sawmill owner, former mayor and richest man in

CHRONO-LOG

Betty Udesen / Seattle Times

Seattle. His "First Grand Lottery of Washington Territory" sold $300,000 worth of tickets, each costing a $5 gold piece, with the promise that the grand-prize winner would get a $100,000 sawmill (Henry's). After distribution of $218,575 in prizes, Yesler said, all profits would go toward building a road from Seattle through the Cascades to Walla Walla.

No money was ever turned over to the county commissioners for the road, and the mill, which nobody won, was later sold by Yesler for $45,000.

Perhaps the Yesler incident could be overlooked as ancient history. But just two years before Jana Dee Page became a millionaire, the media had widely reported what became known as "Gamscam," in which former Democratic House Speaker John Bagnariol, former Senate Majority (Democratic) Leader Gordon Walgren and lobbyist Patrick Gallagher were convicted of racketeering for conspiring to legalize casinos and slot machines in the state for personal gain.

Three years after winning the lottery, Page had bought a $150,000 house with a swimming pool, new furniture, racehorses, stock, diamond earrings and clothes. Her husband quit his job at a sawmill, and she lost her nursing job at a convalescent home after being accused of using drugs intended for patients.

High-stakes mass murder

Shortly before midnight Feb. 18, 1983, three Hong Kong immigrants entered the Wah Mee Club, a high-stakes gambling parlor in Seattle's International District, and murdered 13 people.

The Wah Mee Massacre was the worst multiple murder in state history and one of the bloodiest in national annals.

Using nylon cord to hog-tie patrons of the club at 507-A Maynard Alley S., the killers methodically robbed their victims, then shot each in the head.

Police who broke through the triple-door entryway to the club found five felt-topped gambling tables and, on the floor, 12 men, one woman and an enormous pool of blood dotted with spent cartridges. Several victims were prominent Chinese businessmen.

Wai Yok Chin, the 14th person shot that night, managed to survive head wounds and stagger out into the alley. His testimony helped convict the killers.

The murders stunned and saddened the Chinese community.

Natalie Fobes / Seattle Times
Police chalk marks show the positions of victims of the Wah Mee Club Massacre in February 1983.

Benjamin K. Ng

"Willie" Mak

"Tony" Ng

Although Chinatown had its share of property crimes, assaults and occasional armed robberies, its crime rate generally was on the low side.

A Wah Mee Task Force set up by Seattle police to handle the investigation arrested Kwan Fai "Willie" Mak, Benjamin K. Ng and Wai Chiu "Tony" Ng. The Ngs were not related.

Mak was sentenced to death after being convicted on 13 counts of aggravated first-degree murder. Benjamin Ng was sentenced to life in prison without parole for the same crimes. Tony Ng, convicted of 13 counts of first-degree robbery, got seven life terms.

Police and prosecutors looking back on the case said that since the Wah Mee Massacre, residents of the International District have been less reluctant to report crimes to police. But one detective on the task force noted that despite the massacre, gambling continued to be an integral part of Chinatown's recreational life, as much a part of the area as "sitting on the front porch and jawing."

According to public record, two weeks before the massacre, about the time Ben Ng turned 20, he sat talking with a tong leader. Someone at the table listened as the leader offered to get a special gift for Ng's rite of passage from adolescence. "I can sell you a bullet-proof vest," the older man said.

Ng shook his head. He didn't need protection. "I shoot people," Ng replied. "People don't shoot me."

Wry on the rocks

 When the ferryboat Elwha hit a reef off Orcas Island on Oct. 2, 1983, the cost — nearly $250,000 for damages to the hull, rudder and keel — was enough to make people weep. But there was a wry side.

State ferry-system manager Capt. Nick Tracy blamed a steering failure, which seemed logical since the 382-feet-long ferry's computerized steering system had been plagued with problems.

But passengers and eyewitnesses on the island had a different story. The ferry, they said, unaccountably had gone into Grindstone Harbor — which was off-limits — and was on its way out again when it struck the rocks.

The truth finally emerged.

Billy Fittro, a licensed skipper for 22 of his 38 years with the ferry system, had invited a passenger, Peggy Warrack, to enter the wheelhouse. He had gone into Grindstone Harbor to give Warrack a bayside view of her Orcas Island home. And on his way out, slam-bang-crunch.

It was sensational stuff. Fittro resigned. Tracy was fired for concocting a story to shield Fittro. Warrack called a press conference to emphatically deny rumors she was a "siren of the San Juans."

Warrack firmly denied inveigling her way into the wheelhouse. Fittro had invited her, she said, when she was all settled down as a passenger, sipping coffee and reading a book. Furthermore, it was all Fittro's idea that the Elwha swing by her home. In fact, Warrack said, she was "absolutely horrified to look out and see us heading toward the reefs I knew were there."

The public loved it.

Within a few days the Island City Jazz Band, a popular fixture at the Electric Company Tavern in Friday Harbor, had come up with a song, "Elwha on the Rocks," written by tuba player Gary Provansha and composed by the entire combo during a jazz festival at Ocean Shores.

At the tavern, bartenders served the most popular drink in the house, "Elwha on the Rocks," equal parts of rum creme and straight rum over ice. Customers would shout to the band, "Play it again, play 'Elwha.'"

Postscripts: Just 18 days after the celebrated incident, Capt. Lawrence Brewster, a state ferry skipper for 25 years, unaccountably invited the same Peggy Warrack into the wheelhouse of the Elwha during a trip to the San Juans. He was reprimanded.

Two months after writing "Elwha," lyricist Provansha disappeared while piloting his light plane in freezing rain from Bellingham to Friday Harbor.

Art: Not enough ayes of the beholders

Public art-bashing was elevated to new heights during the '80s.

In the halls of the Legislature, the howl was over an enormous $82,000 mural entitled "The Twelve Labors of Hercules."

In the Tacoma Dome, the battle raged over a $272,000 neon sculpture.

Art, like it or not, lost both encounters.

In March 1982, after months of private and public grumbling, the state House of Representatives voted to tear down or drape the giant black-and-white murals on the gallery walls. The figures, based on Greek mythology, were variously described as inappropriate or obscene or, as one newspaper reporter jested, "powerful enough to conjure up images of 'Debbie Does Olympia' in the hard-core minds of representatives."

The artist, Michael Spafford, a highly regarded UW art professor, said he was outraged and would prefer that the work be destroyed. As 1989 began, the fate of the murals was still undetermined as the Legislature convened.

About 400 "patrons of the arts" gathered in the Tacoma Dome in December 1984, to cast an advisory vote for the City Council on what to do with the sea of pink, orange, blue and apple-green circles, squares, arcs and squiggles designed for the dome's interior by New York artist Stephen Antonakos.

Among the options presented to those who cheered, booed and stomped their feet: remove the neon tubing but retain the backdrop; drape the whole thing with a curtain; remove everything; leave things as they are.

At the end, 32 percent wanted the artwork removed, 68 percent said it should stay.

Antonakos was upset. He said he had spent the past 20 years of his life doing sculpture, and 13 major cities in the United States — including New York, Dallas, Chicago and Atlanta — had been delighted with his neon works.

The final decision didn't make anyone happy. The sculpture was left in place. But those renting or leasing the domed stadium were given the option of turning it on or leaving it unlighted. Most of the time, it is dark.

Postscript: The people of Seattle did take to their bosoms one piece of sculpture that nobody really knew they cared about. World-renowned sculptor Henry Moore's "Vertebrae" — a lumpish blob of metal — had resided outside the SeaFirst Building for years without drawing much attention, except for occasional cracks about what it meant. But when it was learned that a Japanese businessman was going to buy it, a save-the-sculpture campaign was hastily launched and Vertebrae remained.

Greg Gilbert / Seattle Times

The state House of Representatives voted in 1982 to remove or cover this mural, "The Labors of Hercules," because some members thought it in bad taste.

Drastic action was needed. The Legislature came to the rescue, enacting a law that would allow a Washington bank in danger of failing to be merged with a bank from out of state. The new statute enabled BankAmerica of San Francisco, the nation's second-largest bank, to join hands with the shaky Washington state giant and pump in several hundred million dollars in badly needed cash.

By the late '80s, SeaFirst once again was a powerful institution. But with other state banks also having taken advantage of changed merger laws, there was little chance it ever again would dominate the state's financial world.

Nuclear bondage

SeaFirst's financial problems, however dramatic, didn't come close to the largest municipal-bond default in the nation's history.

The latter occurred in August 1983 when the Washington Public Power Supply System, which had undertaken to build far more nuclear-power plants than was practical, declared it would default on $2.2 billion in bonds, leaving about 40,000 investors with faint hopes of recovering anything at all.

The WPPSS saga — sometimes referred to as Whoops — was a case of good intentions running ahead of reality.

In the belief there would be a major energy shortage in the Northwest by the turn of the century, WPPSS had begun building power plants for 88 Northwest utilities in the 1970s. But instead of building just one or two and getting them running, it tried to build five. Cost over-runs became the rule rather than the exception.

Only one plant, WPPSS No. 2 at the Hanford Nuclear Reservation, made it on line — starting up in late 1984, 12 years after ground was broken.

WPPSS No. 1 (Hanford) and No. 3 (Satsop) — to be financed through regional electricity rates levied by the federal Bonneville Power Administration — were mothballed after being partly completed. To finance the start of No. 4 (Hanford) and No. 5 (Satsop), WPPSS sold bonds — more than $2 billion worth — in the logical hope of repaying the bondholders by selling the power generated by the plants.

By the time the original bond money was gone, the cost of the still-uncompleted plants had soared to $12 billion. WPPSS couldn't sell any more bonds.

Although contracts between WPPSS and the 88 utilities called for the utilities to pay off the bond debt if the plants weren't finished, ratepayers howled and the utilities balked at coughing up the $2.2 billion, plus another $4.7 billion in interest for power plants that wouldn't generate any electricity.

The utilities looked to the courts to save them from ruin.

In Oregon, the courts freed 11 utilities from having to pay their share of the debt, saying the companies never had authority to enter into such contracts. The Washington State Supreme Court said essentially the same thing.

WPPSS defaulted on paying off the bond debt. Bondholders sued for $7.5 billion late in '83. Litigation continued through 1988. The majority of the utilities agreed to modest settlements (Seattle's $50 million was the largest); others continued to fight.

Every time Washingtonians drove down I-5 to Vancouver, they could see what might have been. The Trojan nuclear plant, in Oregon — across the Columbia — steadily cranked out power. And it had been completed for far less money than had been spent on the abandoned Washington plants.

Last stand on Whidbey

Until Dec. 8, 1984, Washingtonians had thought themselves insulated from the cross-burnings and Hitler worship of a neo-Nazi group in Idaho.

But on that Saturday, Robert Mathews, leader of a white supremacist organization called The Order, died in a fiery shootout with FBI agents on Whidbey Island.

Out on the loan prairie

Seattle First National Bank was for years *the* bank in Washington state. Born in the safe Dexter Horton kept in the back room of his store, it became a giant among pygmies.

SeaFirst's 50-story office building was the first to dwarf the Smith Tower. It cornered 40 percent of the state's banking market and had assets of more than $10 billion.

But even the mighty make mistakes. SeaFirst went on a loan spree in the late '70s and early '80s, buying up hundreds of millions of dollars worth of energy loans. Many of them were from Penn Square bank in Oklahoma which, as all readers of business pages learned, subsequently failed. Potentially bad loans in Alaska, Louisiana and Mexico followed. By 1982, the bank's energy-loan portfolio had grown to over $1.2 billion — far more than its consumer loans and nearly half its total commercial loans.

In the second quarter of 1982, the unthinkable happened. SeaFirst reported $56.2 million in losses. As the debt continued to mount — to $165 million — chairman William Jenkins and an executive vice president took early retirement, and a senior vice president was forced to resign.

STATE-MENTS

Seattle Times

Bachelor Bill Gates is reported to be high-strung, given to acquiring speeding tickets and an inveterate reader who disdains television.

The byte of Seattle

When Forbes magazine reported in 1988 that William H. Gates III, 32-year-old chairman and co-founder of Redmond-based Microsoft, was one of the wealthiest people in the United States, it was no surprise to Puget Sound residents. People had come to expect great things from skinny, freckle-faced, slacks-and-sweater Bill Gates.

The net-worth figure was, however, worth a few gasps. The computer prodigy's share of Microsoft, the nation's largest software company, was estimated at $1.4 billion. Fortune magazine said of Gates: "He apparently has made more money than anyone else his age, ever, in any business."

With Paul Allen, he'd founded Microsoft before he was old enough to vote, and he'd begun publicly trading his stock only two years before making the Forbes list. Gates, a seventh-grader, and Allen, a ninth-grader, first discovered computers at Seattle's private Lakeside School. They were so enthralled by the new device that they used up the school's annual computer-time budget of $3,000 the first week they sat down to a keyboard. By the time Gates was a high-school senior, he and Allen had been hired by a California defense contractor.

Gates went on to Harvard, Allen to a job with Honeywell. In Gates' dorm room, the two decided one day to attempt what experts said couldn't be done: write a general-purpose computer language (BASIC) program for the newest wrinkle in high-tech, the microcomputer chip. After five weeks, they had produced an 8,000-instruction program that revolutionized the personal-computer industry.

CHRONO-LOG

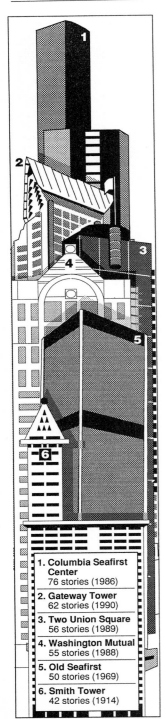

1. **Columbia Seafirst Center**
   76 stories (1986)
2. **Gateway Tower**
   62 stories (1990)
3. **Two Union Square**
   56 stories (1989)
4. **Washington Mutual**
   55 stories (1988)
5. **Old Seafirst**
   50 stories (1969)
6. **Smith Tower**
   42 stories (1914)

Ed Walker / Seattle Times

From the erection of the 42-story Smith Tower in 1914 to 1969, when the original 50-story Seattle First National Bank Building went up, the Seattle skyline stayed relatively static. But it soared to dizzying new heights in the '80s.

1987
$12.9 million addition to UW's Husky Stadium collapses in February while under construction, but no one is injured. New stands completed, however, by season's opener in September.

Mathews was a disciple of the Rev. Richard Butler's Church of Jesus Christ, Aryan Nations. But he had become disenchanted with his Hayden Lake (Idaho)-based leader, thinking Butler long on talk and short on revolutionary action.

Mathews found a ready-made blueprint for action — a 1978 novel by William Pierce, "Turner Diaries," that detailed how a band of white supremacists calling themselves The Order took over the United States government.

According to relatives, the stocky, 31-year-old Mathews refused to carry a gun or hunt as a young man. Now he armed himself and his followers and set out to turn fiction into fact.

The Order engaged in counterfeiting and robbed banks and armored cars in Seattle and Northern California. Members were accused of murdering a compatriot they thought was an informer and of gunning down Alan Berg, a Jewish talk-show host in Denver who was outspoken in denouncing bigotry and racism.

The FBI came close to capturing Mathews in a Portland motel in November 1984. But he escaped in a hail of gunfire, his right hand mangled by buckshot. A few weeks later, Mathews sent a letter to The Newport Miner, a weekly in Pend Oreille County, where his wife, young son and mother lived.

In the letter, Mathews referred to Americans as "cowardly, sheepish degenerates" and called for a reawakening of "racial pride and consciousness." He promised to remove the head from the body of the informant who had betrayed him to the FBI.

"It is logical to assume that my days on this planet are rapidly drawing to a close," he wrote. "Even so, I have no fear. I will leave knowing I have made the ultimate sacrifice to secure the future for my children. As always, for blood, soil, honor, for faith and for race."

Mathews rented a two-story house near Greenbank on Whidbey Island. He and several heavily armed associates laid in a supply of food. A few days later, the FBI closed in. Gunfire was exchanged. In attempting to escape, four men were caught. Mathews stayed behind, vowing to fight to the death. Thirty-five hours after the siege began, the house caught fire. Mathews remained inside. His body later was identified from dental records.

FBI agents seized an Order briefcase that contained a document dated Nov. 25 — 13 days before the shootout. Entitled "Declaration of War," it spelled out how war would be waged against various elements of society in the name of the Aryan Resistance Movement.

Without its driving force, The Order disintegrated. More than 20 members and hangers-on were arrested. All wound up in prison.

Butler and some of his closest associates from around the country survived a federal sedition trial in the late '80s and continued to talk about establishing a white bastion in the Pacific Northwest. But few people were listening.

The heart of the matter

At 10 p.m. March 23, 1983 — after 112 days and 12,912,400 heartbeats — Dr. Barney Clark of Burien died in the University of Utah's Medical Center, where he had become the world's first recipient of an artificial heart.

The retired dentist was within minutes of death from cardiomyopathy Dec. 2 when Drs. William DeVries and Lyle Joyce implanted an air-driven Jarvik-7 plastic heart in his chest. Although it enabled Clark to live, it could do little for lungs damaged by emphysema and vital organs that for too long had been deprived of adequate blood flow.

In the days that followed, Clark underwent several operations. Seizures wracked his brain. His bleeding nose was packed with gauze. At times he was deeply depressed.

Even though his wife, Una Loy Clark — his sweetheart since they met in the seventh grade — occasionally had her doubts about the doctors keeping her husband going, she said later she knew he would not agree to quit. He wanted his experiment to help others in the future.

Clark's funeral at Washington Memorial Cemetery, in South King County, was attended by the surgeons who implanted the heart, by Dr. Robert Jarvik, the artificial heart's principal designer, and by other members of the medical team that monitored his progress. William Ruckelshaus, a Washingtonian who was once U.S. deputy attorney general, twice chief of the Environmental Protection Agency and a past official of the Weyerhaeuser Co., represented President Reagan.

One of the eulogies for Clark, a Mormon, was delivered by a Mormon elder, Neal Maxwell:

Barney Clark, after getting his new heart.

"To those who despair over the meaning of life, Barney represented not someone who would cling to life at all costs, but someone who was willing to endure prolongation — for a purpose."

Three weeks later the state House of Representatives passed a unanimous resolution praising Clark's "great courage."

The rabbi was mortal — in a way

Someone once described Rabbi Raphael Levine as looking like everybody's favorite grandfather: small of stature, white-bearded, leaning on one of his hand-carved canes, eyes twinkling, lips ready to shape very wise words.

It seemed he would go on forever, dispensing wisdom, reconciling divergent viewpoints, smoothing ruffled feathers with a wry smile and a little joke.

But Levine, the Jew who crossed religious barriers to become the conscience of all faiths around Puget Sound, proved mortal after all. He died Nov. 4, 1985, from injuries suffered in a head-on collision on the Mercer Island Floating Bridge nine days earlier.

Born in a ghetto in Poland, he came to this country as a child, graduated from the University of Minnesota Law School and attended Hebrew Union College. As a young rabbi, he served in London, where his synagogue was destroyed in a German bombing raid.

Returning to the United States in the early '40s, he toured the country to speak out on the evils of Nazi Germany. Following a speech before the Seattle Chamber of Commerce, he received a standing ovation — and an invitation to take the position as senior rabbi of Temple De Hirsch Sinai.

He accepted. Almost from the start, his voice reached beyond the synagogue. For 14 years he appeared on a KOMO-TV program, "Challenge," with a Catholic priest and a Protestant minister. Although he never sought the spotlight, it simply followed him.

Levine wanted respect and freedom for Jews. In turn, he extended the same understanding to other faiths. He often did the unexpected:

Praising Pope John XXIII from the pulpit of a Lutheran church; spending weeks making a birchwood altar for St. Patrick's Catholic Church when it was served by the Rev. William Treacy, a priest he often referred to as his son; writing new words for the song "Goodnight Irene," which became the theme of the 1950 Seattle-King County Community Chest drive; enlisting the aid of Charles Z. Smith, one of the city's foremost black attorneys and jurists, to co-chair a Holocaust Study Conference at Seattle University, a Jesuit school that awarded him an honorary doctor of humanities degree.

Everyone — all faiths, all colors — belongs to the same family of man, Levine said in one of his many lectures. "If we can

Seattle Times

Rabbi Raphael Levine seldom was without one of his hand-carved canes.

Balkanize the world," he used to say, "we are not going to save the world. The only way we can do that is by creating greater unity among individuals. We've got to start with religion because that's where we have some influence and that's the business of religion.

"Concentration camps are not a thing of the past, unfortunately — anywhere in the world. It could happen anywhere, given circumstances, given demagoguery."

During times of racial tensions he was on a committee formed to soothe and heal. He won the Brotherhood Award from the National Conference of Christians and Jews.

He got people of all faiths to contribute to a Seattle Brotherhood Forest in Galilee, Israel. He served on the Human Rights Commission, the Council for the Aging, the Washington Society for Crippled Children, the Community Psychiatric Clinic. He helped found Camp Brotherhood in Mount Vernon.

He also wrote constantly and well: "Holy Mountain," "Two Paths to One God, "Israel: A Fresh Approach," "The Wild Branch on the Olive Tree" (with Father Treacy) and "101 Profiles in Service," sketches men and women he felt had made a lasting contribution to the community.

The Rev. Oscar Rolander, who frequently appeared on "Challenge" with Levine, said after the rabbi's death:

"He was living proof that we can differ and still love and respect each other. He wasn't one to paper over our differences. But he was convinced, as I am, that we could talk about them in a loving way."

Matthew Eli Creekmore, in a family snapshot.

With a few songs in his heart

To kick off the 100th birthday party for the Statue of Liberty in New York Harbor in 1986, Frank Sinatra sang one of his biggest hits, "The House I Live In."

Few Washingtonians realized the song was composed by a tall, red-thatched West Seattle High School graduate named Earl Robinson, who also wrote music sung by the country's first internationally acclaimed black baritone, Paul Robeson.

When Robinson graduated from the University of Washington in the Depression '30s, he went off to New York, packing a guitar under his arm and intending to compose songs and become a folk singer. He wrote a song, "Ballad for Uncle Sam," which appeared near the end of a Broadway revue, "Sing for Your Supper." The revue lasted all of five weeks.

But the number became a smash hit a few years later under a new name, "Ballad for Americans," on a television show called "Pursuit of Happiness." The CBS switchboard in New York was lit up for hours after Robeson sang it, and concert singer Lawrence Tibbett incorporated it into his repertoire.

Other Robinson compositions were "Joe Hill," a hymn to the songwriter and radical labor organizer executed in 1914 by a Salt Lake City firing squad, and "Black and White," a song celebrating the Supreme Court's 1954 school-desegregation decision.

"Joe Hill" was revived by Joan Baez at Woodstock in 1970. Sammy Davis Jr. introduced "Black and White," which rose high on the charts in the late '70s when it was performed by a rock group, Three Dog Night.

Robinson's leftist politics got him blacklisted in Hollywood during the 1950s — as they did Robeson — but he returned to favor in later years. He continued to compose at his home on Bainbridge Island.

The death that inspired a law

Matthew Eli Creekmore lived for only three years, two months and nine days. But he probably did more to focus public attention on child abuse in this state than any combination of lawmakers, prosecutors and journalists.

The Snohomish County toddler, who came to be known simply as Eli, was kicked to death by his father, Darren, on Sept. 27, 1986. Before that, the state Child Protective Services had on three occasions removed Eli from his home after receiving reports of abuse. Each time CPS relented and returned him to his parents.

The public reacted. Eli became a rallying point. And child abuse came out of the closet.

As the glare of publicity shone on CPS, the public learned some hard truths: The Department of Social and Health Services agency was overworked and understaffed. Caseworkers were damned if

they removed a possibly abused child from a home and damned if they didn't.

A few months after Eli's death, department officials told legislators the boy's death had triggered a $19 million crisis in the state's foster-care system. Caseworkers, fearful of a repetition of Eli's death, were sending more children than ever before to foster homes — and running out of places to put them.

The Legislature passed an Eli Creekmore Law when it was learned that those who killed children most often got off with a slap on the wrist, while those who murdered adults received stiff penalties. Henceforth, lawmakers decreed, those who inflict punishment on children that results in death would serve a mandatory sentence of 20 years to life.

Childhaven (the former Seattle Day Nursery), an agency dealing with battered and abused children, found ready support for its fourth and newest center when donors learned it would be named the Eli Creekmore Memorial Center.

Darren Creekmore was convicted of second-degree murder and sentenced to 60 years in prison. Eli's mother, Mary, was convicted of family nonsupport, after she admitted she hadn't provided medical attention for Eli when it was obvious he ran a risk of being beaten to death. She was sentenced to 300 days on work release.

Fifteen months after Eli's death, the Eli Creekmore Memorial Center was opened in the Burien-White Center area. Among those who watched as a bronze plaque was unveiled was Eli's maternal grandmother, Myrna Struchen of Edmonds, who had pleaded to have her grandson removed from his abusive home.

The plaque bore a likeness of the little boy and the words: "In memory of Matthew Eli Creekmore July 18, 1983, to September 27, 1986. That all children may have happy tomorrows."

Struchen looked at the picture on the plaque and said: "I'd like to take him out of there and hug him. Just one last hug." Then she added, softly, "I'd never give him back."

The sky's the limit

 Starting in the 1960s, Martin Selig brought about more changes in the Seattle skyline than anything since the Great Fire of '89.

In 1985, Selig opened his monument — the 76-story, 943-feet-high Columbia Seafirst Center — which dwarfed previous claimants to the title of Northwest's tallest structure.

It was, in fact, the eighth-tallest building in the United States. Its 1.5 million square feet of office space, added to what he had already built, gave Selig nearly 4 million square feet to lease.

By the time he was in his 40s, Selig had become one of the premier developers in the world.

Selig's buildings take many shapes. They are short, tall, curved and angular. Several resemble nothing so much as outsized outboard motors. They dominate the Denny Regrade area, add charm to the waterfront at the foot of Queen Anne Hill, hit motorists in the eye as they drive down Interstate 5.

And no Seattle hill is high enough, no cluster of buildings dense enough to prevent his Columbia Seafirst Center from being seen from almost anywhere in the greater metropolitan area.

Selig does not ignore amenities. Many of his buildings front on real-grass parks, suitable for brown-baggers. He spent $872,000 for an Alexander Calder mobile, "Big Crinkly," which now decorates his Fourth and Blanchard Building.

Not everyone liked what he built. Architect Victor Steinbrueck called the Columbia Center "a flat-out symbol of greed and egotism."

But there were others who found the height and the curves pleasing, and almost everyone agreed the interior was exquisite.

The man who remade Seattle's skyline is of short, athletic build, balding and a fierce competitor. He was a small boy when his parents fled Hitler's Germany, crossing Siberia and coming by ship to Seattle. It was sunny when the Seligs arrived, and they decided to stay rather than continue on to San Francisco. With very modest means, the Seligs settled in the Leschi District and opened Empire Children's Wear Co. Martin worked there as a boy.

Early on, he demonstrated a knack for getting what he wanted. One thing he wanted to do was be the first nonconstruction worker to go to the top of the Space Needle before its completion. He presented himself to the foreman, said his parents had a clothing store and he could give the man a T-shirt with the Space

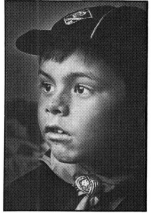
An anonymous donor finally succeeded in sending Billy Joe and his parents to Disneyland, where 50,000 visitors lined the way and the boy reigned as grand marshal of the park's 30th anniversary parade.

A living Scout motto

Freckled-faced Billy Joe Thomas captured imaginations in the summer of 1985. A member of Cub Scout Pack 70 on Seattle's West Queen Anne Hill, the 8-year-old won a trip to Disneyland for four for selling 800 tickets to a Boy Scout show.

It would have been logical for him to take the trip, along with his parents. The family, all but penniless, had purchased Billy Joe's Scout uniform at a yard sale. But without hesitation, he turned in the tickets so terminally ill youngsters at Seattle's Children's Orthopedic Hospital could go to Disneyland in his place. When the word got out, he became an instant celebrity. When gifts poured in from around the nation, Billy Joe responded with a personal letter of thanks and then gave most of them away.

Asked once to explain his generosity, Billy Joe seemed puzzled. Then he replied, "Do your best. That's the Cub Scout motto." The next year, he sold more than 1,000 tickets to British Columbia's Expo as a fund-raiser for the Boy Scouts. True to form, he gave away his prize — two bicycles.

Eighteen months after their son became the most famous boy in Washington state, the Thomases were seen standing in a line outside the Salvation Army at Christmas. They hoped to be given a certificate so they could get two free toys to put under their son's tree.

CHRONO-LOG

Alan Berner / Seattle Times
A sea lion entangled in a fish-protection net drowns at the Ballard Locks fish ladder in 1988 as state and federal agencies escalated their battle to keep the mammals from eating huge quantities of game fish.

1988

Seattle-born Robert Joffrey, founder of world-famous Joffrey Ballet Company, dies in New York. He had returned to Northwest in 1966 and began residency program at Pacific Lutheran University in Tacoma.

Diane Schuur, blind Auburn-born singer, wins second straight Grammy Award in jazz vocal performance.

Needle on the front if he'd take him up. The foreman stalled. Selig upped the ante to T-shirts for the entire crew. Up he went.

While studying at the University of Washington, Selig borrowed some money and made a modest down payment on a building in University Bay Place, later University Village. A year later, "without doing anything to the place," he sold it at a considerable profit.

He took a year off from the university to attend the prestigious Wharton School of Business at the University of Pennsylvania. When he graduated, he entered the family business. It was while working at the store, waiting for a customer to make a decision on whether to spend $15 for a few pairs of gloves, that Selig turned a nice profit, by telephone, on some real estate.

It was obvious, he said later, that developing was more fun than selling gloves. Soon afterward, he went out on his own. His first project was a shopping center in Bellevue's Lake Hills area. Then he began building in Seattle's Regrade. The state's largest city would never be the same.

A faint smell of bitter almonds

The faint odor of bitter almonds led to the discovery in June 1986 that two people — Bruce Nickell and Sue Snow — had died from taking cyanide-laced Extra-Strength Excedrin capsules purchased in stores in Auburn.

Similar pain-killers were swept from store shelves throughout the Puget Sound area. Worried residents scoured their medicine chests and threw away bottles of pain-killer they feared might have been laced with poison.

Two years later, Stella Nickell, 44, wife of Bruce Nickell, was convicted of the two murders. In a sensational trial, the story behind the product-tampering case unfolded.

Bruce Nickell, a 52-year-old maintenance man, had several life-insurance policies, one of which had been taken out by his wife, who forged his signature. A clause in one of the policies provided for $31,000 to be paid to Nickell's widow if he died of natural causes, $136,000 if the death was ruled accidental.

Stella Nickell set out to make her husband die accidentally — by inserting cyanide in Excedrin capsules from several bottles in the family medicine chest.

Bruce Nickell became ill after taking one of the capsules, and was taken to Harborview Medical Center, where he died June 5. The medical examiner's office, however, determined that the cause of death was pulmonary emphysema, which meant the

Seattle Times
Stella Nickell is in handcuffs after her arrest.

lower amount would be paid on a life-insurance policy.

Needing to establish that her husband had died of cyanide poisoning, Stella Nickell poisoned other bottles of Excedrin and placed them on Auburn-area store shelves. One bottle was purchased by Sue Snow, a 40-year-old bank manager. On June 11, she became the second victim.

During an autopsy on Snow, Dr. Corrine Fligner, an assistant King County medical examiner, detected the faint smell of bitter almonds, long associated with cyanide poisoning. Tests proved Snow had died of it and that it had come from the Excedrin.

When the story became public, Stella Nickell came forward and said she suspected her husband also might have died of cyanide poisoning. A test was done on Bruce Nickell's blood serum, and traces of cyanide were found. Both deaths were classified as homicides. A search turned up two more contaminated bottles on June 24.

Less than two months later, an FBI laboratory determined that all five tainted bottles possessed a unique "fingerprinting" identifier, indicating that a single person had done the tampering.

After a lengthy, frequently sensational trial in federal court, the jury for several days stood 11-1 for conviction. The holdout finally voted with the majority to find Nickell guilty.

She was sentenced to 90 years in prison, with no chance of parole in less than 30 years.

A killer so meticulous

In the summer of 1982, the body of 16-year-old Wendy Lee Coffield was found in the Green River where it forms the border between the city of Kent and unincorporated King County.

In the following month, the bodies of four other victims were found in or near the river.

Nobody knew it at the time, but that was the start of an investigation into the greatest unsolved serial killing in the United States — the pursuit of the Green River Killer.

The remains of young women presumed to have been victims of the killer continued to turn up in the months and years that followed. He found new places to dump his victims, too — east of Star Lake, north of the Seattle-Tacoma airport, south of it, near Auburn's Mountain View Cemetery, east of Enumclaw.

Skeletal remains would be carefully tucked away in brush and forest foliage, to be stumbled upon by hunters, fishermen, woodcutters, dirt-bike riders and mushroom pickers. Nearly all the victims were either runaways or prostitutes.

Nearly 18 months elapsed between the finding of Coffield's remains and the formation of a Green River Task Force to sift information and work exclusively on solving the case. Trying to identify the victims — many of whom had a string of aliases — proved almost as difficult as finding suspects. By late 1988, the remains of 48 presumed Green River victims had been found. But only 37 had been identified.

Police speculated they were dealing with a classic psychopath, someone expert at fitting into society, yet forever apart because of a lifetime lack of moral scruples; most likely a white male, aged 20 to 40, experienced in the outdoors. To these they could add two other certainties — he was meticulous and he carefully planned his crimes.

Thousands of tips came in; scores of suspects were questioned. Early in the investigation a prime suspect was put under 24-hour surveillance. When the killings continued, it was obvious he was not the man. Police later searched the home of another "person of interest" under the glare of TV spotlights. Nothing substantial was turned up, and the man sued over the resultant publicity and invasion of privacy.

The task force spent millions of dollars and hundreds of thousands of hours on the case. But as the decade neared an end, investigators seemed no nearer a solution than before.

The long way home

On the 1988 Memorial Day weekend, a green-and-black granite memorial was unveiled on the Capitol Campus in Olympia to honor those from the state killed or missing in the Vietnam War.

The 45-foot memorial, containing more than 1,000 names, was dedicated by Secretary of State Ralph Munro, who said: "To the veterans of the Southeast Asia conflict, welcome home."

Gregory Scott / Seattle Times
Jim Johnson of Everett makes a rubbing of a friend's name at the Olympia memorial to the state's 1,000 dead or missing in the Vietnam War. The memorial was unveiled in 1988.

SOURCES

BOOKS
List includes name of author or editor, title, place and date of publication.

Anderson, Bern, *The Life and Voyages of Captain George Vancouver (Surveyor of the Sea)*, Seattle, 1960
Bass, Sophie Frye, *Pig-tail Days in Old Seattle*, Portland, Ore., 1937
Binns, Archie, *Northwest Gateway*, Portland, Ore., 1941
Boeing Company, The, *Pedigree of Champions, Boeing Since 1916*, Seattle, 1977
Buerge, David, *Seattle in the 1880s*, Seattle, 1986
Clark, Norman H., *The Dry Years: Prohibition & Social Change in Washington*, Seattle, 1965
Clark, Norman H., *Mill Town*, Seattle, 1970
Dryden, Cecil, *History of Washington*, Portland, Ore., 1968
Eells, the Rev. Myron, *Marcus Whitman, Pathfinder and Patriot*, Seattle, 1909
Fletcher, Elizabeth Huelsdonk, *The Iron Man of the Hoh*, Port Angeles, 1979
Franklin, Dorothy, *West Coast Disaster*, Portland, 1963
Harvey, Paul, *Tacoma Headlines*, Tacoma, 1962
Hoyt, Harrold "Jiggs," *Bryn Mawr 1872-1986*, Snohomish, 1986
Jones, Nard, *Seattle*, Garden City, N.Y., 1972
Kalez, Jay, *Saga of a Western Town — Spokane*, Spokane, 1972
Kalez, Jay, *This Town of Ours — Spokane*, Spokane, 1973
LeWarne, Charles Pierce, *Utopias on Puget Sound, 1885-1915*, Seattle, 1975
Lucia, Ellis, *The Big Blow*, Portland, Ore., 1967
Mansfield, Harold, *Vision*, New York, 1956
Martin, Harry, and Kellogg, Caroline, *Tacoma, A Pictorial History*, Virginia Beach, Va., 1981
Martin, Paul, *Port Angeles, A History*, Port Angeles, 1983
McClelland, Jr., John, *Wobbly War*, Tacoma, 1987
Meany, Edmond S., *History of the State of Washington*, New York, 1909
Meany, Edmond S., *Origin of Washington Geographic Names*, Seattle, 1923
Meeker, Ezra, *The Tragedy of Leschi*, Everett, 1905
Meeker, Ezra, *Pioneer Reminiscences of Puget Sound*, Seattle, 1905
Morgan, Murray, *Puget's Sound*, Seattle, 1979
Morgan, Murray, *Skid Road*, New York, 1952
Morgan, Murray, *The Last Wilderness*, New York, 1955
Newell, Gordon, *Rogues, Buffoons and Statesmen*, Seattle, 1975
Phillips, James, *Washington State Place Names*, Seattle, 1971
Sale, Roger, *Seattle Past to Present*, Seattle, 1976
Speidel, William, *Sons of the Profits*, Seattle, 1967
Spencer, Lloyd, and Pollard, Lancaster, *A History of the State of Washington*, New York, 1937

OTHER PUBLICATIONS
Historical Highlights of Washington State, issued by Secretary of State Earl Coe, Olympia, 1950
Landmarks, a magazine of Northwest history and preservation, Seattle
Pacific Northwest Quarterly, Seattle
Portage, published quarterly by Historical Society of Seattle and King County, Seattle
Seattle Post-Intelligencer
Seattle Times
The Vancouver Area Chronology (1784-1958), diary by Carl Landerholm
Washington — A Guide to the Evergreen State, compiled by Work Projects Administration, Portland, 1941
Washington Highways to History, issued by the State Highway Commission, Olympia
Washington Quarterly, Northwest quarterly
Weekly, The

LIBRARIES, MUSEUMS, SOCIETIES
Black Diamond Historical Museum
Burke Museum, University of Washington, Seattle
Chicago Historical Society
Museum of Flight, Seattle
Museum of History & Industry, Seattle
Renton Historical Museum
Seattle Public Library
Steilacoom Historical Museum
University of Washington Libraries, Special Collections and Preservation Division
Washington State Historical Society
Washington State Library

INDEX